Black, White, and Indian

Black, White, and Indian

Race and the Unmaking of an American Family

CLAUDIO SAUNT

OXFORD
UNIVERSITY PRESS

OXFORD
UNIVERSITY PRESS

Oxford University Press, Inc., publishes works that further
Oxford University's objective of excellence
in research, scholarship, and education.

Oxford   New York
Auckland   Cape Town   Dar es Salaam   Hong Kong   Karachi
Kuala Lumpur   Madrid   Melbourne   Mexico City   Nairobi
New Delhi   Shanghai   Taipei   Toronto

With offices in
Argentina   Austria   Brazil   Chile   Czech Republic   France   Greece
Guatemala   Hungary   Italy   Japan   Poland   Portugal   Singapore
South Korea   Switzerland   Thailand   Turkey   Ukraine   Vietnam

Copyright © 2005 by Oxford University Press, Inc.

Published by Oxford University Press, Inc.
198 Madison Avenue, New York, New York 10016

www.oup.com

First issued as an Oxford University Press paperback, 2006

Oxford is a registered trademark of Oxford University Press

Library of Congress Cataloging-in-Publication Data
Saunt, Claudio.
Black, white, and Indian: race and the unmaking of an American family / Claudio Saunt.
p. cm.
Includes bibliographical references and index.
ISBN-13 978-0-19-517631-5; 978-0-19-531310-9 (pbk.)
ISBN 0-19-517631-6; 0-19-531310-0 (pbk.)
1. Creek Indians—History—Sources. 2. Creek Indians—Mixed descent. 3. Creek Indians—v Genealogy.
4. Blacks—Southern States—Relations with Indians. 5. Whites—Southern States—Relations with Indians.
6. Interracial marriage—Southern States—History. 7. Grayson family—History. 8. Southern States—
Genealogy. I. Title.
E99.C9S27 2005
929'.2'08905973850073—dc22   2004057659

9 8 7 6 5 4 3 2 1
Printed in the United States of America
on acid-free paper

Acknowledgments

When I arrived in Oklahoma to begin working on this book in 1999, I was overwhelmed by the warm response I received. Tressie Nealy and Sharron Ashton of the Oklahoma Historical Society took me under their wing when I knew nothing about genealogy. They were extraordinarily helpful and continued to be so right to the end of the project. Also at the Oklahoma Historical Society, I would like to thank Phyllis Adams and William Welge for making the archives so accessible. John Lovett, at the Western History Collections of the University of Oklahoma, and Sarah Irwin, at the Gilcrease Museum, also assisted me in my research. At the Muskogee Public Library, Wally Waits helped me navigate his enormous collection of genealogical resources. Buddy Cox, whom I met at the OHS shortly after arriving, shared his knowledge of Creek history with me and unfailingly offered assistance when I asked. He became a good friend, as did Jack Baker, who is a font of information on the Five Tribes.

I owe Karen Elaine Crook and Harold Grayson Hoppe special gratitude for permitting me to read their copies of Wash Grayson's diaries. I had the pleasure of meeting Karen and her husband, David, in person in Tulsa, Oklahoma. They share my interest in Native American history and are determined that their family story and the larger history of American Indians be preserved.

I would also like to thank all the people who took time to share their past with me: Chester Adams, Joyce Bear, David Cornsilk, Napoleon Davis, Henry Durant, James M. Etter, Henry Evans, Carolin Fox-Mayes, Robert Freeman, Ron Graham, Henry Grayson, Mark Grayson, Robert Handy, C. Jeff Henderson, Rudy Hutton, Gail Jackson, Robert Littlejohn, Adolf Logan, Rena Maxwell, Chinnubbie McIntosh, Wilma Moore, Rebecca Priest, J. C. Scruggs, Marilyn Vann, Ida Wallace, Ruth Woods, and John York. I apologize to those I have inadvertently left out. Other individuals kindly helped me at various points in my research, including David Gerard of the *Muskogee Daily Phoenix*; Angela Walton-Raji, an expert in the genealogy of black Indians; and Creek linguist Jack Martin. William

T. Jurgelski applied his mapping and computer skills to the project and produced two superb maps.

A number of colleagues helped me clarify my thoughts or provided research leads. They include Alexander Byrd, James Cobb, Elizabeth Fenn, Frederick Hoxie, Barbara Krauthamer, Michael Kwass, Laura Mason, Tiya Miles, Celia Naylor-Ojurongbe, Reinaldo Román, Bryant Simon, Steve Soper, Mary Jane Warde, Laura Wexler, Peter Wood, and Gary Zellar. My editor at Oxford, Susan Ferber, offered concise and useful suggestions for revisions.

As always, I owe thanks to Paulette Long. Thanks also to Shep Pollack and Jerry Long for their support.

Rachel Gabara helped me think through a number of problems when I was writing this book. She offered perceptive comments, moral support, and loving companionship. I look forward to working with her on future projects.

Prologue

On a rainy spring day in May 1905, George Washington Grayson sat down to write his autobiography and "incidentally my genealogy as near as I can come to it."[1] It was his sixty-second birthday, and he was spending it at home in Eufaula, a town in the Creek Nation, lying some two hundred miles east of present-day Oklahoma City. Wash, as he was known, was a prominent Creek citizen, a successful businessman, and an influential politician.

Wash did not intend to publish the account but instead wrote "for the information of my own family only."[2] He continued working intermittently on the project until March 1912, when in a burst of energy spanning three months, he wrote nearly two hundred pages.[3] In January 1913, his wife, Annie, read through the completed manuscript. She was, Wash noted with gratification, "greatly pleased with it."[4]

In the 1930s, a copy of the autobiography landed in the Western History Collections at the University of Oklahoma. It was there that J. Leitch Wright, a historian of southeastern Indians, read through it in the early 1980s. In *Creeks and Seminoles*, Wright cited the manuscript. Wash Grayson, he wrote, quoting from the autobiography, "was dismayed by the 'lasting cloud over his family's name.'" Wash's grandmother, Wright explained, "had borne two children in Alabama by a Negro father." In addition, his grandmother's brother had married a female slave.[5] In 1988, two years after *Creeks and Seminoles* appeared, Wash's autobiography was published by the University of Oklahoma Press with a title obviously designed to appeal to Civil War buffs: *A Creek Warrior for the Confederacy: The Autobiography of Chief G. W. Grayson*.[6]

In 1996, when I noticed Wright's brief reference to the manuscript, I headed to the library to learn more from the autobiography itself about this "lasting cloud." In vain, I searched through the published version without finding a single reference to Wash's African ancestry. When I called the Western History Collections and asked to see a copy of the original, I was told it had been withdrawn from the archives in 1987. I wrote the editor of *A Creek Warrior for the Confed-*

eracy, asking if there were missing passages that discussed Grayson's African American forebears. Yes, he confirmed, adding that the original manuscript "was removed from the Smock Collection to prevent that information from being published." "Ten years ago," he explained in 1997, "one of Grayson's grand-daughters still lived in Eufaula, Oklahoma, and the family believed that revelation of the existence of black Graysons would be an embarrassment to her."[7]

In the published version, the missing passages are marked by ellipses. The first such ellipsis occurs when Wash describes Indian agent Benjamin Hawkins's 1796 visit to his great-grandfather, Robert. At the time, Wash wrote, his grandmother Katy "was not yet born. . . ." The sentence has a footnote:

> At the request of Grayson's heirs, brief passages relevant principally to the father have been excised at this point. This has necessitated subsequent deletion of an adjective or two at different places in the text, particularly through n. 15 in this chapter. An ellipsis marks the location of all of the alterations.[8]

The original manuscript is now in the possession of one of Wash's descendents, a retired army officer who lives in Tennessee. When I called to speak with him about it, he hung up. My letters to him were returned unopened.

The autobiography, I later learned, was first planned for publication in the 1930s, when E. E. Dale, a distinguished historian of the Southwest who taught at the University of Oklahoma, visited Grayson's daughter, Eloise Smock, at her home in Eufaula. Dale was impressed by Smock's collection of her father's manuscripts, and he said so in a letter to her in September 1934. "If you should ever decide to publish" the autobiography, he wrote, "I should be happy" to offer "any assistance." "Of course," he added, "if your father's manuscript is published, it should be edited just a little and a few minor passages which might be objectionable to your family left out."[9] Smock immediately accepted Dale's invitation, as long as he agreed to leave out "the objectionable parts."[10]

The preparation of the manuscript continued apace, with constant, even obsessive, reassurances by Dale that it would be edited appropriately.[11] Dale's wife typed the working draft of Grayson's handwritten manuscript so that its "confidential matters" would be kept "perfectly safe."[12] The process dragged on, and not until 1938 did Dale report that he had completed the task of editing. He chose a title for the manuscript, divided the work into chapters, and "edited out of the manuscript and omitted any statement" he thought might be "in the slightest degree objectionable" to Smock or her family.[13]

Even his diligent eye did not catch every passage that Smock found troubling. On one occasion, Wash described meeting a man who appeared to have "negro blood in his veins." "I believe this should be left out for the reason that we never know who might read this book," Smock wrote, "and if any of this mans descendants should read such a statement it would be unpleasant for them as well as perhaps cause us some trouble."[14] "Undoubtedly you are exactly right," Dale responded. "I deeply appreciate the suggestion, which is another evidence of the old saying that two heads are better than one."[15] Other members of the family also vetted the manuscript, and by the middle of 1938, it appeared ready for publication.[16] World War II intervened, however, and Dale abandoned the project. When it was revived in the late 1980s, the manuscript had a new editor, but the family was still adamant about deleting certain passages.

Every ellipsis in *A Creek Warrior for the Confederacy* can seem portentous, hiding dark secrets about the Grayson family, but most are surely insignificant, the insertions of Wash himself or the emendations of the editor struggling to bring logic to the punctuation. On two occasions after the first, however, the editor expressly notes that the ellipses signal omitted material "relevant principally to the family." Referring to Wash's grandmother Katy and her second husband, one sentence reads, ". . . . [T]heir first . . . child . . . was . . . named James."[17] The missing words, marked by four different ellipses and a bracket, spark the imagination. On another occasion, Wash writes about visiting his uncle: "I think we rode some forty miles the first day, stopping over night at old William Grayson's. . . ."[18]

The following chapters attempt to fill in these ellipses.

Contents

Introduction 3

Profile: A Symposium at Dartmouth College 6

1 The Griersons 10

Profile: Native Art, June 2000 27

2 "My negro Woman Judah": William's Decision 30

Profile: Rudy Hutton, September 1999 and June 2000 46

3 Race and Removal: Katy's Compromise 49

Profile: Marilyn Vann, June 2003 and April 2004 64

4 Separate Paths: Katy and William in the Antebellum Creek Nation 66

Profile: Napoleon Davis, June 2000 84

5 "It is negroes that we are killing now": The Graysons' Civil War 88

Profile: Chester Adams, June 2000 108

6 Northern Indians and Negro Slaves:
Wash and the Politics of Reconstruction   111

Profile: Buddy Cox, July 1999 and June 2000   128

7 Hardship and Opportunity: The Fortunes of Emma, Vicey, and Wash   132

Profile: Buddy Cox, June 2000   149

8 Divided by Blood: The Graysons and the End of the Creek Nation   151

Profile: Bob Littlejohn, July 1999 and June 2000   169

9 Wash in the Age of Progress   173

Profile: Bob Littlejohn, June 2002   192

10 The Graysons in a Black and White World   194

Afterword   213

A Note on Sources and Historiography   217

Notes   223

Index   291

Black, White, and Indian

Introduction

The Grayson family of the Creek Nation traces its origins to the late 1700s, when Robert Grierson, a Scotsman, and Sinnugee, a Creek woman, settled down together in what is now north-central Alabama. Today their descendants number in the thousands and have scores of surnames in addition to Grayson: Hill, Finniegan, Bruner, Arbor, McIntosh, Tilly, Harrod, Smock, Fuller, Hansard, Hoppe, Crook, Hudson, Sulpher, Smith, Mitchell, Land—to name just a few. They live in Oklahoma, Tennessee, Washington, California, Texas, Kansas, Hawaii, and probably just about every other state. The story told here is therefore necessarily selective. It focuses on a small section of the family in order to explore a big subject: American history as experienced by native peoples.

The Creeks predate the founding of the United States by a century. In the 1500s and 1600s, Old-World diseases, introduced by Spanish explorers such as Hernando de Soto, decimated the native populations of the South, toppling the extensive chiefdoms that dominated the region. The survivors dispersed into village communities, but by the late 1600s they were once again building larger political alliances. The Creeks, incorporating Hitchiti, Muscogee, Koasati, and Yuchi speakers, owe their formation to this tumultuous time, as do the Choctaws, Chickasaws, Catawbas, and Cherokees. By the end of the seventeenth century, when there were only a few thousand Europeans living south of the Virginia border, the Creeks were a formidable force in the Southeast, controlling much of present-day Georgia, Alabama, and northern Florida.[1]

They held their own against the British, French, and Spanish colonies, protecting their land from squatters and taking advantage of imperial rivalries to secure advantageous trading terms.[2] In fact, for a time in the mid–eighteenth century, the Creeks seemed to be thriving in the presence of the European colonies. Trade goods such as beads and textiles introduced new forms of wealth into Creek communities, and European-manufactured guns made Creek warriors feared throughout the region. But in the 1780s, the emergence of the United States marked the beginning of a long decline in Creek power. While Britain,

France, and Spain had been stretched thin administering colonies all over the world, the United States aggressively brought its agents and armies to bear exclusively on Indian nations in North America. Over the course of the nineteenth century, the United States established on Indian lands a series of states—in essence, colonies—that stretched across the continent.[3]

Between 1790 and 1826, the United States forced a number of treaties on the Creeks that significantly reduced their homelands.[4] The process culminated in the 1830s, when the United States removed the Creeks, along with the Choctaws, Chickasaws, Seminoles, and Cherokees, to lands it designated "Indian Territory," west of the Mississippi River. Indian Territory did not remain free from U.S. rule for long. American states continued to expand westward, and in 1907 the United States dissolved the "Five Civilized Tribes," as they were known, and turned Indian Territory into the state of Oklahoma.[5] Not until the 1930s did these Indian nations have the opportunity to reconstitute themselves, albeit in weakened forms.

The story of the Graysons illustrates how one native family survived in the face of overwhelming American force and how it came to terms with a central American obsession, race.[6] In the South, where the Creeks lived, survival was in fact often predicated on abiding by the racial hierarchy. Though the subject is often underplayed in history books, race was a central element in the lives of southeastern Indians, not just as a marker of difference between natives and white newcomers but as a divisive and destructive force within Indian communities themselves.[7] This book examines how and why race was such a powerful force in Indian lives. It argues that abiding by America's racial hierarchy was a survival strategy—part cynical ploy, clever subterfuge, and painful compromise.[8]

In the case of the Graysons, over the course of the nineteenth century, race drove a wedge between family members, separating those with African ancestry from those without, and driving the two sides apart until they denied their common origins. The story here focuses on two branches. One branch begins with Katy Grayson, born in the Creek Nation in present-day Alabama probably sometime in the 1780s. She had two children with a man of African descent. When this short-lived relationship ended, she married a Creek Indian of European and native ancestry. After removal to Indian Territory, one of Katy's children by this second marriage, James, had a son, Wash, the author of the autobiography. In 1917, three years before his death, Wash became the principal chief of the largely defunct Creek Nation. His son Washie, born in 1883, succeeded him to the office.

The other branch of the family begins with Katy's brother William. Around 1819, William initiated a relationship with Judah, an African American slave belonging to his father. They eventually had several children, including Emma, born in 1823 in the old Creek Nation, and Vicey, born in Indian Territory in 1842. Vicey never had children, but Emma had at least four, including Jeanetta and Eli. Other individuals—sisters, brothers, cousins, nephews, and nieces—appear in this book, but the story remains focused on Katy, James, and Wash on one side, and William, Emma and Vicey, and Jeanetta and Eli on the other.

While conducting my research, I met and talked with a number of Creeks and native peoples in Oklahoma and around the country. Their stories, briefly recounted, precede each chapter. In different ways, each one illustrates how to this day race still haunts both the Grayson family and native people more generally.

This is an American Indian story, but it is an American story, too. The Graysons—Scottish deerskin traders, Native American planters, African slaves, and Creek politicians—may appear foreign. They lived in areas, such as north-central Alabama and Indian Territory, that are rarely included in American histories. They took extraordinary actions—rejecting their children, enslaving their relatives, and marrying their masters—that seem unimaginable today. But, with race, inequality, and conflict at the core of their story, the Graysons are truly American, and in one way or another, we all belong to their family.

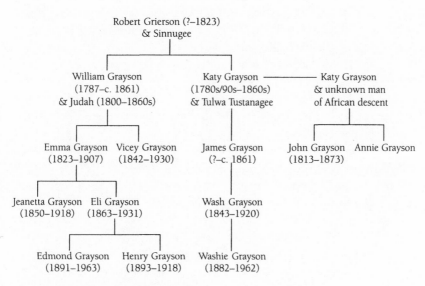

Selected members of the Grayson family.

Profile

A Symposium at Dartmouth College

In late April 2000, the first ever national conference on black Indians convened in Hanover, New Hampshire, at Dartmouth College. The conference was an odd mix of scholarship and group therapy. Participants were welcomed at the opening session by the purifying smoke of sweetgrass. Before the first speeches, people milled about the auditorium, greeting each other and observing others. One dark-skinned man wore a shell choker, buckskin leggings, long feathered earrings, and a gold armband. Four gorgets, shining bright gold—crescent-shaped ornaments frequently worn by eastern Indians in the eighteenth century—hung around his neck. I later learned that he is Don Little Cloud Davenport, cofounder of the Black Native American Association in San Francisco. A woman donned a white buckskin robe with a beaded bandolier hanging by her side. She carried a feathered fan. Another woman wore several medicine pouches hanging around her neck. I spotted a black man with a flaming red, yellow, and black Plains Indian headdress. His shirt was of fringed buckskin. For several minutes he struck a somber pose reminiscent of Red Cloud, the Sioux chief. Then he sat down. He wore a nametag: Chief Sitting Sun. The next day, he would replace his cumbersome headdress with something more sensible, a small, beaded headband.

Some participants arrived with families. Flashbulbs lit up, video cameras rolled. On one side, four or five academics took their seats together. A few college students hunkered down in their chairs, trying to hide their discomfort. In the back, two Indians from the Anishinaabe Nation, dressed modestly compared with some participants, looked on.

After a few introductions at the podium, the dean of the college greeted us in Comanche and told us that being in our presence was a "humbling experience." Donna Roberts, the repatriation and site protection coordinator of the Abenaki Nation, took the stage next, her long gray hair covered by a felt hat that recalled the significance of beaver to her ancestors. Africa has been decolonized, she told us. Canada has begun decolonization—witness the recently created northern land of Nunavit. Central America will be decolonized. And so, too, will the United States. She appealed to the earth mother and the powers of the four directions to bring us knowledge and understanding. Later, after the participants got to know each other better, a black woman told me that she and others felt Roberts to be insincere, a speaker of nice words who actually disdained the African Americans at the conference.

The Dartmouth College chaplain followed with a rendition of a song by Sweet Honey and the Rock, delivered from the podium in a forceful voice. We are a grandmother's prayers, the breath of ancestors, mothers of courage, sisters of mercy, the spirit of god. She concluded with a quotation from Black Elk, the famous Sioux medicine man and guru to New Agers: we must honor the sacred hoop, the world and its spirits.

Finally, the featured speakers took the stage: Don Little Cloud Davenport, Radmilla Cody (Miss Navajo Nation, 1997–1998), and Jewelle Gomez, an activist and author. Davenport, a self-described elder from the seventh generation, recounted the wanderings of his Sudanese ancestor, a medicine man who, he said, ended up with the Seminoles in Florida. Davenport has his own Internet site. Cody, whose father is African American, gave a brief summary of the controversy surrounding her crowning as Miss Navajo Nation. (The Miss Navajo competition is far more rigorous than its Miss America equivalent, for all potential Miss Navajos must compete in fry bread and sheep-butchering competitions.) For her part, Gomez recounted how the lesbian community gave her the strength to search for her Indian roots. The talks were testimonies of personal fortitude and discovery. At night, in the hotel bar, two Indians revealed their disgust for the day's proceedings. "I want to be Afro-American, can I be?" one of them mocked.

African and Indian relationships are as fraught with tensions as those between Africans and Europeans. Historians have worked long and hard to find evidence that these two peoples joined together to fight against their oppressors, but the results are less than satisfying. On some occasions, blacks and Indians did indeed form common alliance, but many other times they fought each other. Today it seems that divisions between blacks and Indians are as deep as they are between blacks and whites. The depth of the divisions between black and Indian peoples became apparent as the conference proceeded.

Many participants attended for what they described as "healing." "There is a lot of pain in this room," said one. They wished to understand their past and make the present come to grips with it. The full absurdity of race in America became apparent as they told their stories. They are African, Native American, and European, but they are only allowed to be black. Some have relatives who go as white. Others have light-skinned cousins who deny any connection to their darker family members. Throughout the conference, they testified to their mixed heritage.

Tension built slowly. In the bathrooms, the black participants grumbled about the panelists and about some of the Indians in the audience. The Indians voiced complaints of their own. The rupture came on the third and last day. It began with a presentation on why the Lumbees of North Carolina, an amalgam of whites, blacks, and Indians without distinct language and customs, should be a federally recognized tribe. Michael, an Oklahoma Cherokee sitting next to me, could barely contain his anger. "They don't even have an origin story," he whispered. The next speaker, Ward Churchill, an American Indian Movement (AIM) activist, provided a temporary catharsis by invoking black power, red power, Gramsci, and Frantz Fanon. A white leftist in his fifties recorded the speech on a tape deck. Sporting cowboy boots, jeans, and an Earth First T-shirt, he vigorously nodded assent to Churchill's assertions. Behind him, a twenty-year-old white college student with short, dyed-blond hair and black-framed glasses sat with a stunned look, mouth agape. "Shit," he gasped, as Churchill launched into a recitation of the FBI's war against the Student Nonviolent Co-ordinating Committee, active in the 1960s civil rights movement. A reference to Leonard Peltier, the AIM activist controversially imprisoned for murdering an FBI agent in 1975, earned applause and cheers. Churchill's final summation, a litany of "U.S. out of . . . ," ending with "U.S. out of North America," brought the crowd to its feet.

But the catharsis was short-lived. After the closing speeches, a black woman stood up. She had spoken the day before, exciting some people and disturbing others with a rambling speech about how the little people come to talk to her at night and how the giant bird formed the mountains of the Earth. Dressed in white buckskin, a white feather in her hair, she now rose to declaim on the Cherokees. "They sold their own people," she said, and another long, disjointed talk seemed about to begin. But from across the hall, Michael could no longer control his anger. He stood up and proclaimed, "I am a Cherokee. Do not speak about my people." She replied, "Your people sold each other." Voices rose, and neither would back down. They began yelling. She would not stop talking, and Michael stormed across the back of the auditorium, in sadness and anger yelling, "Fuck you!" She followed him out the door, and we heard the enraged voices recede down the hall.

In stunned silence, the audience turned to again face the front. Five Native American students from Dartmouth took the stage to sing stanzas of "Amazing Grace" in Navajo, Cherokee, Choctaw, and finally English. Some people were in tears. The audience joined in the last round, "Praise God, praise God, praise God."

The conference ended where it began. In his closing remarks, Robert Warrior read a poem by Nila Northsun, a Shoshone and Chippewa poet, drawn from a volume entitled *Reinventing the Enemy's Language*.[1] Northsun recounts reading, in *Cosmopolitan* magazine, a list of ninety-nine things to do before dying. Forty-seven of them she has already done, and the others are beyond the reaches of "a poor Indian." She consequently decides to make "a list that's more culturally relevant." The list recovers and celebrates Indian ways. Among Northsun's things to do are

> eat ta-nee-ga with a sioux
> learn to make good fry bread
> be an extra in an indian movie
> learn to speak your language
> give your gramma a rose and a bundle of sweet grass
> watch a miwok deer dance
> attend a hopi kachina dance.

Warrior perhaps read the poem as a gesture of inclusion. Black Indians and Native Americans can all participate in these native ways. But one critical passage slipped by most listeners. After learning twenty ways to prepare commodity canned pork, Northsun intends to

> fall in love with a white person
> fall in love with an Indian.

These words caught the breath of the audience's black Indians. The enemy's language seemed to be everywhere.

1 ▪▪▪

The Griersons

Alabama and Georgia seemingly cannot escape their histories. The Confederate cross of Saint Andrew can be spotted on car bumpers, and politicians, even when so inclined, have been unable to erase the Confederate past from state flags without facing the wrath of white voters. These states occupy the heart of the Deep South. Slavery, the Confederacy, the Civil War, and, more encouragingly, the civil rights movement are their legacy.

It is surprising, then, that only some sixty years before the Civil War—that cataclysmic event that defines the Deep South for so many—huge areas of the region, including large portions of Georgia, Alabama, and northern Florida, belonged to the Creek Nation of Indians (also known as the Muscogees). On southeastern maps today, the frequent occurrence of the prefix *oki*, a Creek word meaning "water," attests to the historic extent of the Muscogee Nation. In Georgia, streams, lakes, and swamps are named Ogeechee, Oconee, Ocmulgee, Okapilco, Ochlockonee, Okapilco, Okefenokee, and Ockwalkee. In Alabama, one finds Oakachoy, Oakmulgee, and Oaktasasi creeks. (Okatuppa and Okwakee, also in Alabama, are probably of Chickasaw origin.) In Florida, there are Lake Ocklawaha and the Ochlockonee River. Even as late as 1800, after three centuries of encroachment by European colonists, the Creek Nation still covered the eastern half of Alabama, Georgia west of the Oconee River, and northern Florida. Atlanta, Macon, Columbus, Tallahassee, Montgomery, Birmingham—the major cities of the Deep South—sit on lands that in 1800 belonged to the Creeks.

In the Creek Nation in the heart of the Deep South, no plantations sprawled for acre upon acre. No slaves toiled in vast fields of cotton. No hierarchy divided light-skinned and dark-skinned peoples. This fundamental contrast between the native and plantation South led scores of slaves, day laborers, and other disfavored subjects to flee to the Creek Nation to escape from the oppressive world that colonists were building along the Atlantic seaboard. One of these refugees was named Sinnugee. She came from Spanish Florida and was therefore probably part Spanish, Mesoamerican, and African. A dark-skinned person living in a world that privileged light skin, she (or her mother or grandmother) fled the colony in the 1700s. Or perhaps she was captured by Creek warriors. In either case, she found sanctuary among the Muscogees. By giving her a clan name, they signaled her adoption into the nation; she belonged to the Spanalgee or Spanish clan.[1]

For a time, Sinnugee would fare well in the Creek Nation. But in the early nineteenth century, the Creek world of mixed peoples and small farms would begin converging with the racial hierarchy and sprawling plantations of the southern states. The process would strain Creek communities and would hit Sinnugee's family especially hard. Desperate to survive and prosper in these difficult circumstances, her children would disown their offspring, abandon their spouses, and repudiate their siblings. Her descendants would enslave their own relatives, and brothers would go to war against brothers. By the end of the nineteenth century, Sinnugee's grandchildren would deny each other's existence. But all this seemed unimaginable in the late 1700s. When Sinnugee first started a family with a Scottish immigrant named Robert Grierson, the Creek Nation was a far different place.

Sinnugee's hometown was called Hilabi. It once sat in the upper reaches of the Muscogee Nation on a small waterway called Town Creek, which drains via Hillabee Creek into the Tallapoosa, some fifty miles upriver from present-day Montgomery, Alabama.[2] The land undulates gently and is still largely covered by a mix of longleaf pine and hardwood trees, as it was in Sinnugee's time. Hilabi resembled most other towns in the heart of the Deep South. At its focal point stood a council house, a large rotunda made of logs and plastered with mud that seated hundreds of people. The council house sat adjacent to Hilabi's central square ground, a spacious plaza flanked on each side by open-sided cabins, where town meetings were held in the summer months. Caleb Swan, a New Yorker who visited the Creek Nation in 1791, saw square-ground cabins decorated with eagle feathers, swan wings, scalping knives, war clubs, rotting scalps, bundles of war medicine, and other paraphernalia associated with making war and peace. The structural posts featured paintings of horned warriors, horned rattlesnakes, horned alligators, and other fantastic creatures.[3]

Nearby, there was carved out a flattened ground for playing chunky, a cross between bocce ball and a javelin toss that one U.S. Army medic judged "a most

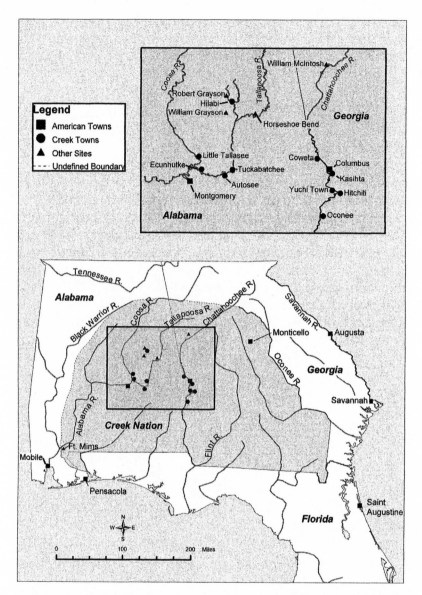

The Creek Nation around 1810, superimposed on a map with present-day state boundaries. Montgomery and Columbus, shown here, would not be established until 1819 and 1828. Map by William T. Jurgelski.

animating and exciting spectacle."[4] William Bartram, a naturalist who traveled through the Deep South in the 1770s, described the average chunky yard. Banks of earth surrounded a sunken field that was as long as two or three hundred feet. In the center stood a thirty- or forty-foot obelisk made of four square pillars. Two far corners of the field were marked by twelve-foot poles, called slave posts because captives were burned on them. "The pole," Bartram noted, "is usually crowned with the white dry skull of an enemy."[5]

You could traverse Hilabi's dirt paths in no more than a few minutes, for there were only some twenty buildings in all.[6] The residential structures were arranged in twos, threes, or fours around small courtyards. On each courtyard, open arbors sheltered women as they tanned deer hides over smudge pots. Storage sheds housed agricultural instruments and hunting equipment as well as corn. A main building provided sleeping quarters for families. It was made of wattle and daub, a lattice of saplings plastered with mud.

"Old Hilabee," as some people called it, had seen better days.[7] In the late 1700s, its residents still numbered five or six hundred, but many of them had recently moved to outlying residences and satellite villages.[8] North of Hilabi, along a marshy creek now called Enitachopco, sat the village of Aunette Chapco, or "long swamp." Farther north on Hillabee Creek, past a three-hundred-foot rise, stood Thenooche Aubaulau, or "over little mountain." In the other direction, about four miles below Hilabi, lay Echuseisligau, "where a young thing was found." And two miles directly south of Hilabi on a large sandbank sat Ooktau-hauzausee, "a great deal of sand," on Oaktasasi Creek.[9] These places started to attract people in the 1780s, when Thomas Scott, Auwillaugee, Robert Grierson, and other ambitious Hilabi residents began raising cattle. Scott, Auwillaugee, and Grierson demanded more space for their ranches than the compact settlement of old Hilabi offered.[10]

Most residents of Hilabi were content to make do with less space and fewer material resources than these entrepreneurs. They grew their own food, hunted their own game, manufactured their own pots from local clay, and tailored their own clothes from deer hides. Nevertheless, since the mid–eighteenth century, they depended more and more on imported items: guns, gunpowder, lead shot, blankets, shirts (checkered, ruffled, white linen), handkerchiefs, scissors, knives, combs, looking glasses (walnut-framed), tinsel-laced hats, ribbons, copper kettles, and beads.[11] Items such as guns were becoming nearly a necessity because of the declining bow-and-arrow skills of hunters. Other items, such as kettles, both sturdier and lighter than clay pots, simply proved more practical. Still others, such as beads, were hardly necessary, but they occupied such a high place in the hierarchy of Creek wants that few Hilabi residents wished to do without them.

The annual busk, a yearly Muscogee ceremony marking the first harvest of corn, brought together a remarkable assortment of people in the town square of old Hilabi. Their names testify to their diversity: Auwillaugee, Thomas Scott, Robert Grierson, Mad Bear, Big Chatter, Reles Eneha, Hilabi Captain, Hilabi Harjo, Hilabi Tustunagee, Paya Lucko, Grence, Saucy Jack, David Hay, Stephen Hawkins, Eneha Thlucco Harjo, Thomas, Opioche Tustunagee, James, Venus, Rachel Spillard, Sinnugee, Fannautotau, Opio Docta, and others. Most of the residents were born and raised in the Creek Nation by Creek parents, but some were immigrants. Thomas Scott and Robert Grierson came to Hilabi from Scotland to set up shop and trade guns, pots, and blankets for deerskins.[12] Other immigrants came from Africa by way of Georgia, South Carolina, or Florida. Two such newcomers arrived in Hilabi in August 1788 after fleeing 225 miles from their owner, Captain Martín Palao of Pensacola. In Hilabi, they joined a growing population of fugitives, including at least one other slave belonging to Palao.[13]

Traders frequently married local women, and Hilabi therefore also counted among its residents a number of people contemptuously called "half-breeds" by white Americans. One North Carolinian, a U.S. Indian agent, singled out Auwillaugee by such a name, although he noted approvingly that she owned seventy head of cattle.[14] By the agent's logic, Sinnugee, in all probability the child or grandchild of a fugitive slave, might have warranted the same designation.[15] Yet the agent called Sinnugee an Indian, for he was blind to the frequent marriages between Native and African Americans.[16]

Still other immigrants were fully African or European American but had lived so long in the Creek Nation that they all but became native Muscogees. John Eades's son Daniel surely fit this description. Born in Wilkes County, Georgia, in 1770, Daniel was kidnapped at the impressionable age of nine by a party of Creeks. Fourteen years after this traumatic event, John hopefully reported that his son was held "captive" in Hilabi. Yet Daniel, then twenty-three, was scarcely a prisoner. He had adopted a new identity and now answered to the name Saucy Jack.[17]

This was Sinnugee's world in the late 1700s. In fact, the vast majority of residents in the Deep South lived in similar communities. The typical town in the region looked a lot like Hilabi: a few hundred Creek residents, several immigrants from Africa and Europe, small farms, and wattle-and-daub houses stocked with locally produced goods.

Around the time of George Washington's stunning victory over Cornwallis at Yorktown in 1781, Sinnugee began a relationship with Robert Grierson. Unlike Sinnugee, Robert sought fortune, not refuge, in Hilabi.[18] Like so many other Scottish immigrants, he moved to the Creek Nation to participate in the deerskin trade. From Hilabi, Robert could purchase skins from the 170 hunters who lived in the area and transport them along the main trade route east to Augusta, which conveniently passed just south of town.[19] As an outsider who offered a service both irresistible and unwelcome, he occupied a precarious place in Creek society. Traders did not simply sell shirts and kettles. They also were purveyors of social change, for by reshaping the economy and transforming the demand for labor, each good traded had significant social repercussions.[20] Even if Muscogees accepted these innovations, they often objected to common market practices, such as traders raising the price of goods if demand so warranted.[21]

Robert's success in the deerskin trade therefore depended on good relations with native peoples and especially with women.[22] Robert surely knew the cautionary story of his predecessor in Hilabi, James Henderson. In 1761, twenty Indians from nearby towns stormed Henderson's store and absconded with the majority of his wares. Hilabi women concealed what remained and returned the merchandise after the immediate danger had subsided, but Henderson's travails were not over. After he reestablished his shop, warriors demanded goods on credit and took them by force when he refused. When Henderson stubbornly stayed on, Hilabi Captain ordered him to leave town and made it plain that other traders were unwelcome as well.[23] Two years later, an unnamed trader, perhaps the unfortunate Henderson himself, was murdered in Hilabi.[24]

The lessons were clear: defer to your hosts and befriend local women, who often acted as a moderating force on rash warriors. But the surest way to avoid trouble was to become an adopted town member by marrying a Creek woman, such as Sinnugee. If Sinnugee brought Robert a sense of security, Robert in turn offered her economic stability and opportunity, especially at a time when Creeks were experiencing a major and unsettling shift toward a new economy based on plow agriculture and ranching rather than farming and hunting.[25] It is worth noting that their relationship began soon after the Muscogees weathered a difficult period of famine and disease.[26] By marrying a trader, Sinnugee assured that in times of want her family would have access to resources beyond the Creek Nation.

Over the course of the 1780s and 1790s, Sinnugee and Robert raised a family of eight: Sandy, Watt, Elizabeth, William, Thomas, Sarah, David, and Katy. The Grierson children grew up in relative privilege. By the 1790s, Robert had accumulated some three hundred head of cattle and operated a thirty-acre farm that stood out as the most advanced of Hilabi's new settlements. The farm, located some three miles upriver from old Hilabi, produced two thousand pounds of cotton every year. When harvest rolled around, Robert hired local

Hilabi women to pick the white bolls. Robert's offer of employment marked the first time wage labor had ever come to Hilabi, and it arrived when there were few other opportunities to make money. The older economy based on the deer-skin trade was collapsing because of a precipitous decline of the deer population. At least some women therefore accepted Grierson's offer of employment. For each thirty-two-pound basket of cotton, they earned a cup of salt, three strands of mock wampum (blue and white beads), or a half cup of *tafia*, a cheap rum distilled from the by-products of sugar. On good days, at the height of the season when the bolls were fully open, they picked between two and three baskets each. Wages from a typical harvest introduced a total of sixty-two cups of salt, 188 strands of mock wampum, or two gallons of *tafia* to the economy of old Hilabi, whose residents were mainly subsistence farmers and hunters. Robert, by contrast, grossed 150 pounds sterling, nearly five thousand times the value of the wages he paid Hilabi women.[27]

The economy of new Hilabi made the Griersons wealthy, but it also drove a wedge between them and their neighbors. Robert's profit-making enterprises were foreign to most Creeks, and many Hilabis resented his close accounting of debt and credit and his affection for private property. Robert whipped Creeks who stole his goods. On one occasion he paid a Muscogee three and a half gallons of rum to administer the punishment. "This is the way we spend our money," he complained. Creeks stole so much property, Robert lamented, that it was impossible to "do my business like one ought to be done."[28]

Nevertheless, by the end of 1796, U.S. Indian agent Benjamin Hawkins could unequivocally report that Robert had "large possessions," among them cattle, horses, and—significantly—"negroes."[29] These "negroes" were probably slaves, but in what sense it is difficult to say. Slavery is a term that describes a wide variety of forced labor. Americans are most familiar with chattel slavery, the form of servitude practiced in the British colonies and the United States, where slaves were defined as property and exploited for their surplus labor.[30] Less well known is kinship slavery, once common in parts of Africa and native America. Kinship slaves were to some degree family members. They cooked, cleaned, collected firewood, farmed, provided sexual services, and were a lot like any other family member. Unlike most chattel slaves, kinship slaves generally did not pass their status on to their children (who, after all, were usually the offspring of masters as well), and they themselves sometimes became full family members. In short, in kinship societies, the line between slave and family was frequently murky.[31] Robert's "negroes" stood somewhere on this indistinct line separating slave and kin. The difficulty in distinguishing between the two would vex his family for generations.

Agent Hawkins himself seemed confused about the matter. He wrote that

Robert "employs 11 hands, red, white and black, in spinning and weaving, and the other part of his family in raising and preparing the cotton for them."[32] Whom did Robert include among his family? In what sense did he employ them? Was each laborer red, white, or black, or red, white, *and* black? Hawkins's other descriptions of the Griersons evince a similar confusion. In the agent's words, Robert "had his family around him ginning and picking cotton." What combination of coercion and cooperation hid behind the ambiguous verb "to have"? Robert "governs them as Indians, and makes them and his whole family respect him," said Hawkins. How hierarchical was a family whose patriarch appeared at least to one observer to draw a racial line between himself and his wife and children? What kind of respect did he demand from them? Robert, Hawkins noted, set up a cotton manufactory with "ten women red and black," *including* his wife, Sinnugee, and their daughter. Red, black, and white, slave and kin—these terms converged and sometimes became indistinguishable in the Grierson family.[33]

Robert's patriarchy and racism may have galled Sinnugee, yet she profited measurably from both hierarchies. By acknowledging at least in part the patriarchal rule of her husband, she conceded a great deal of her own authority and set aside Creek notions of matrilineal control. But in exchange she received material benefits at a time when, because of the shifting economy, many Creek women lived in poverty. Likewise, by recognizing a hierarchy of races, she admitted her own inferiority to whites, but in turn she gained command over blacks. In fact, by 1812, Robert had accumulated between seventy and one hundred slaves, and Sinnugee stood above each one of them.[34] By "Industry and Acconemy," Robert boasted in 1820, "I have procured a property."[35] This tension between being Indian, white, and black, between commanding and serving, permeated the lives of Sinnugee and her children.

Other families in the Creek Nation were less adept at surviving in the new economy. By the early nineteenth century, the uncompromising policies of the United States, widespread poverty, and the unresponsiveness of Creek politicians were weighing heavily on many Indians. U.S. policies were sometimes well-meaning and ill-informed, other times dishonest and self-interested, but repeatedly destructive to native peoples. No matter the details, the end result, if not always the stated goal, of U.S. Indian policy was dispossession. The "gradual extension of our Settlements," wrote George Washington, "will as certainly cause the Savage as the Wolf to retire; both being beasts of prey tho' they differ in shape."[36]

Washington, writing at the conclusion of the Revolutionary War, made the process sound natural, like the changing of the seasons. But, in fact, dispossession demanded a concerted effort by the United States. With government sponsorship, numerous missionaries, schoolteachers, and Indian agents set out to civilize America's native peoples. Benjamin Hawkins, agent among the Creeks, was fondly remembered by one contemporary admirer for civilizing "by example as well as by precept." Hawkins used his slaves to establish a "large plantation," making "immense crops of corn and other provisions."[37] Such instruction, it was presumed, would lead Indians to forgo hunting and depend entirely on farming, thereby freeing up vast hunting grounds for purchase by the United States— never mind that crop yields were notoriously erratic, that unbalanced diets are less nutritious, and that hunting played an integral role in the cultures of southeastern Indians. Named after its foremost exponent, this scheme to civilize Native Americans and appropriate their lands became known as Jeffersonian Indian policy.[38]

Despite Jefferson's hopes, few Indians abandoned their traditions in favor of American practices. Instead, whites squatted on their land, driving off game animals. When Native Americans sought U.S. cooperation to remove the squatters, the federal government refused to take action. When they tried to remove the squatters themselves, however, state militias retaliated against native villages without mercy. Under such duress, Indians had no choice but to cede their lands. In the Deep South, the borders of the Creek Nation were chipped away by a succession of treaties in 1790, 1802, 1804, 1805, and 1811.[39]

Poverty followed in the wake of the land cessions. Periods of starvation, triggered by natural disasters but made worse by continuing land loss, were common in the Southeast, as Indians and others attested: "the Indians this way are nearly starving" (1794); "some of our women and children were actually starved and many so reduced by hunger as to be unfit for any business and a prey to disease" (1804); "the whole land has experienced the want of corn for nearly two months" (1807); "they are likely to experience a very hungry year, as they express it, and what we call a famine" (1810).[40] Creeks understood the problem exactly. Ceded lands gave the United States valuable timber, pasture for cattle and hogs, rich soil for tobacco plantations, and rushing rivers to drive grain and lumber mills. All these things, said the Creeks, were "lasting profits." In exchange, they received "little goods" that, in a year or two, were "rotten, and gone to nothing."[41]

Desperate and angry, Creeks formed a political and religious movement in 1813 dedicated to rejecting U.S. colonizing policies. They called themselves Redsticks, after the war clubs they wielded. Their militancy divided the nation, for many Creeks thought that the Redsticks were rash or simply wrong to oppose the United States. When Creek politicians balked at supporting the movement,

Redsticks attacked them in April 1813. In Hilabi, Robert and Sinnugee found themselves at the center of the conflict. As ranchers, planters, and slave owners, they stood out as glaring examples of the new Hilabi promoted by Indian agents, and many residents were unhappy with their presence.[42] On April 21, with violence spreading, Redsticks murdered Robert and Sinnugee's son David.[43]

Then, in July 1813, warriors struck Robert and Sinnugee's home. "Mr. Grayson is a respectable Scotchman, was in the British service in the War of the Revolution, and had acquired a large property," wrote Agent Hawkins. "One would suppose such a man would be a favourite. But they have destroyed every hog he has, took all his cattle horses and negro's, a few of which only have been recently restored."[44] That was hardly the worst of it. The Redsticks also attacked Robert and Sinnugee's daughter-in-law, an American woman who taught the family how to spin and weave cotton. Warriors stripped her of clothing and destroyed all her possessions.[45] They drove Robert and Sinnugee's son Sandy from the nation, and they murdered Pinkey Hawkins, the child of their daughter Sarah.[46]

In August, tensions erupted again in Hilabi, and twelve more residents died in the violence.[47] That same month, Redsticks killed and scalped three Indians near New Yaucau, a short distance from Hilabi, and in nearby Wewocau they murdered two leading Creek politicians.[48] At the end of the deadly month, Redsticks turned their anger on Americans and murdered 250 settlers who had sought safety at Fort Mims, a U.S. outpost in southern Alabama. The attack, later memorialized melodramatically in *Gone with the Wind*, spurred the United States to enter the war.[49] "Sleep not too hard you must have heard of the massacre at Tombigbee," Robert warned Agent Hawkins after the attack on Fort Mims. "I wish to God to see those magic owls cut down," he exclaimed, while more than two hundred Redstick warriors were gathering in Hilabi.[50] Yet the Griersons stayed on, reluctant to leave their plantation. At the end of October, the Redsticks again attacked their home, this time razing it.[51]

Left "to the inclemency of the weather without food or raiment," Robert appealed directly to Andrew Jackson, the general commanding U.S. troops in the Creek Nation, begging for protection from this "outrageous and lawless band of savages."[52] He and his family fled soon afterward, heading northeast toward U.S. troops and the Cherokee Nation. The trip was arduous, for Robert suffered from paralysis and could not even stand without assistance.[53] Near present-day Rome, Georgia, his fortunes worsened. Cherokee warriors, mobilized to aid the U.S. war effort against the Redsticks, began stealing his slaves. Over a week's period, Robert lost forty-seven of them. "In short," he wrote to Jackson, the assailants left him "both hungry and naked, unable to procure anything to subsist on."[54]

Either shortly before or after fleeing Hilabi, Robert's twenty-six-year-old son, William, decided to enlist against the Redsticks, joining a brigade of Creek soldiers loyal to the United States that served under the command of Generals John Floyd and Andrew Jackson.[55] William's tour of duty brought him to familiar territory. In early November, William's company received orders to march on Hilabi, even though local residents had offered to capitulate to Jackson.[56] At Little Okfuskee, a day's ride from William's home, the troops captured five Redsticks, then set fire to the town. Perhaps in haste to reach his destination, the commanding officer, James White, spared Hilabi's outlying village Aunette Chapco. The soldiers rushed the final few miles to Hilabi itself. On November 18, they surprised the residents, killed 60 people, and captured 250 others. Then they burned it down.[57]

Other battles followed: on November 29 at Autosee, 200 Redsticks were killed; December 13 at Ecunhutke, 30 were killed; January 27, 1814, along the Tallapoosa River, 189 were killed.[58] Then, on March 27, William, serving under Andrew Jackson, participated in the final battle of the war. At a sharp horseshoe bend on the Tallapoosa River, scarcely twelve miles due east from William's childhood home, 1,000 Redsticks gathered from several nearby towns, including Hilabi. Across the narrowest part of the horseshoe, they erected a three-hundred-yard barricade that met the river on both sides of the tight bend. The barricade stood five to eight feet high and was, according to Jackson, nearly impenetrable. "It is difficult to conceive a situation more eligible for defence than the one they had chosen," Jackson remarked.[59] If the position were breached, however, escape would be impossible.

Jackson and his militia pounded the barricade with cannons for two hours, but to no avail. Then he ordered his troops to charge, and they stormed the breastworks, sending hundreds of Redsticks fleeing toward the Tallapoosa. The land drops evenly down to the river, which flows placidly around the bend. The opposite bank, not more than three hundred feet away, rises sharply in places. There, William's company and other soldiers stood, shooting down Creeks who attempted to swim to safety. William's company eventually crossed the river and fought its way through the Creek position. Perhaps 500 died at the hands of Jackson's militia, and another 250 or 300 drowned or were shot down in the river by William's company and other soldiers.[60]

After the battle, William was discharged, and he headed to rejoin his family, which had since taken refuge in Jasper County, now located in central Georgia, but then lying just across the boundary of the Creek Nation.[61] William left behind a land in ruins.[62] More than fifteen hundred Creeks had died in the conflict, fully 10 percent of the population.[63] The loss of life was compounded by loss of land, for in August 1814, Andrew Jackson imposed a treaty on the

Muscogees that seized twenty million acres of their nation.[64] The treaty was signed by William's brother Sandy, among others. "How much was taken from them and how little was left to them constitutes one of the most striking and consequential events in our Indian and Anglo-American annals," said one observer from Georgia.[65] Their fields razed, livestock slaughtered, and houses destroyed, starving Creeks scrounged for corn dropped from the feed bags of General Jackson's horses.[66] Buddy Cox, a Creek citizen who now lives in Oklahoma City, recounts family stories suggesting that Muscogees were even more desperate; they picked undigested kernels out of the horses' dung.[67]

With her family under constant attack during the war, Robert and Sinnugee's sixteen-year-old daughter Katy made an extraordinary decision. Just when the Redstick movement began to polarize the nation and enflame tensions between whites, Indians, and blacks, Katy formed a relationship with a man later described by her grandson as a "negro," and she conceived her first child with him.[68] Katy's partner may have been African or merely of African descent, free or enslaved, a newcomer to the area or a longtime servant to the Griersons. Their child, John, was born in 1813.[69] John's birth challenged the prevailing sentiment among Creek politicians that Africans should be slaves, not spouses.

Katy conceived her second child, a daughter who would be named Annie, shortly after John's birth. Annie's father was also a "negro," according to Katy's grandson, probably but not certainly the same person who fathered John.[70] While Katy lay pregnant, the prospects for dark-skinned Creeks were dimming considerably. Invading U.S. troops were assessing Creek lands for their potential to grow cotton. The Alabama River valley in the Creek Nation, planter and general Andrew Jackson reported ominously in August 1814, "far exceeds any conception of fertility, and advantages that I had conceived." It would produce an annual revenue of at least $30 million, he claimed, estimating the profits of slavery.[71] Years later, one Georgian would recall that after the "formidable Indian had been humbled," "smiling Fortune beckoned" the wealthiest planters to take up residence in Alabama.[72]

In the short term, Katy and her new family would have to survive in Jasper County. The Griersons did not suffer deprivation while in exile. Robert borrowed money from a business partner, Henry Walker, to purchase goods for his family: sugar, coffee, bacon, whiskey, brandy, tableware, and other items. He also bought plantation tools to keep his remaining slaves working. Some of the purchases indicate that Robert wished to keep his family busy as well. He purchased a pair of cotton cards for Katy, for example, allowing her to prepare cotton fibers for spinning. Robert's expenses at this time also included an extravagant twenty-dollar fee paid to Dr. Milton Antony, presumably toward relieving Robert's "Complicated" and "grievous" disease.[73] Antony, who would later found the state's medical college in Augusta, had earned a national reputation by performing an astonishing surgery in which "he successfully excised portions of the 5th and 6th ribs . . . and lung tissue" from a patient.[74] Robert presumably demanded less invasive treatment. During their stay in Jasper County, the Griersons also probably met Reuben Shorter for the first time. Shorter's son Eli, with the assistance of the Griersons, would later play an important role in dispossessing the Creeks of their Alabama lands.[75]

Despite the family's material comfort, the sojourn in Jasper County must have alarmed Katy. It likely marked her first extended experience with the racial hierarchy of the southern states. Jasper County had been carved out of Creek lands taken by treaty in 1805. By 1810, the county numbered 5,700 free residents and 1,800 slaves. Large plantations had yet to come to the county, but with one slave for every three free people, the region contrasted markedly with Katy's hometown of Hilabi.[76] Vicious prejudice was evident everywhere. Slave codes in the state sometimes equated Indians with Negroes and other times referred more generally to "persons of colour," a term that in practice could include anyone with dark skin.[77] The two small children, John and Annie, and perhaps their mother, too, fell under a whole host of racist laws.

With war raging in the Creek Nation, local residents, already predisposed to treat Native Americans with contempt, were living in heightened fear of Indian uprisings and slave revolts. Rumors raced through the South of Indian and black alliances in southern Georgia and Alabama, a prospect so alarming that no public figure could bring himself to write explicitly about the possibility, even though it was on everyone's mind. In late 1812, when fugitive slaves and Indians were joining forces in Florida, Governor David Mitchell of Georgia feared "the very worst evils imaginable," but he refused to elaborate.[78] Four years later, Indian agent William Crawford spoke cryptically of "irritations" in Georgia that "may ultimately endanger the peace of the nation."[79] The national Niles' Weekly Register replaced mention of African American soldiers joining the Redsticks with a more discreet reference to "***** troops."[80]

Because Jasper County sat on the border of the Creek Nation, local whites felt especially vulnerable. In early November 1813, probably shortly after the Griersons arrived, residents were startled by a Redstick attack that left several newcomers dead in neighboring Morgan County. Governor Peter Early sent cavalry to patrol the frontier, and Monticello, the Jasper County seat, served as the staging ground for more than five hundred volunteers who marched into the Creek Nation. Even as tensions dissipated in spring 1814, Governor Early complained about the presence in Georgia of friendly Creeks such as the Griersons. They should travel unarmed and only with a pass from the U.S. Indian agent, he stated.[81]

After living in such a hostile atmosphere, Katy must have been relieved to return to Hilabi at the close of the war, but even there, people were growing more intolerant of mixed relationships. Big Warrior, the Creek leader who emerged victorious after the war, owned a plantation and between seventy and eighty slaves of his own. An acquaintance described him as "a lover of wealth."[82] Moreover, the United States established a military presence throughout the Muscogee Nation, intimidating fugitive slaves and increasing the anxiety of free blacks.[83] In 1816, it launched a military campaign in northern Florida designed to seize fugitive slaves living with Creeks and Seminoles.[84] In short, opportunities for mixed families such as Katy's were rapidly disappearing.

The political sentiment within the Creek Nation was crystallized in 1818 in a code of eleven laws, the first ever put into writing by the Creeks. The third law in the series reads, "It is agreed, that if a Negro kill an Indian, the Negro shall suffer death." "And if an Indian kill a Negro," it continued, "he shall pay the owner the value." The law, as originally drafted, apparently struck U.S. Indian agent David Mitchell as problematic. He scrawled at the bottom of his copy that it was approved after modification "for the further security of the life of a negro," probably not to defend the rights of the accused but to protect more strongly the interests of planters.[85]

On several accounts the Creek law was racist. By stipulating no more than a fine for killing a Negro, it devalued the lives of Africans. By assuming that all Negroes had owners, it conflated Negroes and slaves. Most important, by using the term "Negro," it assumed that there is such thing. There is nothing self-evident or logical about the category, and it dissolves upon even the slightest scrutiny.[86] On the continuum of skin color, where does one draw the line dividing Negroes and others? Why are Papua New Guineans, who most assuredly have dark skin, not considered Negroes? If the term is meant to encompass people from Africa, why does it not include Moroccans? If it is intended to refer to people in sub-Saharan Africa, at what threshold does a barrier become great enough to mark racial divisions? If the Sahara is such a barrier, what about the Alps dividing Switzerland and Italy, or the Sierra Nevadas dividing California and the rest of the United States, or, for that matter, the Hudson River dividing Manhattan and New Jersey?

Negroes exist first only in the eye of the beholder, although the category later takes on a life of its own in law, science, and popular discourse, and even in the minds of those called Negroes. Frantz Fanon famously described how he first recognized that he was a Negro, "an object in the midst of other objects." "I subjected myself to an objective examination," he wrote with bitter sarcasm.

"I discovered by blackness, my ethnic characteristics; and I was battered down by tom-toms, cannibalism, intellectual deficiency, fetishism, racial defects, slave-ships, and above all else, above all: 'Sho' good eatin'.' "[87] The Creek law thus not only deprived Africans of equal rights but also formally recognized the existence of race. Being of European, African, and Creek descent, Katy, John, and Annie were glaring examples of the unsoundness of racial categories. They were also race's potential victims.

This regrettable law may have been directly inspired by an act "for the trial and punishment of Slaves, and free people of Colour," passed by the Georgia legislature when David Mitchell was governor in December 1816, shortly before he became the U.S. agent to the Muscogees and oversaw the passage of the similar Creek statute. The Georgia act sentenced to death all slaves and free people of color convicted of murdering a white person. Like the Creek code, Georgia's specified a favored class (in this case whites, not Indians) and conflated slaves and free people of African descent.[88] There was one difference between the Creek and Georgia slave codes, however. Whereas a Creek who killed a slave needed only to pay a fine, in Georgia, any white person who killed a slave was tried as if he or she had killed a free person, with two significant exceptions. The killer was deemed innocent if the slave died during an insurrection or when receiving "moderate correction."[89] In practice, however, as Frederick Douglass vividly described in his autobiography, southern whites had virtually free license to murder slaves.[90]

Unstated in the Creek law is the precise definition of a Negro. Did Katy's two children qualify? By the Muscogee tradition of matrilineal descent, children traced their line through their mothers. Assuming that Katy's mother, Sinnugee, had been fully adopted into the nation, John and Annie were undeniably Creek, regardless of the identity of their father. Another section of the 1818 code, however, must have given Katy pause: "It is agreed," stated the eighth law, "that when a man dies and has children living, his children shall have his property." "His other relations," it concluded, "shall not take the property to the injury of the children."[91] In a matrilineal society, a man's property descends to his sisters and then to his sisters' daughters. This law, at least in theory if not in practice, overturned matrilineal in favor of patrilineal inheritance. In fact, fathers were becoming increasingly important in the Creek Nation, and it was now uncertain if John and Annie would be able to shake off the stigma of having a father of African ancestry.

Katy faced a bleak future—until her life took a significant turn around 1817. Katy and her African partner went their separate ways, though it is impossible to say why. Perhaps she abandoned him because of the increasingly hostile racial climate or simply because she grew to dislike him. Maybe she was abandoned by him for similar reasons; or he was sold out of the Creek Nation; or maybe he simply died. Wash Grayson's published autobiography evades the issue, noting only that Katy "was living quietly somewhere," presumably with her father, Robert. "[In due time] . . . ," it continues mysteriously, with brackets and ellipses, she married someone else.[92] If the transformation in Katy's family is shrouded in darkness, it is nevertheless certain that it had a profound impact on the Griersons for decades to come. Its reverberations still echo in the family today.

As if to mark the transformation, in 1817 Robert gave his daughters Elizabeth and Katy a number of slaves, out of "natural love and affection" and for their "better support and maintainance." These sentimental reasons were perhaps outweighed by Robert's desire to make "all other bonds and deeds null, and void," for he was involved in a series of lawsuits and desperately wished to clear the title to his slaves. Elizabeth received Dy, Molly, Grace, Grace's child Rina, Ben, Diana, Luamina, Hope, Nelly, Isaac, Lucy, Daniel, Amitto, Amitto Senior, and Rina and her children, Polly, Lidia, Nero, Dick, and Ian. Katy received Will, Dy, Ian, James and his wife, Venus, and their children, Sam, Robin, Amanda, Will, Hector, Mary, Ann, and Abigail, and Abigail's children, Judy, Kit, and John.[93] Robert's gift to Katy made her dependent on the degradation of blacks and, intentionally or not, illustrated a simple choice: be a mother to black Creeks or a master of black slaves. Around this time, the spelling of the Grierson surname evolved into Grayson, more accurately reflecting pronunciation in the Muscogee language. It is ironic that a century later, Wash Grayson would attribute this transformation to the inability of the Grierson slaves to enunciate their master's name.[94]

If Katy struggled with the contradiction between enslaving and bearing the children of Africans, two of her older brothers, Watt and Sandy, showed no such compunction. No matter the ancestry of their mother, Sinnugee, or their nephew and niece John and Annie, Watt and Sandy were certain that they had the right to hold slaves, as Robert conveyed in a pathetic letter to Agent Hawkins in November 1820. His sons Watt and Sandy, he lamented, were accusing him of stealing "thire negroes." "I have Given them a divide of property [and they] have lost it," he explained. They "are ungrateful to the Extream to me," complained Robert, "affording me no relief nor Comfort in old age but the contrary are thratining abuses of all Kinds to myself and the three other Children at home." His wayward sons struck an agreement with William McIntosh, one of the wealthiest Creeks in the country and a slaveholder himself. McIntosh would use his political leverage to confiscate Robert's slaves, and in turn McIntosh, Watt, and Sandy would divide the bondmen and bondwomen between them. Big Warrior, the head of the Creek Nation, soon intervened in the dispute against Robert. According to Robert's account, Big Warrior (said by one acquaintance to be of "great size" yet "not so corpulent as to be either unwieldy or ungainly") ridiculed and abused him "in the most Violent and absurd maner" before reaching an "arbitrary" decision. The entire affair, Robert concluded, was "more then I can bare."[95]

Robert could at least console himself with the presence of his three youngest children, Elizabeth, Katy, and William. They "are disposed to treat me humane and tender and as becomes Children to a parent," he said, declaring that he was "Antious the[y] should be Rewarded [for] thire Kindness to me."[96] Elizabeth and Katy had indeed been rewarded with slaves in 1817 and would be again at Robert's death. There is no record, however, of William receiving any gifts from his father. The reason may have to do with Judah, a slave woman belonging to Robert. After William returned from the Redstick War, he and Judah began sleeping together. In 1819, they had a child, William Jr. (Billy).[97] Like his sister Katy, William had to make a decision. Would he be Judah's master or Judah's partner?

Profile

Native Art, June 2000

Old Robert Grierson has inspired scores of his descendants to become amateur genealogists. Searching through genealogy Web sites, I found numerous queries and postings from people around the country regarding their Grayson ancestry. Many Web visitors claimed to be descended from Elizabeth Grierson's marriage to William McIntosh. Elizabeth was Katy's older sister. William is renowned in the Creek Nation for corruption and graft, but outside of the Creek Nation, he embodies a combination of Indian dignity and Scottish highlands vitality. One nineteenth-century portrait by a white admirer shows him gripping the hilt of a sword, visage flanked by sideburns that would do any Scotsman proud, and head adorned with a feathered turban announcing his eminent status among the Creeks. Unfortunately for amateur genealogists claiming to be both McIntoshes and Graysons, there is no contemporary evidence attesting to Elizabeth's and William's marriage, and some documents even weigh against it.

The enthusiasm with which some people embrace dubious connections to William appears to rise in proportion to the vigor with which they deny their better-documented connections to black Creeks. Christie Schultz is a rare exception. Katy Grayson's great-great-great-granddaughter, Christie now lives in Washington State. "I'm totally open to all relations, and think it's a matter of history that needs to be documented accurately," she wrote me. Her great-grandmother Christie Grayson, born in 1858, was "always very adamant about there being 'no persons of color in our family,' " she revealed. Christie Grayson even refused to let her four daughters wear patchwork " 'because the Blacks wore that.' " Did Christie's great-grandmother protest too much?[1]

Unfortunately, other Graysons were less accommodating when I inquired about their family history. One direct descendant of Wash's has a collection of valuable family manuscripts that he will not share with historians. When I phoned him, he hung up after I introduced myself. News had already spread that I was writing a book about *all* the Graysons. I fared slightly better with another Grayson descendant, a successful artist who lives in Muskogee, Oklahoma. She is a great-great-great-great-granddaughter of Robert Grierson and Sinnugee. When I called her, she said that she would love to talk to me, and even over the phone she began recounting stories about her family. We set up a time to meet in two weeks at her home. Later that same day, she called me back. She had talked to her brother and now insisted that there was little point in my interviewing her.

Interview or no interview, I was off to Oklahoma City for a research trip, and since I arrived on a Sunday, when all the state archives are closed, I headed for the Red Earth Festival, an annual celebration of Native American culture featuring several days of dancing and drumming. As I wandered through the stalls of Indian arts and crafts, a name on one placard caught my eye. It belonged to the Grayson descendant from Muskogee. She had been designated the "Honored One" by festival organizers, and there she was standing before a display of her paintings and greeting old friends and passersby. Her work is figurative and symbolic; it features landscapes of full moons and dark, long-haired women. I approached her and introduced myself. She was welcoming and profusely apologetic for canceling our meeting. We chatted amiably. I did not feel it was appropriate to raise her troubled family history in the context of this chance encounter, but the subject nevertheless arose briefly. "I don't understand why people are so afraid of having African ancestry," I said, naively ignoring the fact that, in many communities, African ancestry remains a serious liability. She replied that, had I been born black, I'd know.

On my departure, she gave me a copy of the 2001 Cherokee Heritage Calendar, "produced," as it says, "for the purpose of supporting the art of artists with Cherokee descent—whether enrolled members or not." Her work is featured in the month of December. In her paintings, she employs Indian iconography, addresses Indian themes, and, most important in the art market, identifies herself as Indian. Indian identity is so critical to the reception of this genre of art that Congress passed the Indian Arts and Crafts Act of 1990, which threatens artists who falsely market their work as Indian with a fine of $250,000 and up to five years in federal prison. The act defines an "Indian" as "any individual who is a member of an Indian tribe" or who is "certified as an Indian artisan by an Indian tribe."[2] The marketing of Indian art is therefore potentially dangerous business, and the calendar's editors offer a worried disclaimer: "O-SI-YO Truthart does not represent or suggest either expressly or implied that any given artist is a registered tribal member or certified as an Indian artist by any Cherokee tribe, or any other Indian tribe." "The determination of all such matters is left to the discretion of the public," the editors warn, implying that a powerful painting of a full moon and howling wolf would somehow be less powerful if produced by someone without Indian ancestry. It certainly would be less valuable in the art market.

David Cornsilk learned the value of Indian identity the hard way. A Cherokee citizen, native Oklahoman, and professional genealogist, Cornsilk became suspicious that many Cherokee artists were not in fact citizens of the Cherokee Nation. He traced the genealogies of the ten most renowned Cherokee artists in Oklahoma and found that not one could claim a relative who appeared on nineteenth-century Cherokee censuses. He published his findings, and one day when he was campaigning in a Wal-Mart parking lot for a position on the Cherokee National Council, one of the ten artists pulled his car up to Cornsilk and popped the trunk. The artist slid out of the front seat, approached the puzzled Cornsilk, slugged him, and threw him into the open trunk. Fortunately, Cornsilk escaped before his assailant could close the hatch.

The great-great-great-great-granddaughter of Robert Grierson and Sinnugee need not take such dramatic action in defense of her undeniable Native American ancestry. Her Indian background is rewarding, in terms of both personal identity and real income, yet its profitability underscores the cost of denying African Americans their Indian heritage. Robert Grierson has other descendants who find it difficult to win public or legal recognition of their Indian ancestry because they are part African. If you have a drop of Indian blood, then you may claim to be Indian, explained David Cornsilk—"unless you are black."[3] But if all Americans could map their genealogies back to 1500, millions would find that they are enmeshed in a tangled web of African, European, and native peoples. Too often, we stand at the crown of a branching family tree and trace our ancestors back to a single trunk of sturdy and supposedly pure stock, the Robert Grierson of the family. A more revealing exercise would place us at the base of the tree and follow the branches of our ancestors back in time as they divide and subdivide, finally encompassing not merely Robert Grierson but also all other forebears, African and Indian alike. The revelation of a national family tree would dissolve the racial divisions within the Grayson family. The revelation might persuade Americans to abandon the idea of race altogether.

2

"My negro Woman Judah": William's Decision

In mid-August 1828, Creek warriors kidnapped three Muscogee women, stripped them of clothes, and bound their hands and feet. Stringing a rope over a tree limb, they hoisted their victims off the ground and whipped them until their breasts were "cut to pieces." The women's crime, living with white men, might have gone unnoticed in less stressful times, but in the late 1820s, some Creeks were near starvation, and the very survival of the nation was in question. That same month, warriors severely beat four or five Creeks who stole food to "supply their immediate wants." One elderly woman, "reduced to a perfect skeleton," was whipped "till her bowels might be seen" merely for taking a few ears of corn—"whipped to the hollow," said reports circulating around the nation.[1] By 1831, according to the *Milledgeville Reporter*, emaciated Creeks, barely sustained on a diet of roots and tree bark, were begging for bread. In Columbus, Georgia, "haggard and naked" Creeks went door-to-door in search of food.[2]

Not only were Muscogees starving, but they were under severe pressure to cede their remaining lands in the Southeast. In 1802, Creeks owned 19.6 million acres in Georgia alone. By 1824, after a series of coercive land cessions, that number had shrunk to 4.8 million acres. A year later, the Georgia lands were gone, leaving the Creek Nation with a small share in Alabama of its once vast homelands.[3] Alabama, greedily eyeing Georgia's victory, soon after began the final push to cleanse the Southeast of Creek peoples.

The violent actions of Creek warriors underscore the desire of people to shore up their defenses, sometimes in counterproductive ways, when they feel threatened. Muscogees wished to purify their communities by drawing a distinct and impermeable line between themselves and their black and white neighbors. As a consequence, the wrath of Creeks fell hard on the Graysons. The family frequently and openly associated with white Americans, and, as the owners of scores of slaves, they sponsored the presence of blacks in the nation.

For William, the political and social movements that formed in the Creek Nation in the 1820s were alarming. He and Judah, his father's slave, now had a young son. Given the turbulent situation in the nation, it was unlikely that they could avoid attracting attention. By abandoning Judah and his son to a life of slavery, William might turn even a once consensual relationship into one that, in retrospect, appeared coercive to both parties. Such an action would relieve the pressure on him to conform to social norms. William was thus forced to make a decision. Was his relationship with Judah casual, akin to the numerous forced sexual encounters between planters and slaves throughout the South? Or was his relationship a long-term and serious commitment? Whatever his decision—to abandon or to embrace Judah and his child—he could be sure that it would have repercussions for generations to come.

In the second and third decades of the nineteenth century, the Graysons did little to make themselves welcome to other Creeks. Business demanded that they maintain close ties to outsiders, and they spent many days beyond the borders of the nation, buying and selling slaves and, as fate would have it, arguing in court to clear clouded title to their human property. Henry Walker, Robert's old friend from the days of the Redstick War, sued Robert in Georgia superior court for the cost of supporting between seventy and one hundred of his slaves during the conflict. In late summer 1817, Henry won a judgment of nearly $8,000 against Robert. When the Creek Nation refused to honor his claim, Henry sold it to William McIntosh, a powerful Creek slave owner who lived along the Chattahoochee River in Creek territory. McIntosh intended to seize at least nineteen of Robert's slaves as payment, but Robert sent his favorite daughter, Elizabeth, with his slaves over the line to Montgomery County, Alabama, hoping to find legal protection in U.S. jurisdiction.[4]

These cultural and geographic border crossings caught the attention of Creeks at a time when political pressures demanded that they tamp down on such transgressions. In January 1818, in the first land sale since the Treaty of Fort Jackson, Creeks were forced to part with tracts of land in Georgia and Alabama. These cessions were relatively small, but they marked the beginning of a concerted campaign by the state of Georgia to remove the Creeks once and for all.[5] Perhaps in light of these new political pressures, Muscogees began to harass the Graysons. The family's dealings with white and black Americans set them apart from most other Creeks. Moreover, some of the Grayson children had close ties to William McIntosh, who played a prominent and increasingly dishonest role in every land cession after the Treaty of Fort Jackson. In addition to political allegiance, the Graysons were joined to the McIntoshes by marriage.[6] In early February 1819, a number of Hilabi warriors, from the Graysons' own hometown, raided Elizabeth's plantation, stealing one mare and five axes. Nearly a year later, they returned, taking seven weeding hoes and five plows.[7] It is impossible to know the precise motivation behind these raids, but at the very least, they suggest that the Graysons were out of step with other residents of Hilabi. These were open political acts, not furtive thefts of private property, and they were intended to send a message.

The blows fell harder on the Graysons. In October 1821, Hilabis again raided Elizabeth's plantation, this time making their message more pronounced. Instead of a handful of inexpensive tools, they took seventy-five hogs, seven pairs of trace chains (for harnessing draft animals), and twenty pounds of soap, amounting to nearly $400 worth of goods. Two months later, they returned, making off with ten sheep, thirty-five more hogs, ginned cotton, spun wool, and an assortment of tools.[8] In 1823, the raids were even more widespread. Watt Grayson, one of Robert's sons, lost more than $1,000 worth of livestock and goods. Samuel Hawkins, Elizabeth's nephew, was robbed too.[9] But nine slaves belonging to Elizabeth bore the brunt of the attack. They may have fallen victim to a law, first recorded in 1825, that forbade slaves from holding property. Lawmakers "may do as they please with the property," read the act.[10] Each slave was robbed of hundreds of dollars of goods, ranging from moccasins and pantaloons to rings and broaches. William's partner, Judah, had $128 worth of goods stolen.[11] One slave named Dick lost nearly $800 of goods, including a pair of "fine shoes," a fiddle, and a fur hat.[12] Robbing these slaves was a way of robbing their owner. The theft also marked Dick and the others as outsiders, who threatened the integrity of the nation at a time of crisis.

Robert, the aged family patriarch, died of natural causes that same year, adding personal tragedy to the growing social problems confronting the Graysons. Fittingly, the final disposition of his estate reflected the racial turmoil engulfing the Creek Nation. The nation appointed William McIntosh to oversee the disposal of Robert's property. Each of Grayson's children received a share of slaves except for William. William was mentioned only once in the disposition of the estate: Elizabeth, the settlement read, "may loan or bestow to Wm Grayson the negro woman Judy and her son William, at her pleasure."[13]

The phrase—whether originating from patriarch Robert or from William McIntosh—cut two ways. It cruelly placed the ownership of William's partner and child in the hands of his sister, and at the same time it called attention to the reason for his exclusion from his father's estate. Two years later, William McIntosh's son Chilly would codify in writing a Creek law seemingly aimed at William and Judah. "If any of our people have children and Negros and either of the children should take a Negro as a husband or wife," wrote Chilly, "and should said child have a property given to it by his parent the property shall be taken from them and divided among the rest of the children." The law's conclusion—part of the desperate effort of hard-pressed Creek leaders to conform to the values of the South's planter elite—left little room for ambiguity: "It is a disgrace to our Nation for our people to marry a Negro." McIntosh's code further degraded black Creeks by stipulating that Indians who killed "negros" need suffer no punishment if they "pay the owner the value."[14] By conflating Negroes and slaves, McIntosh made it clear that African ancestry was now to be indelibly associated with bondage. Yet William Grayson ignored the hostility, as was visible to all at the time of his father's death. Judah was then pregnant with their second child, Emma. If, after the settlement of Robert's estate, Judah had difficulty envisioning a future for her growing family, her pessimism was only confirmed when Hilabis raided her house during the violence of 1823.[15]

Slavery lay at the core of the Graysons' troubled relationship with the Creek Nation. Losing his slaves would be "the next thing to Death," Robert once wrote, revealing just how intertwined he and his children had become with their human property.[16] That was precisely the problem, many Creeks believed. The Graysons were caught between two political camps that formed in response to the constant pressures on their land and sovereignty in the early nineteenth century. One camp wished to strengthen the nation by eliminating outside influences. The corrosive effects of Christianity and American culture demanded a retrenchment, its adherents maintained. The other camp adopted Christianity and American culture—if only strategically—and argued that sovereignty was best served by conforming to the practices of the slave South, where whites measured civilization by the abundance of slaves and the rigidity of the racial hierarchy. Slavery "is our moral strength," said Governor George M. Troup of Georgia, William McIntosh's relative.[17] This camp consequently promoted slavery but kept slaves at a distance socially and culturally; the other camp kept them not at all. Slaves such as Dick, with his fine shoes, fiddle, and fur hat, were unwelcome in both camps. Dick was too much Creek and not enough slave for one side, and not enough Creek and too much slave for the other.

No matter the efforts of Muscogees, white Georgians were resolved to drive them out, and no one worked against the Creek Nation more tenaciously or with more fervor than William McIntosh's own cousin, George M. Troup, elected governor of Georgia at the end of 1823. Some northern newspapers were soon describing Troup as the "mad Governor of Georgia," and even Georgians had to admit that he was "peculiar and somewhat eccentric."[18] Upon inauguration, Troup immediately sent a message to the state legislature, calling for the removal of the Creeks. The United States recognized "temporary usufruct only in the Indians," he declared.[19] By bullying and bribing Creek politicians, Troup finally got his treaty in February 1825. William McIntosh, the slaveholder and controversial Creek politician, headed a group of unknown Creeks who signed away every foot of Creek land in Georgia, as well as a large tract in neighboring Alabama.[20] "My friend, you are now about to sell our country," Opothleyahola warned McIntosh at the treaty signing. "I warn you of your danger."[21] Opothleyahola later went down the list of men who had signed the treaty, assessing the status of each of them: "a broken or dismissed Chief," an "underling Chief," "no Chief," "an Indian merely," "no chief, a Clerk," and so on.[22] Troup nevertheless stated that "no Indian treaty has ever been negotiated and concluded in better faith."[23]

The treaty aggravated the already difficult position of the Graysons in the nation. A few weeks after the cession, two of McIntosh's allies were run out of the country. Creek warriors "threatened to kill them—cut their throats and set up their heads by the road for a show," learned Chilly McIntosh.[24] These threats were directed at the Graysons, as well. Samuel Hawkins, the grandson of Robert and Sinnugee by their daughter Sarah, was one of the main targets. In April, Creeks ransacked his plantation house and set it afire, taking fifteen slaves with them.[25] Sarah reported that she lost clothes and kitchen utensils in the attack, as well as a collection of books that included *Gulliver's Travels* and *Robinson Crusoe*.[26] (One wonders if she identified with Defoe's protagonist shipwrecked among savages or with Crusoe's native servant, Friday.) William Grayson, a frequent visitor to the house, also lost a few possessions.[27]

On May 1, Creeks made good on their threats. They surrounded McIntosh's house, set it afire, and shot William to death when he tried to escape. Shortly afterward, they hung Samuel Hawkins and threw his body into the Tallapoosa River, making him the second of Sarah's three sons to be murdered. (Pinkey had died at the hands of Redsticks in 1813). Sarah's third son, Benjamin, escaped with only a bullet wound.[28] The next day, Creeks stopped Sarah and her husband, Stephen, as they made their way along a trading path. Seizing all their possessions, including two slaves, the warriors sent Sarah and Stephen fleeing for their lives to Montgomery, Alabama.[29] They "have never to this day returned to the nation to live," reported Creek chiefs a year later.[30] Other Graysons remained unharmed until October 1825, when Creek warriors caught William visiting Judah on his sister Elizabeth's plantation. Judah was pregnant with another child, Henderson—or perhaps had recently given birth. The warriors bound and flogged William and "carried away and Kill.d every thing on the plantation of any value."[31]

While the Graysons were singled out for their symbolic and real threat to the integrity of the nation, black Creeks also became targets. As early as 1823, free black Creeks recognized the growing uncertainty of their status in the nation and the increasing importance of skin color. In that year, a few of them took steps to reaffirm their freedom. Sakay Randall got a number of Creek leaders to declare in writing that she was "free from Slavery or servitude to any person whatever togeather with all the Issue of her body." Careful to attend to the interests of her children, Sakay clearly feared for the future of black Creeks in the nation. The brothers Alex and Sampson Perryman went before the local Indian agent that same year to secure written confirmation that they were "born free and ever since have been so."[32] Though free since birth, they evidently believed that the hostile climate of the 1820s placed their status in jeopardy.

Randall and the Perryman brothers had reason for concern. In the mid-1820s, Muscogees began attacking the rights of their black relatives, friends, and slaves. The campaign arose in anger at the dissolving strength of the nation, but it also served as a desperate, last attempt to halt that dissolution. The "utmost of the rights and privileges which public opinion would concede to the Indians," said Governor Troup of Georgia, "would fix them in a middle station between the negro and the white man." As "long as they survived this degradation without the possibility of attaining the elevation of the latter," he asserted, "they would gradually sink to the condition of the former; a point of degeneracy below which they could not fall."[33] It seemed fruitless to attempt to challenge such racism, so deeply rooted in Georgia's history.[34] Instead, Creeks tried to operate within its framework, elevating themselves at the expense of their black neighbors, desperately trying to avoid that lowest point of degeneracy predicted, in fact actively encouraged, by Troup.

The campaign focused on the actions of missionaries, who, by instructing black Creeks in Christianity, made them bad slaves and bad Muscogees, unwelcome to both Creek planters and Creek traditionalists. Although Creeks were in general hostile to missionaries, they especially resented their meddling with slaves. Instruction not only made for rebellious bondmen and bondwomen, as Frederick Douglass later illustrated so persuasively in his autobiography, but also gave Christianity a toehold in the nation. Many black Creeks were born in the southern states, and they were more open to the gospel than were other Muscogees. Living in a nation that excluded people on the basis of kinship, blacks Creeks welcomed the universalism of Christianity.

In September 1826, a Baptist missionary reported that one of the most powerful politicians in the Creek Nation had threatened blacks who attended prayer meetings with "the direst penalties."[35] Apparently the threat was serious, for into the following year congregations of slaves had to meet on the sly or not at all.[36] Then, in 1828, only a few months before Creek warriors whipped three women for living with white men, as many as thirty Muscogees broke into a prayer meeting at Withington Station, on the border of Georgia and Alabama, and bound and tied the black participants. They led the worshipers one by one to a post in the yard and beat them.[37] According to one account, a twelve-year-old girl was forced to witness the proceedings. Later, the warriors pulled her dress over her head, flogged, and sexually molested her.[38] When missionaries asked for justice, one Creek leader asked "if it were worth while to shed blood for a *few old negroes.*" One of the slaves' owners expressed satisfaction at the punishment meted out, regretting only that her other slave women had escaped.[39] Prayer meetings continued, but in secret and in fear.[40]

The hostility toward black Indians reflected the worries not only of slave owners but also those of Creeks who wished to purge the nation of outsiders. The violence was so brutal because of the impossibility of drawing lines between Creeks and black Creeks. "There is an number of Black free fameleys that seems to be in Every way Identifyed with these people," wrote one puzzled U.S. official who had been told in 1832 to take a census of Creeks. Who was Creek, he wondered, when "the only difference" between black Creeks and Muscogees was "in the coler."[41] What was he to make of Polly from Coweta, "half negro and having a negro slave for a husband named John"? Or of Nero, a free black man married to a Creek woman with a family of three?[42] Or, for that matter, of the two young Creeks recently orphaned and now in the sole care of a black woman who was also their property? "Very many such cases has presented themselves," the official noted.[43]

Shortly before the brutal attack at Withington Station, a congregation "consisting of almost every variety of colour" gathered not far from the Graysons' hometown to honor the death of a black Creek. A leading chief in that part of the nation also attended, but he stood a short distance apart. Though "he could not hear all that passed," he watched intently.[44] Like this reluctant yet respectful mourner, Creeks were drawn toward their black friends and relatives but were hesitant to embrace them fully. In the 1820s, Creeks struggled to resolve the social tensions in their communities and families. This struggle occupied the minds of Muscogee leaders and set entire communities throughout the Creek Nation against each other; it also played out in families and in individual lives. As slave owners and as husbands and wives of Afro-Indians, the Graysons embodied the larger tensions within the nation.

William McIntosh's Treaty of Indian Springs, ceding all Creek lands in Georgia, was hastily annulled by the United States when a war seemed imminent between Georgia and the Creek Nation. One well-placed Georgian would later reproach "mawkish philanthropists of the North" for the treaty's annulment and would single out President John Quincy Adams for blame: the "furtive wariness of his small gray eye, his pinched nose, receding forehead, and thin, compressed lips, indicated the malignant nature of his soul."[45] Governor Troup insisted on the integrity of the treaty. He pulled the state to the brink of war with the federal government, and the United States gave in and sought a new treaty ceding nearly the same land. The Treaty of Washington, signed in January 1826, left to the Creeks one million acres in Georgia, though Muscogees were soon cajoled into ceding these lands as well.[46] Unwelcome in the remaining part of the Creek Nation, roughly 750 of William McIntosh's closest followers struck out for Indian Territory (the present-day state of Oklahoma) in November 1827. They arrived nearly three months later, settling on the Arkansas and Verdigris rivers, not far from the future site of Muskogee, Oklahoma.[47] Even before the Creeks departed, Georgia began surveying their lands and distributing them by lottery to white men. "What had been savage wilderness, was now becoming a garden," wrote George M. Troup's biographer in 1859.[48]

The Graysons stayed in what remained of the old Creek Nation in Alabama, but they were not secure in their homeland for long. Inspired by Georgia's roughshod treatment of the Creeks, Alabama passed two acts in January 1827 intended to drive native peoples west of the Mississippi. The first extended civil and criminal jurisdiction over that portion of Alabama lands ceded in the 1825 Treaty of Indian Springs and since returned to the Creeks by the federal government. (The state legislature soon abandoned all pretense of legal procedure and extended jurisdiction over every square foot of Creek lands.) The second act of 1827 prohibited Indians from hunting, trapping, or fishing within the settled limits of the state, on pain of arrest, forfeiture of guns or traps, and, on a second offense, imprisonment.[49] In tandem, these two acts denied Muscogees the right to pursue their economy on lands that, according to the federal government (not to mention the Creek Nation), belonged to them. Creeks explained their dilemma:

> We are injured in our property, we are told to go to the protection of the Alabama laws—to present our case before an Alabama court. We present our case, and we are not permitted to be heard in behalf of each other. Our cause is adjudged by a jury of Alabama, under the direction of a court of Alabama, administering the law of Alabama. The law, if it

contains a single provision which can protect the Indian from outrage, or can redress his wrongs when they have been sustained, is, to this extent, unknown to us. We know it only as an instrument by which we are oppressed, and as opposing an insurmountable obstacle against our obtaining redress.[50]

The Graysons' hometown, Hilabi, was now subject to Alabama law, and whites began flooding into the region, settling close by the Graysons.[51]

At the same time, emigration officers began plying the Creek Nation, looking for potential clients. The Graysons, hoping to leave behind the hostility of both their fellow Muscogees and white Alabamans, expressed interest. But once again, they found themselves at odds with the Creek Nation. In early 1828, Creek leaders resolved to execute anyone who enrolled to emigrate. One young man who signed up for Indian Territory barely escaped with his life when a chief pointed a cocked rifle at his chest. In the Graysons' neighborhood, an emigration agent successfully enrolled thirty Creeks in a single day, but after one of them was badly beaten, only a lone volunteer remained a few days later.[52] Such instances were widespread, reflecting the intense pressure Creeks were under to circumscribe dissent.[53] Warriors threatened one potential emigrant, John Dannely, with death. His children, an elderly Creek prophet named Menaway told him, "should be raised up as other Indians were, and then they would comply with the customs of the nation." Menaway's intolerance, though perhaps understandable under the circumstances, left no room for opposing views. "This should be the fate of all his men who spoke of going to Arkansas," he concluded.[54] The Graysons, in light of such threats, remained quiet, not wishing to draw attention to their already compromised position. In September 1828, after a Creek leader threatened one of the emigration agents with a knife, the United States sent a company of infantry to keep order.[55]

Creek Indian agent John Crowell reported in spring 1829 that Creek leaders maintained a "settled obstinancy of purpose" to defeat removal, but by the fall, at least a few Creeks had privately expressed their desire to leave Alabama.[56] The Graysons were likely among them, though Crowell could not yet list names. They "are afraid to Speak it publicly untill I am prepared to protect them," he wrote.[57] By spring 1830, Elizabeth, Watt, William, and other Graysons had enlisted to emigrate. Whites were becoming more aggressive in Creek country, stealing Afro-Creeks with impunity, a serious problem for black Graysons, whether slaves or family members, who might suddenly find themselves in chains headed for a Georgia cotton plantation.[58] Consequently, Elizabeth enrolled her twenty-six "family" members, including slaves, for emigration to Indian Territory. Watt and William enrolled their families as well.[59] Watt, anticipating his imminent departure, did not plant crops that year, nor did his brother Sandy.[60] Phil Grayson (whose parents are unknown) had eighty hogs stolen from him "inconsciquence of his enroleing to emigrate."[61] Sandy also was stripped of sixteen head of cattle.[62]

It is not clear if Elizabeth and others had the foresight to plant their crops. If not, the Graysons must have suffered during the ensuing winter, for the planned emigration never took place. The federal government failed to organize the resources necessary to transport the Creeks. At the end of June, when it was clear there would be no mass removal to Indian Territory during 1830, Indian agent Crowell observed indifferently that would-be emigrants "seem to be quite uneasy about Their Situation and think they are not well treated."[63] Thomas Grayson was so frustrated that he and his family struck out for Indian Territory on their own, financing the trip themselves.[64]

By August, Crowell's indifference had turned to alarm. Unless would-be emigrants such as the remaining Graysons were removed at once, he said, "they will be in a state of starvation."[65] Thousands of whites moved onto their lands, notching trees to mark their claims, sometimes in the middle of cornfields actively cultivated by Creeks.[66] The Graysons contended with at least two intruders, Henry Towns and Mr. Rhoden, but they surely encountered others. A squatter named Peter Lendly, for instance, ran a public house and operated a ferry across the Tallapoosa River, not far from the Graysons. "Old Mr. Logan," another intruder, also spent time in the Graysons' neighborhood, passing counterfeit money and rustling livestock. "Indians state they have lost latterly by him and his coleagues upwards of one hundred head of Horses, and more than that number of Cattle," noted one government agent.[67]

Other Creeks, who frequently visited to "scold at, and abuse" emigrants, offered little solace. In some cases, as the Graysons well knew, Creeks threatened the lives of emigrants and "destroyed their stock and other property."[68] By the end of 1831, Muscogees were desperate. "Your White children are fast settling up my country," one leader wrote to President Andrew Jackson. "They are building houses, Mills making field [sic] and destroying all my timber and games."[69] Neha Micco, a prominent Creek chief, confessed, "We expect to be driven from our homes."[70]

With few options before them, Creek leaders signed their final treaty in the Southeast in March 1832, a last-ditch effort to secure land title for their people. The treaty provided for the distribution of half-section tracts to every household head in the nation. Ninety Creek leaders each received an entire section (one square mile). Five years after allotment, land title would become fee simple, allowing Creeks to sell their property as they wished. Before then, they could sell only with the approval of the federal government. Muscogees hoped the treaty would guarantee possession of their remaining lands; the United States hoped it would hasten their dispossession. Accordingly, the federal government promised to pay the transportation costs of emigrants to Indian Territory and to maintain them for a year after their arrival west of the Mississippi.[71]

The Graysons—mother Sinnuggee, siblings Sandy, Elizabeth, Watt, and William, as well as Sinnuggee's grandchildren—took their half-section allotments within a few miles of each other.[72] Others accepted similar terms, and by January 1834, fully 2,187,200 acres of land had been allotted. That spring, all the remaining land in the Creek Nation, 3,012,800 acres, was transferred to the United States.[73]

Immediately after allotment, Creeks were permitted to sell their lands in accordance with regulations established by the federal government. Parties to a land transaction had to appear before a certifying agent, appointed by the United States, who personally interviewed the seller, established that the price was just, and verified that payment was made. If the transaction met with the agent's approval, he issued a certificate, and upon authorization by the president, the sale became final.[74] One government investigator charged with reviewing the procedure found it admirable: "It would be difficult to imagine a system more wisely arranged for the honest and beneficial fulfilment of our covenants, more perfectly adapted to the protection of Indian incapacity, or more carefully devised for the exclusion of fraudulent operation upon the interests that we had undertaken to preserve."[75]

In fact, however, the land sales brought on a torrent of speculation, fraud, and theft. While Creek allottees and federal officers engaged in violent battles against white squatters, emigration agents (including Chilly McIntosh, who had returned from Indian Territory for the occasion) trolled the nation, now motivated by the prospect of purchasing Indian allotments on the cheap. Promised wagonloads of silver or the "vast wealth" in the vaults of Georgia's banks, Creeks unfamiliar with the market soon parted with their lands.[76] White observers could not find words to describe the extent of the fraud. "I have never seen corruption carried on to such proportions in all of my life," said one.[77] "Strikers," as the perpetrators of fraud were known, openly defied "all regard for morality and decency," wrote one government officer in an otherwise staid report.[78] Another officer asserted, "A greater mass of corruption, perhaps, has never been congregated in any part of the world."[79] This was hyperbole, no doubt, but even the thieves thought themselves participants in a historic event. "The harvest is nearly over," said one striker, "and perhaps there will never be another such a one."[80] Such abundance called for a toast, overheard in a gathering of strikers: "Here's to the man that can steal the most land to-morrow without being caught at it."[81]

The methods of theft were several. Locating agents, who were charged with assigning plots of land to individual Indians, sometimes gave homesteads to minors and to absent or even dead Creeks, with the intention of purchasing the lots themselves.[82] Other strikers dispensed with legal ruses and simply ran the rightful residents off their land and set fire to their houses.[83] Two methods of fraud surpassed all others in frequency. Creek leader Opothleyahola described the first. A "fiendish designing scoundrel" would hire an Indian to impersonate the owner of an allotment. After certification of the sale, the impersonator returned the money to the purchaser, save five or ten dollars, "given to the Indian as a premium for his rascality." Opothleyahola concluded that in this way "a few hundred dollars and four or five Indians could sell all the land in the Creek purchase."[84] Impersonation became so common that in March 1835 strikers saw fit to remove a potentially incriminating clause from land sale certificates in Russell County, Alabama: "And the deponent saith further, that he believes the Indian who has been introduced before the agent is the true holder of the location described in the foregoing deed."[85] In the other common method of swindling, strikers would purchase land from the rightful owner. By force or fraud, they later recovered the payment from the seller.[86] Said one striker, the "best of it was" that this method allowed him to recoup his entire outlay.[87]

The theft reached its greatest proportions in the first three months of 1835, just before charges of corruption led the government to suspend all sales. One might expect the Graysons to have survived the onslaught, like most Creeks, quietly and desperately. A few Creeks did not survive at all. They starved to death, died in drunken brawls, or were shot down by white intruders. But, remarkably, at least two of the Graysons, rather than falling victim to the strikers, became their collaborators. Watt, the brother of Katy and William, was one. The other is identified as Bailey Grayson; his parents are unknown. Watt and Bailey were associates of Eli Shorter, the Graysons' old acquaintance from Jasper County, where the family had spent the Redstick War. Shorter led a group of land speculators and thieves. Early in 1835, he feverishly exhorted his partners to steal as much land as possible before the suspension of sales. "It is important that you press this subject immediately upon the attention . . . of the Griersons," he wrote. Watt and Bailey Grayson were to "spread it among the Indians" that if Creeks did not sell this moment, they would be "cheated out of their rights." Shorter compared the operation to an amorous conquest or a military campaign. He urged one partner to "give up the beautiful Miss Jenny" and told another to "swear off from the society of ladies." "Every man should now be at his post," he exclaimed.[88]

The Graysons' role in the crime was central. One partner underscored twice

that M. A. Cravens, an associate in crime, "must be certain to come with Wat &
Bailey."[89] Watt and Bailey gathered as many Indians as they could and escorted
them to the office of the certifying agent. Several miles from their destination,
they pulled their victims off of the road and set up camp to await Shorter. Watt
and Bailey were "kept out constantly drilling the Indians," instructing them in
their responses to the agent and promising them ten dollars for participating.
Shorter arrived sometime later with the certifying agent and a pocketful of cash,
ready to reward any Indian who would step forward to sign a contract, no matter
his or her true identity. "*Stealing* is the order of the day," Shorter shamelessly
confessed. The scene was chaotic. At times, as many as one thousand Indians
were crowded into the camps of the speculators.[90]

If Shorter had pangs of guilt, there is no such evidence, for he only lamented
that his company did not steal as ruthlessly as its competitors: "When I see such
men, with so few advantages, getting so much valuable land at $10 per tract,
and how much money *we* have paid out, the *power* we have had, and see the
quantity and *quality* of land we have received, and particularly when I think of
the *reason* why these things are so, I can almost tear my hair from my head."[91]
The slightly comic tenor of his lament illustrates the festive mood of the strikers,
who were amassing tremendous fortunes with minimal effort. Benjamin Tarver,
who joined Watt, Bailey, and Eli in the theft, shared Eli's jubilance: "Now is the
time, or never! Hurrah boys! here goes it! let's steal all we can. I shall go for it,
or get no lands! Now or never!"[92] Shorter's and Tarver's euphoria may not have
been tempered by doubts, but it is difficult to imagine that Watt and Bailey did
not have second thoughts about their actions. They were profiting at the expense
of their friends and neighbors, and the larger costs to the Grayson family remained unknown.

It is unclear how much Watt and Bailey profited from the fraudulent transactions they helped to organize, but given their active participation in the land
frauds, it is not surprising that the Graysons did well for themselves in the sale
of their own allotments. Elizabeth, William, Watt, Sandy, and seven other family
members who took allotments around Hilabi sold their lands for an average of
$600 each. (It must have galled them that two of the purchases were made by
Henry Towns, who had intruded on their lands since 1831.) By contrast, on
average the forty-two other heads of households in Hilabi sold their allotments
for scarcely half as much. Thirty-two of these allottees parted with their property
for less that $350, whereas no Grayson sold for less than that value. Samson
Grayson, whose father Thomas had emigrated in 1832, earned $2,300 for his
tract, fully $700 more than the next Hilabi resident.[93]

Most surprising is that Elizabeth herself purchased two allotments from
nearby residents, spending $905 on the transactions.[94] Elizabeth may have

wished to help out neighbors in need of cash. (One observer noted the " 'stag-gering walk,' the blood shot eye, and the clotted and bloody garments" of many Muscogees.) Or she may have been engaged in speculation. Or perhaps, despite the swarms of squatters, the hundreds of desperate and starving Creeks, she thought that her family could still remain in the Southeast.[95] Creek leader Opothleyahola would later recall that until the graft reached intolerable propor-tions, "a great many Indians" intended to remain in Alabama, raise their families, and become citizens of the state.[96] Elizabeth's experience in the courts, frequent trips to Montgomery, and practiced market skills must have given her a confi-dence that many other Creeks lacked. Seventy-three of her Hilabi neighbors fled north to the Cherokee Nation rather than face the process of allotment, and an "enormously large" number of Creeks hanged themselves in despair.[97] The foun-dation of her confidence—a plantation with improvements worth $1,300, ready cash to purchase other lands—was built by her black slaves. Elizabeth's border crossings had been profitable, but they came at great social cost.

William and Judah knew those costs well. "It is a disgrace to our Nation for our people to marry a Negro," Chilly McIntosh had written in 1825. Many of the costs of disgrace, emotional and psychological, cannot be measured by the documentary fragments that still exist. But those that can are startling in their enormity. William McIntosh had excluded Grayson from his father's estate and transferred Judah like a farm animal to Elizabeth's ownership.[98] Creek warriors had singled out and robbed Judah when she was pregnant with her second child. Later, on a return visit to the slave quarters, Creeks had bound and whipped William. In the 1830s, white intruders made William's and Judah's lives even more perilous by threatening to kidnap Judah and her children. As racial ten-sions rose in the Creek Nation, it came time for William to make his decision. Katy and her black partner had parted ways. Would William abandon Judah to a life of slavery?

Other possibilities for black and Indian relationships existed in the Creek Nation. In late summer 1823, Thomas Perryman had freed his partners Judy ("heretofore reputed my slave") and Molly, as well as their children.[99] The prob-lem for William, of course, was that Judah did not belong to him, and Elizabeth had shown no willingness to part with her human property. In 1819, she had granted Dick "his time and lawful freedom" but only at her "decease," a feeble act that revealed her dependence on slavery.[100] Decades later, Dick was still waiting for freedom. What, then, would William do? Perhaps William had al-ways foreseen his choice, or perhaps he struggled to reach it for years. Either way, his decision came in three parts, each more momentous than the previous one. The first occurred sometime before winter 1834, when William convinced Elizabeth to part with Judah, possibly by silent perseverance more than reasoned argument. In the ten years since their father's death, he and Judah had had five children, making seven in all. Most slave owners would have been pleased with the rapid increase in their assets, but Judah's offspring were Elizabeth's own nephews and nieces. Even if their aunt felt little compunction about enslaving her close relatives, William's constant presence in the slave cabins may have made her uneasy. "It is said that when no pursuasion [sic] would induce him to abandon her," Wash would later recall about William and Judah, Elizabeth "was forced to release her from slavery and grant her full freedom from bondage."[101]

Now the legal owner of his own wife and children, William made the second part of the decision that would determine the fate of his relationship with Judah. In late 1834, William and his family, master and slaves, set off at their own expense for Indian Territory.[102] The decision to emigrate had serious implications for William's future. Both literally and figuratively, it divided him from his siblings. Only William's brother Thomas had emigrated before him, and no relatives accompanied William, Judah, and their children on the journey west.[103] Thomas's son Samson, with thirty-four slaves, traveled to Indian Territory that same season to join his father, but Samson chose to travel in a party escorted by a U.S. Army officer rather than in the company of his uncle and aunt. William would never again live next to his siblings.

Unfortunately, no account records the ordeals that William and Judah, a mixed-race couple with seven children, must have faced traveling through the antebellum South in late 1834. Like Samson's party, William and Judah weathered an unusually harsh winter, whose freezing temperatures forced emigrating Creeks to halt six or seven times a day to warm their children before fires. Only 469 of the original 630 Creeks in Samson's party survived the three-month journey.[104]

When William and Judah arrived in Indian Territory in early 1835, they settled in the gently undulating prairie country bordering Butler Creek, just a few miles south of the present-day city of Muskogee, Oklahoma. Two miles north of their new home stood Chimney Mountain, named for its peculiar shape. Despite the fact that it rises only a few hundred feet above the surrounding country, the peak, noted one nineteenth-century visitor, "seemed to preside over the prairie and to watch every passer-by." "For twenty miles or more," this visitor wrote, "it is seemingly about you; you cannot escape it . . . you feel haunted and then attracted; and when at last some rival mound, aided by distance, hides it from your vision, you feel as if you had looked for the last time on some old familiar landmark, or had bidden a friend farewell."[105]

Soon after settling down, William took the last step in his extraordinary three-part decision. On April 16, as spring weather was warming the land, William took a day trip to Fort Gibson, a U.S. outpost near the junction of the Arkansas, Verdigris, and Neosho rivers. There he transformed his relationship with Judah in a remarkable declaration: "Be it known to all persons whom it may concern that I William Grayson of the Western Creek Nation from motives of humanity and benevolence and for faithful services tendered do hereby emancipate set free and forever release from Slavery my negro Woman Judah aged twenty eight years and her seven children." "I do hereby give grant and release unto the said Judah and her children," he continued, "all my right title and claim of in and to her or their persons labour and services and to the Estate and property which she or they may hereafter acquire."[106] William had a copy of his statement entered into the national record book of the Creek Nation, where it remains to this day.

William's decision stood in stark opposition to Katy's, and as William knew, it would have a tremendous impact on his life. "To debauch a Negro girl hardly injures an American's reputation," observed Alexis de Tocqueville after touring the United States in the early 1830s; "to marry her dishonors him."[107] Perhaps William believed that by moving to Indian Territory, he could escape both his family's opprobrium and the unforgiving racial hierarchy in the United States. But Katy would soon follow him west, and the United States would continue its continental expansion. In the two years separating Katy's and William's emigration, Katy would witness horrific events in Alabama. Her experience there would only strengthen her resolve to enslave blacks rather than befriend them. It would lead her and her children to deny that they had any connection at all with Judah and her descendants.

Profile

Rudy Hutton, September 1999 and June 2000

Rudy Hutton resembles a koala bear, stocky, round faced, and immediately likable. He is a career military man but shows none of the expected sternness. Hutton later worked for the Veterans' Administration hospital, which perhaps explains why he chose to meet me not far from the Oklahoma Historical Society in a hospital cafeteria, where, he said, you can get a "cheap breakfast." He dug into a plate of biscuits with scrambled eggs and gravy on top as he talked about his family history. Hutton is informed and well-read, as immediately became clear when he mentioned a recent article in the *Chronicles of Oklahoma*, the state's historical journal, normally perused only by academics.

Hutton's great-great-great-grandparents were Jim Grayson (also known as Chinny Chotke) and Venus, both the property of Robert Grierson. Jim was "a half breed, half indian and half colored," according to one of his sons, and Venus was a black woman.[1] In 1817, Grierson transferred Jim and Venus to his daughter Katy, perhaps to reward her for abandoning her Creek and African husband and their children. Robert also deeded to Katy Jim and Venus's children: Sam, Reubin, Arnold, Will, Huton, Maryanna, and Abigail. And he deeded Abigail's children: Judy, Kato, John, Will, and Diane.[2] In 1825, Jim and Venus had another child, Joe, Hutton's great-great-grandfather. Joe belonged to a Creek woman named Nancy Hutton, a half sister to some of the Graysons. During removal, Nancy and her husband, Jim, settled in Van Zandt County, Texas (fifty miles east of present-day Dallas), so that Jim could avoid punishment for a crime he had committed in the Creek Nation. Joe must have been separated from his friends and family at this time, but occasionally he returned to the Creek Nation with Nancy to transact business. They would stay at Watt Grayson's, in the Choctaw Nation.[3]

After the Civil War, Joe returned to the Creek Nation with a young son named Jim, Hutton's great-grandfather. Joe first farmed a plot of land on Watt

Grayson's plantation, perhaps as a sharecropper. Later he settled close to Sodom, a small town southwest of Muskogee.[4] Despite his long ties to the Creeks and to the Grayson family, Joe had trouble establishing citizenship in the nation. Wash Grayson asserted that, after living for a time among "Uncle Wat's niggers," Joe tried to pass himself off as someone else, thereby establishing residency and citizenship.[5] Joe was Creek, Rudy asserted, "but he had hell getting on the rolls." "We have to control these sons-of-bitches," Hutton imagined the Creeks saying; "we don't want any ties to them at all." "Special attention" was always given to Creeks like Joe, Hutton claimed. Black Indians were "radical folk," and Hutton traces a connection between radical Creek politics in the Redstick War and the radical politics of his ancestors. Despite Joe's troubles, after a number of protests and appeals, he successfully secured his Creek citizenship.

By 1882, Joe's son Jim had left his father's household and started his own family. One of his children was named Everett, Hutton's grandfather.[6] Both Jim and Everett voted in Creek elections, alongside other citizens, but by 1899 there were signs of growing ostracism and exclusion. That year, Jim's ballot for principal chief was rejected, on the grounds that Jim was a "doubtful" citizen.[7] Their status continued to decline. By 1904, Everett's son Pilot, Hutton's father, was enrolled in the Coon Creek Day School, created by the Creek Nation to educate black students.[8] The family was now known to Wash Grayson as "the Hutton negroes," reflecting their reduced status in the nation.[9] The racial segregation did not sit well with Pilot. He left Oklahoma when Rudy was a child, declaring that he refused to live in a racist state. Hutton recalled his father's words: "Sonny, I don't ride on the back of no son-of-a-bitch's bus." Pilot worked in auto plants in Detroit and later found employment in Chicago. During his final illness, as Hutton drove his father to his childhood home in Huttonville, Pilot began speaking Creek, though he always maintained he had forgotten the language. When Pilot was in the hospital, Hutton received a call from the nurse: his father was speaking something unintelligible. Hutton suspects it was his childhood language.

Hutton has little good to say about the Creek Nation. His family has continued to have problems with government. In the 1970s, Claude Cox, the principal chief, offered to help Hutton's uncle get a Certification of Degree of Indian Blood card (commonly referred to as a CDIB card in Indian country), but Cox was unsuccessful. Hutton believes that Cox's motive was far from benevolent. He suspects that Cox hoped to prevent the Hutton family from mounting a more serious challenge to the citizenship rules. Cox "wanted to make damn sure that he never got on the rolls." There was another reason Cox took a personal interest in Hutton's family. Hutton's grandmother was Delilah Haynes, and the Haynes family is related to the Cox family. It "was about getting that cleaned up," Hutton told me. "Those SOBs at Okmulgee," he said of the Creek capital, "they won't give you nothing unless you're a white guy."

Hutton believes that among the working class, there still is some interaction between Creeks of European, Indian, and African descent. "They know they're related even if they don't say it," he observed. "It is the upper class like G. W. that drew boundaries," he said, referring to Wash Grayson. Wash was of the "patrician class, archetypal of his group." "There are three important things to know about G. W.," he told me: "First, he fought with the Confederacy, two, he was a primary proponent of allying with whites, and three, he controlled the media." G. W. was "going European." "He became a more radical Indian on behalf of Indians, in some sense—but in the white man's way."

"I'm not bitter about it, but my uncle is," Hutton concluded. The older generation remembers, and they lived through the racial politics of Jim Crow. "They've got white first cousins," observed Hutton. He quoted his uncle: "A son of a bitch who won't recognize his own is no better than a dog."

3

Race and Removal: Katy's Compromise

Slavery "is our moral strength," Governor George M. Troup of Georgia once proclaimed. In the 1830s, Katy Grayson decided to adopt Troup's axiom as her own. Soon after she and her black partner went their separate ways, Katy married Johnnie Benson, whose Creek name was Tulwa Tustanagee. Tulwa Tustanagee was the son of Intakhafpky, a medicine man from Hilabi, and Mary Benson, a white woman from Georgia who had been taken prisoner as a small child.[1] Tulwa Tustanagee's grandson later described him as "of medium build, rather below the medium in stature, a little inclined to be bow legged, coal black hair inclined a little to curl, with all the ways and manner of a full blood Creek Indian."[2] As a former Redstick partisan, Tulwa Tustanagee offered Katy respectability in the community of Hilabi Redsticks who, less than a decade earlier, had singled out the Graysons for abuse. As a Creek and a European, he also satisfied Robert Grierson's racial criteria. Shortly after their marriage, Katy and Tulwa Tustanagee had their first child. They would have ten in all, six girls and four boys.

The historical record tells little about Katy and Tulwa Tustanagee's early life together, except that they continued to live in Hilabi. It also remains nearly silent regarding Katy's relationship with her black son, John, revealing only that by the time he was nineteen, he was living in a separate residence a few miles from his mother.[3] Her daughter Annie disappears from the record altogether.[4] John and Katy's proximity to one another suggests that they continued to keep in contact. Yet John, even if confident with his status as a Hilabi, must have looked at his mother's family with some bitterness. The only black Creeks now in Katy's household were slaves, fourteen of them in 1832.[5]

When William left in late 1834 for Indian Territory, Katy, Elizabeth, and other Graysons may have hoped that allotment fraud would ease in the following year, but instead it continued to escalate. One observer noted in a letter to President Andrew Jackson that in the sales of allotments, the "real owner is not brought up more than one time out of twenty."[6] By mid-1835, Jackson had called for an investigation, but government officials could neither alleviate the famine sweeping through the Creek Nation nor allay the growing desperation of Muscogees. One traveler through the nation reported that Creeks had barked oak trees along the road "to get the inner rind as a substitute for bread." In their hunger, they ate diseased swine and cattle and even devoured rotten carcasses.[7] Whites had nearly exterminated their game, forbidden them to hunt what remained, and invaded their farms.

In early May 1836, Creeks murdered five whites in lower Alabama, setting off well-planned retaliations that have been dignified as the "Creek War of 1836."[8] The conflict proved a one-sided atrocity from its squalid origins and shameful prosecution to its ignominious conclusion. To William Schley, the governor of Georgia, the cause of the war was simple: the "great majority" of Creeks were "idle, dissolute vagrants."[9] In fact, the seeds of the conflict were sown by Schley's own constituents, for it appears likely that land speculators from Columbus, Georgia, were behind the hostilities.[10] "Of this I know nothing, and have no evidence on which to form an opinion," said Schley in the timeless language of politicians.[11] According to testimony, one Philander R. Broad, a white man, led the initial attack against whites at the behest of Columbus land companies.[12] Sitting in a jail in Mobile, Alabama, after his foray, Broad reportedly received several visitors who urged him not to divulge his secret. Yet one contemporary, an army officer named John Hogan, confidently pieced together the outlines of the plot. When investigations into fraudulent land sales began in April 1835, speculators hoped to "raise a fuss" or "a chunk of war," he said. President Jackson, Hogan dryly noted, "would then kill all the Indians off and that would close the matter." But the war spiraled out of control, and to hide their villainy, they became "furious partisans to put down the war."[13]

Despite the conflict's origins, the United States pursued it as if the very survival of the Republic were at stake. Secretary of War Lewis Cass immediately sent in General Thomas Jesup to reduce the Indians. "The great object is to remove them immediately," Cass wrote, "and to this, other considerations must yield."[14] In fact, the murderers had little support in the Creek Nation, and Creek leaders quickly gathered three hundred, then nine hundred, warriors to put down the wayward Creeks. Among these warriors was a group from Hilabi.[15] Within a month, nearly all rebellious Creeks had surrendered, with the exception of one hundred stalwarts who were still on the run, hoping to join the Seminoles in Florida.[16]

The army's cleanup operation was vicious, and it reflected the contempt that whites felt for native peoples. On numerous occasions, soldiers murdered their Indian prisoners. One such incident came to the attention of General Jesup. In July 1836, an Alabama militiaman named Scroggins captured three or four Creeks from Yuchi Town. With the prisoners marching behind him, Scroggins followed a footpath as it ascended a small bluff. When he reached the top of the rise, he turned and shot dead the unsuspecting Creeks. Scroggins acted "in mere wantonness," concluded his commanding officer.[17] A few weeks later, troops encountered a party of twelve Yuchis, who fled into a swamp, abandoning their bundles of bed quilts, sheets, and clothing, as well as ammunition. Soldiers killed four of the Yuchis in the skirmish.[18]

Famine, warfare, and terror drove Creeks to commit increasingly desperate acts. On one occasion, a Yuchi, unable to escape from his white pursuers, pulled out a knife and slit his own throat.[19] On another, fugitive Creeks reportedly killed their children who could not maintain the pace of flight.[20] The plight of one Eufala woman (whose hometown was on the Chattahoochee not far from Columbus, Georgia) illustrates the depth of the Creeks' desperation. U.S. troops invaded her small camp in early September 1836, overturning pots of boiling corn and roasted meat. Though the men escaped, soldiers took the women and children prisoner. The following day, a commanding officer sent out the woman to persuade the remaining fugitives to surrender, carrying his dubious assurances that the Creeks would be "treated with kindness." She was caught on the horns of a dilemma, for the officer was holding hostage her two children, a nursing baby and a two-year-old, belying his assurances that the Creeks would be "treated with kindness." She parted with her children reluctantly, "evidently much affected," but remained silent until out of camp. Then she broke into tears. She never returned for her two children. Shortly after her disappearance, "volunteers" tracked down her camp, shot dead four men, and wounded, if not killed, several women and children. The fate of the child hostages remains unknown.[21]

By mid-July 1836, troops held 2,300 Creek prisoners, purportedly participants in the war. They were marched under armed guard to Montgomery and then shipped down the Alabama River, some in handcuffs. Soldiers, stationed on the hurricane decks of the steamboats, had orders to fire on Creeks who "evince a hostile spirit," and one Muscogee was shot dead and another bayoneted before their arrival in Mobile at the mouth of the Alabama a week later. From there, the prisoners were shipped off to New Orleans and up the Mississippi River to the mouth of the Arkansas, where the overland journey to Indian Territory began.[22] A second party of 193 Creek prisoners fared even worse, as suggested by a terse "journal of occurrences" left by one U.S. agent. Two children died on the three-day trip down the Alabama River. Arriving at Mobile at 3:00

A.M., the Creeks were transferred immediately to another steamboat, which left the next afternoon for New Orleans. After a three-day delay in the Crescent City, agents secured a boat for the trip up the Mississippi River, beginning a five-day journey to the mouth of the White River. Weeks of exposure to malarial mosquitoes, poor sanitation, and scant food had left the Creeks weak and sick. The entire party suffered from "Congestive and intermitent fever," and several people died on the Mississippi. Because of a shortage of transports, at the mouth of the White River, the healthy were divided from their families "with great reluctance" and sent on a forced three-day march through the swamps lying between the Mississippi and White rivers. Only a passing flatboat loaded with whiskey provided any relief; the entire party drank itself senseless. Reunited with their relatives, the prisoners then set off to cross Arkansas by foot. Exhausted Creeks were "constantly dropping," and torrential rains, broken by two days of scorching sun, worsened their plight. More than fifty were ill; "death occasionally carries off the weakest," noted the agent. The two-month odyssey ended on October 3. Nineteen Creeks had died along the way, and nine were missing "from some unaccountable cause," a casualty rate of 15 percent.[23] So ended what is now known as the Creek War of 1836.

Most of the wartime violence occurred south and east of the Graysons' hometown of Hilabi. Five Graysons enlisted to fight the dissident Creeks, but even if the Graysons did not go to war, the war inevitably came to them.[24] Though soldiers did not raid their homes or drive them into swamps, the presence of troops marked all Creeks as enemy peoples and encouraged local whites to mistreat them. Shortly after the beginning of the war, white men living close to the Graysons gathered in nearby Socapatoy (a town south of Talladega National Forest, now situated on Highway 280) to discuss the "uprising." Noting the "sour disappointment" of area Creeks at the failure of the government to remove them as promised, whites demanded an investigation into the conduct of emigrating agents. Hardly one of the more hostile groups of whites, they nevertheless demanded the removal of every Indian, whether unfriendly or not.[25] Other whites were even less circumspect. General Benjamin Patterson demanded "the *immediate* removal" of all Creeks, explaining that their "nature and habits are averse to a discrimination between those who are guilty and those who. have been innocent."[26]

U.S. officers moved quickly to round up innocent Muscogees. Shortly after July 20, a federal agent visited the Graysons and instructed them to prepare to depart in a few weeks. Resisters would face General Patterson, who passed through the area to "take measures to correct all difficulties that may arise."[27] By mid-August, agents across the state were gathering Creeks into six major camps in preparation for removal.[28] The Graysons, including Katy, her recent family, and her son John, were in the sixth detachment. In the last week of August, they were finally turned over to the Alabama Emigration Company, which had won a contract to provision Creek emigrants. Because its profits derived from the difference between actual cost and contractual payment, it frequently skimped on supplies and often delivered rancid meat and rotten corn. The sixth detachment and the Graysons left their homeland in September 1836 in a party of 2,830 people.[29] They traveled some three hundred miles on foot, setting off every morning at eight and walking until four or five in the afternoon. Food contractors padded their profits by driving the pace. Averaging about twelve miles a day, the detachment reached Memphis near the end of October.[30]

By the time it reached Memphis, the Graysons' party was still relatively healthy, but conditions soon began to deteriorate. The disbursing agent failed to obtain fresh meat, and provisions became few and far between. One subagent abandoned his charges together. His supervisor later found as many as four hundred Creeks spread out for miles along the road leading south from Memphis to the mouth of the White River. "Some were tired and sick and had no transportation," the agent wrote. "Others had had no provisions issued to them, since leaving Memphis" a full two weeks earlier. "Dead Horses and Indian ponies" littered the length of the road.[31] After most of the emigration detachment regrouped, it set off by steamboat for Little Rock, arriving in late November.[32] There, as the weather turned colder, the Graysons suffered a blow when Sandy's young daughter died on December 2.[33] (Sandy was Robert Grierson's grandson, the son of Sandy Grayson Sr.) With provisions running low, they could not afford to stop and mourn. Instead, they took to the road again, and finally, on January 23, 1837, they arrived at Fort Gibson in Indian Territory.[34]

Overall, the detachment was relatively fortunate. Of the original 2,830 emigrants, only the Grayson child and 14 other people died. Nevertheless, they were now homeless, without supplies and provisions, and facing freezing weather. Their situation was "truly distressing," an Indian agent noted a few days after the Graysons' arrival. Upwards of ten thousand Creeks were camped around Fort Gibson. Many were "naked," making the issuance to the Graysons of a single blanket per family both welcome and disgraceful. With the thermometer hovering around the freezing mark, Indian agents and Creeks alike anxiously awaited an additional shipment of blankets from New York.[35] Within a month, snow lay four to eight inches deep across the land.[36]

The United States had promised to provision the emigrants for a year after their arrival in Indian Territory, but graft, incompetence, and general indifference made the promise worthless. One man named A. J. Raines outlined the extent of the corruption. The provisioner of the Creeks was paid $44,000 every month to feed 16,200 Indians. The provisions cost the company $50,000, but instead of losing $6,000 every month, as would be expected, the company made a profit of nearly $6,000. How did it obtain such remarkable results? According to Raines, the methods were simple: issue cattle that weighed far less than stated, dole out corn in short measure, and bribe the Indian agents to overlook violations. On those frequent occasions when the provisioner had neither skeletal cattle nor rotten corn to offer, he attempted to quiet the desperate Creeks with a small amount of cash. Muscogees complained "powerfully," reported William Grayson, who witnessed the fraud, but they "got no satisfaction." (Raines later withdrew his accusations after receiving a bribe of $13,500 from the provisioner.)[37]

The scanty provisions hit the Creeks hard. "The Indians were obliged to dig for the wild potato, in the prairies," said one witness. A "good many died, and but for the wild potato, a great many more would have died."[38] Another reported seeing the Creeks "gather wild salad and boil it and eat it, when they had nothing else to live upon." "When the corn and pumpkins came in season for planting," this witness stated, "the Indians lived almost entirely upon them."[39]

The impact of removal is difficult to assess, but one story, recounted in 1937 by an eighty-four-year-old Creek woman named Elsie Edwards, suggests how traumatic the experience was. The elderly Edwards was interviewed for an oral history collection called the Indian-Pioneer Papers, funded by the New Deal's Work Projects Administration. Edwards launched into a story that she has learned as a child. "Somewhere upon the banks of the Grand River near Ft. Gibson lies an old grave of an old lady whose name was Sin-e-cha," Edwards began. "I could lead you to that grave today." Sin-e-cha was from Ketchapataka, a Hilabi settlement; she was very possibly Sinnugee, the ancient matriarch of the Grayson family.[40] According to Edwards, Sin-e-cha journeyed west, and "with shattered happiness she carried a small bundle of her few belongings." "Reopening and retying her pitiful bundle" on a steamboat plying the Mississippi River, "she began a sad song":

> I have no more land, I am driven away from home, driven up
> the red waters, let us all go, let us all die together and
> somewhere upon the banks we will be there.[41]

Edwards's powerful secondhand recollection of removal a century after the fact illustrates the great weight of the experience, yet it is not enough simply to acknowledge the trauma. Removal was not solely an emotional experience. By painfully illustrating the intensity and power of American racism, it had long-term social consequences that shaped the Creek Nation. The racism that underlay U.S. policy in the Southeast seemed to demonstrate the truth of George Troup's axiom: Creeks could aspire to be white, or else whites would see to it that they became black. Some black Indians, aware of the extraordinary pressures within Creek communities to whiten the nation, made the risky determination to remain in Alabama rather than migrate west.[42] Their decision might be ascribed to imprudence, but it perhaps reflects the equally uncertain future that blacks faced both in the Creek Nation and in Macon County, Alabama. Katy, who personally experienced the trauma of forced removal, felt these same pressures. They strengthened her resolve to distance herself from her black relatives. Scarred by the experience, she perhaps recognized that by embracing slavery she could secure a promising future for her new family. If she aspired to be white, then perhaps her young children would not have to live their lives at the bottom of America's racial hierarchy. Yet the cost was high. She would have to sacrifice her relationship with her older children, John and Annie, and with her brother William.

As historians have long recognized, removal policy reflected a new American fascination with the science of race, and this evolving pseudoscience, as much as removal itself, shaped the world of the Graysons in the 1830s and 1840s. All through the eighteenth century, leading American scientists and philosophers had believed that Africans, Europeans, and Indians were merely different varieties of a single species. Two pieces of evidence strongly supported their position. The first rested on simple observation. One species could not produce fertile offspring with another species, scholars believed, and everyone knew that in the Americas people of all sorts were multiplying rapidly. In fact, the terms to describe these offspring—"mulatto," "mestizo," "zambo," "quadroon," "octoroon," and so on—proliferated as well. Clearly, then, Africans, Europeans, and Indians must be different varieties of a single, unified species. The second piece of evidence seemed equally unassailable. Species were said to be by definition immutable and primordial. Unless there were multiple creations of humans at the beginning of time, eighteenth-century people perforce had to belong to the same species. Were there multiple creations? Genesis, the foundational text of natural history for Europeans, strongly suggested not.[43]

The origins of human variations puzzled eighteenth-century scientists, but by far the most popular theory held that environmental factors such as the sun and wind were responsible for the visible differences between people. The standard-bearer was clearly Samuel Stanhope Smith, whose *Essay on the Causes of the Variety of Complexion and Figure in the Human Species* appeared in 1787 and was reissued in expanded form in 1810.[44] For Smith and other leading scientists, skin color was merely a product of the environment. As evidence, environmentalists cited the famous case of Henry Moss, a black former slave whose name became almost as renowned as that of John Adams, Thomas Jefferson, or James Madison. To the great satisfaction of environmentalists, Moss's skin began turning white in 1792, shortly after he moved north and took up residence in Philadelphia. Most were content to attribute the transformation to the northern climate and to the benefits of freedom. Benjamin Rush, America's preeminent medical doctor, went further, observing that dark skin was a result of leprosy and that Moss was undergoing a spontaneous cure. Africans not blessed with nature's cure might rely on Rush's: tight clothes, friction, bleeding, "Oxygenated muriatic acid," and, among other things, the "juice of unripe peaches."[45] Whether undergoing a spontaneous cure for leprosy or experiencing the whitening effects of the Philadelphia sun, Moss seemed to demonstrate that skin color was determined by environment.

Environmentalism led white Americans to formulate policies—including intermarriage—that held out the possibility of amalgamation. "You will become one people with us," Thomas Jefferson told an Indian audience; "your blood will mix with ours; and will spread with ours over this great island."[46] Environmentalists could still be virulently prejudiced. "The blacks may be of the same species, for the mixed progeny will breed," conceded one author in the *Southern Literary Journal* in 1835. "But they are an inferior variety of the animal, man."[47] Yet belief in the unity of humankind permitted radicals to question the justice of inequality and slavery. African Americans and black Indians could find personal solace and some public protection in the eighteenth-century Enlightenment faith in human unity and progress. In the early 1800s, however, belief in the unity of humankind began to crumble under the attack of scientists.

The first sustained campaign was launched in an 1811 review article by Dr. Charles Caldwell, a native of North Carolina, graduate of the University of Pennsylvania, and professor of natural history at his alma mater. Caldwell deemed Smith's *Essay* "one of the most fallacious productions I have ever perused."[48] Caldwell later expanded his attacks in *Thoughts on the Original Unity of the Human Race* (1830), where he charged that Smith was both a "bigot" and a "fanatic."[49] In this diatribe against human unity, Caldwell asserted that "Caucasians" were the "most perfect" race, a perfection evident in their physical form and in their cultural achievements, for they authored "all great and important discoveries, inventions, and improvements." "[W]e say *all*, and do not speak extravagantly," wrote Caldwell. "The African and Indian races have not made one." Well, even Caldwell had to admit to one: Sequoyah's invention of a Cherokee syllabary, or writing system, in 1826. But Caldwell rescued his argument by attributing Sequoyah's genius to the "Caucasian blood in his veins." This kind of virulent and uncompromising racism led to conclusions about the future of the Indian in America that Caldwell found not at all troubling, endorsed as they were by the cold, hard truth of science: "The years of his race are not only numbered; they are comparatively few."[50]

Caldwell's unwavering conviction that he was on the side of truth rested on the discoveries of the new science of phrenology, a discipline that would be discredited only decades after its emergence. Phrenologists divided the brain into thirty-five different faculties or organs and from the shape and size of the skull presumed to determine the subject's character and intelligence. Was the patient sanguine, bilious, nervous, or lymphatic? Prone to malice or benevolence? Inclined toward immoral or moral behavior? From their experience examining crania, phrenologists concluded that Africans and Indians tended toward the low end of the spectrum of desirable qualities.[51] When their leading practitioner, Englishman George Combe, toured the United States in the late 1830s, he stopped at Catlin's Indian Gallery, in Boston's Faneuil Hall, where he studied portraits of America's native peoples. "The best, Mr Catlin suspected to be half-breeds," Combe wrote, "but the great mass of pure Indians present the deficient anterior lobe, the deficient coronal region, and the predominating base of the brain, by which savages in general are characterized."[52] Later, in an examination of the brains and skulls that once belonged to native Hawaiian Henry Nye and Indian Daniel Freeman, he found that both brains "shewed a proportionately large development in the animal region."[53] Indians, his brief studies revealed, were "deficient in Conscientiousness, Benevolence, and Ideality" and "inferior in their moral and intellectual development." Morally and intellectually, he concluded, Indians were "inferior to their Anglo-Saxon invaders, and receded before them."[54] In this way, Combe made Indian dispossession and annihilation a law of nature rather than a public policy.

During his tour of the states, Combe met Samuel George Morton in Philadelphia, then one of the country's leading natural scientists. Morton was at the time busy collecting and measuring skulls, eventually amassing 867 crania from around the world, a collection that the Swiss scientist Louis Agassiz deemed alone worth a visit to America.[55] Collecting the skulls was "perilous business," according to one grave robber, for Indians did not seem willing to desecrate their burial grounds in the name of science.[56] It was also gruesome. In 1826, one witness reported seeing a grave digger arrive at Fort Brady army hospital with a head wrapped in a handkerchief. That evening, large kettles over flame were spotted in the hospital, and "a most abominable stench" wafted over the grounds, thought to be the effects of boiling the flesh off of the day's acquisitions.[57] Despite its sordid origins, Morton's enormous collection and his meticulous measurements yielded a magnum opus in 1839, *Crania Americana*, a detailed study of the size and shape of hundreds of Native American skulls. The work did two things: by measuring skull size, it established a hierarchy of races, with whites at the top and Indians and blacks at the bottom; and by comparing ancient and modern skulls, it claimed to demonstrate the permanency of the differences between Africans, Indians, and Europeans.[58] Morton's work, rooted in the science of measurements rather than the art of phrenology, gave race a new scientific legitimacy, and by illustrating permanent differences across great spans of time, it undermined the very foundations of environmentalism.

These rarefied scientific debates about human difference may seem far removed from the Graysons, but Indians could not ignore the growing hostility toward their presence in the United States, nor could they avoid the unwelcome attention of natural scientists. In fact, the debates waged in learned journals were far more meaningful to Indians than they were to most other North Americans. "[W]e are convinced that the only method to protract the existence of that people, as a distinct race, is to send them into the wilderness," concluded Charles Caldwell.[59] T. Hartley Crawford, the commissioner of Indian affairs who oversaw the Creeks' removal from the Southeast, echoed Caldwell's conclusions. "It is late in the Indian's day," he asserted, "and his sun, it is feared, will soon set. . . . The only atmosphere through which it can much longer light his way, is west of the great river."[60] In some cases, the impact of science's new obsession was felt even more directly. Morton's *Crania Americana* included a full-page engraving of the skull of Athlaha Ficksa, reportedly "a full-blood chief of the Creek nation." A veteran of the Creek War of 1836, Athlaha Ficksa died in 1837 in Mobile, where a navy doctor removed his head, cleaned it of flesh, and mailed it to Morton's Philadelphia laboratory. Morton judged it a "remarkably fine head" and carefully measured its "parietal diameter," "inter-mastoid arch," and "occipito-frontal arch."[61] Athlaha Ficksa had served in war alongside five Graysons; in this nation of some twenty-two thousand people, the Graysons surely knew him, if not personally then by reputation.[62] The removal of his head must have alarmed and disgusted Creeks.

Morton had other Creek skulls in his collection. Item number 441 in his catalog had once belonged to a "Creek Warrior of Alabama," and number 751 had belonged to a "Creek woman from Georgia." Number 408 reputedly came from a Choctaw Indian, but Morton observed that "the skull strongly indicates a mixture of the Negro," a remark that indicated the direction of scientific racism.[63] The next decade would see a new obsession with "hybridity," the mixing of peoples, a phenomenon understood to have measurable and lamentable consequences. One article from 1842 would carry the title "The Mulatto a Hybrid—

Probable Extermination of the Two Races If the Whites and Blacks Are Allowed to Intermarry."[64]

It would be satisfying to assume that Creeks ignored the poor science and apologies for slavery that emanated from America's centers of learning. It might even be expected that they passionately despised the propaganda of their colonizers. Yet Creeks could not escape the South, with its racial hierarchies and vast slave plantations. Nor could they avoid recognizing the racial hierarchy that had already taken root in their own nation. The primacy of this hierarchy can be illustrated by careful examination of the social world of the Creek Nation, but it is also possible to explore the Creeks' own deliberations about race and to trace their ultimate rejection of the unity of mankind. Some Creeks, it appears, not only shared the beliefs of scientific racists but in a sense even anticipated their arguments.

Naturalists such as Samuel George Morton provided the scientific evidence to overturn the long-held belief in the unity of the humankind, but this belief did not rest solely on observation of the physical world. It was also grounded in faith, for Genesis stated clearly that humans were descended from Adam and Eve. This conflict between religion and science embarrassed a number of naturalists. Some sidestepped the issue by denying that their theories conflicted with the Bible. The races, distinct and immutable, surely existed, they said, but their origins remained a mystery. Others, by contrast, took glee in rejecting the historical validity of Adam and Eve's travails.[65] Surprisingly, despite their great investment in slavery, white southerners never rejected the biblical doctrine of the unity of humankind. They were unwilling to commit heresy, even if that heresy made slavery unassailable on scientific grounds. Their rejection of separate creations did not rest solely on a foundation of piety, for they well knew that the Bible also offered ample evidence in defense of slavery.[66] With less investment in the Bible, however, a southern people who fancied themselves masters and not slaves would have fully embraced the notion of separate creations, thereby dissolving the tension between foundational beliefs and empirical observation.

As southern slaveholders with little interest in the stories of Genesis, the Creeks were just such a people. Their willingness to believe in separate creations suggests that they understood Indians, Europeans, and Africans to be intrinsically different. In the early eighteenth century, Creeks did not bother to account for the existence of Africans and Europeans.[67] When, by the 1760s, they began mentioning Europeans and Africans in their narratives, they frequently did not specify how these newcomers came to be, but when they did, they spoke of a single creation. Both "red and White Men spring from the same God," one Creek said in 1765, suggesting that they were born in a single creation, although his ambiguous statement allowed for multiple creations as well.[68] In 1793, a Seminole leader (culturally affiliated with the Creeks) was similarly vague about the specifics of creation. "I was told the great water divided the world in seven parts, and this part (America) was given to the *red people*," he said. "And when the white people first came to this part," he continued, "the red people was afraid of the white people."[69] That same year, a Creek leader named White Lieutenant offered more detail. All "the people in the world" were descended from a single couple, his forefathers had learned from the Spanish.[70] Here was the doctrine of unity, stated explicitly.

In considering these examples, it must be taken into account that Creeks were speaking to a white audience in a politically charged atmosphere. White Lieutenant and others flattered their listeners by telling them what they wanted to hear. Hence, all these early origin stories mirror the accounts in Genesis, and all seem to be in the tradition of a single Edenic creation. It is all the more striking, then, that in 1818 and twice more in 1823–1824, Seminoles recounted stories of *separate* creation. Neamathla's story, told to the governor of Florida in 1823 or 1824, is the most complete of these narratives. God made a white man first, Neamathla explained. Displeased with his "pale and weak" creation, he made another, but this one was too black. "The Great Spirit liked the black man less than the white," Neamathla reportedly said, "and he shoved him aside to make room for another trial." Then he made his favorite creation, "the red man." Neamathla explained that the "Great Spirit" set three boxes on earth and allowed the white man as his first creation to choose his fate. The white man opened the boxes and selected "pens, and ink, and paper, and compasses." When the black man stepped forward to make his choice, the Great Spirit said, "I do not like you," and ordered him to stand aside. The red man then selected "tomahawks, knives, war clubs, traps, and such things as are useful in war and hunting." The black man took what was left: "axes and hoes, with buckets to carry water in, and long whips for driving oxen." Neamathla concluded that "the negro must work for both the red and white man, and it has been so ever since."[71] With its description of "pale and weak" white men, of a god who worked according to trial and error, and of separate creations, this was hardly a tale to flatter a white audience.[72]

The racial content of these stories cannot be attributed merely to the presence of a white audience, for Creeks and Seminoles spoke of separate creations at a time when only a mere handful of whites shared their views.[73] Why had Indians taken up the belief of separate creations and of immutable and distinct races? The racial climate in the South had much to do with the formation of their views. Unburdened by Christian dogma, they adopted their stories to explain what they saw and thought to be true. In a world where skin color was closely correlated with status, they concluded that Africans must indeed be a different sort of human. White Americans saw the same social world and developed an entire science to justify its existence, but despite their deep-seated and vicious prejudices, they could not so easily dismiss the tenets of Christianity. (Their struggles to reconcile faith and what they believed to be the natural world resembled those of educated Europeans in the age of Copernicus or Galileo.) Ironically, Africans also may have contributed to the emergence of a Creek belief in separate creations. There are African precedents for Neamathla's story that date back to 1698, and some folklorists believe that the long history of cultural convergence between blacks and Indians in the Southeast gave rise to accounts of separate origins.[74]

Though influenced by both whites and Africans, Indians ultimately drew on their own traditions and experiences. One scholar suggests that color symbolism in the native Southeast, where red and white were commonly understood to be opposites, gradually took on racial connotations.[75] Others have noted that southeastern Indians frequently dismissed all outsiders as nonhumans.[76] It is not difficult to see how this disdain for others might have led to the conviction that plantation slaves were separate and distinct beings. Whatever the underlying precedents, the Creek belief in separate creations anticipated the direction of America's scientific racists. In a country of growing hostility toward nonwhites, Creeks rejected assertions of Indian inadequacy, but many accepted those of black inferiority. Even Creeks who were resolutely opposed to the science of their enemies may have harbored doubts, if only momentarily. Perhaps blacks were inferior; perhaps whites were more naturally gifted at studious pursuits; perhaps the admixture of white blood did hold the only chance of long-term survival for Indian peoples. These thoughts, no matter how briefly entertained, would have weighed heavily on families such as the Graysons.

The growing distance between Creeks of African descent and their relatives is nowhere better reflected than in a critical decision that Katy made upon her arrival at Fort Gibson in early 1837. She established her first home along the Poteau River, which flows southwest from its origins at Fort Smith. By 1843, she and several of other Grayson emigrants had moved deeper into Indian Territory, settling in the Choctaw Nation on land now flooded by the southern arm of Eufaula Lake.[77] William, of course, had already established a homestead in Indian Territory. He had weathered the first difficult years and would have been of immense assistance to his newcomer siblings. But William was settled some thirty miles north on Butler Creek (near the present-day town of Oktaha), and his sister Katy, brother Watt, and other relatives chose to live a full day's journey away. More telling, they settled across the Canadian River, whose current was at times too strong to cross.[78] In the old Creek homeland, by contrast, Katy, William, and the others had all lived within a few miles of each other.[79]

Three factors may have influenced Katy's unusual decision to live so far away from her brother. First, she may have been unwelcome in the Creek Nation after her family's participation in the preremoval land frauds. Second, the Choctaw Nation was generally more accommodating to slaveholders. During removal, some Choctaw leaders had reaffirmed their commitment to the institution by selling their allotments and using the profits to purchase slaves.[80] Their invest-ment in slavery was reflected in the laws they adopted shortly before Katy arrived in Indian Territory. Choctaw leaders passed legislation forbidding slaves from owning property and, to deter abolitionist missionaries, prohibiting others from teaching slaves to read or sing without the consent of their masters.[81] Creek legislators were slower to draft their own set of slave laws, and they would struggle over the matter well into the 1850s. Finally, Katy may have settled in the Choctaw Nation simply to place some distance between her and her black

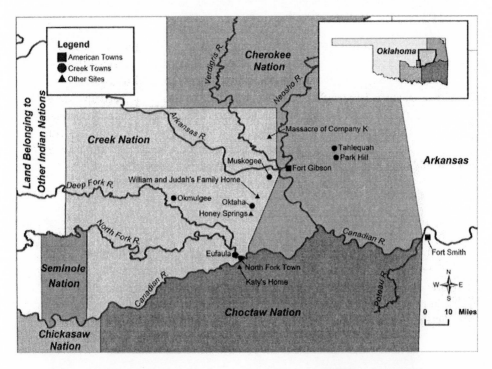

The Creek Nation and Indian Territory in the 1860s. Map by William T. Jurgelski.

relatives. In a sense these three factors were related. The participation in white land frauds, the investment in slavery, and the rejection of black family members reflected a more general decision to join white America.

The growing science of race and the enthusiasm with which whites applied it to Indians drove a wedge between the Graysons during the removal era. Davy Grayson, of Creek and African descent, discovered as much. He kept a long list of grievances culled from his removal experience. The "whole of the way from the old nation, clear to Fort Gibson," Davy had worked as a teamster, but he "never received a cent for it," he complained. Nor had he received any provisions. Moreover, he continued, he "never received a dollar of the annuity" in the four years since moving to Indian Territory. Asked why, "he said he didn't know, but he has colored blood in him he says, and some have told him that was the reason."[82]

Profile

Marilyn Vann, June 2003 and April 2004

Marilyn Vann bears one of the most famous surnames in the Cherokee Nation. Before his murder in 1809, James Vann, whose columned, brick mansion still stands in northwest Georgia, was one of the wealthiest and most powerful Cherokees in the nation. Marilyn Vann is descended from one of his two hundred slaves. From her physical appearance, it is easy to imagine that she has Cherokee, African, and European ancestry. I first met Vann in June 2003 at a conference on black Indians that was inspired by an organization she founded, the Descendants of the Freedmen of the Five Civilized Tribes. The conference took place in Norman, Oklahoma, in a sprawling training facility for federal postal employees, operated by Marriott.

The featured speakers largely were descendants of freed people and were active in the cause of citizenship for black Indians. Some told engaging family stories; others waged spirited attacks against racial injustices in the Five Tribes (the Creeks, Cherokees, Choctaws, Chickasaws, and Seminoles). Vann stood out for her detailed and precise knowledge of the federal legislation, legal decisions, and treaties that bear on the political status of freed people. Middle-aged and wearing thick glasses and a plain T-shirt, she was the picture of seriousness.

Although her mother is descended from Chickasaw slaves and her father from Cherokee slaves, Vann grew up in Ponca City, not far from the Kansas border, on land that once belonged to the Ponca Nation. As a child, she occasionally visited the Cherokee Nation. Her great-grandmother had moved west with the Cherokees in 1838, and her father was on the Cherokee freedmen rolls. He was already sixty when she was born, however, and he died before she was old enough to learn much about her family's history. Over the years, she asked elderly family members about her ancestors. Finally, by September 2001, Vann had collected enough information to submit a citizenship application to the Cherokee Nation. A month later, she received a rejection letter.

At the time, Vann had no idea about freedmen or by-blood rolls—lists of ex-slaves and Indians compiled by the U.S. government in the 1890s—but she went to work trying to understand the origins and history behind the disenfranchisement of ex-slaves. She was methodical and rigorous in her research, qualities that came easily to her, given that she has a degree in engineering and a job with the federal government that frequently takes her to law libraries. The depth of her knowledge was reflected in our discussions. She spoke casually of Title 25, the federal Indian code, and referred freely to numerous court cases that she had uncovered with Westlaw, a database of legal journals. At one point, she told me, she even drove from Oklahoma City to Tahlequah, the Cherokee capital, to read the trial record of a case on the citizenship of freed people then pending before the Cherokee Supreme Court.

While reading up on black Indian history, Vann began looking around for organizations that shared her interests, but she found none. After she wrote a series of articles on the subject for black newspapers, such as the *Ebony Tribune* and the *Tulsa Eagle*, black Oklahomans began contacting her. They had been waiting for someone to speak out, they said. In January 2002, only a few months after her rejection letter from the Cherokee Nation, she called a meeting in Oklahoma City at the Ralph Ellison Library. About twenty-five people showed up. A few months later, she called a second meeting, and more people attended. By October 2002, Vann had created a board of directors and incorporated her fledgling organization, the Descendants of the Freedmen of the Five Civilized Tribes. She has been "spreading the message and trying to fight ever since," she told me.

Vann wishes to open up a dialogue with Cherokee citizens. Many Cherokee citizens and even tribal officials simply do not fully comprehend the situation of the descendants of freed people, she observed. "There is a lack of knowledge, a lack of understanding," she said. Many people believe that black Indians have more connections to Africa than to the Five Tribes. Yet most descendants of freed people "know a lot more about a stomp dance, hog fry, and wild onion dinner than anything about Africa."

If Indian nations continue to violate their promises to freed people, Vann astutely observed, the United States may use these violations to justify terminating its own relationship with the Five Tribes. "I believe in sovereignty," she asserted, "but just as they want the United States to live up to what the United States says, we want tribes to live up to their commitments." Cherokee slaves "paid their dues." They cleared fields and built houses for the Cherokees. "Is this now the deal, now that they're no longer useful?" she asked. "It is repugnant to me."

4 ▪▪

Separate Paths: Katy and William in the Antebellum Creek Nation

Indian Territory at first seemed a place of affliction. "Billious fever," "oppressive drought," "extraordinary floods," and "dreadful famine" were regular occurrences, worsened by the Creeks' unfamiliarity with the land.[1] Sometimes the country appeared cursed. In the harsh winter of 1858–1859, packs of "mad dogs" made nighttime excursions dangerous if not fatal.[2] On occasion the pestilence reached immense proportions. When grasshoppers descended on Indian Territory in spring 1856, missionary John Lilley was reminded of the plagues of biblical lore. The insects devoured entire cornfields and destroyed them again after Creeks had replowed and planted anew. Lilley noted that in "some places the ground is almost covered" with grasshoppers. "In passing along the road their motion on the dry leaves sounds like rain."[3] The costs of these afflictions can be measured starkly. In 1832, there were nearly twenty-two thousand Creeks, not including slaves; by 1859, there were barely fourteen thousand.[4]

Much like the floods, droughts, and epidemics in the region, a deteriorating racial climate also hit the Creek Nation, damaging communities and dividing families. Population statistics measure the rapidity of this deterioration. In 1832, Creeks held about nine hundred slaves.[5] By 1860, that number had doubled to eighteen hundred.[6] In short, before removal, slaves made up roughly 4 percent of a vigorous and growing nation; thirty years later, they made up 13 percent of a much smaller, weaker nation. These numbers, which reveal that the slave population rose as quickly as the free Creek population declined—as if the figures were linked in inverse proportion to one another—neatly capture the circumstances faced by the Graysons in the two decades before the outbreak of the Civil War.

In the shadow of removal, when white southerners had used race to justify the appropriation of Indian lands and the expulsion of Indians, Katy Grayson and her family embraced slavery as both a private confirmation and a public display of their own racial superiority. Indian slaveholders usually bore the designation of "mixed-blood," a step above the "full-blood" Indians in the nation.[7] As if to emphasize both their closeness to whites and their distance from other Indians, some "half-breeds" in Indian Territory reportedly referred to themselves as "white Indians."[8] In many cases, there were in fact visible physical differences between slaveholders and nonslaveholders. "Some of them Creeks was mixed up with the whites," recalled former slave Mary Grayson in 1937. Some of "the big men in the Creeks" who visited her master, Mary recalled, were "almost white, it looked like."[9]

She might have been thinking of the Graysons. Katy's spouse was the son of Mary Benson, a white woman. Of Katy's and Tulwa Tustanagee's five children whose marriages are known, all had white or "mixed-blood" spouses. James, for example, married Jennie Wynne, a woman of mixed European and Creek ancestry.[10] Their first child, Wash, born in 1843, had "exceedingly red hair" and was "quite white in complexion."[11] He would marry Annie Stidham, the daughter of G. W. Stidham, of Scotch-Irish and Creek descent and one of the five largest slaveholders in the nation before the Civil War.[12]

Wash's uncle (Katy's son) sometimes drew attention to his nephew's looks by dressing the young boy in a turban and tying rags about his legs, in imitation of "the full blood Creeks of that day." Wash remembered the game as "innocent amusement," but the ironic contrast between Wash's physical features and his clothing touched on serious matters. Wash, like his parents, disdained white Americans. In fact, he said he "regretted" his light complexion.[13] In later years he would recall with disgust the features of one unwelcome traveling companion: "He was a blond—blond hair, eye lashes, moustache and gray eyes, in fact blond all over." He had, he admitted, "a repugnance to blonds of all degrees."[14] Yet Wash's hatred of white Americans existed uncomfortably with his family's own history of marrying them. With each passing generation, Katy's descendants more closely resembled the Creek Nation's enemies.

The Graysons' keen awareness of injustice toward Indians committed in the name of race seems only to have fortified their desire to prove Americans wrong on their own terms. If whites treated him like the "Wild man of Borneo," Wash would later confess, he would "do as Rome does."[15] Rome, in this case, owned slaves. Slave ownership not only flattered the Republic's white citizens but also confirmed the slave owner's rank in the hierarchy of races. Many whites wildly imagined that slavery and whiteness existed in a proportion determined by the laws of nature. Surely, they reasoned, "full-blood" Indians had neither the talent nor the wherewithal to be planters, for how could natural subjects be made into masters, or children turned into fathers? A tincture of white blood might grant would-be Indian planters the qualities needed to lord over their slaves with some effectiveness. And a preponderance of that blood might even turn Indians into respectable planters, whose superiority would be manifested by the efficient subjugation of Africans and measured by the profitable expropriation of their labor.

Such logic led to self-confirming observations. "Between the wealthy half-breed with his slaves . . . and the unclad Indian, there is a great disparity," observed one visitor to Indian Territory in 1838.[16] Ethan Allen Hitchcock, who traveled through the area in the 1840s, deemed "full-bloods" to be poor and lazy. "A slave among wild Indians," he said, "is almost as free as his owner, who scarcely exercises the authority of a master, beyond requiring something like a tax paid in corn or other product of labor."[17] Other white visitors noted that the bondmen and bondwomen of "full-bloods" were slaves "only in name."[18] Observation unsurprisingly confirmed preconception, as it so frequently does in matters of race. Samuel Morton, the naturalist whose studies lent scientific validity to race in the 1830s, had been a victim of the same distorting power of prejudice. He assumed that Caucasian skulls would be more capacious than others, and his meticulous experiments, carried out with earnest integrity, seemed to prove him right. We now know that he unconsciously mismeasured his gruesome specimens so that they conformed to expectations.[19]

Yet the observed connection between European ancestry and slavery, though mired in the confused racial logic of nineteenth-century America, contained some truth. Katy and her light-skinned descendants had the option of marrying whites, whose economic advantages facilitated the accumulation of slaves. William's children, by contrast, could have found white spouses only with difficulty. Moreover, Katy and numerous others made conscious decisions to pursue a survival strategy that was shaped by the antebellum South. The strategy demanded that Indians emulate whites by becoming the masters of blacks. Emulation sometimes led to marriage to white Americans, even if families such as the Graysons occasionally revealed their distrust of whites. Forged in race and slavery, this strategy had predictable success. As one former slave recalled, the Grayson slaveholders were "big people" in the Creek Nation "and with [the] white folks too."[20]

The Graysons were not alone in their decision. In the mid-nineteenth century, out of a free population of fourteen thousand, some 255 Creeks owned as many as eighteen hundred slaves. The number of slaveholders seems small, but it means that one of every ten families enslaved other humans. Of these slaveholders, 47 owned more than ten slaves, and five families owned more than forty slaves.[21] The Graysons were related to two of the five largest planters in Creek country. Sam and Pink Hawkins, who jointly owned forty-one slaves, were the descendants of Sarah Grayson and Stephen Hawkins. Jane Hawkins, who owned seventy-six slaves, was the widow of Samuel Hawkins, Sarah's son.[22] After emancipation, the Graysons would marry into a third of these five families.[23] In addition, Katy Grayson, across the Canadian River in the Choctaw Nation, owned at least fourteen slaves.[24] Watt Grayson, patriarch Robert's son, was also one of the largest slaveholders in the area.[25] In all, Graysons owned at least seventy-nine slaves.[26]

Often portrayed as corporate and kin-based, benign and even inconsequential, slavery in Indian Territory was far more diverse.[27] Slaves were a common sight in the Creek Nation. They served as interpreters, messengers, and guides. Some slaves were hired out to missionaries. Missionary Mrs. Lilley found it impossible to manage her "Indian raised Negress," though her friend Mrs. Thompson tried by the whip. Their fellow missionary Mr. Ballentine similarly became "very much annoyed at the way the negroes worked."[28] Missionary William Robertson admitted that "slavery is hateful," but did "not wonder that darkies get whiped," given their "slow stupid motions."[29] These opinions, so common among white Americans, suggest that Indian slaves were much like their southern counterparts. Working against their will, they worked as little as possible.

Small Creek slaveholders used their human property for routine farming and household tasks. When Katy gave a slave named Wilson to her son James (Wash's father), Wilson provided real material assistance to the family. After his death, children and parents felt the increased workload.[30] On larger plantations such as Katy's, slaves worked as both unskilled and skilled laborers. Most "of the labor among the wealthier classes . . . is done by negro slaves," said one traveler, "for they adopted substantially the Southern system of slavery." Another noted that it was not uncommon to see twenty or thirty slaves at work on a single Creek plantation.[31] Katy's slave Paro Bruner was one of the skilled slaves, plying his trade as a blacksmith. By repairing plows and other iron tools, he made possible the work of the much more numerous unskilled slaves who labored in corn, cotton, or rice fields, "raising large quantities of surplus for sale." Some planters sent their surplus as far abroad as Ireland.[32] Other skilled slaves spent their days carding and spinning wool and cotton. They dyed the yarn with sumac and copperas for a rich tan, indigo for a deep blue, and sycamore and red oak for shades of pink and red. Skilled slaves also made shoes, using hog bristle needles to sew together the uppers and employing wooden pegs to secure them to the leather soles.[33] After planting in July, field labor declined until the September harvest, but slaves were expected to work to clothe and feed themselves during this period.[34]

Though numerous observers and ex-slaves testified to the relative kindness of Indian masters, some Creek planters brutalized their bondmen and bondwomen.[35] Alex Haynes recalled that when his father failed to pick five hundred pounds of cotton each day, he was whipped. "My father has said that he came through the slave days with much whipping and blood shed," Haynes stated.[36] Ed Butler, a former slave in the Choctaw Nation, where Katy and other Grayson planters lived, remembered being treated well but confessed that his master whipped slaves occasionally, if "always in moderation."[37] Slave master Pleasant Porter, who later became the principal chief of the Creek Nation, did not fare so well in the memory of Tony Carolina. By his bedside, Porter kept a long whip, which he wielded when his slaves moved too slowly for his taste. "My mother said he used to whip her even if she did all that he asked her to do," Carolina remembered.[38]

No matter how painful the whip, slaves often lived in greater fear of the trading block. It is impossible to measure the frequency of slave trading in the Creek Nation, but qualitative evidence suggests there was an active market.[39] In 1827, Watt Grayson sold an entire family of nine to his brother Thomas for $1,500.[40] Watt again entered the market in 1839, when he purchased "certain Negroes." Four years later, he sold the slaves to his brother Sandy, who returned them a year later for fear of clouded title.[41]

These seemingly simple economic transactions wounded enslaved blacks so severely that the scars still showed a century later. In 1937, John Harrison recounted how his enslaved mother had moved west with the Creeks one hundred years earlier. Shortly after her arrival in Indian Territory, she was sold "on the block" to Mose Perryman, a powerful and wealthy Creek planter. Perryman later purchased Harrison's father but just before the Civil War sold him to a "slave buyer." "No one ever know what become of him," said John.[42] Lucinda Davis recalled that her parents ran away or bought themselves, leaving her behind as a small girl. Her owner sold her soon after to attend to the child of another Creek.[43] Jordan Folsom recounted how his grandmother Sylvia, a young woman in Alabama with one child, was sold to a slave trader. "Sylvia's mother was there and was crying but it did no good," Folsom said; "they were just chattels and were sold, regardless of what any of the relatives said or did." Sylvia never saw her mother again, for the trader drove them to Indian Territory, "just like cattle," to sell to wealthy planters. Soon after Sylvia was sold to a Choctaw slave owner, her child died.[44]

Though one former slave claimed that most Creeks would not sell their slaves, a few actively profited from the slave trade.[45] Comanches sometimes sold black captives from Texas to the Creeks. Creek planters were occasionally the end purchasers, paying up to $500 for each slave. At other times, they served as go-betweens, buying the captives for as little as $150 and making a quick $300 profit. Two young and bewildered boys, Abram and Sambo, followed this path: stolen by Comanches in 1839, they were purchased by a party of Cherokees and Creeks and then quickly resold to a Creek and white family for a healthy profit.[46]

Though 90 percent of families owned no slaves, bondage underlay every encounter between Muscogees and black Creeks. Sometimes, as when Creeks whipped other humans, slavery was manifest, but even when Muscogees and black Creeks met on seemingly equal terms, the daily labor of slaves, the painful punishments, and the slave-trading block remained a silent subtext of the conversation. The conversation grew more strained in the two decades after removal. As Katy Grayson and others struggled to climb from the bottom of America's racial hierarchy, they distanced themselves from their darker relatives. They married light-skinned Creeks, and they worked their slaves harder, punished them more brutally, and sold them when they proved too intractable. The space for compromise was becoming smaller and the distance between Creeks and their black relatives even greater.

Just north of the present-day city of Muskogee, Oklahoma, the first Presbyterian mission established in the western Creek Nation seemed to hold some promise that black Creeks and Muscogees would find common ground. In 1831, both groups could be seen worshiping and receiving communion together.[47] A year later, the Muskogee Baptist Church hosted similarly mixed congregations. One night in October 1832, the church's minister baptized eight or ten Creeks together with some twenty-six to twenty-eight slaves.[48] The uncertain numbers reflect the minister's confusion over who was black and who was Indian. To some outsiders, this land of racial harmony seemed nearly Edenic. Washington Irving, who traveled through the region in 1832, a dozen years after writing *The Legend of Sleepy Hollow*, encountered a scene at a trading post in the neighboring Cherokee Nation that inspired his pen. On the banks of a "beautiful, clear river," Irving wrote, "Indian nymphs" lay "half naked," Indian men roasted venison, and "negroes" ran to greet him. His impressions came quicker: "half breeds— squaws—negro girls running & giggling—dogs of all kinds—hens flying & cackling—wild turkeys, tamed geese." "In these establishments," he joyfully observed, "the world is turned upside down—the slave the master, the master the slave."[49]

But the social and racial confusion that intrigued Irving troubled leading Creeks, newly arrived from the Deep South. Many Creeks wished to establish a racial hierarchy, some to eliminate a source of white contempt, others to satisfy a deep-seated sense of superiority. Missionary David Rollin unwittingly gave voice to white contempt at the same time as he identified Creek racism: "the more enlightened Indians," he said, "are far from considering themselves on a level with blacks."[50] These Indians were "more advanced in intelligence" than most, said another white man.[51] Whether motivated by expediency or conviction, Creek leaders made a concerted effort to elevate Indians to masters and reduce blacks to slaves. The campaign started in 1833 when the multiracial congregations in the Creek Nation came to the attention of Muscogee chiefs. The Presbyterians offered Sunday school for both Indians and their slaves, and some Creeks found the situation intolerable. Missionary John Fleming described a visit from one Creek leader: "the first cheif [sic] assaulted me . . . with great fury for teaching their slaves, and said it was contrary to their laws." Fleming protested but finally decided against teaching slaves.[52] Though in fact the Creek Nation had yet to pass any laws prohibiting the education of slaves, Presbyterian missionaries reported in 1835 that schools for Creek slaves had been entirely disbanded.[53] William Grayson's emancipated children, recent arrivals in Indian Territory, would have been affected only indirectly, but the political climate in the nation could not have been reassuring.

Though Katy was a slaveholder rather than a former slave like her sister-in-law Judah, she also could not have been entirely reassured when she arrived in 1837. The Creek Nation had yet to entirely eradicate the stirrings of abolitionism. Across the Canadian River to the south, by contrast, the Choctaw Nation absolutely prohibited any interference with slaves. In 1836, Choctaws banned abolitionists from the nation, prohibited people from teaching slaves to read, write, or sing without the master's permission, and forbade ministers even from sitting at the same table with slaves.[54] These draconian laws may have contributed to Katy's decision to settle in the Choctaw Nation.

In the Creek Nation, the campaign against abolitionists was more protracted. In August 1836, Principal Chief Roley McIntosh complained to the U.S. commander at Fort Gibson that missionaries were "encouraging our slaves by teaching them and telling them, that they should be free." He demanded that the missionaries be removed "as *soon* as *possible*."[55] By one report, three white men, resident in the Creek Nation, wrote the letter and urged Creek leaders to sign it.[56] But two years later, Creeks drafted a similar document. They first complained about white men who pursued "a course of life but little calculated to advance the condition of their families." They banned all white men from the nation unless permitted to remain by the chiefs in council but reserved their harshest words for "a Class of individuals styling themselves free negroes," who were "more objectionable both in character and in there [sic] conduct." Free blacks, they wrote, were "arrogating to themselves privileges to which they are not entitled" and were setting "bad examples to our slaves subversive to our authority over them." As with whites, exceptions could be made for certain individuals to remain with permission of the chiefs. But otherwise, Creek leaders banned all free blacks from the nation and vowed to expel those not in compliance.[57] Samson Grayson, owner of thirty-four slaves, looked on as the letter was drafted, and he signed at the bottom as a witness. By traveling to Indian Territory separately from William, Samson had distanced himself from his uncle four years earlier. This letter turned that act of rejection into active hostility. Samson must have known that the letter he witnessed could, if honored, expel William's wife, Judah, from the nation.

These acts against outsiders reflected the belief of lawmakers that "the time has arrived when we should free our community from all who are not immediately identified in interest and Blood."[58] Yet their defense of community was reactionary, for it confronted slavery merely by cracking down on the subjugated population. A more imaginative response—one pursued by many Creeks, as suggested by the mixed congregations of the 1830s—would have been to incorporate black Creeks into the nation. In the National Council, however, the small minority of slaveholders dominated, and state policy never considered this political possibility. Early in October 1839, missionary Charles Kellam was called before the National Council and questioned about his activities. Kellam crudely paraphrased the slaveholders' grievance: "Our niggers be sp[o]iled by preachers, send em to work, they sit under tree and read book, sp[o]ilt nigger now." The National Council demanded that he refrain from preaching to blacks.[59] According to Kellam, those few planters who approved of the missionaries' activities did so in the hope that Christianity would make slaves "feel tender towards their masters."[60] Kellam continued to preach to slaves after dark, sometimes all through the night, and the resolve of the National Council only intensified the devotion of the audience. Some who attended gave Kellam their few hard-earned dollars; others sent Kellam small livestock; still others offered room and board. These "are highly interesting seasons," the minister reflected.[61]

Creeks had long disdained the proselytizing efforts of missionaries. Katy's son James, for example, was opposed to the Christian churches in Indian Territory, a sentiment likely inherited from his Redstick father. It did not help their cause that in 1836 one minister had seduced, or perhaps raped, a Creek woman, who became pregnant with his child.[62] In the past, Creeks had deflected the patronizing lectures of ministers with a perfunctory "Yes, yes, I know." "Oh, yes, yes, yes, I know it," said one impatient Muscogee in 1810 after listening to a speech on "the love of God and of Jesus Christ."[63] But now, missionaries had established a permanent presence in the nation, and their impact on slaves could not be so easily dismissed. Four months after instructing Kellam to halt his abolitionist activities, Creeks shot at his partner, J. A. Mason, and, "armed with a large knife," chased the "damd negro Missionary" into a thicket.[64] Roley Mc-Intosh, the principal chief of the Lower Creeks and the owner of sixty people, explained that Creeks opposed Kellam, Mason, and others because "they have acted in such a manner as to make us believe they were Abolitionists, by their paying more attention to our slaves than our own people."[65] Two years later, the National Council, led by McIntosh, allowed the Presbyterian Board of Foreign Missions to establish schools in the nation only on the condition that the missionaries not "interfere in any manner, with the relation existing between master and slave, by learning them to read."[66]

Following the lead of their Choctaw neighbors, the Creek pro-slavery leadership generated a written code of slave laws in the 1840s and 1850s. Unfortunately, the statutes cannot be dated precisely, but they confirm a general trend of harsher and more oppressive laws aimed at black Creeks. The earliest legislation seems to have been drafted shortly after a slave uprising in the Cherokee Nation in 1842 spurred the Cherokees to draft a number of oppressive slave laws. Soon after the revolt, two Quaker missionaries who visited the Creeks observed that Muscogees intended "to enact more rigid laws for the government of their slaves, and for binding their chains more strongly upon them."[67]

One law prohibited enslaved blacks from owning horses, cattle, or guns, and another mandated harsh punishments for Creeks who harbored fugitive slaves. (It is not clear if this act preceded or followed the Fugitive Slave Law passed by the U.S. Congress in 1850.) Three other laws—all resembling legislation passed in various southern states—were intended to drive free blacks out of the nation. The first made future acts of emancipation illegal unless the slave in question was removed from the nation. The other two were aimed at ex-slaves emancipated before the passage of the first law. These laws levied special head and property taxes on freedmen and freedwomen who had not been adopted as Creek citizens.[68] If the taxes were enforced, they were debilitating. Sophy and Jim Kennard of North Fork Town, for example, would have had to pay eight dollars per year (in effect, one of the three cows they owned), nearly 15 percent of the total value of their possessions.[69] At times of crisis, planters in the slave states passed similar laws aimed at free blacks, most famously after Nat Turner's rebellion in Southampton, Virginia, in 1831.[70] Such laws reflected the belief that free blacks, in the words of Creek slaveholders, exercised "a very pernicious influence" on slaves.[71] But rather than confronting the unsettling truth that slavery itself was the problem, the statutes both in the Creek Nation and elsewhere merely reassured self-deceived planters that outside agitators were to blame.

Judah and seven of her children were ex-slaves, but their connection to William probably exempted them from head and property taxes. Nevertheless, three additional laws drew attention to their compromised status in the nation. One of these laws seemingly covered criminal behavior: it mandated one hundred lashes for "any Negro, slave, or free," who "shall abuse any Indian citizen of the Creek Nation."[72] The law's wording was meant either to preclude Negroes from being Indian citizens or to create two classes of citizens, Negro and Indian. Where did William and Judah's son Henderson or Katy's children by her first marriage fit in this law? Were they free Negroes liable to be convicted of abusing Indian citizens? Could they be one of the Indian citizens so abused? Could people of African descent even become citizens?

The wording of the final two laws manifests a similar confusion. One prohibited any "negro," slave or free, from having sexual intercourse with a Creek woman. Negroes caught violating the restriction were to receive one hundred lashes, Creek women fifty. The last statute made it unlawful for Indian men to marry black women. Any "citizen" who broke the law was to be flogged.[73] Neither act prevented masters from sleeping with their slave women. The legislators intended to codify a social movement, their dark response to the antebellum South and removal. By very clearly branding all black Creeks with the mark of slavery, Creek lawmakers denied their African heritage and raised themselves from the bottom of America's racial hierarchy.

For Judah and William, the laws must have been horrifying. They were now living together illegally. The status of their children, however, remained ambiguous. Were they black? In 1840, their sons Billy and Henderson turned twenty-one and fifteen, respectively. Would they be flogged for dating Creek women? Emma was now seventeen. Was she a Creek woman, risking fifty lashes if she slept with a black man? Or was she herself black, proscribed from marrying Creek men? In 1840, Judah and William had another daughter. They named her Judy, courageously identifying their baby with her black mother.[74] What would Judy's future hold?

Despite a Creek government policy to bind slaves more strongly to their chains, many Muscogees drew on egalitarian political traditions to make a community without divisions between black and Indian, slave and free. In January

1842, Ethan Allen Hitchcock found a congregation of "Creeks, half-breeds and negroes engaged in prayer and singing psalms." Their clothing—coats, vests, leggings, moccasins, and turbans—reflected their shared, yet diverse, culture, one caricatured by the Graysons when the young Wash dressed in "innocent amusement" like a "full blood."[75] The congregation sung hymns in Creek to Creek music and in English to Methodist and Baptist melodies. One black participant "made a prayer with considerable energy."[76] Elsewhere, prayer meetings of "Indians and negroes," frequently led by black preachers, were reportedly "filled to over flowing," and hundreds of people, "red white and black," were receiving baptism together.[77]

Some slave masters professed to believe that Christianity would make their slaves "better men and women," and one even cynically suggested that "his negroes" were "worth twice as much as they were before they become religious."[78] But their tolerance ran low in 1843. That year, a rump National Council decided to forbid all blacks and Indians from preaching and to admit only licensed white missionaries. Violators would receive fifty lashes on the bare back, and on the second offense they would receive one hundred.[79] Fifty lashes with slender hickory branches known as withes, twisted into a cord at least an inch in diameter, would cut flesh almost to the bone; one hundred lashes might permanently disable, if not kill, the victim.[80] The law may have had little support outside the wealthiest planters, but at least one black man, Moses, felt the sting of its judgment on his back.[81]

In the neighboring United States, the growing controversy surrounding slavery made Creek politics even more volatile. A series of U.S. land acquisitions in the 1840s destabilized the sectional compromises that had held the Union together. In 1845, Congress admitted Texas as a slave state. The following year, it signed a treaty with Britain, dividing Oregon Territory at the forty-ninth parallel (the current Canadian border). And, in 1847, it invaded Mexico, seizing from its neighbor a huge section of North America that was eventually divided into California, New Mexico, Nevada, Utah, Arizona, and parts of Wyoming and Colorado. The United States would spend the next half century fighting wars to conquer the indigenous peoples who lived in this area. The formal annexation of these new lands called into question the Compromise of 1820, which had permitted slavery only south of 36°30'. Pro-slavery and antislavery forces rallied to their causes, and the West became the great object of victory.[82] In the North, antislavery advocates started the Free Soil party in 1848, dedicated to making the West a white man's land, where white farmers and artisans could seek their fortunes.[83] In the South, planters cracked down on dissent, pulling antislavery tracts from the U.S. mail and producing their own spirited defenses of human bondage.[84]

Creek slave owners feared that Indian Territory, bordering the unorganized territory of Nebraska (eventually divided into Nebraska and Kansas) and the two slave states of Texas and Arkansas, might be swept up in the storm. The continuing free associations between blacks and Indians presented one threat to stability in the Creek Nation. Another arose in 1845, when the Creeks agreed to permit Seminoles to settle on their lands. The U.S. government had long striven for such an accord, but slavery proved to be a sticking point. Seminoles feared that their black citizens and slaves would be seized by Creeks, who claimed that hundreds of their bondmen and bondwomen had taken refuge with the Seminoles before removal. Creek families were remarkably persistent in their quest to regain these fugitive slaves, in some cases continuing the effort from one generation to the next. The 1845 agreement simply avoided the matter by leaving future property disputes subject to the determination of the U.S. president.[85]

The treaty created unexpected problems, however, when large numbers of free blacks and fugitive slaves from Indian Territory and the surrounding area began building communities in the southeastern corner of the Creek Nation, not far from the residences of both William and Katy Grayson. Creek leaders were determined to break up the settlements and to expel all free blacks from their nation. Free blacks, asserted several of the wealthiest slaveholders, exercised "a very pernicious influence not only on our own negroes but on the lower class of our people."[86] Their fears may have reflected racial and class bias, but they were not mere fantasies. "Creeks, Seminoles, Whites, Blacks, all mingle together, distinctions are unknown," one missionary wrote of prayer gatherings in the winter of 1848–1849—"at least in the meetings," he added.[87] William, Judah, and their children may have attended these gatherings.

The oppressive political conditions in the Creek Nation, the denials, lies, and violence that leaders used to control the "pernicious influence" of black and Indian associations, could not entirely overcome the decades of close, intimate relations between the two intermingled peoples. Jennie must have confronted her own self-deceptions when she attended Baptist meetings with her first child, Wash.[88] There she shared religious experiences with black Creeks. Her baptism took place in a local waterway, not long after one visitor encountered a Baptist congregation of "Creeks, half-breeds and Negroes" in the area.[89] But even in the world of transcendence, contemporary political conditions infringed. In the mid-1830s, one Baptist preacher named David Rollin had noted, "Even those who profess religion bring into the church more or less prejudice." He observed the workings of racism in seemingly trivial incidents involving church seating. Indians wished to sit in front, Rollin wrote, but blacks refused to cede ground. The struggle over pews assumed such large dimensions that Indians began avoiding the church altogether. Rollin suggested that Indians and whites congregate at one house of worship, blacks at another.[90] The advice went unheeded, but by 1848, when Jennie was bringing young Wash to church, black and Indian Baptists were beginning to separate. In that year, Baptists replaced a black preacher named Jacobs with a white man, Americus L. Hay, who soon set up a school near James and Jennie's residence.[91] Katy quickly built several nearby cabins to provide a temporary home for her younger children and grandchildren who would attend the school. While Wash and his brother Sam learned to read and write in English at Hay's school, one of Katy's slaves cooked and cleaned house for the students.[92]

The growing separation of Indian and black Baptists preceded a concerted effort on the part of Creek slaveholders to root out Afro-Indian children from the sectarian schools in the nation. In 1851, a number of Creek leaders objected to the enrollment of black Indians at Koweta school, about twenty-five miles northeast of William and Judah's home. Those who were "quarter blood" or more, said the politicians, using the language of scientific racism, should be dismissed, for Creeks would "never agree to have their money appropriated to such a school." "Eighths are admissible," explained one missionary.[93] Yet these kinds of fictitious racial boundaries were difficult to draw. Out of a student body of thirty-five, teachers counted eleven Creeks with African ancestry at Koweta school. The high number, nearly one-third of the entire group, attests to the long history of African and Creek interaction. The "African and Indian are so confounded that it can-not be told when one race ends, or the other begins," wrote M. L. Price, a Presbyterian missionary, though she noted that Indian marriages to blacks within the Creek Nation were "becoming more unpopular as they advance in civilization."[94] Many of the pupils with African ancestry at Koweta came from well-known families. As Price suggested, however, Creeks would deny this heritage with great vehemence in the coming years.[95]

For William and Judah, the growing hostility to black Indian education had a direct impact on their family. Most of their children grew up at a time when there was little formal schooling in the nation, but Judy, born in 1840, and Vicey, born in 1842, reached school age just as politicians were purging Koweta of its black pupils. With a mother widely known to be an emancipated slave, Judy and Vicey had little chance of receiving an education in the Creek Nation. Powerful families might deny or minimize their African heritage, but Judy and Vicey had no choice but to acknowledge it. They perhaps felt the same way as one "unruly" black Indian at Koweta school. Though by the accounting of Creek politicians this student was only one-eighth African, he not only acknowledged his heritage but also turned it from a detriment to an advantage. He did not want an "*Indian* teacher," he asserted. His tutor, frustrated with the boy's cockiness, complained, "Those *mixed people* think themselves superior to the Indians!"[96]

These daily forms of resistance—black Creeks sitting in the front pews, Afro-Indian students refusing to show the expected humility—went only so far in combating the slaveholders' political agenda. The slaveholders' response to the free black communities that took root after the 1845 Seminole agreement revealed to all Afro-Indians the limitations of pride and self-assertion. These settlements, composed of blacks and Indians of African descent, some free, some enslaved, many somewhere in between, were sometimes bought wholesale by aggressive slave traders. In November 1853, Creeks and white traders joined together to purchase an entire community, some fifty miles southwest of where James and Jennie Grayson were living. One night, a company of armed men, led by two Creek preachers, stormed the town, tore the residents out of bed, and locked them in chains. One father, separated from his children, was knifed when he tried to rejoin his family. The captives were marched to North Fork Town, where Wash was attending school, and there they were auctioned off. One black observer reportedly saw the children of one mother divided and sold to several different buyers. As he recounted, "[The family] was all scattered and she would walk from one to another putting her hand on their heads saying in a pitiful tone Oh! Lord, Oh! Lord! untill she fell down in a swoon and in that state she was put in a wagon by a white Baptist minister, and drove off."[97]

In 1859, amid growing antiabolitionist fervor in the Creek Nation, sixteen-year-old Wash Grayson joined his father, James, on an extraordinary journey that both reflected the past divisions in the family and presaged the ones to come. Wash and six other young scholars were selected by the Creek Nation to attend Arkansas College (a "small and weak school," Wash called it) in Fayetteville. The honor presumably rewarded Wash's hard work, but as he recognized, it also came about because of the connections of his mother's family to Moty Kennard, one of the Creeks' principal chiefs.[98] Setting out in late summer for Fayetteville, about seventy-five miles northeast of their home, Wash, his father, James, and his cousin Valentine N. McAnally rode forty miles the first day, stopping overnight, remarkably, at "old William Grayson's."[99] William, now sixty-nine years old, must have been ailing, for within a year Judah and her oldest daughter, Emma, would be living and working as servants in the household of a white stock raiser and slaveholder who resided in the area.[100]

During the visit, Wash perhaps met William and Judah's nine children, Wash's first cousins, once removed. The contrasts would have been striking.

Wash, "white and red headed," scarcely resembled Judah and William's children.[101] These differences in appearance reflected several generations of marriage choices, shaped by social forces of racism that divided light-and dark-skinned people. The contrast would have been made all the more apparent by the presence of Saucer Brady, Emma Grayson's husband. Saucer was African, Indian, and probably part European as well, the son of Steptney and Mary Harrod.[102] Wash knew the surname. It was the same as his maternal grandmother's, whose family probably owned Saucer's parents or grandparents. Also obvious to the guests and hosts at William's house must have been the cultural contrasts not only between families but also between generations. Wash's father, James, always wore a turban fashioned out of a shawl, like many other Creeks and like many blacks, too.[103] To one visitor, these shawl-turbans gave black Creeks a "pseudo-Moorish Character."[104] Wash only wore turbans in jest.

In nineteenth-century America, these cultural and physical differences gave Wash an immense advantage over his darker cousins, one that must have been all too apparent during this particular visit. The advantages of the slaveholding Graysons over William and Judah's family can be quantified. Thirty-four-year-old Henderson Grayson, William and Judah's second son, had married and set up his own household.[105] He owned 4 horses, 25 cattle, 80 hogs, an ox, and a small house, totaling $1,185 in value. Judy and Vicey had recently moved out as well, settling nearby with their Cherokee husbands. Judy's household counted 5 horses, 19 head of cattle, 2 oxen, and 9 hogs, amounting to $830 after the value of her house and furniture was included.[106] Vicey was a little better-off. She had 7 horses, 100 head of cattle, and 150 hogs, and her total possessions were valued at $3,230.[107] Compare these figures with the value of Simpson Grayson's possessions. Twenty-nine-year-old Simpson Grayson, whose father had refused to travel west with William in the winter of 1834–1835, owned 25 horses, 350 head of cattle, 250 hogs, 25 sheep, and 3 oxen. His belongings totaled $8,930, nearly eight times the value of Henderson's.[108] The material objects reflected in these numbers would have left Wash with a powerful impression. Simpson was vastly more wealthy than any of his black relatives. In fact, his black relatives were scarcely better-off materially than some of the slaves owned by his own family.[109]

The poverty that Wash encountered at William and Judah's would have reinforced impressions formed during his childhood and early years in Indian Territory. As revealed by the claims of 1,523 Creeks for property destroyed in the Civil War, Indians identified as "half-breeds" were substantially wealthier than others. They on average claimed $4,434 worth of belongings. "Full-blood" Creeks on average claimed $3,743. Free black Creeks, such as Henderson, Judy, and Vicey, claimed an average of $2,274, and at the very bottom, slaves claimed on average $849 worth of belongings.[110] These numbers cannot be taken as precise measurements of the possessions of all Creek Indians, but they do reflect the very real separations that had grown more marked in Creek society. Wealth, privilege, and advantage were distributed in a hierarchy that placed white Creeks at the top and black Creeks at the bottom.

Wash was off to college, a privilege extended in part because of his mother's political connections, and his education would only widen the economic gap between the two sides of the family. Judy and Vicey, William and Judah's children who were closest in age to him, could only dream of such an advantage. Some Creek girls, including Katy's daughters Caroline and Adeline (supported by their mother's slave), did receive formal educations at the time.[111] But while Wash was learning algebra and parsing Latin sentences in preparation for his higher education, Judy and Vicey were tending to their households.[112] Neither sister ever learned to write.[113]

The differences between the two sides of the family, once negligible, were now enormous. They had grown slowly but steadily. Katy's separation from her black husband and subsequent inheritance of sixteen slaves gave her children the means and realistic ambition to rise above the majority of Creeks. Her son James married a Creek woman of European descent, whose family connections played a part in the selection of Wash to attend college. And Wash received the necessary preparation because the work done by Katy's slaves allowed him to attend school instead of laboring for the family farm.

If Wash and his relations still had enough in common to spend an evening socializing, Wash's departure the next morning made clear how far apart the two sides of the family were moving. After leaving William and Judah's, Wash, his father, and his cousin Valentine headed east into the Cherokee Nation to Park Hill, the home of some of the wealthiest planters in Indian Territory. The Murrell and Ross mansions, Wash later recalled, were "in all respects keeping with the homes of the rich in the states, with walls and paling yard fences all beautifully painted." Wash remembered that they were "by far the most beautiful I had ever seen," and they "lent him some idea of the great and grand things I had always suspected as existent in the outer world, and which I longed to see."[114] The Murrell plantation was owned by a Louisiana sugar planter who had married a daughter of John Ross, the principal chief of the Cherokee Nation. The Murrells lived in a style befitting the great planters of the slave states. They traveled in a coach manned by liveried slaves. Mr. Murrell dressed in "the old Southern style," while his wife, one visitor recalled, wore a voluminous flounced-silk dress, "with the mantle heavily bedecked with spangles which glittered in the sunlight with every movement." Well-appointed with mahogany furniture and four-poster beds, their mansion could not have contrasted more strikingly with William and Judah's cabin. The source of the wealth was also arresting, given Wash's recent visit with Judah: slaves.[115]

Wash, James, and Valentine stayed not at Mr. Murrell's but at the nearby home of John Ross. Wash left his impressions:

> Entering the house we were ushered through corridors into rooms covered with brussels and plush carpets and rugs of such richness and beauty as quite bewildered me. The upholstery of the lounge chairs and other furniture I knew no name for was exquisitely enchanting and not calculated to make me feel much at home.[116]

Wash was at once amazed and overwhelmed by what he saw. William and Judah's children lived in houses with furniture worth no more than fifty or seventy-five dollars. John Ross, by contrast, walked on carpets worth that much. Ross alleviated Wash's unease with "hearty good will and cordiality," and by the end of the visit, the guests felt "quite at home." Wash easily made the journey on horseback from William and Judah's to the Murrell and Ross estates, but to

The George M. Murrell home, Park Hill, Oklahoma. Courtesy of the Research Division of the Oklahoma Historical Society.

turn this two-day trip from subsistence to grandeur into lifelong ambition would demand a concerted effort of deception and self-fashioning. Recalling Ross's Brussels carpets many years later, Wash's precise vocabulary for things once so unfamiliar indicates the success of his endeavor. It would begin in earnest during the impending Civil War. In unexpected ways, the war would force the Graysons to confront their family's troubled history.

Profile

Napoleon Davis, June 2000

If you follow South Seventy-fourth Street as it leaves Muskogee and heads west, you will soon find yourself driving through a sparsely populated country-side of fields and pastures. Then on the left in the distance, your eye will catch the prow of a ship breaking through a sea of grass. As you approach, the prow will rise out of the field and be revealed as the apex of a conical roof, brilliant white in the summer sun. It is the Oklahoma Freedman's Shrine, constructed by Napoleon Davis. When I arrived in June 2000, eighty-eight-year-old Davis, who lived next door to his creation, ambled over to his Cadillac and drove the hundred feet to the door of the shrine to greet me.

Born in Bristow, thirty miles southwest of Tulsa, Davis attended school only rarely, when he had free time between planting, weeding, and harvesting crops on the family farm. Later in life, he received an eighth-grade GED, but Davis remained conscious of his lack of formal education. During my visit, he confessed that he was embarrassed about the way he spoke (although I did not notice anything unusual about his diction), and he requested that his English be "cleaned up like they did to Joe Louis." Davis pursued many lines of work before he became the founder of a shrine. As a young man, he served in the U.S. Navy and, upon discharge, settled in San Diego, where he found a job in con-struction. At different times, he owned a barbecue restaurant, a grocery store, a dry-cleaning operation, and a feed and seed store. But for most of his life, he was a brick and stone layer, skills he learned in the 1930s on a Works Progress Administration project. After retirement, he returned to his birthplace to found the Oklahoma Creek Freedman Association and shrine.

Davis's family has a long history with the Graysons. His great-grandfather was Aaron Grayson, very possibly the same Aaron Grayson whom Thomas in-herited from his father, Robert Grierson, in 1823. Sometime before the outbreak of the Civil War, Aaron earned his freedom. He was a prosperous carpenter by the 1860s, but by the 1870s, he was described as "blind and destitute." He died soon afterward.[1] His son Hardy, born in 1841, was Davis's grandfather.[2] Hardy married Peggie, an ex-slave, who gave birth to Lucy, Davis's mother. Hardy wrote a remarkable letter to the principal chief of the Creek Nation in 1882, asking for remuneration for property damaged or destroyed by Creek soldiers. He asserted his right to government assistance on two accounts. First, he wrote, "I am a citizen of this nation and . . . I am entitle [sic] to its protection of my Person and property"; second, "I have always ben Loyal to its Laws and Constitution."[3]

At the entrance to the shrine built by Hardy's grandson Napoleon, a pink granite wall announces the building's purpose. "My Roots Oklahoma Creek Freedman Association & Shrine," and "African American Cultural Heritage Center, Napoleon Davis, Founder," the wall reads. One section is inlaid with four white stone stars, each carrying the name of Davis or one of his siblings. At either end of the wall sit the tombstones of Davis's maternal grandparents, Hardy and Peggie Grayson.

Napoleon Davis, June 2000. Photograph by the author.

The shrine is a single cavernous space—an "African American tepee," Davis called it—flanked by two short wings. A bowling ball and a pair of rusty skis lay just outside the entrance. Inside, the hot, stuffy room was filled with odds and ends. One table carried two cans of Raid wasp and hornet spray. (The dead wasps on the floor attested to their usefulness.) Another was covered with books on African American history. Two large magazine displays held back issues of *Ebony*. The upper walls of the shrine were lined with pictures of Davis's ancestors and of prominent African American leaders, including Malcolm X, Martin Luther King Jr., and Jesse Jackson. On the lower walls, lacquered plaques listed every ex-slave in the Creek Nation alive in the 1890s.

Davis began constructing this shrine in 1976 after seeing Alex Haley's *Roots*, but its seeds are much older. In America, Davis said of himself, he is "a non-person, like a sack of wheat or rice." He first reached this ugly conclusion at the early age of eleven or twelve, when a white boy challenged him to a debate in front of the local store. Davis argued that no race was better than any other, that whites should not have enslaved blacks. He thought he made a good case, but the white boy did not bother to engage with Davis's argument. Instead, he dismissed Davis altogether. "You are nobody," the boy said, "a negro, and no one cares what you think." Davis was speechless. At home, his grandfather sat him down and said that it was true; he was nobody.

"Still yet to this day I am trying to prove that I am somebody," Davis said. His efforts took several directions. One, manifested in the very construction of the shrine, involved the recovery of the history of Creeks of African descent. The stories he heard from his grandmother (born in 1848) never jibed with what he read in books and newspapers. She praised Indians for the treatment she received and asserted that she never felt like a slave. Another direction involved his persistent campaign to have the federal government declare that blacks are "African Americans." "Black" is negative, Davis told me, used "to make us always feel inferior to our master." A corner table was stacked high with his correspondence on the subject, including letters to Presidents Bush and Clinton. The first President Bush never responded to Davis's request, and President Clinton's response was formulaic and generic: "Thank you for your letter. Our nation faces many complex challenges, but these challenges are less daunting with the help of the many Americans who are concerned about the welfare of our nation and are trying to do something about it." Undeterred, Davis sent another letter, asking if the matter was on Clinton's agenda for consideration in the near future.

Regarding Graysons who say they are white, Davis paraphrased Desmond Tutu: "Anytime you see a man standing above, he's standing on someone's shoulders." Creeks are helped by the U.S. government now, he explained, but they are doing the same thing to African Americans that the United States did to Indians. "Until we establish ourselves as human beings, they don't want to be associated with us." He concluded the interview with a simple assertion: "I like the word 'dignity,' and I like to practice it." Davis died in late 2000, shortly after I visited him. The shrine is now falling into disrepair.

5 ▪▪

"It is negroes that we are killing now": The Graysons' Civil War

Wash Grayson arrived in Arkansas shortly before John Brown led his October 1859 raid on the federal arsenal in Harpers Ferry, Virginia. Brown stormed the arsenal, intending to distribute its arms to local slaves. The attack, Brown hoped, would spark a conflagration that would sweep across the South, destroying slavery root and branch, but the event unfolded somewhat less dramatically, certainly not as the messianic Brown had intended. Nearby slaves recognized the folly of the plan and ignored his call to arms. Brown was easily captured, tried for murder and treason, and hanged. Though Brown failed to burn down the South's great plantations, he did galvanize the emotions of northerners and southerners. White planters condemned Brown and listened with horror to northern luminaries such as Emerson and Thoreau, who sang his praises. By contrast, Wash's homeland was noticeably less inflamed. The "agitation" of the slavery question among the Indians, wrote Wiley Britton, a white Union soldier, was "so feeble that it never excited the interest that it had among the people of the States of the Union."[1] No doubt, Wash found a much more volatile political climate in Fayetteville, Arkansas, but Indian Territory was not entirely insulated from the firestorms raging on its borders.

Britton noted that the "considerable majority" of Indians were "indifferent" to the fate of slavery.[2] Yet a significant minority (the 13 percent who were enslaved and the 10 percent who owned them—nearly one-quarter of the entire population) were deeply interested in the future of the institution. Moreover, because slave owners controlled the Creek government, the business of the nation was the business of slavery. An 1865 compilation of 148 Creek laws shows that 44 of the statutes dealt specifically with slavery or blacks. Two of these laws were passed by the government in May 1859, a few months before Wash visited his uncle William. They had serious implications for William's family. The first revoked the citizenship of people "of negro origin." The second stated ambiguously that "the children of Creek woman [sic] by negro men when they are not of more than half negro shall be considered bonafied members of the Creek Nation." Were the children or their fathers to be not more than half Negro?

These laws in some ways were the Creek Nation's own Dred Scott case. That famous and shocking decision, handed down by the U.S. Supreme Court in March 1857, denied that African Americans were or could ever become citizens of the United States. The Scott case, originating in nearby Missouri, challenged the fundamental American tenet of universal citizenship. Likewise, the 1859 Creek laws violated deeply held notions of community and membership that lay at the foundation of Muscogee society. By revoking the citizenship of Creeks "of negro origin," the first law denied clans the right to adopt black members. In the past, indeed, for as long as anyone could remember, clans had been the ultimate arbiters of community membership. Each clan had the authority to adopt any person it wanted. Once adopted, that person was considered fully Creek by all members of the community. But now, according to the first of the 1859 laws, the power of clans was circumscribed in the name of racial stratification. People "of negro origin" were no longer citizens.

The second law was equally revolutionary. Muscogee society was traditionally matrilineal, meaning that Creeks traced descent through their mother. Consequently, children of Creek women belonged to Creek clans, no matter the origins of the father. This custom explains the large number of Creeks of European ancestry in the nineteenth century; these white Creeks were the offspring of Creek women and European fathers. The second 1859 law violated this tradition by making kinship partially determined by race. Blacks could now become Creeks only when they were the children of Muscogee women *and* not more than half or a quarter African (depending on how the statute's ambiguous wording is understood). After 1859, William and Judah's children were legally foreigners in the land of their birth.

It is unlikely that the 1859 laws had a direct effect on William and Judah's family. The absence of a state bureaucracy and the indifference of most Creeks toward slavery made these laws unenforceable. One politician recalled that the laws were not printed or even written down until after the Civil War.[3] Nevertheless, the Creeks' 1859 decision reflects the convictions and fears of the wealthiest, most powerful, and best-educated men in the nation. Similar convictions and fears were tearing at the social fabric of the United States. Abraham Lincoln's 1860 campaign for the presidency and the prospect of slavery's demise led white supremacists to play on the white public's paranoid fantasies about the fall of the color line.[4] One cynical political operative in New York even coined a new word, "miscegenation," to fuel the public's growing alarm about interracial sex.[5] A Latin construction literally meaning the mixing of the races, "miscegenation" was a product of the scientific racism of the mid-nineteenth century and of the charged atmosphere of the 1864 presidential campaign. Creeks were blown by the same winds. In August 1860, there reportedly was "considerable excitement" among Muscogees about "a great number" of fugitive slaves who had taken refuge in the nation.[6] Creeks threatened to tar and feather one missionary accused of abolitionist sentiments.[7] At the same time, Creek leaders unleashed their own attack against "miscegenation." In fall 1860, a member of the Perryman family who was widely known to be part African became engaged to a Miss Garrison, a white woman who worked at one of the Presbyterian schools in the nation. Whites and white Creeks in the area were enflamed by the prospect of the marriage, and a Presbyterian missionary quickly shuttled Miss Garrison out of the country. Garrison returned, however, and the marriage proceeded as planned. By November, the excitement of white Creeks had ebbed, perhaps because many feared that their own ancestry would come under similar scrutiny.[8]

Yet racial tensions did not fully subside. On December 20, South Carolina seceded from the Union, and six other southern states followed before Lincoln's inauguration on March 4. Texas, on the southern border of Indian Territory, was the final of these seven to secede, joining the Confederacy on February 1, 1861. A few weeks later, Creek leaders met in council. There is no record of their debates, but their sentiments are clearly evident in a series of twenty-two draconian laws passed during the meeting. The majority of the laws clamped down on the freedom of movement of slaves. Without a pass, slaves were prohibited from traveling at night or more than two miles from their plantation during the day, and they were forbidden from trading goods. More generally, "negros," meaning both free and enslaved people, were prohibited from preaching to Indian congregations and from worshiping outside the presence of a free person "not of negro origins." Legislators encouraged enforcement by threatening to fine uncooperative planters and to flog disobedient slaves.[9]

If Judah and her children could dismiss this section of the legislation as yet another ineffective attempt on the part of Creek planters to impose racial hierarchy on the nation, they could not so easily ignore the remaining laws. One stated that all "Free negroes" had to choose an owner by March 10, or else be sold by the Creek Nation to the highest bidder. Accompanying laws attempted to mitigate the excessiveness of this act and perhaps to encourage compliance. Free blacks put into slavery could be held in bondage for only twelve months, and they could not be sold during this period.[10] These laws "didn't make them a slave," one Creek politician later recalled, "but simply made them responsible to some person." If "the question of slavery came up," he said, "they wanted to have track of every negro."[11] But the injustice of the law could not be so easily dismissed. Laws directed at slaves now applied to every single person of African descent in the nation. Judah and her children (who, according to the 1859 citizenship laws, were not Creeks) had to choose owners. Judah and her oldest daughter, Emma, listed respectively as black and mulatto on the 1860 U.S. census, were at the time working and living in the household of Leroy Job. But as a white man, Job was excluded by the Creek statute from being a master of newly enslaved blacks.[12] Judah and Emma, along with Judah's other children, probably ignored the law or arranged informally to become the slaves of a Creek neighbor. (Ironically, the children's cousin Wash would have met the law's requirements as their owner.) But if they drew the ire of local officials, they might have suffered the consequences at the hands of the Creek light horse companies, charged with enforcement. After describing this extraordinary legislation, one white resident in the Creek Nation resorted to sarcasm: "So you see we are getting along in the world."[13]

While his cousins struggled to understand the implications of the 1860 laws, Wash Grayson set out for his second year of studies at Arkansas College. "I had now become well acquainted with the people and their ways and manners," he wrote, "and being freely accorded entree to some of the best families where I enjoyed the amenities and hospitality of the refined, I was in this way very much benefited."[14] In early 1861, however, talk of war closed the campus, and Wash returned home. His adjustment to his "humble cabin home in the quiet forests" was difficult, for he had become accustomed to the excitement of a commercial town. "The thought of remaining here in these quiet solitudes was distressing indeed," wrote Wash, and he soon decided to move to North Fork Town, a few miles from his family's residence. There he took a job as a salesman at a general merchandise store run by a white man, S. S. Sanger.[15]

South Carolina troops shelled Fort Sumter in the Charleston harbor on April 13, marking the onset of the Civil War. On May 25, five days after North Carolina seceded to become the last of the eleven Confederate states, the Chickasaws announced their alliance with the South. They sided with the Confederacy in part because the United States had spent the previous seventy-five years violating their sovereign rights. But they also did so because their leading families identified with the southern cause: "our geographical position, our social and domestic institutions, our feelings and sympathies, all attach us to our Southern friends," declared the Chickasaw legislature. Like other slaveholders, Chickasaw leaders feared that the war might surpass "San Domingo in atrocious horrors," referring to the violent Haitian Revolution in which slaves had won their freedom on the French sugar island in the late eighteenth century.[16] Chickasaw planters, with 18 percent of their population enslaved, had good reason to dread an uprising.[17] The Choctaw Nation followed suit and declared its independence on June 14.[18] The Cherokees, Creeks, and Seminoles were more circumspect in their actions.[19] When one Confederate officer tried to curry favor with the Cherokees by condemning U.S. Indian policy, John Ross, their principal chief, retorted that both the North and the South favored "the acquisition of Indians lands, and that but few Indians now press their feet upon the banks of either the Ohio or the Tennessee."[20] Yet elsewhere, Ross, anxious to balance pro-North and pro-South factions and unify Cherokees in a neutral position, condemned "abolitionism, free-soilers, and northern mountebanks" and assured that "the Cherokee people will never tolerate the propagation of any such obnoxious fruit upon their soil."[21]

The Cherokees were still neutral when Creek leaders gathered near North Fork Town to meet with Confederate Indian agent Albert Pike in early July 1861. The timing of the meeting was unusual, for several prominent Creeks, including Opothleyahola, leader of the upper towns, were out west meeting with "Prairie Indians."[22] Moty Kennard, Wash's relative through his mother's line, pushed forward with the meeting, however. Watt Grayson ordered his slaves to drive in cattle to feed the attendees, and S. S. Sanger, Wash's employer, supplied groceries. The Creek negotiators, Wash's wife, Annie, would later recall, "owned many negro slaves and were otherwise wealthy."[23] The meeting concluded with a treaty of alliance between the Creek Nation and the Confederacy, and the Cherokees joined them soon after.[24] When Opothleyahola and others returned from their embassy, they were horrified by Kennard's actions, and though they tried to remove him from office, the southern faction proved too powerful. At least three of the treaty's signatures (no more than x's with a name printed adjacent) were forged; they belonged to Opothleyahola and two other chiefs who were not present at the meeting and who refused to sign after they returned. "That was the way with many Indians," one Creek noted dryly; "their names were put to treaties when they were not there."[25]

The treaty confirmed that Creek slavery was legal and asserted that it had existed since "time immemorial."[26] One of the treaty articles between the Creeks and the Confederacy foreshadowed what the future would hold for William and Judah's children should the South emerge victorious. Creeks could testify in southern courts, the article read, "unless rendered incompetent from some other cause than their Indian blood and descent."[27] By southern state laws, blacks (defined differently in different states) could not testify in court. More important than the particulars of this legal practice, however, was its general obsession with race and blood. During the war, Judah and her children would witness firsthand the deadly consequences of this southern obsession.

The decision of Kennard and others to ally with the Confederacy came easily. As a matter of strategy, it made sense to join the South. The United States had withdrawn its troops from the region, and the neighboring southern states had declared their allegiance to the Confederacy. A Union alliance consequently would have exposed the Creeks to Confederate attack from both Arkansas and Texas, as well as from the Choctaw and Chickasaw nations.[28] Moreover, nearly all Creek national investments (deposits from land cessions over the years) were invested in southern state bonds.[29] The nation thus had a direct financial interest in the fate of the Confederacy. The Creeks' declaration of independence from the United States also gave the nation the opportunity to reappropriate some of the prerogatives of sovereignty that it had lost over the years to the federal government. One additional consideration led to the Creek alliance with the Confederacy: most Creek politicians believed deeply in the cause of slavery.[30]

In 1937, Jim Tomm, a former slave, summarized the situation in Indian Territory at the time of the Civil War: "The Indians really didn't want to fight on either side but their sentiment was with the south because they came from the south to this country and some of them owned slaves."[31] Though Creeks never shed their identity as Indians, they were southerners, as Tomm suggested, and over the previous century they had come to share many of the South's obsessions with slavery and race. G. W. Stidham, who owned Jim Tomm's parents, was a case in point. Stidham purchased Tomm's parents in New Orleans and brought them to his plantation in the Creek Nation. (One ex-freedman, J. W. Stephens, recalled that Creek planters spent "many thousands of dollars" buying slaves at the New Orleans slave market.)[32] During the war, Stidham would transport his slaves across the border into Texas, where he bought six thousand acres near present-day Texarkana.[33] Stidham asserted his commitment to slavery and to the South by signing the Creek treaty with the Confederacy and by becoming an officer in the Confederate Indian brigade.[34] William A. Sapulpa, a wealthy Creek slaveholder, expressed a similar devotion to the South by investing one thousand dollars in gold in the Confederate states. He rose to the rank of lieutenant in the Confederate army.[35] Abraham Foster did the same, purchasing $1,300 in Confederate state bonds. He disinherited his daughter Sally when she refused to support the Confederacy.[36] Foster's dedication to the southern cause is not surprising; he had lived in Alabama until 1846, when he relocated with his thirty-nine slaves to Indian Territory.[37]

In the Choctaw Nation, where Katy, Watt, and other Grayson slaveholders lived, some residents showed a similar devotion to the Confederacy. The Choctaw General Council declared that the "natural affections, education, institutions, and interests of our people . . . indissolubly bind us in every way to the destiny of our neighbors and brethren of the Southern states."[38] According to one Confederate officer, the Choctaw principal chief, Samuel Garland (elected in 1862), was "a man of wealth and influence," "a slave-holder," and "a true Southerner."[39] In the Cherokee Nation, some people expressed similar feelings. One Cherokee soldier and member of the National Council declared that he was "a Southerner" who abhorred "the negro-fraternizing spirit of abolitionism of the North."[40] The bonds of southern identity were strong enough that when some Indians became disaffected with William Steele, a brigadier general in the Confederate army, they charged that he was "Northern-born, and had no true feeling of sympathy with the South."[41] The Chickasaw legislature thought much more highly of Steele's replacement, Douglas Cooper. Cooper, the legislature declared, was "a true patriot, no mercenary, no Northern man with Southern principles, but a true son of the South, with true patriotism imbedded in his heart."[42]

After the Creek Nation signed its treaty with the Confederacy, the Graysons—Katy and her children and grandchildren, and Judah and her family—followed the examples of many other Creeks. They remained at home and hoped that the conflict would pass them by. But for Judah and her children, the war came quickly. Southern Muscogees soon organized a regiment of soldiers commanded by Daniel N. McIntosh, and thereafter no black Creek could afford to ignore the fighting.[43] (Later, a second regiment was formed, commanded by Daniel's half brother Chilly McIntosh.) With no threat of northern aggression, the troops turned to the local population, terrorizing those who refused to support the cause. They especially singled out black Creeks. Joe Fife lived three miles from North Fork Town, and in October 1861 McIntosh's regiment, "robbing and murdering the loyal negroes of the Nation," forced him to flee for his life.[44] Numerous other black Creeks told similar stories. Gilbert Lewis, who lived only ten miles north of Judah Grayson's family, fled at the same time. Confederate Creeks "would not allow the negroes to remain at home in possession of their property," he said, "and they were being killed because they were not in sympathy with the Southern rebellion."[45] Fife and Lewis were slaves at the time, but free blacks such as Thomas Bruner came under attack as well. Confederate Creeks imprisoned Bruner and would have sent him south into slavery had he not escaped.[46] With William's recent death in 1860, Judah, Billy, Emma, Henderson, Judy, Vicey, and the other children must have felt especially vulnerable to the raids and kidnappings aimed at black Creeks. Yet they, along with hundreds of other black Muscogees, remained in the nation, unwilling to abandon their homes and possessions.

Their temporary security was shattered by the fate of Creek refugees who headed north late in 1861. Joe Fife, Gilbert Lewis, and other black Muscogees joined hundreds of Creeks in a mass exodus for the Kansas border. The refugees were led by Opothleyahola, a Creek leader and slaveholder.[47] Opothleyahola's mass exodus raised alarm among southern Creeks. On the last day of October 1861, they decided to put an end to the "hostile movements" of their fellow Muscogees. Moty Kennard, Wash's relative who helped him gain admittance to Arkansas College, outlined their plans. They intended to attack the refugees. All captured slaves would be sold on the open market, except those belonging to members of the Confederate expedition, who would be returned to their owners. More shocking was the fate of *free* black Creeks. Kennard explained that he and his comrades would enslave them and put them up for sale alongside known slaves.[48] Opothleyahola, by contrast, promised to free the slaves who had joined his party.[49] Suddenly, slavery and abolition among the Muscogees moved to the forefront of their war.

In mid-November, Creek and Confederate troops under Douglas Cooper set out for Opothleyahola's band. The poorly armed refugees, now composed of 1,000 Creeks and Seminoles and up to 300 fugitive slaves, hoped to reach the safety of Kansas without a major engagement. In December, as the weather grew colder and sleet began to fall, the two sides skirmished several times. Then, on December 26, Cooper's men scored a decisive victory at Chustenahlah, some forty miles from the Kansas border. They reported killing 250 people and capturing 160. These numbers are assuredly too high, but scores died, and numerous others succumbed to exposure and starvation.[50] The survivors broke up into small parties and continued north, "in blood and snow," one Creek later reported. Clothed only in rags, some refugees froze to death in the bitter weather.[51] By the end of January, more than 3,000 Creeks and 1,000 other Indians had straggled into refugee camps on the Verdigris River in southern Kansas. Some were sheltered only by makeshift tents of switches and rags, others had no clothing at all, and almost none had shoes or moccasins. Many lost their toes or feet to frostbite.[52] Over the next two months, more than one hundred amputations would be performed, and 240 Creeks would die. "I saw a little Creek boy, about eight years old, with both feet taken off near the ankle," wrote one witness, "others lying upon the ground whose frosted limbs rendered them unable to move about."[53]

Judah and her children had been wise to remain at home, yet the viciousness of the encounter between Opothleyahola's refugees and Confederate Creeks gave notice that Muscogees could no longer merely dismiss the conflict as a white man's war. The hatred that led Creeks to chase their neighbors into Kansas had deep roots in the Redstick War, the land swindles of the 1830s, and Indian removal, events themselves nurtured by Creek politics, family feuds, and old factional disputes. In fact, the McIntoshes had despised Opothleyahola ever since the murder of William McIntosh in 1825.[54] Nevertheless, though no one maintained that Creeks fought in the Civil War for precisely the same reasons as their American counterparts, they could not deny that race played a significant role in the conflict in Indian Territory. How could it not have, given how greatly it had shaped the previous one hundred years of Creek history? By 1861, no corner of Creek society remained unaffected by race and slavery.

For the moment, Katy and her brother Watt remained safe in the Choctaw Nation. Jennie and her children, including Wash, also were unscathed by the conflict. The "enemy," reported Wash, "was no where threatening the peace or safety of our territory."[55] Of course, dark-skinned Creeks reported a different story. Even after the mass exodus led by Opothleyahola, Confederate Creeks continued to attack black Muscogees. In April 1862, two or three miles from Judah's residence, Daniel McIntosh's troops drove Joseph Cooney, a prosperous free black Creek, out of his home in the middle of the night.[56] A few weeks later, they fell on the Graysons. McIntosh ran Emma Grayson (Judah's oldest daughter) and her husband, Saucer Brady (or Bradley), out of their home. They fled to the Kansas border, where Saucer enlisted in the First Kansas Colored Infantry Volunteers, a regiment formed in late 1862 out of fugitive slaves and volunteer blacks.[57]

Saucer Brady was variously described in later years as a "freedman" and a "Chickasaw" Indian.[58] John Myer, Saucer's acquaintance, was once asked for clarification. Was Saucer an Indian or a freedman? Myer responded, "No sir, colored."[59] Saucer's decision to join the First Kansas Colored Infantry Volunteers reflects the ambiguous identity of black Indians. Most Creeks, black Creeks, and Creek slaves joined the First Indian Home Guards, initially mustered in May 1862 in Le Roy, Kansas, about one hundred miles southwest of present-day Kansas City. Slaves of white men, by contrast, joined the First (and later the Second) Kansas Colored Infantry.[60] Perhaps Saucer's dark skin color relegated him to the Colored Infantry, or perhaps chance—a ready opportunity with the Colored Infantry, the temporary absence of the First Indian Home Guards—placed him there. In either case, he had a companion in Franklin Grayson, who also joined Company I, and in Sack Grayson of Company C. Both Franklin and Sack were probably slaves of the Grayson family.[61]

As the intense heat of summer settled on the southern plains, the Union launched a grandly named "Indian Expedition," with the intention of retaking

Indian Territory and resettling the refugees camped along the Kansas border.[62] Among the participants were the First Indian Home Guards. The First Indian Home Guards and other Union troops (many of them Indians and black Indians who had fled with Opothleyahola) pushed south as far as Park Hill, where Cherokee leader John Ross lived. "I have great difficulty in restraining the Indians with me from exterminating the rebels," confessed one officer.[63] Confederate forces fought back under Stand Watie, a southern Cherokee commanding an Indian regiment. But Watie's soldiers were outnumbered, for the bulk of Confederate troops in Indian Territory, then under the dubious command of Arkansas politician and poet Albert Pike, remained stationary south of the Canadian River. In mid-July, Pike, paralyzed by irresolution, resigned. "I am altogether too corpulent to ride much on horseback," he admitted, "and, besides, am subject to neuralgia in the back."[64] Two months later, Douglas Cooper, a junior officer, would place him under arrest on the grounds that Pike was "partially deranged."[65]

As the Indian Expedition marched south, numerous Creeks revealed their Union sympathies, and large numbers of slaves fled from their owners, heading for "the promised land," as some called Kansas.[66] Confederate troops responded with renewed attacks on the Creek population. About ten miles north of Judah's family, planter Benjamin Marshall tried to force his slave Lewis to work as a teamster for Daniel McIntosh's Confederate troops, but Lewis fled toward Union soldiers. He was severely injured by Confederates during his escape, but he reached Kansas, where he found work as a teamster for the quartermaster at Fort Scott.[67] Confederates were "engaged in Killing the loyal freedmen of the Nation and destroying their property," reported Harry Island, who "was compelled to leave his home in haste."[68] Southern Indians also attacked Robert Grayson, "a free man of color," at his house at the mouth of the Little River, roughly forty-five miles southwest of Katy's plantation. Robert's parents were, as one son said, "a half breed, half indian and half colored," named Chinne Chotke (Little Jimmy), and a "black woman" named Venus.[69] Robert was well-known to Judah, Katy, and Wash, for he and his parents had once belonged to patriarch Robert Grierson and had been deeded to Katy in 1817.[70] (Venus and her family were later transferred to Sandy Grayson.)[71]

Unfortunately for black Indians and pro-northern Creeks, Union leadership proved as uninspired as its Confederate counterpart. In the midst of the Indian Expedition's thrust south, subordinate officers arrested their commander, William Weer—a "mutiny," one Indian agent called it—and ordered a retreat of all white troops, leaving behind only three Indian regiments to defend the vast territory.[72] For a time, Indian soldiers held on to the land north of the Arkansas

River, but by early August they were in retreat.[73] Large numbers of slaves and refugee Indians trailed after the retreating army.[74] Bands of "mixed Indians and whites" followed at their heels, terrorizing Union Creeks and slaves.[75]

Amid the devastation, slave owners lamented the flight of their servants. Their contempt for black people was fortified by the sudden recognition that now they would have to fetch their own water, cut their own firewood, and prepare their own meals. Hannah Hicks, a missionary living at Park Hill in the Cherokee Nation, complained that her black servants had left her "without any help," at least until God's intervention. When "Aunt" Edie's horse ran off, forcing Edie to return to Hicks, Hicks considered it "specially ordered by a kind of Providence."[76] The contempt for blacks and Afro-Indians reached into the Indian leadership as well. Cherokee Stephen Foreman wrote, "It was hard to see my negroes taken off, and harder still to see my own negroes take off my horses." He wished for a southern force to "rout all the would-be free negroes."[77] Creek planter Mose Perryman tried to cow his slaves into submission. After his bond-men slipped off, Perryman descended on the slave cabins in a rage, waving his shotgun and yelling for the women to assemble immediately. "We're going to take all you black devils to a place where there won't no more of you run away!" one ex-slave recalled him shouting. Soon after, Perryman drove his slaves south into the Chickasaw Nation, where they worked for the duration of the war.[78]

By the end of 1862, neither Creek country nor the sprawling refugee camps in Arkansas and Kansas offered escape from wartime suffering. In Arkansas, displaced Indian and black families huddled in makeshift tents, while four or five inches of snow lay on the ground.[79] Thousands more braved the winter near Leavenworth, Kansas.[80] One attending physician listed the predominant diseases in the crowded camps: "pneumonia, intermitting, and remitting and typhoid fevers, scorbutis, ophthalmia, syphilis and gonorrhœa." He added that "Paratitus and mosbili" were also becoming common.[81] Creeks who remained at home, including Judah's and Katy's families, may have avoided the diseased refugee camps, but they too struggled through the cold weather. A drought during the summer of 1862 had scorched the corn crop, and what survived was destroyed by Confederate troops as a matter of military policy. Consequently, few Indians had surpluses to help them through the winter.[82] By November 1862, some Indians were destitute and in danger of starving or freezing to death over the winter months.[83] In the Cherokee Nation, residents sometimes went several days without eating grain or bread.[84] When army supply trains laden with flour and meal arrived, emaciated Indians swarmed over the wagons to obtain scarce supplies.[85] At the end of the year, a final thrust by Union Indian troops into the territory between the Arkansas and Canadian rivers, where Judah's family lived, sent Confederate Creeks fleeing South, seeking to escape starvation as much as the invading troops.[86]

It was in this context that Wash Grayson decided to join the Confederate army.[87] Pro-southern Creeks had been formed into two regiments numbering about sixteen hundred, according to the inflated estimate of their commander, Albert Pike. The new troops, who were mounted on ponies and armed only with common rifles or ordinary shotguns, received only sporadic pay for their service.[88] It "seems to me that no effort is spared to alienate them [Indian troops] and lose the whole country," wrote Pike in June 1862.[89] Yet they continued to fight, less out of any devotion to Jefferson Davis and his Richmond-based government than out of a commitment to their town leaders. The "organization by regiments is all nonsense," said Pike, recognizing the importance to Creeks of kinship and loyalty. "They ought to go by towns, in bands of different numbers, under their chiefs and captains."[90] These chiefs and captains, people such as G. W. Stidham (Wash's future father-in-law), were large slaveholders. Tustanarkchopko, a Union Creek, gave a partisan appraisal of their motives: "Some of our money loving leaders have joined the rebels merely for speculation."[91] Such unfavorable assessments of Confederates meant that Union Creeks would give them no quarter. Stidham himself warned that if pro-northern Creeks retook the countryside, they would "kill him and the other half-breeds." "They found out he talked of moving his negroes to Texas," Pike reported, "and they notified him that if he did they would follow him and kill him."[92]

Daniel N. McIntosh and Chilly McIntosh, who commanded the two Confederate Creek regiments, represented the worst of this slaveholding class. Daniel had led the antiabolitionist movement in the Creek Nation in the years leading up to the Civil War. "It was his work that reduced the free blacks to slavery, broke up our missions, led the Creeks to revolt and finally introduced civil war," wrote missionary William S. Robertson. Robertson's hatred for the man burst forth when he received unconfirmed (and mistaken) news of his death: "If the report is true, he has found his reward for the troubles and misery he has brought upon his people."[93] Chilly McIntosh had an equally checkered past. He did little to endear himself to other Muscogees when he took refuge "amongst his white friends" after the murder of his father, William, in 1825.[94] Nor did he serve himself well during the land scandals in the 1830s, when, in the words of one government investigator, he was "either the dupe or the tool of a set of heartless speculators."[95] After removal, he lent his tarnished name to numerous efforts to enslave free blacks living in the Seminole Nation.[96] It was Chilly's regiment that Wash decided to join in 1862.

Wash's decision was perhaps surprising only for its delay. Wash's peers from

Arkansas College had already joined; in fact, two of them, Billy McIntosh and Saladen Watie, were children, respectively, of the highest-ranking Creek and Cherokee officers in the Confederate army. Saladen's father, Stand Watie, would eventually become a brigadier general and the most trusted Confederate officer in Indian Territory.[97] Unlike Billy and Saladen, however, Wash did not come from a wealthy family, and, with the recent death of his father, Wash initially felt obligated to support his family rather than rush off to fight the war. But by the end of 1862, conditions were changing. The Union's Indian Expedition was driving Confederate Creeks south and making the need for manpower more pressing.[98] Moreover, malicious gossip began to spread that Wash was shirking his duties.[99] His induction into the Confederate army, seemingly routine, would put him on a collision course with his black relatives.

Wash's Confederate troops and the Union opposition skirted each other in late 1862 and early 1863, but slowly they converged on the center of the Creek Nation, exactly where William and Judah had settled their family in early 1835. Confederate Creeks spent the end of the year around Fort Gibson, "robbing and murdering all the loyal men they could find," in the words of one black Indian.[100] The First Indian Home Guards passed the coldest months, January and February, in camp at Bentonville, Arkansas, where they weathered the sleet and snow.[101] Then, in early April, they moved west and captured Fort Gibson, just north of Judah's home. Stand Watie, a Cherokee officer who signed his letters as the "Principal Chief of the Cherokees," could not resist making a disparaging remark about the "hostile Indians" and "negroes." "This mongrel force," he wrote with contempt, "has laid waste our country."[102] A few months later, Watie returned to this theme in a letter to Moty Kennard, the leader of the Confederate Creeks. The Five Tribes must be "resolved never to be enslaved by an inferior race," he wrote. "Shall we suffer ourselves to be subjugated and enslaved by such a class? Never!"[103] Yet this "mongrel force" of blacks, Indians, and guerrilla troops from Kansas known as Jayhawkers now controlled the area north of the Arkansas River. Confederates occupied the area south, and both sides seemed intent on joining battle at Chimney Mountain, where Watie's drunken scouts and several Union spies were reconnoitering the terrain. Judah's family lived near the foot of the mountain, and local residents were reportedly "uncertain and fearfull" of what lay ahead.[104] It seemed as if decades of racial strife, witnessed both in individual families such as the Graysons and in the Creek Nation itself, would come to a head at Judah's doorstep.

Union officers slowly gathered their forces. In late May, the First Kansas Colored Infantry joined the First Indian Home Guards at Fort Gibson.[105] The number of troops totaled over three thousand.[106] It is impossible to know which soldiers were present and on active duty, but it is certain that members of the Grayson family, including Emma's husband, Saucer Brady, were serving in both the First Indian Home Guards and the First Kansas Colored Infantry.[107]

Some twenty miles south of Fort Gibson at Elk Creek, a river that passed through Henderson's, Judy's, and Emma's neighborhood, Confederate troops were amassing. By one account, six thousand men were stationed along the waterway.[108] Among them was Wash Grayson, who by mid-July had been camped in the area for several weeks.[109] The terrain was of course familiar to Wash, for he had visited William and Judah's children only four years earlier, on the road to college in Arkansas. Oddly, in his autobiography, Wash gave no hint of either ambivalence or resolve to destroy his family members. In fact, he failed to comment at all on the presence of his black relatives. It was as if they had ceased to exist between his first visit in 1859 and his return in 1863.[110]

The battle took place on July 17, just two weeks after the momentous defeat of Lee's Confederate army at Gettysburg in southern Pennsylvania. Before sunrise, a messenger rode through the area, giving word that battle was imminent. Planters rushed to secure their slaves by relocating south of the Canadian River, which was firmly under Confederate rule. Lucinda Davis recalled how her owner, "old Tuskaya-hiniha," directed her to load wagons with meat, corn, pots, and kettles. The male slaves had already run off, including Lucinda's brother Abe, who joined the Union army.[111] Nonslaveholding families, by contrast, took action only to escape the immediate danger of the battle. Judah's family climbed to the top of Chimney Mountain, where they could watch the soldiers from afar.[112]

The sky soon grew dark, and a light rain turned into a torrential downpour. Confederate troops pushed their heavy guns through the mud, readying themselves for the onslaught.[113] At 10:00 A.M., the Union soldiers formed two columns and advanced on foot toward the mile-and-a-half Confederate line. The wet weather prevented many of the cannons from firing, but the fighting was nevertheless "unremitting and terrific," according to one Union officer.[114] Lucinda Davis recalled taking refuge in a cave, where she spent the morning listening to the reverberations of the gunshots.[115] Wash was stationed in the rear lines at the bottom of Elk Creek, under a cover of dense foliage. "Here we remained listening breathlessly at the rattle of small arms," he later recalled. He was "anxious to take a hand in the affray, but could do nothing without orders."[116]

Then came word to retreat. Emma's husband, Saucer, and other Union soldiers had broken through the enemy line, and Confederate troops began withdrawing. Two miles south of the front line, pursuing troops from the First Kansas

Colored Infantry came across the Confederate depot buildings. Saucer was perhaps present when they inspected a cache of three or four hundred handcuffs, reputedly intended for black prisoners. The soldiers set the buildings afire and then chased the Confederate troops for another three miles.[117] The Union had scored a decisive victory at the Battle of Honey Springs, killing 135 to 150 Confederates, wounding 400, and taking between 47 and 77 prisoners. Only 13 Union soldiers were killed and 67 wounded. By the next morning, the Confederate troops had retreated south of the Canadian River. The commanding Union officer, James G. Blunt, singled out Saucer's regiment for particular commendation. "Their coolness and bravery I have never seen surpassed," he wrote.[118] Eli Grayson, Emma's first son, who was born in 1863, later recalled how his family found dead bodies and abandoned equipment around its house after Wash and the other Confederate soldiers had withdrawn.[119]

The stunning victory of the "mongrel force," half the size of its Confederate opposition, must have infuriated southern troops, and they took their anger out on black Indians who lived in the neighborhood of Wash's family.[120] They pursued "all the negroes to take them South," said one black Creek.[121] Aaron Grayson, a former slave of the family, fled for his life shortly after the battle.[122] So, too, did former slave Matilda Grayson, with her two children, Mary and Clarissa. They "went away secretly and in a hasty manner, and repaired to the Camp of the Refugees at Gibson."[123] Some slaves were not so fortunate. Soda Hawkins escaped, but his wife and children were seized and carried south by their master, Lafayette Marshall. Soda's wife died soon after the war.[124] When Mory Marshall was taken south after the battle, his wife fled to the Union lines, but Mory did not escape until spring 1864.[125] One refugee stands out among the numerous victims of Confederate troops: John Grayson, the son of Katy and her black husband. John had done well for himself. He had a family of at least four full-grown children, and he lived quite comfortably.[126] Yet his status as a free black Creek and as the son of one of the most prominent planters in the area did not protect him. He abandoned property worth nearly $4,000, and the hurried flight took a toll on his family. John's wife of twenty years, Lotti Hillaby, died soon afterward, perhaps in one of the disease-ridden refugee camps behind Union lines.[127]

The refugees flooding into Fort Gibson aggravated an already serious problem. Thousands of Indians were camped around the fort, living in temporary shelters and barely surviving on scanty provisions. Sanitary conditions were horrendous. In the hot summer months, human waste poisoned the water supply, and cholera spread through the population.[128] Just before the Battle of Honey Springs, one visitor to Fort Gibson estimated that there were six thousand refugees camped around the post. "These Indians, in part, were lying under trees and on the wayside, exposed to the hot sun, half starved and naked, and a great many of them sick with dysentary and diarrhœa," he wrote. Smallpox also broke out in the crowded settlements.[129] In August, Cow Tom, a free black Creek, took charge of the camps and tried to bring some order to the population, but refugees continued to die.[130] In the cold winter months, "absolute starvation" set in, and desperate Creeks picked through dung dropped by the army's horses and mules, searching for undigested corn kernels.[131]

The great number of deaths devastated families, creating a population of single parents and orphaned children. Forty-four-year-old Billy Grayson, William and Judah's first child, died in 1863, as did his wife, Maria. They left behind two children, Robert, age thirteen, and William, age ten.[132] Martha Grayson, married to Wash's uncle, watched her husband die in the camps in early 1864, leaving her with a six-year-old daughter to care for.[133] At times, the deaths hit several generations of a single family. Jacob Bruner, the husband of slave Mary Ann Grayson, died at Fort Gibson. So, too, did her grown daughter Matilda, leaving the care of Matilda's two children, Mary and Clarissa, to Mary Ann. Mary Ann's son also died, orphaning two infants. Somehow, Mary Ann survived the multiple blows.[134] One of her children, Mitchell, would later marry William and Judah Grayson's granddaughter.

The Battle of Honey Springs uprooted southern Creeks as well. Wash returned to his mother's house soon after the Confederate retreat, and there the family mulled over its options. His mother, Jennie, wished to remain, hoping that northern Creeks would spare her, but Wash's brother Sam prevailed. The family loaded a single wagon and set out for the Red River, which today marks the southern boundary of Oklahoma. Grandmother Katy and Katy's brother Watt joined them on the road south with their slaves. Union troops scoured the countryside, but the Graysons safely reached the Confederate camps at Wapanucka Academy, a Choctaw school located about ten miles west of Boggy Depot.[135] When Wash returned to the Creek Nation with a scouting party, he found the countryside nearly deserted. Freshly dug roadside graves attested to the Battle of Honey Springs.

In his autobiography, Wash brought a neat symmetry to this turning point in the war. He signaled its onset by omitting mention of Judah and her family, even though he was stationed in their immediate neighborhood for several weeks. Conversely, he marked the battle's closure with an act of inclusion. He described passing by the house of the Bensons, his mother's Creek and white relatives. He "lingered some few minutes," he wrote, remaining with the family for a time after his command had departed.[136] (The Bensons would soon head north to join other refugees.)[137] Both the omission and the inclusion must be considered significant, given the incongruity in the narrative's structure: the dramatic encounter with his black relatives is left out, but the inconsequential visit with his white relatives is not. Perhaps the Battle of Honey Springs marked a turning point for Wash as well as for the war itself. He had traveled a great distance since his 1859 visit with William and Judah. Faced now with the hard reality of throwing down his weapon or trying to kill his black relatives, he chose the latter. As if in response to Wash, William and Judah's son Henderson enlisted in the Union's First Indian Home Guards a few months after the battle. The muster rolls alternatively describe his complexion as "black" or "copper."[138]

If there had once been a spirit of compromise between northern and southern Muscogees, it was broken by late summer 1863. In early September, northern Creeks signed a treaty with the United States that recognized the Emancipation Proclamation, Lincoln's directive freeing slaves in lands under Confederate rule. In the treaty, Creeks averred that "henceforth slavery in their midst shall cease." They granted ex-slaves and black Creeks "the right to occupy and possess such portions of land as may be set apart for their use by the chiefs." And they stipulated that "the laws of said nation shall be equally binding upon all persons of whatever race coming therein."[139] In this way, northern Creeks anticipated both the Thirteenth Amendment and the Fourteenth Amendment by several years. According to the commissioner of Indian affairs, northern Creeks also agreed (or insisted?) on excluding rebel Creeks from "all offices of profit and trust in the nation." Opothleyahola, sometime after his trek out of Creek country in the bitter winter of 1861–1862, had had an interview with the commissioner of Indian affairs. One superintendent reminded his superior of the conversation: "You suggested to him, whenever he and his people did return to their own country, to be merciful to their brethren who had differed with them, and more particularly spare the women and children." Opothleyahola reportedly answered that "when a man has a bad breed of dogs, the best way to get rid of them is to kill the bitch."[140] Opothleyahola died in fall 1863, but the anger and hatred did not.

The Confederate effort in the Creek Nation was largely over. Farther south in the Confederate-controlled Choctaw Nation, the economy had collapsed. Goods were so scarce that coffee sold for up to ten dollars a pound, sugar for two dollars a pound. The Confederate currency was nearly worthless. Two dollars in silver could purchase a Confederate five-dollar bill. One Creek soldier named Joseph Perryman reported that "men are so discouraged that they wont fight." Creeks, he suggested, "would soon lay down their arms if it was not for the sweet talk and lies of the superior officers." Disillusioned and angry, Perryman himself had recently abandoned the Confederate cause. When "I was on the Secesh side," he wrote, "I did not know what I was fighting for without it was for a few negroes that some few proud rich folks had."[141] In the Creek Nation, people were desperate. "We can see nothing but Starvation before us," wrote one Indian.[142] Yet some Creeks, including Wash, continued to fight. His autobiography recounts a series of courageous encounters with the enemy in 1864, each one a seeming vindication, as Wash wrote, of Creek "manhood."[143] Wash had been made a captain, but his perseverance came at a cost. In September 1864, he confronted his family's past one last time on the battlefield.

The encounter took place two miles north of the present-day town of Wagoner. Some 2,000 Confederate troops, including Wash, were moving through the area, in search of Union supply trains. On September 16, they stumbled upon 195 men—white, Indian, and black soldiers. Forty-five of them were from Company K of the First Kansas Colored Infantry Volunteers. Company K was employed cutting and hauling hay to Fort Gibson and providing guard for the operation.[144] Soldiers from other companies may have been present, including Wash's in-law Saucer Brady and former Grayson slaves, Sack and Franklin. The Union soldiers were scattered over a three-mile prairie, cut through by a network of narrow channels and shallow pools and lagoons. Small willow trees hung over the precipitous banks of the lagoons, and water lilies floated gently on the water's surface.[145] These details proved critical to the nine men from Company K who survived.

When the Confederate soldiers charged the field, Company K was cut off. The ex-slaves buried themselves in the prairie grass and along the banks of the waterway, Wash recalled, but "the men proceeded to hunt them out much as sportsmen do quails." "Some of the negroes finding they were about to be discovered, would spring up from the brush and cry out, O! master spare me." They were shot down. Others, hiding in the water, were shot and left on the riverbank. The nine survivors escaped by concealing themselves in the lagoons. One lay for hours in the water below the overhanging willows, leaving just his nose exposed. Another slipped beneath the water lilies. "I confess this was sickening to me," wrote Wash, yet he was "powerless" to stop what he termed "unnecessary butchery," at least until a young white soldier was discovered. "Should we not kill him too?" Captain Grayson was asked. No, he said, "it was negroes that we were killing now and not white men."[146] This awkward phrase hints at the dark decision that Wash made during the war. He tried to purge his family of its black ancestry, both literally and figuratively.

A terrible irony both motivated and thwarted Wash. No matter how much he struggled to succeed, no matter if he disowned his black relatives, no matter if he shot them down himself, white Americans would never accept him as an equal. Katy had discovered as much during the era of removal. So, too, would her grandson. The irony was laid bare at different points throughout the war. "The Creeks are about equal in scale of intelligence to the Delawares of Kansas; they are inferior to the Cherokees," said their commanding Union officer.[147] After the March 1862 Battle of Pea Ridge, near Leetown, Arkansas, Union troops reported that Confederate Indians had scalped some of their men and plunged knives into the hearts and necks of others.[148] An investigating committee concluded that the "warfare was conducted by said savages with all the barbarity their merciless and cowardly natures are capable of."[149] Such attitudes inspired one officer to suggest sending Confederate prisoners into war against rebellious Sioux Indians in Minnesota in late 1862. The secretary of war was delighted with the plan. It is "excellent," he wrote, and "will be immediately acted upon."[150]

If Wash thought that his commitment to the Confederacy would somehow grant him a degree of equality, he was wrong. In early 1864, one incident involving a white soldier, L. M. Martin, of the Fifth Regiment of Texas Partisan Rangers, encapsulated the racial views of most Confederates. Martin refused to report to Tandy Walker, a Choctaw slaveholder commanding the Second Indian Brigade, and Martin's protest eventually worked its way up to General E. Kirby Smith, commanding the Trans-Mississippi Department. To Martin, the matter was simple: the dispute brought up "in practical form the old question of the relative grade of races, upon which there is now being waged sanguinary war between the North and South of the old Union." "The Indian is physiologically recognized as an inferior race," Martin confidently asserted, and no white officer with "a proper respect for the natural dignity of his race" would report to an Indian. Moreover, the "well-known mental incapacity" of Indians, especially in operations which require "promptness and concentration of mind," made them unfit officers. Even Indians themselves recognize their incapacity, he insisted, for they "of their own impulses" prefer to be led by the "superior mental acuteness of the white man." Martin smugly expected Smith to confirm these truths. If not, Martin would resign immediately rather than "renounce the self-respect of a gentleman, and subordinate" himself to "an individual of an inferior race." He added that other members of the Texas Partisan Rangers shared his sentiments.[151] White southerners and northerners may have differed on the virtues of slavery, but they agreed that this was a white man's country.

In fact, after the Battle of Honey Springs, Union officers, freed from the urgency of planning troop movements and organizing supply trains, began contemplating the future of Indian Territory. They scanned the countryside and envisioned factories, farms, and mines worked and owned by white men. "I have been specially struck with the vast resources of all the Indian Territories," wrote Samuel Curtis, commanding the army's Department of Kansas. "In soil, climate, prairie, timber, coal, salt, and probably copper and lead, I know of no such country."[152] William Phillips, in charge of the First Indian regiment, agreed. He suggested that the United States consider admitting Choctaw, Chickasaw, and part of Cherokee and Seminole country as a state. It is "magnificent country," he wrote. "I do not discuss the question of throwing open the whole Indian nation, because I do not deem it expedient to argue it here, and now especially," he added ominously, "as I have no white troops."[153] From behind Confederate lines, one officer accused the Union's General James Blunt, commanding Indian Territory, of being "an old land speculator." Blunt, he said, believed it would be "a good thing" to extinguish Indian title.[154] But that would have to wait. In the meantime, Union troops stole everything but the land itself. Kansas merchants, in league with U.S. officers, drove more than twenty thousand head of cattle out of Indian Territory.[155] Even William Phillips, who had greedily assessed the value of Indian lands, was disgusted by the behavior of his comrades. "Most of the white regiments that have entered the Indian Nation commit more or less depredations," he wrote. "They treat it as if it were an enemy's country."[156]

This terrible irony marked the entire war. It drove Wash to disown his relatives, but to no avail. It drove Saucer Brady, Henderson Grayson, and others to fight for the Union, in search of an emancipation from the racial hierarchy. But their dedication did not prevent northerners from eyeing their land—surely better exploited by industrious white men—even before the war had ground to a close. The irony permanently scarred both southern Creeks and black Muscogees. It scarred the Graysons, too. Despite this common experience, the war set them farther apart than ever. After exchanging shots on the battlefield, after Wash had returned to William and Judah's home armed as a Confederate soldier, how could they ever bring themselves to recognize their connections? How could they even live peacefully in the same nation?

Profile

Chester Adams, June 2000

In 2000, Chester Adams lived in a small, dilapidated, ranch-style house off of a gravel road in Beggs, Oklahoma. I pulled open the broken screen door and knocked. A rail-thin black man answered, pointed me to the back room, and then sunk back down on a stained couch, before a television loudly broadcasting the day's stockcar race. I cautiously entered the dark house and was struck by the sour smell of urine. In the back room, Adams was lying across an unmade bed watching a college football game on television. An oxygen machine puffed next to him, and he wore the tubing over his nose throughout our meeting. Medicine bottles lay scattered across the night table. The floor was covered in shag carpet, in shades of orange and brown.

Adams was seventy-nine when I met him. He had receding gray hair, dark honey skin, and an easy laugh. Betsy Grayson was his great-great-grandmother. Although various documents reveal that Betsy was an intimate relative of Katy, Watt, William, and Elizabeth (the children of Robert Grierson), her precise relationship to them remains unknown. Betsy had three children by an unnamed man. ("Father: don't know," reads one government record from 1916.)[1] Her daughter Mahala married Thomas J. Adams, a Creek of African descent born in 1842. Adams became the chief justice of the Creek Nation in the late 1800s, suggesting that some black Muscogees still wielded significant power. Their children were visibly of African descent, and they spoke Creek fluently.[2] One of them, Louis, was the father of Washington, and Washington was the father of Chester, who sat before me on a bed strewn with newspapers, socks, medicine bottles, and other odds and ends.

As a child in the 1920s, Adams went to a black school and a Methodist church attended by blacks and a few Creeks. "I had two cousins who tried to go to white school, but were not allowed," he recalled. "They later went to Haskell," an Indian boarding school established by the Bureau of Indian Affairs.

The Creek Council house in Okmulgee, Oklahoma, in the late nineteenth century. Thomas J. Adams, the chief justice of the Creek Nation and the great-grandfather of Chester Adams, is standing in the foreground. Courtesy of Chester Adams.

When he was twenty-one, he moved to Detroit and took a job as a bus driver. Later, he got a job with General Motors, where he worked for twenty-four years building Pontiacs. In 1975, he returned to Beggs. In Detroit, he observed, he lived in an all-black neighborhood, and although he used to hunt with a number of Cree friends on the Cree reservation in Canada, he was identified as black in strictly segregated Detroit. Nevertheless, he found the big city liberating. "In Detroit," he remembered, "you said what you wanted and if you could buy it, you could get it."

The racial situation in Oklahoma, by contrast, was more complicated and perhaps ultimately more frustrating. "Down here I was aware of the fact that I wasn't white, I wasn't black," he told me. In fact, some of his cousins go as white, others go as black. Adams's maternal cousin, for example, is blond and goes as white. Although she lives in nearby Tulsa, they last spoke to each other in 1937, but when they were kids, she visited him regularly in Beggs. "They came to stay with us for all the summer," to ride horses and be outdoors, Adams recalled. "Today, you call her an Indian and she wouldn't speak to you." "When you go down the street and see someone with a head full of blond hair, you'd never think they were Indian or black," he observed.

Adams was careful to say "go" instead of "pass," as most white Americans do. The phrase "passing for white" implies that any African ancestry at all makes you black, and Adams saw the absurdity of such an assertion. Yet as a child, he struggled to fathom the illogical rules of racial segregation. "I could never understand the fact that when I was with my cousins, I had to sit in different places according to who was visiting." "When I went to the store with my black cousins," he said, "we sat in the segregated section. When I went with my white cousins, we sat in the white section." When he went alone, he sat wherever he wanted.

The conversation turned to the racial situation in the Creek Nation. He explained that many Creeks go as white because of the multitude of advantages whiteness brings in America. To a large extent, he sympathized with their decision to distance themselves from their ancestry. Claude Cox, a controversial Creek chief in the 1970s who oversaw the disenfranchisement of black Creeks, went as white before he became chief, Adams noted. Cox was a pole man for the rural electric company, and only white men could get these desirable jobs. Yet Cox himself had African ancestry. "Years ago it meant something," Adams said. "Blacks could only teach or farm. A few were mechanics or bricklayers." Then he added, "Today, if you were trying to go into business and you needed a loan, it would make a difference. You'd be a fool to deny yourself this advantage."

But eventually Adams revealed a hint of frustration. Cox "never had nothing to do with black people." Cox disliked George Grayson, one of Adams's friends, because he was black. "I know some Indians who are real black who won't talk to black people. And white people won't talk to them." "When I run into someone who denies his black ancestry," he concluded, "I remind him of one of his cousins I know."

Adams died in January 2002, about a year and a half after I interviewed him.

6

Northern Indians and Negro Slaves:
Wash and the Politics of Reconstruction

In late 1864 or early 1865, Wash Grayson attended a dance with his friend and fellow Confederate soldier Pleasant Porter.[1] Like Wash, Porter was highly educated and a devoted southern partisan, as his battle scars attested.[2] Porter was shot on two different occasions. One bullet passed straight through his cheek; another left him with a permanent limp. Both of his brothers died in the conflict, and Porter himself murdered his Unionist cousin, James McKellop.[3] Wash and Porter, comrades-in-arms, interested and informed citizens of the Creek Nation, probably discussed the question that must have been foremost on their minds: How would their nation rebuild itself, and how could it defend its sovereignty after many of its wealthiest and most influential members had gone to war against the United States?

In the former Confederate states, other southerners asked themselves the same question. Creeks and white southerners were both fighting against the supremacy of the federal government, with one significant difference. In the South, the contest against the federal government was meant to protect a way of life that was wholly premised on racial hierarchy. Southern states drafted black codes to return ex-slaves to a state of servitude, and where law failed, violence took its place.[4] In the Creek Nation, by contrast, the contest against the federal government protected a way of life that depended only partially on racial hierarchy. In fact, many Creeks could not escape the simple fact that they had African forebears. Wash and Porter were well aware of the mixed ancestry of the nation's citizens. Porter himself was of African descent; on occasion, he even bragged that he had the "meanest mixture of blood there was."[5] Wash of course only had to recall his 1859 visit to William and Judah's to remind himself of his own family's mixed heritage.

Yet some southern Creeks came to identify with their white counterparts. "The work of reconstruction," Wash recalled, "proved to be a most difficult task." "Southern Creeks," he wrote, "could not brook the idea of being dominated and governed by the ignorance of the northern Indians supplemented by that of their late negro slaves."[6] His language resembles that of the redeemers of the former Confederate states. Southern Creeks such as Wash, convinced of their superiority, believed that the fate of the nation depended on the subjugation of the northern Creeks and the disenfranchisement of their black allies. The "intelligence" and the "little wealth" that remained, Wash asserted, belonged to southern Creeks.[7] When the federal government demanded that Creeks incorporate their ex-slaves into the nation, the struggle was on. The integrity, indeed very survival, of Creek sovereignty, southern Creeks insisted, rested on the disenfranchisement of black Indians.[8] For the Graysons, and for the larger Creek Nation, the results were long-lasting and disastrous.

In September 1865, U.S. commissioners and representatives from the Creeks (as well as from other nations) met at Fort Smith, not far from where Interstate 40 now crosses the state line between Oklahoma and Arkansas. The commissioners had come to reestablish relations between the Indian nations and the United States, formally ending the war. Each treaty, they hoped, would meet several conditions, including the emancipation of slaves, the reconciliation of northern and southern tribal factions, and the creation of a territory-wide government, encompassing all Indian nations living in Indian Territory.[9] The consolidated territorial government, Native Americans and whites recognized, would throw open Indian lands to exploitation.[10] It "will do great injustice," said one senator.[11] But without it, an army officer observed, ten or twelve thousand ex-slaves living among the Creeks, Choctaws, Chickasaws, and Cherokees would be without any government.[12] The resolution of this matter would shape the future of free black Creeks such as Emma, Judy, and Vicey, three of William and Judah's children who lived through the Reconstruction era.

In 1865, ex-slaves occupied an ambiguous position. Many Indians denied that they had any place in the nation. Creek slaves were alert to the potential dangers they faced at the close of the war. As early as February 1864, Monday Durant, a free black Creek, wrote to the commissioner of Indian affairs regarding the matter. "I ask in behalf of the loyal Africans from Creek Nation that they have guaranteed to them equal rights with the Indian," he stated. Under his signature, as if to anticipate the objections to his request, he wrote, "Sixty years in the Creek Nation."[13] Sixty years may have been long enough to become a citizen in Monday's view, but his assertion touched on all the difficult issues faced by Creeks in the postwar years. Monday and many other blacks were not members of Creek families and therefore not Creek, some objected, although everyone knew that black-Indian relationships were common, from rape to long-term commitment. Yet, if ex-slaves were incorporated into the nation, Creeks feared, they might remain apart, only weakly supportive of Indian sovereignty.

Such fears were not entirely unfounded, as Monday's own letter suggests. Monday requested Creek citizenship, but he made that request to a U.S. officer. The United States should intervene, he suggested, not only because he and other black Creeks had lived in the Indian nation for decades but also because "all of our boys" served in the U.S. Army.[14] Black Creeks sometimes identified both as Creeks *and* as Americans, and ultimately their incorporation into the Muscogee Nation could weaken it and perhaps even lead to its demise. This dilemma was a problem of the Creeks' own making, for their leaders had spent the previous four decades oppressing Creeks of African descent, forcing them to become a people apart.

Leading the northern Creeks at Fort Smith was Oktarsars Harjo, Opothley-ahola's successor. In addition, at least five black Creeks represented ex-slaves at the proceedings.[15] Southern Creeks arrived late at the conference, bringing with them not only a hostility toward their northern counterparts but also an expressed contempt for black Indians. Because of the difficulty of settling treaties with the numerous and deeply divided Indian nations present at Fort Smith, U.S. commissioners asked for only a preliminary agreement that recognized the "exclusive jurisdiction" of the United States over the Indians and looked forward to future negotiations settling all outstanding issues.[16] After some negotiation, both northern and southern Creeks consented to the preliminary agreement. (The Fort Smith agreements were never ratified by the Senate and therefore do not have the status of treaties.)

The negotiations at Fort Smith left black Indians between bondage and freedom, both legally and practically. Though some U.S. officials believed otherwise, the commissioners had merely called for measures to be taken to emancipate black Indians. "I have not learned that any 'measures' in relation to this matter have made emancipation in the Indian Country an accomplished fact," concluded one agent from the Freedmen's Bureau in December 1865.[17] Similar confusion surrounded the reach of the Emancipation Proclamation and the Thirteenth Amendment. Though the Emancipation Proclamation did not mention any of the western territories in its list of subject areas, in September 1863, the northern Creeks agreed to "cheerfully accept and ratify" the proclamation for their own nation.[18] Few people anywhere were aware of this act, however, and in any case, the authority of these Creeks to legislate for the entire tribe was in question. A better case might have been made for the applicability of the Thirteenth Amendment.[19] Yet confusion reigned even in the federal courts, where one judge asserted that both the Emancipation Proclamation and the Thirteenth Amendment applied to Indian Territory.[20] Later, a higher court rejected his finding.[21]

Given the uncertainty surrounding the status of slaves, emancipation proceeded haphazardly. In some areas, freedom came quickly to slaves; in other areas it did not come at all. It was felt least in the Choctaw and Chickasaw nations, where Wash Grayson and his relatives remained until early 1866. U.S. officers sent back alarming reports to their superiors about the conditions there. In October 1865, an agent of the Freedmen's Bureau received "reliable information" of "a most deadly persecution upon the colored people" in the Choctaw and Chickasaw nations, part of a larger campaign of violence against freed people in the South.[22] Some Choctaws and Chickasaws were reportedly beating their former slaves to death.[23] "Many negroes have been shot down by their masters" in the Choctaw Nation, one officer wrote.[24] By early 1866, when Wash and his relatives set out for their old homes in the Creek Nation, most blacks in the Choctaw and Chickasaw nations were still enslaved.[25]

Although Wash and his brother Sam apparently no longer had any slaves, they were accompanied by their sisters Adeline and Caroline, who owned a number of people.[26] On the trek back to the Creek Nation, some of these slaves accompanied the Graysons. Wash, recalling the journey forty years later, referred to them as "servants," but it is impossible to know what mixture of affection, desperation, and coercion preserved the bond between the Graysons and their slaves.[27]

Judging from surviving records, affection between master and slave was in short supply. "Old Ben was not going to free the slaves when the war was over," recalled former Cherokee slave Sarah Wilson in 1937, "but about that time he died and went to hell where all other slave owners ought to be."[28] For the Graysons' ex-slaves, the simple act of choosing a surname was both a statement of contempt for their former masters and an assertion of independence. When census takers were at work in 1866, one ex-slave vehemently insisted that they erase his Grayson surname because "he wasn't an Indian and his daddy was a negro." Because the freedman did not know his father's name, he asked to be known only as "Old Suttin."[29] George Grayson had a similar moment of revelation. At some point after serving in the Union army, George abandoned his master's surname in favor of his father's, Tobler.[30] The hatred was mutual. Alice Robertson, a missionary in the Creek Nation, remembered that after the war, in places where ex-slaves remained in their modest cabins, planters "disdained to come back, and sought new homes elsewhere."[31] Despite this evidence of mutual hostility, years later, Wash Grayson's daughter would remember nostalgically not Old Suttin or George Tobler but an "old Negro slave named Prince, who, when the Negroes were freed, would not leave" her family.[32]

Desperation and coercion, rather than affection, were probably far more powerful forces in preventing freed people from leaving their former masters. Ex-slaves did not have homes, tools, or seed of their own, and so for their very survival, they sometimes remained with their former owners. The risk entailed by striking out on one's own was compounded by the general scarcity of provisions in the Creek Nation after the Civil War. Many Indians were starving, too weak even to plant crops.[33] Mary Ann Grayson and her sister Sykie Hawkins, two former slaves, probably faced no more difficult a time than many others. Mary Ann Grayson's husband had died during the war, and she was left with the care of two grandchildren and a young child of her own. From Texas, Sykie wrote her sister asking for money to return home, but Mary Ann could only advise her to "make cotton" until she had accumulated enough cash for the trip to the Creek Nation. Only a day or two after Sykie's return, Mary Ann "told her to lets work," and they began clearing a field in preparation for planting onions. It "was cold," Mary Ann recalled, "but we would wait until the Sun got up." When Sykie received news that her husband in Texas was near death, she went around "begging for money" to help her go back. "I told her I just had one lone five dollar," Mary Ann remembered. Sykie's husband died before she could set off, leaving their children stranded in Texas.[34]

Coercion was more common in the Chickasaw and Choctaw nations, where Wash and his relatives were living, than in the Creek Nation. One Choctaw slave owner, Michael Laflore (whose surname today graces Le Flore County, Oklahoma), kidnapped four of his former bondmen in Arkansas and bound and beat them during the abduction to his plantation. In late September 1865, Laflore was reportedly still buying "colored people" for one hundred dollars in gold.[35] Creek planters resident in the Choctaw and Chickasaw nations followed suit, driving Daniel Hawkins to steal a horse from his owner, Louis McIntosh, in August 1865 and flee to Fort Gibson.[36] At the end of the year, ex-slaves petitioned U.S. officers at Fort Smith for military escorts to visit their enslaved families in the Choctaw and Chickasaw nations, where it was still too dangerous for black Indians to travel.[37]

Several months after the 1865 treaties, the U.S. government called delegates from the Five Tribes to Washington to conclude another round of treaties settling all outstanding differences. Each 1866 treaty had four principal points: the rec-

onciliation of northern and southern factions, the emancipation and incorporation of slaves into Indian nations, the compensation of Union Indians for
property losses, and the cession of lands to be used for the settlement of other
native peoples.[38] Some of the land cessions were enormous. The Seminoles
turned over their entire domain, more than two million acres, in exchange for
lands in the Creek Nation. The Creeks themselves ceded more than three million
acres, with only modest compensation. In addition, each of the Five Tribes
granted rights-of-way to railroads.[39] The railroads sparked a destructive chain
of events: economic development, an invasion of white colonists, and public
pressure to dismantle the Five Tribes.

The status of freed people was one of the most contentious issues in the
settlement of these treaties. Northern Creeks acquiesced to the incorporation of
their former slaves, but their southern counterparts, far more heavily invested
in slavery, vehemently objected. Confederate officer Daniel N. McIntosh fired
off an angry letter to the commissioner of Indian affairs on behalf of his peers.
Without a hint of irony, he wrote, "Our people were *proverbially* kind to their
slaves." Creek servitude was "merely nominal," he insisted, and slaves "possessed
plenty" and were "contended and happy." Adopting the paternalist rhetoric of
southern planters, he insisted that the "ancient care and kindness" of Creek
masters would guarantee the well-being of ex-slaves. Legal equality for black
Muscogees was therefore unnecessary and even wrong: "we can never recognize
them as our equals," he wrote. "It is, we conceive, contrary to nature and nature's
laws." McIntosh concluded his impassioned plea with a reference to Jeremiah
13:23, a favorite biblical passage of nineteenth-century scientific racists:

> The antipathies of race among Indians are as strong, if not stronger than
> they are among the whites. The Government of the United States . . .
> may force us to things repugnant to our nature; but it cannot change
> our honest conviction and faith, any more than it can change the skin
> of the Ethiopian, or the spots of the Leopard.[40]

When McIntosh learned that southern Creeks might be excluded altogether from
the treaty, he and his fellow Confederate James Smith agreed to sign it despite
its unequivocal language: the laws of the Creek Nation, the treaty read, "shall
be equally binding upon and give equal protection to all such persons, and all
others, of whatsoever race or color, who may be adopted as citizens or members
of said tribe."[41] Wash later described this clause as "distasteful."[42]

If southern Creeks had lost the war, however, they had not lost the cause.
As one of the few Muscogees with an advanced formal education, Wash played
a central role in securing the government for southern Creeks. His political

allies—Sam Checote, Una McIntosh, Sam Callahan, G. W. Stidham, Sanford Perryman, and others—were described by their opponents as "officers in the Rebel Army." The characterization is not entirely fair, for Una had earned the moniker Union McIntosh for his allegiance to the North.⁴³ For the most part, however, Wash's allies were indeed Confederates. Checote signed the Creek treaty with the South in 1861 and for a time commanded the Confederacy's First Creek Regiment.⁴⁴ Sam Callahan also fought in the Confederate army and in 1864 traveled to Richmond, Virginia, to represent the Creeks in the Congress of the Confederacy. (At his death in 1911, he would be buried in his faded and tattered Confederate uniform.)⁴⁵ G. W. Stidham, merchant and former slave owner, also signed the Confederate treaty.⁴⁶

These brief war biographies suggest that Wash had teamed up with unregenerate slaveholders to "redeem"—the favorite word of defeated Confederates— the Creek Nation, to save it from northern Creeks and their black allies. This is surely part of the story. But it is only part. In the Creek Nation, there could be no simple redemption, for the Creeks themselves already stood near the bottom of America's racial hierarchy. Wash's politics and the politics of his allies must be understood in this context. They wished to redeem the Creek Nation not only to save its racial hierarchy but also to save the nation itself.

Wash's political ally Sanford Perryman embodies the contradictions and terrible ironies of Creek politics. Perryman was both a Creek nationalist and a racist, and he considered the two not only compatible but interrelated. He was also visibly part African. In the prewar years, his ancestry had been a burden, no doubt. In 1852, for example, he was identified as a student of African descent when Creek leaders were threatening to expel from school those more than one-eighth African. But the prominence of his family—Mose Perryman was one of the largest slaveholders in the nation—offered protection and reassurance, at least until the 1860s. During the Civil War, Confederate Creeks set out to capture Sanford and his relatives and take them south into Texas to sell into slavery. Sanford's family narrowly escaped only with the assistance of a minister, who sent the pursuing Creek troops in one direction and the fleeing Perrymans in another.⁴⁷

After the Civil War, Perryman initially refused even to consider readmitting Confederate Creek leaders to the nation, but his resolve did not last.⁴⁸ By 1868, he had taken scissors to his curly hair, the most visible sign of his African heritage, and begun wearing a wig of "straight dark Indian hair." His prominent hairpiece attracted "the ill will of every colored man in this nation and plenty of Indians besides," said one disapproving acquaintance. Then Perryman went out and made a political alliance with his erstwhile enslavers. The deal soon made him speaker of the House of Warriors.⁴⁹

Sanford Perryman. Courtesy of the
National Anthropological Archives,
Smithsonian Institution.

Perryman's behavior seems only an extreme example of the cynical politics
embodied by Wash Grayson and others, but their manipulation of race was not
entirely self-serving. They were Creek nationalists who understood a critical fact
about postbellum America: white abolitionists and civil rights advocates had no
use for difference. White reformers desired all people to be equal before the law,
and they demanded that the law be universal. William Graham, a white reformer,
abolitionist, ardent advocate of civil rights, and vocal opponent of the Ku Klux
Klan, epitomized this viewpoint. He condemned Sanford Perryman for insisting
that Creek schools teach Muscogee rather than English, and "National" or Creek
rights rather than federal supremacy. Reformers like Graham believed that the
English language and American law were the universal standards of measure-
ment.[50] Muscogee, he snorted, "is a mere gibberish and no language at all."[51]
Facing such hostility, Sanford, Wash, and their allies reasoned that for the Creeks
to survive as a separate and distinct nation, they had to embrace states' rights
or risk being swallowed up by the federal government.

The opposition to Wash's political party formed around Oktarsars Harjo.
Also known as Sands, he found his support among poor Creeks—he called them
"full-bloods"—and ex-slaves. This party did not recognize any distinction between Creeks and ex-slaves.[52] In fact, Oktarsars Harjo was particularly vocal
about incorporating black Muscogees into the nation. Northern Creeks and ex-

slaves were "as brothers," he said, "and they wish this friendship to continue." Southern Creeks, he charged, were "opposed to the Freedmen."[53]

The balance of power between northern and southern Creeks rested in the hands of ex-slaves.[54] In late 1867, Muscogees drafted a constitution, modeled on that of the United States, that provided for a principal chief and second chief, elected by the majority of male citizens over age seventeen. The principal chief governed in conjunction with the House of Kings, composed of one representative from each town, and the House of Warriors, composed of representatives apportioned by town population.[55] Ex-slaves and other black Creeks, who congregated in the towns of Arkansas Colored, Canadian Colored, and North Fork Colored, could swing votes in both the houses. They made up 15 percent of the voting population and for national candidates represented the difference between victory and defeat.[56]

Wash's allies therefore set out to disenfranchise their opponents. In late 1866, U.S. agent J. W. Dunn had begun taking a census of the Creek Nation for the purpose of distributing $200,000, as stipulated in the recent treaty. Checote wrote to the superintendent of Indian affairs to propose the novel argument that the second article of the treaty entitled ex-slaves to an interest in soil and national funds, but not in "special funds" such as the $200,000. When the treaty intended to refer to ex-slaves, reasoned Checote, "the word Freedmen is always used in contra-distinction to the words Indians or Creeks."[57] Checote's careful argument found support from the commissioner of Indian affairs, and in March 1867, Dunn distributed the $200,000 to persons listed on his census who were not ex-slaves.[58] The standards of exclusion were not always exacting. Judah received a payment, as did her children, suggesting that, despite their status as former slaves, they maintained an undeniable bond to the community of Hilabi.[59]

The move to exclude ex-slaves had significant consequences that long outlasted the small per capita payment of $17.34. First, it antagonized ex-slaves and northern Creeks. Ex-slaves retained the services of a missionary and agreed to pay him four hundred dollars if he successfully secured their share of the payment.[60] Northern Creeks, led by Oktarsars Harjo, complained vehemently to government officials. According to the 1866 treaty, asserted Sands, "the colored citizens of the Creek Nation, were to get the same rights as others, and they have not got it."[61] The treaty was clear, he said: "we were all one Nation, and would share the money equally, colored people and Indians."[62]

Ex-slaves and northern Creeks appealed to the U.S. government for direct intervention in the affairs of the Creek Nation, and U.S. officials were happy to oblige. J. W. Dunn protested to the commissioner of Indian affairs.[63] O. O. Howard, the head of the Freedmen's Bureau, requested that Secretary of War Ulysses S. Grant intervene.[64] Finally, Congress took action by withholding Creek annuities until ex-slaves received a share of the $200,000.[65] Southern Creeks responded first by requesting that Dunn be removed from his post as U.S. Indian agent.[66] Then they asked the commissioner of Indian affairs if the act of Congress required the assent of the Creek Council.[67] They received an unambiguous reply: the U.S. government cannot "to any extent, be influenced or modified by any action which the creek council may think proper to take in the premises. The assent of the creek council is not required to make the law operative, and the withholding their assent will not suspend or delay its execution."[68] In June 1869, Dunn paid $17.34 to each of 1,781 former slaves.

The conflict between Muscogees placed southern Creeks in a difficult position that the nation to this day has not fully abandoned. By refusing to dismantle the racial hierarchy they had built in the antebellum era, southern Creeks, like advocates of states' rights, defended racial hierarchy in the name of sovereignty.[69] White southerners were disingenuous and had little reason other than racism and the privilege that it spawned for defending the power of the state against the federal government. Indians, by contrast, were undeniably engaged in a struggle against imperialism. The actions of southern Creeks were thus especially costly. They allowed the United States to colonize in the name of emancipation and to do so with the support of black and northern Creeks.[70]

In one other important way, the dispute over $17.34 proved to have long-term consequences. It resulted in two lists: one of Creek citizens who received payment in 1867, and another of Creek citizens who received payment in 1869. These two lists, known as the Dunn Roll of Creek Citizens and the Dunn Roll of Freedmen, gave bureaucrats the means to discriminate between Muscogees, and they have formed the basis for all subsequent divisions between Creeks and their ex-slaves, right down to the present day. (Later discriminatory censuses depended on the Dunn rolls.) The Dunn Roll of Freedmen explains on its first page that it enumerates "such persons" who were refused money for being "of African descent."[71] It thus owes its very existence to the racist politics of the 1860s. The discrimination between people who were, in Oktarsars Harjo's unequivocal words, "all one Nation" is troubling enough, but even if tribal membership should be based on kinship, as some Creeks maintained (and still maintain), the Dunn rolls are indefensible. Many ex-slaves were the children of their Creek masters. Planter Lewis McIntosh was particularly notorious in this regard. He fathered both Arceny Wofford and Prissie Carruthers, and probably many others, by his slaves. "My grandfather used to devil us," said Prissie's friend Ella McIntosh, "and say she [Prissie] was our young mistress." "I asked him how and he said she was Lewis Mcintosh our young masters daughter."[72]

Creek descent is now traced bilaterally, and either a Creek father or mother is sufficient to establish citizenship. But even if kinship is defined strictly along matrilineal lines, a number of people on the Dunn Roll of Freedmen should be considered Creek. Arceny Wofford stated that her mother "had Indian in her."[73] So too did Prissie Carruthers, though Prissie appeared on neither Dunn roll.[74] Moreover, by the rule of matrilineality, a number of people on the Dunn Roll of Creek Citizens should *not* be considered Creek kin, including Judah and her children.

The inconsistency of the Dunn rolls is compounded by the numerous marriages between persons on the two lists. These marriages belie all reasons for drawing lines between citizens and ex-slaves. William and Judah's daughter Emma, for example, appears on the Dunn Roll of Creek Citizens, while her husband Saucer Brady appears on the Dunn Roll of Freedmen. Their child Mollie appears on the Dunn Roll of Creek Citizens. Mollie would later marry Bob Daniels, who is listed on the Roll of Freedmen.[75] Emma's daughter Jeanetta (by a Creek citizen named Jack Gabler) also appears on the roll of Creek citizens. Jeanetta, too, would later marry a freedman, Mitchell Grayson, a former slave of Watt Grayson.[76] Mitchell was the son of Mary Ann Grayson, who had weathered the deaths of her husband, a daughter, and a son at Fort Gibson during the war, and who had planted onions in the cold spring of 1866.

While Creeks were fighting over the future of their nation, they were also rebuilding their homes. Nearly all Creeks—northern and southern, former masters and ex-slaves, light-skinned and dark—suffered in the years immediately following the war. Wash described how he and his brother Sam went to work with "a will and desperation," splitting rails, raising fences, and clearing fields. He recalled "terrible hardships and privations" and described fighting off hunger while he labored to plant crops.[77] The travails of his cousins Emma, Henderson, Judy, and Vicey (William and Judah's children) were no less difficult. They had likely been among the five thousand refugees camped at Fort Gibson in spring 1865 who were "absolutely on the verge of starvation."[78] In early 1866, they were probably still drawing rations from the fort, along with eighty-five hundred other Creeks.[79] That summer, just as Wash and Sam were preparing their fields, they must have been doing the same in Oktaha, some twenty miles north of their cousins.

The strenuous conditions took their toll on both sides of the family. Wash's little brother James died sometime during the war.[80] In William and Judah's family the toll was higher. Billy (William and Judah's first child) died in 1863. Then between 1866 and 1871, their children Henderson, Mitty, and Judy, who

was only thirty-one at the time, died.[81] Henderson's wife, Abby, also died during
this period, orphaning her three young children.[82] By 1871, at least five of
William and Judah's eleven children had died. Forty-eight-year-old Emma was
now the senior member of the family. She depended heavily on her youngest
sister and neighbor, twenty-nine-year-old Vicey.

Emma and Vicey, uneducated, dark-skinned, and poor, had few opportunities to improve their economic status in the nation, and their cousin Wash
had all the advantages they did not. As long as the southern Creeks did well,
Wash stood to benefit. In 1867, Sam Checote, Wash's old Confederate commander, won the first postwar election for principal chief, and Wash became
his official clerk. Though at first Wash worked without pay, the benefits of his
position were immediately apparent. Because of his favorable standing with the
Creek government, his credit was good around the nation. "I was able soon to
aid materially toward providing a livelihood for Mother and the children," he
noted. At the same time, he began working as a salesman for a merchant, Gray
E. Scales, a white man who operated a general merchandise store. Wash recalled
earning about twenty-five dollars per month, the equivalent of a workhorse or
two heifers. Two years after becoming official clerk, Wash, skilled in both writing
and arithmetic, was appointed treasurer of the nation.[83]

By 1869, Wash was employed as a salesman in the general merchandise
store of G. W. Stidham. He further improved his fortunes in 1869 by marrying
Stidham's daughter, Georgeanna, known as Annie. "In wealth, beauty, education
and social standing," he wrote, "she was at that time far ahead of any Creek or
other young lady."[84] Annie's parents were slave owners before the war, reported
an 1892 guide to the leading men of Indian Territory, and "she was brought up
in affluence and ease, knowing nothing of hardships until the war swept away
everything."[85] A photographic portrait from 1866 shows her seated, clothed in
a black dress of either alpaca or velvet, and wearing a pocket watch, ostenta-
tiously chained to her collar.[86] The watch, a common middle-class accessory at
the time but rare in Indian Territory, confirms the sitter's status in a portrait that
otherwise reflects the difficulty of the immediate postwar years.[87] If the watch is
a concession and gesture to the time-obsessed industriousness of white America,
Annie's long, unfashioned hair is defiantly Indian.

As Wash rose to prominence in the Creek Nation, the fortunes of his part-
African relatives declined. The two trends were related, for Wash's success was
tied to the power of the southern faction, and southern Muscogees depended
on the disenfranchisement of dark-skinned Creeks, at least so charged their
opponents. After Sam Checote's election in 1867, Oktarsars Harjo (Sands) voiced
a number of grievances: southern Creeks never announced the slate of candidates, in some towns they recorded a unanimous ballot on the basis of four or

Annie Grayson. Courtesy of the
Western History Collections, University of Oklahoma Libraries.

five voters, and on occasion they counted the votes of unborn infants.[88] As a
result, he claimed, Checote "was elected by his own party only."[89] Most egregious
was the violation of the rights of ex-slaves. According to the 1866 treaty, he
stated, "the colored citizens of the Creek Nation, were to get the same rights as
others, and they have not got it."[90] Checote's party, he charged, did not consider
ex-slaves to be citizens.[91] A U.S. agent reached the same conclusion. Black
Creeks, he said, "have been ignored in the matter entirely, and are now clamoring
for their rights, as given by said treaty."[92]

In 1869, the two political factions nearly erupted in a civil war, and, according to Oktarsars Harjo, several of his supporters were murdered by Checote's party.[93] The threats of violence intensified in the election year of 1871,
when Oktarsars Harjo and three hundred armed supporters stormed the Council
House and held it for four days, before peacefully ceding the election to Checote.[94] "Whether the result of the Ballot was reached with equity and accuracy
or otherwise," a government investigator noted, "it is evident, a large relative
number of Indians and Freedmen, *believe* they were wronged therein." Checote's
party, he concluded, "should evince a more liberal appreciation of the ability
and fitness of the colored members of their nation to participate in the administration of government."[95]

Their disenfranchisement led ex-slaves and black Creeks to organize a group dedicated partly to political protest and partly to organized crime, reflecting the inextricable ties between politics and economic inequality. Checote accused this "squad of young men" of being horse thieves and sent the light horse and then the cavalry after them. "The so called thieves," said one missionary, "are a set of smart active fellows that had hard masters in the days of slavery and could not be easily controled then." Since the war, he observed, "they consider themselves abused with their government." "Good government and fair treatment," he concluded, would best remedy the situation.[96]

Creek records reveal very little about these dissidents, but two black Creeks who appeared numerous times in court for stealing horses were the "ringleader" Alfred Grayson and his brother Jim, the sons of John Grayson, Katy's first child.[97] John's family must have fallen on hard times, for before the war, John had been relatively well-off. After several difficult years rebuilding their homes, Creeks became desperate in 1874, when a drought and then a plague of grasshoppers destroyed crops around Muskogee. An unusually severe winter followed, and a large number of black Creeks died of starvation, exposure, and pneumonia. Some survived on a diet of roots and tree bark, and crime—now a matter of survival—burgeoned.[98] That winter, Cyrus Herrod, a freedman married to Henderson Grayson's daughter Cilla, was accused of stealing a pocketbook containing forty-five dollars.[99] The following year, Jim Grayson stood trial and was convicted of theft for the third time, punishable by one hundred lashes on the bare back or death. A prolonged whipping could in itself be fatal. Remarkably, a number of Creeks, including Daniel N. McIntosh and several Graysons, petitioned for the pardon of this "poor fellow man."[100] They were apparently successful; two years later, Jim Grayson was again in trouble with the law.[101]

Neither willing to accept black Creeks fully into the nation nor able to expel them, Creek nationalists such as Wash Grayson and his political allies found themselves in a bind. They were unable to resolve the tensions between race and sovereignty. The problem was inherited from the United States, which constructed Indian sovereignty in terms of race.[102] When two Creek freedmen murdered an unidentified Grayson in 1871, the secretary of the interior determined that the culprits were not Indians and should be tried by U.S. and not Creek courts. "It is the *race* to which that proviso refers," he wrote, referring to the Intercourse Act of 1834, "and the prisoners are not of the race of Indians, although they may be members of the Creek tribe, or nation."[103] Principal Chief Sam Checote recognized the potential significance of the case. By accepting that Creek courts had no jurisdiction over black Muscogees, Checote would compromise the sovereignty of the nation, but by rejecting the secretary's decision (thereby embracing them as citizens), he would place the nation's distinctive status as a separate people in jeopardy. The politics of the postwar years demanded that Indians assert their racial distinctiveness or else risk being incorporated into the American republic.[104] Checote opted to defuse the more urgent threat to his nation, the immediate extension of U.S. courts over Creek territory. "We claim full jurisdiction" over black Creeks, Checote therefore asserted.[105] The secretary of the interior initially rejected Checote's position, then reversed himself. Black Creeks cannot be called Indians, he concluded, but they are to be protected by and subject to Creek law, "precisely as if they had been native Creek Indian citizens."[106] This was hardly a victory either for Checote or for black Muscogees.

This strategy of keeping black Creeks at arm's length only served to alienate Muscogees of African descent and to encourage their self-identification as black people and not as Indians. With the founding of black towns such as North Fork Colored, Canadian Colored, and Arkansas Colored after the Civil War, settlement patterns became highly segregated. So, too, did public spaces. In 1872, Wash's own hometown, North Fork, established a separate school for black citizens.[107] A few years later, Afro-Creeks, who once could be observed praying and singing psalms in a party of "Creeks, half-breeds, and negroes," separated from their Creek and white counterparts to create the Freedmen Baptist Association, an indication of the growing distance between Creek citizens.[108] The southern states witnessed a similar process when blacks withdrew from biracial churches in the 1870s.[109]

Inevitably, the alienation of black Creeks grew. In 1879, Turner Duncan, an African Baptist preacher, traveled to Muskogee, Creek Nation, from Dallas, Texas, and began telling black Muscogeans "that they ought to have colored teachers and not Indians and etc. also colored Doctors." His message created "discord and domestic strife" among the "colored citizens," some Creeks reported. Duncan's oratory, one Indian agent noted, "takes hold of the lost sheep of the house of Ham, and brings them to repentence by the dozens and scores."[110]

It is impossible to tell if Emma or Vicey Grayson or one of William and Judah's other children attended Duncan's sermons, but it is certain that they were aware of the growing violence against black Creeks in the Muskogee area. In the 1870s, neighboring Cherokees, who lived only a day's journey from Emma's and Vicey's homesteads in Oktaha, were frequently crossing into the Creek Nation and attacking black residents. The Creek government failed to take notice. In early May 1879, Ed and Cobb Vann and George Lowery, in drunken revelry, shot three black residents in Muskogee. The local paper described the incident in a breezy and humorous blurb.[111] Black Creek John Kernal responded with a petition demanding protection as "citizens of the Muskogee Nation." "As it is now," Kernal wrote, we cannot "go to the Town of Muskogee on business in pursuance of our civil occupation without being shot at, and etc., for no other cause than our color." As the violence escalated, black Creeks from several towns gathered at Pecan Creek, west of Muskogee, "for the purpose of suggesting the best method of uniting our people together and secure a perfect union and live together in accordance to law of Muskogee Nation."[112]

But despite their efforts, their troubles continued. At the end of 1879, Afro-Creeks belonging to the Creek light horse were accused of killing John Vann. Vann was a scion of one of the wealthiest slaveholding families in the Cherokee Nation and a relative of James Vann, who led a campaign in the Cherokee Nation against adopting ex-slaves.[113] After the murder, Afro-Creeks renewed their plea to the National Council. "Our lives are threatened insomuch that we cant stay at home," read one petition, "and we are constantly on guard, as we are likely to be shot down at any moment."[114] Cyrus Herrod, Henderson Grayson's son-in-law, "was forced to leave his home, in Muscogee, from the too frequent attacks upon his house." He "is now living as best he can on the charity of his relations, as he cannot return to his home for fear of being murdered." Ben Barnett fared just as poorly. Cherokees torched his house and then fired through the front door, intending to kill the fleeing residents. Barnett narrowly escaped by leaping through the back window, but his niece was hit twice. "We can bear this no longer," a number of black Creeks declared. "Already four of our people have been killed, and six wounded." Their desperation and growing frustration with the inaction of the Creek government is reflected in a final plea: "*Nothing Done.* 'Tis niggers.' We cry for justice. In one accord: '*Give us Justice.*' "[115]

Yet the violence continued to escalate. An altercation in July 1880 between Afro-Creeks and Cherokees left several people dead on both sides. Two black Creeks, innocent according to a Muscogee judge, were taken into custody by the Cherokees and sentenced to hang.[116] During the trial, Cherokees referred to the accused as "darkeys," "black men," and "niggers." Daniel Lucky, fighting for his life in court, was identified as a "copper colored nigger."[117] The constant reference to skin color undermined his status as a Creek citizen, a point not lost on Afro-Creeks. Their petitions to the Muscogee government frequently empha-sized the citizenship of the accused. A murder victim was "our citizen in the Creek nation"; nine "Creek Citizens" in all were killed. One sentence pointed to the apparent lack of concern shown by Principal Chief Sam Checote. "We Con-sider the Lives of those three men are of vital importance to us and Should also be to you as . . . the Honord and Supreem Ruler of the Muskogee People."[118] Nevertheless, black Creeks recognized that "there is a great deal of prejudice felt against the Colored portion of the Creek Citizens."[119] A lawyer for the Afro-

Creeks would later conclude, "There is hard work a head to save those Boys from the *gallos*."[120] One was later pardoned. The fate of Daniel Lucky is unknown.[121]

The struggle to save the Creek Nation during Reconstruction forced Creeks to make difficult political decisions about how to survive in the age of federal supremacy. The strategy pursued by Wash and other Creek nationalists in some ways resembled the campaign of white southerners to redeem former Confederate states. It was both elitist and racist. Wash and his allies were undoubtedly able to handle the treacherous negotiations with federal officers better than other Indians, but their defense of Muscogee sovereignty came at a price. Its elitism, built on racial and economic hierarchy, alienated poor, uneducated Creeks and disenfranchised those with African ancestry. Wash's nationalism divided Creek communities and made reconciliation increasingly difficult, as would become apparent in the Grayson family in the coming years.

Profile

Buddy Cox, July 1999 and June 2000

"Why black Indians?" Buddy Cox asked when I first told him about my research. Buddy lives in Oklahoma City, where he is a lineman for OGE, the state power company, but his real interest is in improving the lives of the state's Indian citizens. He is the director of the board of the Indian Health Service in Oklahoma City and keeps close tabs on Creek politics and Indian affairs in Washington, D.C. He is also an avid student of the history of the Creek Nation, where his uncle Claude Cox was principal chief in the 1970s. His interest in history coupled with his generosity and warmth led us to strike up a friendship. He has an irrepressible spirit that never ceases to amaze me. Two years after I met him, he sent me an e-mail stating that, at age fifty-one, he had decided to go to Paris for a week. His friends thought he was crazy. He had never before been out of the country, but he went anyhow and now wants to move there.

Shortly after we met, Cox appeared one evening at my room at ExtendedStay America in northwestern Oklahoma City with a stack of books under one arm and a box of Creek documents under the other. We talked until midnight about Creek history. Despite his puzzlement about my interest in black Creeks, he displayed a lenient attitude toward the subject: "We owned some, we were some, and we slept with some," he said about black slaves.

A year later, we were headed to Okmulgee, the Creek capital, where Cox thought he might be able to introduce me to some of the Grayson family. Shortly after we hit the interstate, he casually revealed that there were rumors that his own family has African ancestry, perhaps through the black wife of Abraham Mordecai, an eighteenth-century Jewish deerskin trader to whom Cox is related. In fact, he said, most Creek families have some black ancestry, but no one will talk about it. He explained that this fact became a dirty secret when he was a young man. In 1962, the U.S. government settled a lawsuit by the Creeks seeking payment for lands stolen from them in Alabama and Georgia in 1814. The Court of Claims awarded the Creeks $3,913,000. Each person who could prove that he or she had a relative on one late nineteenth-century census stood to share in the settlement. When the award was finally dispersed in 1972, per capita payments amounted to a mere $112.13. Despite this paltry sum, the settlement precipitated a flurry of genealogical research in Creek country, and Cox said that rumors soon began to fly about families that had uncovered black ancestors. "Did you hear who's *estelusti?*" Creeks asked their neighbors, using the Muscogee expression for "black man." The embarrassing revelations became so frequent that Creeks soon began to joke about the subject. They rushed up to friends and, as if they possessed a choice piece of gossip, asked with excitement, "Did you hear who's *not estelusti?*"

Somewhere on I-40 between Oklahoma City and the Okmulgee exit, Cox dropped the subject of his black ancestry, and I did not pursue it any further. After reaching the Creek capital, our first stop was the site of Cox's childhood home. In the Creek tradition, several small log houses belonging to different families once stood around a central square. New Hope Church sat at one end. Children had once played together all day in the square, interrupted only by occasional requests from family matriarchs to fetch water at the well. His family had nothing, Cox recalled. Cox's father was a laborer, frequently away at work, and when home, drunk. One of his aunts recalled that Cox, as a young child, wore tattered, dirty clothes. He often went without food, and Cox even remembers eating ashes mixed with water to stave off his hunger. Despite the deprivation, Cox recalled with some wistfulness the old Creek community, now long vanished. Everyone spoke Creek, and they gathered around the fire each evening to share stories. The church still stands, but nothing remains of the houses and the busy talk of this once active community.

We moved on to the tribal headquarters, where we met an officer in the government of the Creek Nation. While I looked over some files, Cox examined a turn-of-the-century photograph of the Creek council house. As he peered at the blurry figures standing before the building, the officer joined him. "They all look *lusti*, don't they?" she asked under her breath. "Thank god for Claude slipping that constitution past." Claude Cox, Buddy's uncle, had overseen the passage of a new Creek constitution in 1979, still in effect today, that disenfranchised the descendants of Creek slaves.

At lunchtime, we joined the officer at a sandwich place in central Okmulgee. We talked about black Creeks, and Cox, who is known around the nation for his independent opinions, warmed to the task at hand. He said in Creek, "I'm *estelusti*." Cox had broken a taboo, and the officer responded in kind. "My family is part black, too," she said in English. "But I don't show it, do I?" she asked, presenting her profile in both jest and anxiety. I listened as they joked lightly

Buddy Cox standing at the site of his family's home in 1867, now New Town Cemetery, in Okmulgee, Oklahoma, June 2002. Photograph by the author.

about the subject. After lunch, we stood before the restaurant saying good-bye,
and the subject again turned to the *estelusti*. "A number of Creeks have black
blood, not just the Graysons," the officer observed. "Don't we all?" asked Cox.
"Not me" were her last words to us before she turned down the street and walked
away.

In the evening, we visited Cox's father-in-law, Robert, in his cluttered three-
room house in Okmulgee. Robert was ensconced in a Lazyboy recliner watching
The Undefeated on TV, starring John Wayne and Rock Hudson. When Robert
learned of my interest in black Creeks, he joked that I should talk to Buddy, an
expert on the subject. Throughout the evening, Robert and Buddy laughed about
Buddy's rumored black ancestry. Buddy said he wanted a *"lusti* card" attesting
to his black blood, just as the Certification of Degree of Indian Blood (CDIB)
card, issued by the Department of Indian Affairs, attests to a holder's Native
American ancestry. Robert replied that Buddy liked his soul food. Buddy said
he liked black women, too.

The jokes and ribbing, along with the Creek officer's private revelation and
then public denial of her African ancestry, reveal that even today, Creeks self-

consciously maneuver in the white racial hierarchy. In public, they maintain a distance from their black relatives. This stance is a matter of survival. In private, however, they admit that they are all related, and few people seem overly concerned about the matter. One thing did puzzle me, however. Robert seemed to be making much of Buddy's black heritage, although there appeared to be only circumstantial evidence of his African ancestry dating from the late 1700s. There was more to the story, as I would soon discover.

7

Hardship and Opportunity:
The Fortunes of Emma, Vicey, and Wash

By several measures, southern Muscogees did remarkably well overseeing the reconstruction of their nation. In 1865, the Creek Nation was depopulated. Few houses remained standing, most fields were choked with weeds and bushes, and nearly all the livestock had been driven off or slaughtered. The refugees who returned in 1865 were penniless and starving.[1] By the 1880s, new homes, surrounded by well-kept cornfields, filled the land, and cattle once again grazed in the pastures. In 1886, the commissioner of Indian affairs described one Creek estate that he had visited. It contained one thousand acres under fence and featured a "costly residence," as well as several "large commodious" barns and stables. It produced twenty-five thousand bushels of corn and "large quantities" of hay, and every year it sent two hundred head of cattle and three hundred head of hogs to market.[2] Even humble residences showed a vast improvement since the devastation of the Civil War. One Creek who died in 1888 left behind a three-room cabin, forty acres under cultivation, a stable, a small fruit orchard, five head of cattle, and twenty-two pigs.[3] He was by no means well-off, but neither was he desperate.

Yet reconstruction had its costs as well as its benefits, and they were not shared equally by Creek citizens. White observers liked to charge that the Indian nations, rife with corruption, were like baronial fiefs, in the "grasping hands of moneyed monopolists and powerful and influential leaders and politicians."[4] Their newfound interest in social justice was nurtured by the desire to dismantle the Five Tribes and open their lands to capitalist exploitation. The height of hypocrisy must have been Grover Cleveland's 1896 meeting with Muscogee delegates, at which he expressed his concern for monopolies and "inequalities of property-holding" in the Creek Nation. This belated concern by the president who had ordered U.S. troops to crush the Pullman strike of 1894 seems misplaced.[5]

If Indian Territory was not the despotic place imagined by whites, however, neither was it the land of close-knit communities and families that so many Indians remembered from before the war. The thousand-acre estate visited by the commissioner of Indian affairs in 1886 might very well have been Wash's residence, since Wash and his brother Sam would have more than sixteen hundred acres under fence in 1891.[6] "The proprietor grows annually richer," the commissioner wrote of his unnamed Creek host, "while the laborers, his own race, joint owners of the soil, even of the lands that he claims and individually appropriates, grow annually and daily poorer and less able to assert their equal ownership and tribal claim."[7] The commissioner's assessment of matters was overly crude and certainly motivated by his desire to dismantle the Muscogee Nation. Yet the fractures within Creek communities and families were widening. White Creeks, as they deemed themselves, were rising, and their darker-skinned cousins were falling. While Wash found opportunity in the reconstructed Creek Nation, Emma and Vicey found hardship.

The early eighties marked a time of growing social stratification within the Grayson family and the Creek Nation. A drought in the summer of 1881 pushed Muscogee farmers to the brink of starvation. Few had either corn or beef to help them through the winter, and one observer wondered aloud how most managed to survive.[8] When the wet winter receded in early March 1882 and the muddy, impassable roads dried, Creeks began clearing fields for their early crops, but some were too famished to undertake the labor.[9] Compounding the problem was smallpox, which spread through the weakened population and took its toll especially on poor black settlements.[10]

Wash Grayson must have fared better than his cousins Emma and Vicey. In 1874, he and his brother Sam had opened a general merchandise store in Eufaula with Edmond Grayson, the son of Uncle Watt. Watt put up the capital, and Wash and Sam provided the know-how. Watt died the next year, and Edmond was killed by a gunshot to the head in 1878, leaving the business in the hands of the Grayson brothers.[11] Selling farm equipment, "Traveler's supplies, Prints, Hosiery, Boots, Shoes, Hats, Caps and all the etceteras requisite to a First Class Western business House," Grayson Brothers Mercantile Store grew quickly.[12] In 1877, Wash and Sam purchased a cotton gin, and three years later, they replaced the mules turning the gin with a new twenty-horsepower engine.[13]

Grayson Brothers Mercantile in Eufaula, Oklahoma. Courtesy of the Western History Collections, University of Oklahoma Libraries.

At the same time, they began adopting advanced farm equipment then spreading through the region: expensive but efficient reapers, mowers, seeders, and cultivators.[14] Wash and Sam also took advantage of new opportunities offered by the Missouri, Kansas, and Texas Railroad.[15] Connecting the Creek Nation to St. Louis and Kansas City, the Katy Railroad, as it was known, made the export of cattle and cotton profitable. When railroad engineers decided to place a depot in North Fork Town (not to be confused with North Fork Colored), populated largely by "full-bloods" and black Creeks, Wash, Sam, and several other leading citizens in the area reportedly bribed the manager of the railroad with one thousand dollars to relocate the site several miles west, where their farms and stores were situated. The depot, completed in 1872, became known as Eufaula.[16] Eufaula "is destined to be *the city* of the Territory," remarked one missionary in 1878. "It is a station on the M.K.T.RR, and is the center of a considerable trade, which is increasing every year."[17]

If, from the perspective of Wash, the country looked like it was headed in the right direction, many Creeks were not so sure. Isparhecher carried on the protest tradition of Opothleyahola and Oktarsars Harjo. He and his allies—disaffected Muscogees and black Indians—refused to resign themselves to Sam

Checote's administration, and they increasingly operated as a shadow government. In July 1882, a minor exchange between Isparhecher's men and Checote's police force turned into a larger conflict when Checote called up more than one thousand men to put down the opposition. Several skirmishes occurred before the violence dissipated.[18] Checote offered a general amnesty, and Creeks looked forward to settling the matter by the ballot box.[19]

Yet the election in the fall of 1883 only further divided the nation. Isparhecher ran on a platform that promised to enfranchise everyone who married into the nation, "irrespective of race or color." The chairman of the committee that drafted these words was one Robert Grayson, either a descendant of a Grayson slave or the grandson of William and Judah.[20] The popular vote appeared to put Isparhecher in the Creek council house ahead of Joseph M. Perryman and Sam Checote, but with Wash Grayson's public support, an election committee, headed by Wash's father-in-law, G. W. Stidham, threw out the votes of Arkansas Colored Town and two others, swinging the results from a 37-vote victory over Joseph M. Perryman to a 155-vote defeat.[21] One observer witnessed the debate raging in the Creek council house in Okmulgee: "The heated discussions carried on by the Indians and negroes—there were almost as many negro as Indian members in the house of warriors—were immensely interesting."[22] When the newly elected warriors took office, they reversed the results once again, making Isparhecher principal chief.[23]

The dispute taught Creeks a "useful lesson," Isparhecher told the council: "every Muskogee citizen, whether his skin be red, white or black, has equal rights and privileges in this nation; and the most abject, poor and ignorant is entitled to equal consideration with the most distinguished, rich and learned at the hands of our officers."[24]

Not all saw the lesson so clearly, as was evident in the Grayson family. Wash described the election as one between the "soldiers of the South" and the adherents of the North, although he admitted that affairs had become "somewhat mixed" when politicians began making "strange compromises."[25] Twenty-two Graysons voted for Isparhecher, the majority of them living in North Fork Colored Town, a few miles east of Wash's residence in Eufaula. Four Graysons from Hilabi voted for the southern stalwart Sam Checote. Clearly, race, privilege and political position were strongly correlated. Only Burney Grayson of Okfuskee (parents unknown) and Emma's son Eli voted for Perryman.[26] Perryman was a southern Creek but not as objectionable to disaffected Muscogees as was Checote. In Canadian Colored Town, for example, Perryman garnered seventy votes, Isparhechar seventy-five, and Checote zero.[27]

In January 1884, Wash Grayson became personally involved in the election dispute. He, Sam Checote, and Isparhecher, accompanied by two other Creeks, boarded a train for Washington, D.C., where the secretary of the interior intended to settle the controversy. The train ride must have been tense. Checote, making one of the "strange compromises" described by Wash, had thrown his support for Isparhecher. Wash, originally a Checote supporter, was now working on behalf of the Creek Council for Perryman. Only a few months earlier, he had publicly declared Isparhecher an "agitator and malcontent." Isparhecher's supporters, he asserted, were "largely an aggregation of horse thieves and other violators of law, and hence opposed to all order and progress."[28]

Once in Washington, the delegates began jockeying for favor. Wash feared that the secretary, under the impression that Perryman was educated and had the appearance of a white man, might favor Isparhecher. U.S. officials frequently charged what they called "mixed-blood" Indians with abusing their power and misleading the "full-bloods." Wash therefore wired Perryman, who in fact was "very dark complexioned" and a man of "limited education," to come to Washington at once.[29] Perryman's appearance would disabuse the secretary of his misperceptions, which were probably reinforced by Wash's own appearance and comportment. According to a white man who met him in Washington, Wash Grayson was "an Indian with only a few drops of Indian blood."[30]

The secretary of the interior did indeed eventually decide in favor of Perryman, but Isparhecher suspected that it was the light skin of Grayson and others that got Perryman the job, not Perryman's dark complexion. Isparhecher charged that the Bureau of Indian Affairs (BIA) report on the election was "full of abuse to myself and friends—criticising the complexion of our skin, but extolling Mr. Perryman and his friends in the most complimentary terms." Though he chose to abide by the decision and suggested that he held no animosity toward his political opponents, he singled out Wash for condemnation. Grayson, he charged, told the secretary that the Indian Office had been "too lenient" toward Isparhecher and his allies. It should be "more rigid and prompt," he recalled Wash saying. "The plain English of this language," concluded Isparhecher, "is, 'put the lash to my people and let them learn they have a master.' "[31]

The political divide between the Graysons, one defined by race and privilege, had a counterpart in the courts. In the postwar years, the Graysons ran into a series of legal difficulties. Wash, the respected politician, was accused of embezzlement and fraud, and his relatives, living on the margins, of theft and murder. For Emma, Vicey, and their families, their legal problems began one afternoon in mid-June 1879, when E. L. Kellam's dog picked up a bone along the bank of Butler Creek, about three hundred yards from Emma's house (located on old Highway 69, five miles southwest of Muskogee). Kellam looked closer and saw that the bone was human. Farther down the bank, he found a boot, standing upright next to a pile of muddy clothes. A skull sat at some distance from a spine; other bones, a hip, lower jaw, and femur, lay scattered about. Emma's neighbor Edmund Fleetwood believed he knew whose body it was. A German immigrant had passed through the area in March, stopping for three days at Fleetwood's house. Emma had made a contract with him: ten dollars for a month's worth of labor on her farm. The immigrant worked for ten days and then disappeared.

Soon after Kellam's gruesome discovery, Emma's daughter Jeanetta, along with Tacky Grayson, whose mother had been a slave of Wash's, were charged with murder in the federal court of the western district of Arkansas.[32] (The victim was a white man, and therefore U.S. courts had jurisdiction.) On February 8, 1880, they were arrested and held in jail in Fort Smith until the hearing, nine days later. Emma and Jeanetta, but not Tacky, were put on trial. Could the immigrant merely have drowned and his bones washed high up on the riverbank? "The creek frequently gets up very high," testified Kellam, although he added that one five-year resident had never heard of anyone drowning in it. Fleetwood stated that at the time of the immigrant's disappearance, Butler Creek was low. About ten days before the discovery of the skeleton, it had risen, but not as high as the skull's final resting place, atop a hill alongside the river. Fleetwood provided a motive. Two of his horses had been stolen, and the immigrant, "from the way he acted," had seemed to suggest that he wanted to tell Fleetwood something about the theft. Fleetwood tried to talk to him on April 4, but could not do so in private. The next morning he went to Emma's and was told that the immigrant had departed without warning. Emma claimed that the immigrant had "gone down the railroad."

Fleetwood's testimony was tainted. He admitted that he and Emma had "quarrelled" several times, though at present they were "so far as I know friendly." In fact, either shortly before or after the trial, twenty-four of Fleetwood's neighbors, including Emma's son Eli and her nephews Seaborn and Robert, sent a complaint to Principal Chief Sam Checote demanding Fleetwood's "immediate removal." Fleetwood, who was not a Creek citizen, was causing "a great deal of trouble," they stated. The verdict: Emma and Jeanetta were not guilty.[33]

Guilty or not, Emma Grayson and her family were vulnerable in a way that Wash was not. Both she and Wash faced intrusive and aggressive white invaders, and both could fall victim to the prejudice of an all-white jury in the federal court in Fort Smith. Yet Wash's education and material wealth granted him a degree of protection and privilege. Emma and her close relatives, by contrast, lived closer to the margins. They were more likely to come under the purview of the courts and less likely to be able to defend themselves. Between 1870 and 1885, Tacky was indicted three times, for murder, assault, and selling tobacco without a license. Emma's son Eli was indicted for larceny. Also indicted were her son Adam Brady (twice for bootlegging and once for theft); nephew Seaborn (larceny); niece Cilla (bootlegging); niece's husband Cyrus Herrod (bootlegging); and cousin Jim Grayson, Katy's grandson by her black husband John (theft).[34] These were the crimes of people living on the margins of the economy. Even Emma's accused murder might be so interpreted. Emma, a single woman in need of assistance on her farm, contracted with a drifter.

At least two other murders touched the Grayson family. Jim Hutton (also known as Jim Grayson), the son of Robert Grierson's slaves Jim and Venus, shot dead John May, a black man from the states. "God Damn the Indian Nation and the Indian niggers," May was overheard to say, after he and Hutton had argued. May purchased a six-shooter and followed Hutton out of town. When he found Hutton, Hutton shot him in the mouth, and the bullet lodged in the back of May's neck. Hutton was found not guilty.[35] The nature of the dispute remains a mystery, but Jim's identity as an "Indian nigger" seems to have played some role in the altercation.

Then, in February 1883, Mitchell Grayson, Jeanetta's husband and Emma's son-in-law, shot his brother Josh. Mitchell was tried for murder and acquitted. No record sheds light on the motive for the shooting, but whatever its source, the tensions between Mitchell and Josh must have been aggravated by their constant struggle to make ends meet. Mitchell's reputation as a horse thief was "*well known*," said one witness, and in fact, three years later, Eli Grayson, Emma's son, would post a bond worth $183, the total value of his possessions, to secure his brother-in-law's release from prison, this time for larceny.[36] As bootleggers and horse rustlers, these men must have regularly carried guns. With an eye toward reducing accidental shootings, the Muskogee *Indian Journal* frequently published editorials urging its readers to leave their firearms at home. Moreover, difficult economic conditions might lead anyone to commit desperate or foolish acts. When Wash and Sam faced a mountain of debt years later, Wash would confess that he felt driven to drink or even to kill himself. He resisted both temptations, but Sam took to the bottle and was often drunk for days on end.[37]

Wash and Sam faced neither economic marginalization nor political alienation, but they too became tangled in the Creek courts. Their problems started in 1880, when Wash was accused in the Muskogee newspaper of embezzling money from the national treasury.[38] The charge was never made in court, but suspicions continued to linger that Wash was taking advantage of his privileged position in the Creek Nation. Two years later, both Wash and Sam were called before the Creek Supreme Court when a number of Uncle Watt's descendants sued them for control of Grayson Brothers Mercantile. After Watt and his son Edmond died, Wash and Sam had simply assumed possession of the enterprise—illegally, according to the plaintiffs, who claimed to be the rightful heirs.[39] There is no record of the court's decision, but since Wash and Sam continued to run the store long after the suit, it is clear that they either won the case or settled out of court.

Suspicions about Wash Grayson's probity would not die. In 1890, he was again suspected of embezzlement during an official trip to Washington. Some Muscogees feared that he intended to skim 25 percent ("fees") off of a $400,000 payment due from the United States to the Creek Nation. Creeks suspected that Wash and his fellow delegate Roley McIntosh "might do something that is contrary to the will of the people," wrote one Muscogee. "All the confidence of people are lost in those two men."[40] Whether or not Wash intended to claim 25 percent in fees, he would profit from the government payment. Faced with a food shortage in 1890, poor and destitute Creeks had traded with local businessmen on credit, and these merchants stood to collect their debts when the payment was distributed. In 1891, Addie Grayson (possibly William and Judah's granddaughter) wrote a note to the treasurer of the Creek Nation. There is no better illustration of the contrasting economic positions occupied by the Graysons. She requested that her per capita payment of twenty-nine dollars be turned over directly to Grayson Brothers Mercantile. "I run short of means and the above firm accomodated me for the full amt in mdsc [merchandise]," she wrote.[41]

Like so many public men in the late nineteenth century, Wash lobbied government perhaps too actively, and he was suspected, rightly or wrongly, of crossing the indistinct line separating political engagement and personal enrichment. The other side of the family pursued its interests by theft and liquor running, measures commonly adopted by the poor and disaffected. Wash would later characterize William and Judah's children as "the most humble and withal rather worthless citizens," but he merely reflected his own class biases. "I know little more about these people," he admitted, "as we have never met them on full social equality."[42] A more accurate assessment would recognize that from opposite ends of the social spectrum, all the Graysons, rich and poor, used the tools available to them to survive. Sometimes they skirted the bounds of propriety; in desperation and on rare occasions, they committed acts of violence.

The Swift-Chase refrigerated railcar would seem an unlikely candidate to spark a confrontation between the Graysons, but it did just that by allowing for the efficient transportation of butchered beef from the West to eastern cities.

After the Civil War, cattle ranching boomed in the United States in response to the needs of rapidly growing urban areas. Books such as Joseph McCoy's *Historic Sketches of the Cattle Trade of the West and Southwest* (1874) and James Brisbin's *Beef Bonanza; or, How to Get Rich on the Plains* (1881) popularized stories of self-made millionaires, and investors rushed to get a piece of the action. Like other parts of the West, Indian Territory experienced a rapid growth in its herds. Between 1860 and 1880, the number of cattle in Indian Territory climbed from one hundred thousand to five hundred thousand.[43]

There was a logjam in the industry that limited growth and profits, however. Butchered beef could only be shipped in refrigerated cars, and before 1879, cuts of beef lay for days directly on blocks of ice, leaving meats partially decomposed and unappetizingly discolored. Cattle were therefore shipped live in small lots to butchers scattered around the country. The process was costly, for 60 percent of a live animal was waste product, meaning that most of the tonnage shipped on railroads never reached market. In 1879, the Swift-Chase car revolutionized the industry by permitting butchered meat to be shipped profitably and efficiently across the country. At the same time, the total mileage of railroad track increased significantly. In 1865, the United States had 35,000 miles of track. By 1880, that number had grown to 93,000 miles, and in 1900, it reached 193,000 miles.[44] Some of those tracks crossed the Creek Nation, where the Katy Railroad gave Muscogees access to markets in St. Louis and Kansas City.

In the 1880s, Creeks who looked to improve their lot therefore turned to livestock. Because land was still free for the taking—one needed only build a fence to lay claim to thousands of acres—ranching looked immensely profitable. In the early 1870s, Emma Grayson and her immediate relatives and Wash and his brother Sam each owned only a few dozen cattle.[45] They stood to make a great deal of money if they could expand their herds.

In this enterprise, Wash and Sam had two significant advantages over their relatives. First, they were both educated, giving them the skills to operate successfully in the market and to fulfill broad ambitions that were beyond the realistic expectations of Emma and her children.[46] Equally important to the success of Wash and Sam was their close relationship with Uncle Watt, one of the wealthiest men in the Creek Nation. He was among the largest stock raisers in Indian Territory and every year branded several hundred new calves. Watt provided the capital to allow his nephews to enter cattle ranching on a large scale.[47]

By contrast, Emma and her relatives lacked education and therefore the skills to balance books and read contracts. They also lacked capital. Unable to purchase new stock, they could not market their small numbers of cattle profitably. Instead, they were forced to trade their surplus cattle to merchants such as

Grayson Brothers Mercantile in exchange for store goods. These merchants pooled cattle from different farmers until they had a number sufficient for the market.[48] The cash profit went to the merchant. Small-scale farmers earned only clothing, sugar, coffee, agricultural tools, and other necessities.

Limited capital not only squeezed profits, but at times of scarcity, when poor Indians suffered disproportionately, it made it difficult to sustain any kind of ranching operation at all. In the mid-1870s, during a lengthy drought and insect infestation, many Creeks were forced to sell their breeding stock in order to survive.[49] In the early 1880s and again in 1886–1887, they faced the same situation.[50] The winter of 1886–1887 proved particularly devastating to ranchers all across middle America. Heavy snowfall in November followed by a severe storm in January dropped temperatures to fifteen below zero as far south as the Texas panhandle. In what was known as the "big die-up," tens of thousands of cattle froze to death, five times what might have been expected in an average winter.[51] When crop failure followed in the summer of 1887, subsistence farmers such as Emma and Vicey were forced to slaughter or sell the few cattle remaining in their herds.

The result of these relative advantages and disadvantages is that, between the 1870s and the end of the century, Emma and her relatives do not appear to have increased their stock.[52] By the mid-1870s, in contrast, Wash and Sam were already shipping cattle on the Katy Railroad to St. Louis. They eventually formed ranching partnerships with G. W. Stidham, Joseph M. Perryman, and Hugh Henry.[53] By 1891, Wash and Sam had $18,000 in equity in four thousand head of cattle.[54]

The successful cattle operation of Wash and Sam might not have troubled their cousins living near Oktaha, but for two qualities of ranching: it demanded an enormous amount of land, and the immense numbers of cattle devoured pasture used by the livestock of local, small-scale ranchers. Cattle could only be contained by miles of sturdy fences. Barbed wire was scarce, and to split the rails needed for a single square-acre fence, one man would have to labor for forty-eight days. He was then only half done, for he still had to transport the rails from the forest, distribute them along the line, and erect the enclosure.[55] Even then, fences were no guarantee of safety. One resident of Indian Territory recalled witnessing a stampede of ten thousand cattle. The herd trampled fences and destroyed three houses.[56] "Lots of us have no stock of any kind such as horses, cattle, hogs," stated one Creek, "but do have some children that we were afraid might be killed."[57]

In the 1880s, pastures began to assume enormous proportions. Often Creeks acted merely as frontmen for American ranchers who wished to fatten their cattle on Creek land. Huge amounts of capital, some of it coming from overseas, were invested in the industry. At one point, Standard Oil even entered the business, running twenty thousand head of cattle in the Cherokee Outlet, a strip of land owned by the Cherokee Nation.[58]

The eastern part of the Creek Nation was particularly appealing to ranchers. Not only was it lush and verdant, but the Katy Railroad passed through it, allowing easy access to eastern cattle markets. In addition, it was populated by poor, often black, Creeks, making the appropriation of lands all the easier.

Ranchers such as H. B. Spaulding, a white man married to a Creek woman, clearly took advantage of the vulnerability of these people. In early 1890, he filed suit against Mollie Grayson, Tacky's cousin, for encroaching on the passway around his pasture. Mollie claimed to have fenced off her small plot first. She and her husband had cleared the land "when no one had ever thought of fencing it." Mollie foresaw the difficulty of her position. Once before, she protested, her citizenship had been challenged:

> I can prove that I am a Citizen of this Nation myself if Tackey Grayson is a Citizen I am I think and if old aunt Jennie Grayson was citizen I think that I am Because that is my grand mother also Tackey Grandma if the truth was told I presume that you will find Mrs. Spaulvin a Citizen of the United States her self.[59]

The resolution of this particular case is unknown, but Spaulding continued to cause trouble for the area's black residents. Five months after Mollie defended herself, H. C. Reed, a leading Afro-Creek, penned a letter of protest to the district judge about Spaulding's ranching practices.[60] Two years later, the Creek Nation would finally take Spaulding to court.[61]

Vicey Grayson, William and Judah's daughter, faced similar problems. "Parties is about to fenceing my place and public roads in leading to muskogee," she complained in 1892, offering to feed any officer sent down to investigate.[62] Her neighbor Nannie Grayson, widow of Seaborn (William and Judah's grandson) and herself the daughter of a Grayson slave, also penned an appeal to the district judge: "I have bin on this place 5 years and now Willis Yarsar is finceing me in Pleas tell me what to do."[63] The problem, as Judge E. H. Lerblance explained it, was that one of the guilty parties was William F. McIntosh, the chief justice of the Creek Nation, who was building a pasture of three square miles near Oktaha, near where Emma and her relatives lived.[64] "I think a person who seems to think so little of his oath would not be likely to treat a little District judges orders with any great deal of respect," Lerblance wrote to the principal chief.[65]

In 1893, in partnership with G. W. Stidham, Wash and Sam filed for their own pasture on the southern border of the Creek Nation.[66] A year later, they filed for two more pastures that totaled sixteen thousand acres, or twenty-five square miles.[67] By 1896, Wash would have sixty-four thousand acres, or one hundred square miles, under pasture.[68] The cattle industry affected all the Graysons, but in profoundly different ways. For some it was a boon to business; for others it was a threat to their livelihood and even to their lives.

With regard to William and Judah's family, it is evident that women predominated in both the Graysons' run-ins with the law and their relationship to the cattle industry. They posted bond, ran liquor, and, perhaps, murdered. They farmed, owned cattle, and wrote letters of protest to Creek officials when ranchers intruded on their property. By contrast, despite the prominence of members of the other side of the family and despite their formal education, not a single letter exists in the archives of the Creek Nation from any of the women. In 1914, when Annie, Wash's wife, wrote an article for the Eufaula *Indian Journal*, she published under the name of Mrs. G. W. Grayson.[69] Wash, and Sam ruled the family.

In the eighteenth century, Creeks lived in family groups that reflected older traditions, especially matrilineality and matrilocality. In other words, they traced their lineage through their mother, and men moved into the households of their wives rather than the other way around. By the end of the 1700s, some Creeks had begun forming patriarchal, nuclear families, but the structure of the family, the basic building block of society, is slow to change.[70] This gradual transformation is difficult to trace, although it can be followed to some degree by examining naming practices. In the Grayson family, contrary to matrilineal custom, all of patriarch Robert's children used his surname. At the time, however, few Creeks had last names, and it was not uncommon for children to take the surname of their European father and at the same time identify with their mother's clan, the most important marker of Creek identity.[71]

The second generation of Graysons followed both matrilineal and patrilineal customs. All of Robert's sons passed their surname on to their children, even in cases where their wives had surnames of their own. At marriage, his daughter Sarah probably took the Hawkins name from her husband, and Sarah's children took the name of their father.[72] Katy, however, kept the Grayson name and passed it on to her children. If there was still some commitment to matrilineal naming practices, it disappeared by the next generation. All of Katy's daughters from her second marriage used the surnames of their husbands: Carr, Blackburn, and McAnally.

In Wash and Sam's family, patrilineal practices also predominated. As children, they took the Grayson surname rather than their mother's name, Wynne.

Their sister Louisa, following the custom of American citizens, took the name of her husband, Charles Smith.[73] All of Wash's children followed patrilineal naming practices. Matrilineality had not been entirely extinguished, for Wash identified with his mother's clan and town. Yet the power and position of women were clearly changing. In his private diaries, Wash referred to his wife as "Mrs. Grayson," subsuming her name under his own.[74]

Among William and Judah's descendants, there was also a trend toward patrilineal naming practices, but it was slower and less consistent. All of William and Judah's children, male and female, kept the Grayson name, even after marriage, although Vicey occasionally used her husband's name, Witherspoon. Emma passed on the Grayson name to all but one of her children. Her sister Judy passed on the surname to one of her two children. By the next generation, however, matrilineal naming practices disappeared altogether.

The choice of a name is suggestive, but more informative are the many public documents where William and Judah's female descendants sued, posted bond, and petitioned. It is clear from these records that women headed their households.[75] In fact, by comparison to Wash's neighborhood in Eufaula, where the leading citizens were all men, the area around Oktaha and Summit appears to have been run largely by women. When Emma needed help on the farm, she hired an itinerant laborer (and perhaps later killed him).[76] When she felt she had been cheated out of a ten-acre farm, Emma went to court, and her sister Vicey put up a bond to pay for the appearance of witnesses.[77] When it came time to file with the BIA for title to her land, she herself went down to meet with government officials.[78]

In running their households, Emma and Vicey could draw not only on Creek traditions, in which women ran the household, but also on the heritage of their mother, Judah. Most slave families in the United States were matrifocal, meaning that women supervised households where the father was either absent or only occasionally present. Matrifocality was not solely a response to the conditions of slavery, for most families in precolonial western Africa were also matrifocal.[79]

On the occasions when the Grayson women revealed something personal about themselves in their letters, the tone reflects hardship and resilience. "I work very hard for what I get," wrote Mollie Grayson, Tacky's cousin, "and I gets it by the sweat of my eye Brow Because old saying says by the sweat of they eye Brow thy shall eat Bread and a poor woman the only way I make my living."[80] Julia, William and Judah's granddaughter, seemed equally insistent on her rights and confident of her authority. When she was accused of letting her cattle eat a neighbor's crops, she wrote to the district judge, "If the cattle ate up the hay it was because they fence around it was no account." She offered to

A Creek freedwoman standing with a child before her home in the late nineteenth century. *Annual Report of the United States Indian Inspector for the Indian Territory, 1899* (Washington, DC: Government Printing Office, 1899), opposite 106.

produce witnesses. As for Aunt Emma's cattle, "I do not know anything about," she wrote, for "they never botherd me any."[81] Yet Nannie Grayson, William and Judah's granddaughter-in-law, revealed just how difficult it was for women to survive as subsistence farmers. "I am a widow and no bodey to help me," she wrote, when her neighbor fenced her inside a cattle pasture. "I have in a small farm so dear sir please let me know what to do."[82]

If the women on Wash's side of the family remained silent, photographs nevertheless reveal that their lives were markedly different from those of William and Judah's female descendants. A portrait of his family, taken around 1884, shows Annie and her children, dressed in their best clothes. The girls and their mother wear stylish hats, and Annie carries a pocket watch, as she did in her 1866 photograph. The most striking feature of the photograph is its subject. This portrait of a mother and her children seems unremarkable, yet it reflects the values of the American middle class. The photograph presents Annie solely as a mother, thereby suggesting that she had the leisure to lavish attention on her children in the way that white Americans idealized in the nineteenth century.[83] Emma and Vicey, by contrast, were unlikely to identify with the composition of the photograph. They were as much ranchers and farmers as mothers.

The travails of the women of Oktaha and Summit are nowhere better represented than by the case of Bettie Chambers, Emma and Vicey's neighbor. Bettie was married to William Chambers for fourteen years, and by her account, the union brought her nothing but trouble. William never worked—he "dont do anything for his children," she charged—and then he ran off, leaving Bettie and her four children in a decrepit, rotting log house. "Buy god," Bettie quoted her husband, "if this one fall on you I dont give a dam I never will make a house for you buy god if you want it have it done yourself." So she went to work, purchasing lumber, sealing, nails, and boards, and hiring a man to finish it for her. The "children will have to have some place to live if they live," she wrote, sadly acknowledging the likelihood of one of her children dying before she did. After finishing the house, Bettie repaired the fence around her farm. "I have to work so hard to keep up my place," she lamented.

When William returned, Bettie's troubles only mounted. According to her accusations, he ordered her out of the house so he could sell it; when she refused, he tore down her fences, allowing hogs to enter her fields and consume the crops that fed her and her children. Then he threatened to kill her. "I want to left a home for my children when I dies," Bettie wrote; William "never did work for the advantage for me he work to keep me down all the time." She asked for a divorce.[84] He refused. If "the people would let her a lone we would never part or have any trouble," he claimed.[85]

William admitted that he carried a pistol, but he insisted, "i dont mean to heart noboddy with it."[86] He may have been sincere in his professions, but Bettie had reason to fear, for acts of domestic violence were common in the Creek Nation. Sharper Grayson, a former slave of the Graysons, shot and injured his wife after she overcooked some meat. "He told me that I must say I did it myself to keep from going to court," his wife testified, "and I did say so because I loved him and had a child by him and did not want to see him punished."[87] Molly Grayson was shot to death by her husband when he accused her of being "too intimate" with other men.[88] Billy Island raped his fourteen-year-old stepdaughter, and the young girl became pregnant.[89] Sunny Grayson, a former slave of the Graysons, raped his mother-in-law, an "old Ladie" named Vicey Morrison.[90]

Two qualities of the women-headed families of Oktaha stand out: the depth of poverty and the frequency of violence. In the present-day United States, the correlation between poverty and households headed by women is easily explained. Women earn lower wages for comparable work, and they make up a disproportionate share of the unskilled workforce. In the Creek Nation in the late nineteenth century, the poverty of women-headed households had a different source. All Creek families had once been headed by women. When white colonists began stealing Creek lands in the eighteenth century, nearly every family struggled, and the few that thrived actively adopted the economic practices of their antagonists. Economic organization is inseparably linked to other facets of life, including politics and family structure. The colonial economy was premised on the organization of society into patriarchal, nuclear families, and the more closely Creeks conformed to this model of social organization, the better they fared economically.[91] The result was that by the mid–nineteenth century, Creek families that were organized along more traditional lines lived in poverty; patriarchal families, by contrast, were better off. Emma's and Vicey's families were poor because they were normal, and Wash's and Sam's families were prosperous because they were anomalous. If white reformers and some Creek politicians would later blame women-headed households for their poverty, they were politicizing a complex historical transformation.

The violence seemingly prevalent in the families of Oktaha also had complex causes. It is tempting to attribute wayward fathers and spousal abuse to a kind of pathology, but there are other explanations, rooted in the daily lives of Emma and Vicey. The men in their families did not have steady work, and it was advantageous and even necessary for them to seek opportunities whenever and wherever they arose. For Wash and Sam, by contrast, opportunities rested at home, where they were deeply invested in the success of Grayson Brothers Mercantile. Employment practices may explain the frequency of absent men, but they do not explain the seeming prevalence of spousal abuse in the families of Vicey and Emma, an offense nowhere charged to the patriarchs of the Grayson family. Yet this difference may be more apparent than real. Strong women were more likely to report abusive husbands to the courts, whereas women living in patriarchal households were more likely to suffer the abuse silently.

When women in patriarchal households did seek assistance, they did so from male relatives who had the power to help them. May, Sam Grayson's wife, for instance, sought help from Wash in 1906, when her husband's drinking became unbearable. She threatened to leave Sam, an unusually bold move that reflected the seriousness of the situation. Wash was sympathetic but advised her to "bear longer with him."[92] Her complaint never made it into the public records and exists only in Wash's private diaries. On other occasions, Wash could be notably unsympathetic. When serving as a translator for a Creek woman who desperately wanted a divorce, Wash advised her to "make one more effort," even though her husband had shot and wounded her.[93] It is impossible to know how many similar calls for help went unrecorded or were dismissed by family patriarchs.

Despite their contrasting fortunes in the Creek Nation, Wash, Emma, and other Muscogees would contend with a common threat in the 1890s. The U.S. government implemented a formal policy to dissolve Indian nations and incorporate their peoples into the general population. Rich or poor, light-skinned or dark, all Native Americans faced an uncertain and daunting future.

Profile

Buddy Cox, June 2000

After spending a day in Okmulgee, Buddy Cox and I headed back late in the evening to Oklahoma City. A year earlier, Cox had expressed puzzlement at my interest in black Indians. In the morning when we left for Okmulgee, he had mentioned rumors of his own black ancestry. Now, as we drove down I-40, he related a rich and detailed story that revealed even more. When he first got interested in his family's history, his father warned him, "You better stop while you're ahead. You might find something you don't like." His father and his paternal uncle, Claude Cox, knew more than they ever admitted, Buddy later learned. Cox's own black ancestry may come from the deerskin trader Abraham Mordecai and his African American wife, but, Cox discovered, it is also more recent. His grandfather, Porter Cox, was half black and half white, from Tennessee. Porter married into the Creek Nation and went as white until 1912, when he was discovered and beaten up by the Klan. As a result, he lost his lucrative job for the city of Okmulgee. The sudden reversal of fortune is reflected in the arbitrary but powerful racial designations imposed by the U.S. government. In 1910, the census taker listed Porter as white; in 1920, Porter was listed as mulatto.

Decades ago, Porter Cox traveled with two of his daughters to Tennessee for a brief visit. His daughters told Buddy about meeting Porter's white father, but his mother was mysteriously absent. They instead visited a "nursemaid" who had raised Porter. She was black, and Buddy suspects that the woman was in fact Cox's mother. The African ancestry was always denied in the family, Buddy said, but they talked about it in private, sometimes with shame. The fear of public exposure even led one family member to paint a hat on an old photograph of Cox, thereby covering up his curly hair.

As we approached Oklahoma City, Buddy followed this remarkable story with another. He is also related to the Lerblance family, he told me. E. H.

Lerblance was a wealthy businessman in the late nineteenth century who married into the Creek Nation. Family tradition recounts that Lerblance's mother was Catawba Indian and French, his father a French marquis. But, after looking into the story and examining records from the 1830s, Buddy believes that it is far more likely that Lerblance's father was an overseer and his mother a slave. "The Lerblances are prejudiced people," Buddy concluded, "which is a good indication that they might be black."

Cox suspects that the black community in Okmulgee always knew about his family's African heritage. As a child, he occasionally hung around with blacks, as did many other Creeks. Oklahoma was a dry state until 1959, and Creeks frequently visited both black and white speakeasies. Cox remembers spending entire nights in black bars with his father. Some of his black friends ribbed him, "You must be a nigger!" Buddy took it as a joke. Did his friends know the truth about his family history? He suspects they did.

8

Divided by Blood: The Graysons and the End of the Creek Nation

Most Americans have an abiding faith in the merits of freedom.[1] Certainly during the era of the Civil War, the fervent belief of some Americans in freedom culminated in an astounding transformation in the United States. Lincoln famously captured the import of this transformation in his Gettysburg Address in 1863. He declared that it was now for Americans to dedicate themselves to the promise of equality in the Declaration of Independence, so that the nation "shall have a new birth of freedom." Unfortunately, this abiding faith in freedom can be a pretext and justification for imperialism, permitting the United States to violate the sovereignty of other countries in the name of philanthropy.[2]

Such thoughts were probably far from the mind of the renowned abolitionist Wendell Phillips in summer 1870, when he stood before a Boston audience to take stock of the recent expansion of freedom in the United States. The Fifteenth Amendment was indeed a great victory, he stated. Yet its "truth, that all men are created equal," demanded further action, for the amendment applied only to blacks and whites. "With infinite toil, at vast expense, sealing the charter with 500,000 graves, we have made it true of the negro," he told his listeners. "With what toil, at what cost, with what devotion, you will make it true of the Indian and the Chinese, the coming years will tell."[3] As Phillips surely knew, some Radical Republicans had already suggested extending the Fourteenth Amendment, granting civil rights, over Native Americans as well as African Americans.[4] These sentiments did not belong merely to a handful of fervent abolitionists. In the late nineteenth century, Indian reform was premised on the incorporation of Native Americans into the Republic. Using a language of rights drawn from the Declaration of Independence and the Bill of Rights, reformers sought both the extension of U.S. citizenship to Native Americans and the equality of all races before the law.[5]

Paradoxically, the reformers' fervent faith in citizenship and equality gave rise to an unforgiving campaign against indigenous cultures. The American commitment to equality and universal citizenship left little room for difference.[6] Reformers, although purportedly benevolent, were aggressively expansionist, and in the extension of U.S. sovereignty, they saw only the victory of liberty, not the demise of once sovereign peoples. When Indians expressed their objections to becoming citizens of a foreign nation, reformers redoubled their efforts to compel them to receive the blessings of democracy.

In the early 1890s, these broad political trends little concerned Emma Grayson and her family, for they were too busy worrying about short-term survival. Her son Eli spent the latter part of May 1891 watching over his cousin Cilla (William and Judah's granddaughter by their first son, William Jr.). Cilla's friend was murdered that month, shortly after warning Cilla that there were "parties" against her.[7] This mysterious incident perhaps passed quickly, but the danger of being overrun by cattle ranchers continued through the middle of the decade. Wash and his brother Sam, by contrast, had assets worth more than $76,000, and the threats to their livelihood came directly from U.S. plans to dissolve the Creek Nation.[8]

The dissolution came rapidly. On April 22, 1889, the "unassigned lands," a large tract in what is now central Oklahoma, were opened by Congress to colonization. "Vast crowds of home-seekers gathered on the borders," wrote historian Angie Debo, "and when that wild day was over the lonely wilderness had become a settled land of tented cities with soaring ambitions, and staked claims ready for the plow."[9] That same year, the United States established an Indian Territory court in Muskogee, Creek Nation, with jurisdiction over civil and minor criminal cases involving U.S. citizens. The court made it virtually impossible for Creeks to keep intruders off their lands. It assumed jurisdiction over probate cases involving marriages between Indians and Americans and recognized the right of U.S. citizens to inherit Creek property. By 1893, a real estate office had opened in Muskogee, a remarkable development considering that by the laws of the Creek Nation, all lands belonged to the Creek people in common, even if some citizens had fenced off larger tracts than others.[10]

President Cleveland sealed the fate of the Creeks in 1893 by creating a commission, headed by former Massachusetts senator Henry L. Dawes, to negotiate with the Five Tribes. Dawes had been instrumental in the passage of the General Allotment Act of 1887, which granted the president the power to extinguish native nations by dividing their lands into small tracts and granting the plots to individual Indians, a process called allotment in severalty. Because of complications concerning land title in Indian Territory, this imperialist act had excluded the Five Tribes. Now Dawes was charged with extending it over them as well, finalizing their absorption into the United States.[11] "Remember that your work is not for the regeneration of a locality, but for a race," Dawes told a group of Indian reformers in 1897. Until in every Indian home "the wife shall sit by her hearthstone clothed in the habiliments of true womanhood," he proclaimed, "and the husband shall stand sentinel at the threshold panoplied in the armor of a self-supporting citizen of the United States—then, and not till then, will your work be done."[12]

Wash followed the work of the commission closely and traveled several times to Washington, D.C., to represent the Creeks in negotiations. Early on, he stood firmly against allotment. Asked in 1878 how many Creeks favored allotment, he responded, "I do not know a single man." Allotment, he argued eight years later, would dispossess Indians of their lands, turning them into "shifting sores upon the public body."[13] By 1894, however, after witnessing firsthand the bad faith of the federal government in protecting Creek land title, he had changed his mind. "I am confident that our only safety lies in allotment among ourselves of all our land," he wrote in a local newspaper. "Then we could hope to get rid of the intruders."[14] An agreement based upon hard bargaining with the United States, he hoped, would preserve the Creek government after the allotment of lands, but unfortunately, he was not able to contribute his talents to negotiations. In 1895, the National Council impeached Wash's brother Sam, the treasurer of the nation, for financial irregularities, and Wash's reputation plummeted.[15] That year, Wash ran as a candidate to represent Creeks in a pantribal council to discuss a united response to the Dawes Commission. Of the ten candidates before the Creek assembly, Wash received the fewest votes.[16]

The federal government continued dismantling the Five Tribes, creating a morass of misrepresentations and flat-out lies to justify its broken promises and punitive laws.[17] The web of deception led to "An Act for the Protection of the People of Indian Territory," passed on June 28, 1898. The Curtis Act, as it was informally known, brought Indian Territory under the laws of the United States and authorized the Dawes Commission to take a census of the Five Tribes and allot their lands regardless of the sentiments of the act's victims.[18] A year later, the president of the Lake Mohonk Indian Conference, an annual meeting of Indian reformers and government officials, assessed their progress. "In what spirit and by what methods shall Americans deal with the less-favored races?" he asked. Recent experience with "the Negro, the Indian, and the Chinaman," he concluded, illustrated unambiguously "that we have been chosen as instruments to inculcate ideas of justice and to establish social sympathy and good government among less-favored nations."[19] Wash had a different opinion. Why was the Creek Nation dissolved? The "ruthless restless white man," he asserted, "hoped and expected to obtain for a song, lands from ignorant Indians."[20] The "last and final swindle is now in process of consumation," he concluded.[21]

In July 1898, the Dawes Commission set up shop in Okmulgee, the Creek capital, and began taking a census of Muscogee citizens in preparation for allotment.[22] The families of Wash and Emma each set aside days to appear before the commission. For Wash and his family, enrollment was a simple procedure: the commission checked their names against Creek payrolls from 1890 and 1895, filled out a census card, issued citizenship certificates, and directed them to another office to select 160-acre allotments.[23] For his cousins, however, the process was troubling.

The commission produced two rolls, one enumerating Creeks "by blood," the other enumerating "freedmen," the former slaves of the Creek Nation. Much was at stake in these designations because Creek leaders continually threatened to curtail the rights of freed people by proposing that they receive reduced allotments and no share of the nation's treasury.[24] Although in some cases it was easy to determine who should be on which roll, in many others it was impossible. By law, applicants who appeared on the 1869 Dunn Roll of ex-slaves were enrolled as freedmen or freedwomen; those who appeared on the 1890 and 1895 rolls as Creek citizens were enrolled by blood. It was expected that those enumerated on the Dunn Roll would appear on subsequent rolls as members of one of the three Creek "colored" towns, but this was not always the case. Some applicants appeared on the Dunn Roll as ex-slaves and on the 1890 and 1895 rolls as members of one of the ancient Creek towns. Others appeared on the 1890 and 1895 rolls as members of one of the three Creek "colored" towns but not on the Dunn Roll. Still others had been born years before to free women and enslaved men or to enslaved women and free men. A final group included children of parents whose status was indeterminate. How should these people be categorized, commissioners wondered.

U.S. officials had encountered a similar problem in 1890 when they were taking the eleventh census. "A serious difficulty was met in the answer to 'Are you an Indian?' " wrote a census officer in Indian Territory. "Under the laws of The Five Tribes or nations of the Indian territory," he explained, "a person white in color and features, is frequently an Indian, being so by remote degree of blood or by adoption." Yet, he noted, many whites in Indian Territory were not Indian citizens. In addition, he continued, "Negroes are frequently met who speak nothing but Indian languages, and are Indians by tribal law and custom." Others, however, "call themselves Indians" but are not so recognized by the nations. The U.S. census, acknowledged one officer, listed some Indians as whites and blacks, and some blacks and whites as Indians.[25]

Even Creeks themselves could not agree who was who. Town rolls were notoriously unreliable. Ex-slaves were purportedly enrolled only in the three "colored" towns, but, as numerous Creeks testified, people frequently switched from one town to another. "You will find a great many colored people" on Creek town rolls, said L. C. Perryman, a principal chief of the nation; "it is to their choice mostly."[26] William McIntosh, one of the leaders of Arkansas Colored Town, admitted that "whenever I had one on my roll that wished to be transferred to another town, it was the custom to do it."[27] Even Wash participated in these transfers, placing Prince Stidham, a former slave of his wife's, on the Coweta town rolls.[28] Some town leaders reportedly demanded money to place people on the rolls.[29] Others participated in a "kind of a trade," exchanging citizens who wished to be enrolled elsewhere. When disputes arose between towns, however, the same town leaders were known to scratch these exchanged members off of their rolls.[30]

Creeks attempted to bring order to their rolls in 1895 by forming a citizenship committee called the Colbert Commission, but racism proved an insurmountable barrier to reaching any accord. Creeks accused the leaders of the "colored" towns of selling places to noncitizens.[31] These leaders in turn suspected the Creek government of destroying the rolls of ex-slaves.[32] No doubt, race played a significant part in determining the success of each applicant. "If this woman was half white in place of half colored and the other half Indian," a U.S. official observed of one applicant, "no objection would be raised to her claim to citizenship."[33] Paro Bruner, a blacksmith who once belonged to Wash's grandmother Katy, later recalled in colorful language that the "Creek Council contested a many of colored ones citizens rights." The Colbert Commission, he declared, cared no more for the law "than a crow cares for Sunday in the light of citizenship."[34] The commission only made matters worse when it assumed the authority to remove names from town rolls with scissors.[35]

Wash appeared before the Colbert Commission on at least one occasion. Testifying in the case of Joe Grayson, a former slave of Katy's, he seemed irritated when asked if Joe was an Indian or a "colored man." "Well," he replied, "there is an Indian person by the name of Joe Grayson, but then there is a nigger by the name of Joe Grayson."[36] Wash wished to keep the lines clear in his family, but Joe testified that in fact his father Jim Grayson, known as Chinne Chotke (Little Jimmy), was "a half breed, half indian and half colored."[37]

The problem of determining who was a freed person and who was Creek by blood was compounded by outright fraudulent applications, submitted by ex-slaves from the states and white people who desired a share of Creek lands. Wiley, "evidently a white man," according to one Creek, appeared before the Dawes Commission in Muskogee and claimed to be black, a member of Arkansas Colored Town.[38] Maria Richardson wrote the commission from Helmick, Kansas, to recount how her grandmother was stolen from the Creeks "in old Virginia," enslaved, and forced to marry a "Colored man." Maria wished to know if she would be receiving "any Dowry from her Creek Indian kin."[39] Others, claiming to be distant descendants of the Creeks, wrote from Alabama to reestablish ties now that the nation was being despoiled.[40]

One such applicant knocked on Emma's door in summer 1895. He introduced himself as Thomas Grayson and said he and his brother Henry were greatgrandsons of Emma's father, William. "My daddy told me about it," Emma testified before the Colbert Commission that same year. "He told me on his death bed that I must look out for these two children." On further questioning, Emma seemed less certain. She met Thomas for the first time when he recently appeared at her door, she confessed. "Who did he say his father was?" she was asked. "I think he said John," came the response.[41] A Creek officer later revealed that in 1895 Thomas identified himself as a noncitizen and had agreed to pay a tax to reside in the Creek Nation as a foreigner.[42]

Eliminating charlatans was straightforward. The Dawes Commission interviewed each applicant, summoned witnesses, and demanded documentation. Determining who was a freed person or a Creek, however, was more difficult. The Dunn Roll and the 1890 and 1895 payrolls frequently gave contradictory or incomplete answers, and in such cases, the commissioners made decisions based on testimony. Yet even the most forthcoming witnesses could not help them draw distinctions between slavery and kinship in the Creek Nation. "Do you know whether or not she was an Indian?" they asked one applicant about his mother. "I don't know anything about it; never had anything serious to think over it." The commissioners insisted on an answer:

Q. What did she look like? Full colored woman?
A. My mother?
Q. Yes.
A. Oh, my mother is 3/4 Indian.
Q. You are willing to make affidavit to that?
A. Yes, you couldn't hardly tell the difference between her and full blood; she could not use the English language whatever, hardly.
Q. Still, she was a slave?
A. Yes.[43]

Should a woman of Indian descent, fluent in Muscogee, yet a slave be enrolled as a freed person or a Creek by blood?

Unable to arrive at a hard-and-fast rule, the commissioners relied on racist impressions. They believed that from physical observation they could deduce an applicant's approximate proportion of "Indian," "colored," and "white" blood. They usually assigned those with a high degree of colored blood to the freedmen rolls. Was Jane Owen colored? they asked one witness. "I couldn't say that she was, and I couldn't say that she was not." Certainly, Owen "had tolerable nice straight hair and looked like the rest of the Indians," but "her hair was not as straight" as the witness's.[44] Hair proved to be of special interest to the commissioners. "Was his hair curly at all?" they asked about Nelson McIntosh's father. Didn't he have "kinky hair" and "whiskers"? In this case, the commissioners looked directly at McIntosh and recorded that he "has every appearance of being a negro"; "Has kinkey hair, flat nose, thick lips and dark skin and every indication of a full blood negro." McIntosh's attorney objected to the description being placed on record.[45]

Ex-slaves proved particularly hostile to the commissioners' racist presumptions, perhaps because they knew from their own families that many Creeks and freed people were of mixed ancestry. William McIntosh, patronizingly called "uncle William" by the commissioners, refused to label Richard Adkins:

Q. What was Richard Adkins, was he an Indian or a colored man?
A. He was half, mixed some way.
Q. Half—what do you mean?
A. Half-breed, either half white or—
Q. Well what was he? Half Indian and half colored or half Indian and half white?
A. I don't know exactly. I never knowed.[46]

McIntosh's friend Paro Bruner was equally uncooperative. As a former slave of Katy's, he knew personally that families in the Creek Nation were mixed, free and slave, Indian and African. He seemed particularly irritated with the commission's line of questioning about Liza Parker, who was sitting in the room with him:

Q. What is the color of Liza?
A. She—there she is.
Q. What blood?
A. Well, she shows some mixed.

Q. Mixed with colored?

A. Yes sir.

Q. Right much so, isn't it?

A. Well—

Q. More colored than Indian, aint it?

A. No sir; more Indian than it is colored, if I have the say so.[47]

Bruner's sharp retort exposed the authoritarian relationship between the government commission and the mostly uneducated African and Indian peoples who came before it.

The commission's imperious attitude toward applicants and witnesses reflected the belief of U.S. officials that they knew what was best for the world's "less-favored races."[48] This paternalistic and racist attitude was enshrined in federal law in 1886 when the Supreme Court ruled in *United States v. Kagama* that Congress's power over Indian affairs is unlimited by treaty rights or tribal sovereignty. Indian tribes, wrote the court, "*are* the wards of the nation." "They are communities *dependent* on the United States." The court concluded, "The power of the General Government over these remnants of a race once powerful, now weak and diminished in numbers, is necessary to their protection, as well as to the safety of those among whom they dwell."[49] (The doctrine of plenary power, as Congress's absolute and exclusive authority over Indian tribes is called, is still law today.) Secure in their political authority and convinced of their racial superiority, the Dawes commissioners resented any challenge to their power. "Creek colored people," said the supervisor of the allotment office Edward Miller, often "come in with the intention of telling the Commission where they could improve their methods." They were "fresh," "impudent," "impertinent," "unreasonable," "swaggering," and "impolite." "Every employee in the Creek office will tell you the same thing," Miller stated.[50]

For Emma, Vicey, and Emma's two children, Eli and Jeanetta, their visit to the Dawes Commission in late 1898 must have been intimidating. Although Emma apparently had no problems enrolling on the by-blood rolls, Vicey ran into trouble. She insisted that she was freeborn, but the commissioners, perhaps eyeing the tone of her skin and the curl of her hair, decided she was "colored" and put her on the freedmen rolls.[51] When Eli went before the commissioners, they described him as "colored" but enrolled him by blood. Sometime later, they checked his name against the Dunn Roll and found an entry for "Elie Grayson"—not Emma's son but an ex-slave with the same name. Nevertheless, the commissioners crossed Eli off the by-blood card and placed him on a freedmen's card.[52] Their decision was capricious. Perhaps Eli had an experience similar to Prince Stidham's. In July 1898, the commissioners enrolled Stidham as a by-

Chickasaw freed people filing for allotments. Courtesy of the Research Division of the Oklahoma Historical Society.

blood member of Coweta Town. A month later, after he visited the commissioners "with a crowd of negroes," they reenrolled him as a freedman.[53]

By the time the census was finalized, Vicey and Eli had joined Emma on the by-blood rolls, but the rolls still lacked any kind of consistency. The census listed each citizen's degree of Indian blood (full, three-fourths, one-half, and so on). These pseudoscientific and racist fractions would later become enormously important. In the early twentieth century, Congress, acting on the belief that so-called half-breeds were more competent than full-bloods, would exclude people with a low proportion of Indian blood from legislation designed to protect Native Americans from dispossession of their land. Creeks were frequently at the mercy of the Dawes Commission when it came to calculating these numbers, for with a handful of exceptions, they were unable to add and divide fractions. "If your Grand-mother was a half-breed how much Creek blood have you?" one Creek was asked. "I dont know how you count blood," came the response.[54] Eli and Jeanetta were listed as three-quarters Indian, Emma as one-half, and—inexplicably—Emma's sister Vicey as a "full-blood."[55]

No one in the family witnessed the Dawes Commission's capriciousness more than Jeanetta. She first visited the commission on November 24, 1898, with her husband, Mitchell, and their three teenage sons, Robert, Ben, and Charley. Mitchell was a former slave of Watt Grayson's, Jeanetta's great-uncle. The commissioners enrolled the entire family by blood in the town of Ketchapataka. Jeanetta, they noted, was one-half blood, and her husband and children "colored." (On the final rolls, Jeanetta is listed as three-fourths blood.) Sometime afterward, the commissioners crossed off Mitchell, Robert, Ben, and Charley and moved them to the freedmen's roll.[56] They remained on the freedmen's roll on the final census, even though by the Creek tradition of matrilineality and by the commission's own rules, Jeanetta's children should have been enrolled by blood.[57] Jeanetta had another child, Onie, by a white man named Phil Finniegan. In an explicit display of racism, the commissioners placed Onie on the by-blood roles. With a white father and a mother who was purportedly three-quarters blood, Onie should have been three-eighths. Illogically, they listed him as one-half Creek.[58] The enrollment of Robert, Ben, and Charley as freedmen and their half brother Onie by blood shows how deeply racism permeated the decisions of the Dawes commissioners.

The Dawes rolls marked an important step toward the allotment of Creek country, part of a concerted effort by the United States to divest Native Americans of their lands. Between 1887 and 1934, Indian America shrank from 140 million acres to 52 million acres, more than a 60 percent reduction.[59] Among the Five Tribes, the theft of lands was disproportionately severe. Between 1890 and 1940, land belonging to the Five Tribes shrank from nearly 20 million acres to a mere 1.8 million acres, an astounding loss of more than 90 percent in the space of fifty years.[60] The dispossession drew a flood of white colonists into what had once been designated as perpetual Indian Territory. The 1890 census enumerated 109,000 whites, 18,636 blacks, and 50,055 Indians in Indian Territory; by 1900, the white population had tripled to 340,000.[61]

By the terms of the Creeks' agreement with the Dawes Commission, each citizen received a tract of 160 acres of his or her choice. Emma, Vicey, Eli, and Jeanetta each took an allotment near William and Judah's old homestead, located between present-day Oktaha and Summit. As the matriarch of the family, Emma selected a tract containing the family cemetery, a burial ground that included her nephew Seaborn, who had died in 1888 at the age of twenty-one.[62] Emma was surrounded by her family. Vicey, Eli, and Jeanetta selected neighboring allotments.[63] So, too, did Onie (Jeanetta's son) and Emma's niece Julia and nephew John.[64] A few relatives had moved away to join their spouses. Emma's niece Adeline now lived about twenty miles east of present-day Seminole,

Oklahoma, a good two-day journey from Emma's residence.[65] Another niece, Elizabeth, lived just southwest of Checotah, about ten miles from Emma.[66]

For Wash, allotment was in some senses much more unsettling. Emma and her family simply selected tracts that included their modest 30-and 40-acre farms. Wash, however, as a partner in Grayson Brothers Mercantile, owned several thousand head of cattle on pastures enclosing two and a half square miles.[67] Allotment forced Wash to cede this enormous pasture in exchange for a 160-acre allotment, hardly sufficient for a homestead, farm, and pasture for thousands of cattle. Many whites charged that the Five Tribes' stubborn resistance to allotment was orchestrated by ranchers like Wash who stood to lose so much. In fact, poor Creeks were equally opposed to allotment, though perhaps for different reasons.[68]

Facing the imminent loss of their pasture and deeply in debt, Grayson Brothers Mercantile declared bankruptcy just before the onset of allotment, when Creek laws still had jurisdiction. Laws in the Creek Nation forbade noncitizens, including creditors, from seizing land and improvements, such as homes, farms, and businesses.[69] Divested of his pasture, Wash selected a string of adjoining tracts for himself and his family that stretched along the north fork of the Canadian River.[70] Together, the allotments covered the 400 acres he had under cultivation.[71] Today, because of damming, the area is inundated by Eufaula Lake.

The allotment of Creek lands—3 million acres divided into nearly nineteen thousand tracts—immersed the Graysons in a sea of greed and corruption. Each allotment was separated on paper into a 40-acre homestead and 120 acres of surplus land. All homesteads were held in trust by the U.S. government for a period of twenty-one years from the date of allotment; surplus land remained in trust only until June 30, 1907. Creeks neither paid taxes on nor had the right to sell their homesteads and surplus lands during these periods.[72] Yet, in various ways, the allotments gradually moved onto the open market, subjecting the owners to the blandishments and intimidation of unscrupulous speculators. By special application to the Bureau of Indian Affairs, a few hundred Creeks gained the right to sell their lands.[73] Many more allotments became available for purchase when Indians died, for, with a few exceptions, their property became unrestricted.[74]

Congressional legislation turned thousands of other allotments into marketable real estate. In April 1904, Congress removed restrictions on the surplus land belonging to all adult members of the Five Tribes who were on the freedmen rolls, overnight converting more than 550,000 acres of Creek land to fee-simple ownership.[75] "If they sell their land and squander the proceeds they can go to work," wrote teacher Alice Robertson, born in the Creek Nation to a missionary. "A large proportion of them would be better off if this stress of necessity were placed upon them," she concluded.[76] In May 1906, Congress extended restrictions on surplus and homestead land belonging to "full-bloods" to 1931, but it let the restrictions on 400,000 acres of surplus land belonging to "mixed-bloods" expire in 1907.[77] Finally, in May 1908, Congress removed all restrictions on both homesteads and surplus land for ex-slaves and all Indians having less than "half Indian blood." It also removed restrictions on surplus lands of Indians with at least half Indian blood but less than three-fourths Indian blood. Homesteads of this group and all lands belonging to people who were three-fourths Indian or more remained protected until 1931.[78] By 1909, well over 1.5 million acres, one-half of the Creek Nation's holdings, were no longer protected by the federal government.[79]

In 1940, not long after the orgy of theft had abated, Angie Debo's magnificent book *And Still the Waters Run* detailed how Oklahoma's leading citizens had stolen Indian lands. The methods were as varied as they were shameless. Some grafters, as the thieves were known, secured profitable leases from illiterate Indians for nominal fees. Lumber dealers, who specialized in such leases, clear-cut the lands, leaving them denuded and worthless. Other grafters made a living by exploiting minors. In the Creek Nation alone, nearly 500,000 acres belonged

Children of Creek freed people sitting before a mound of cotton, late nineteenth century. *Annual Report of the United States Indian Inspector for the Indian Territory, 1899* (Washington, DC: Government Printing Office, 1899), opposite 106.

to children.[80] Each child by law needed a competent guardian. Real estate developers hired young Indians to go door-to-door in poor communities in search of parents who would sign a guardianship waiver for as little as five dollars. One land speculator unsuccessfully applied for the guardianship of 161 Choctaw children. The timber on their land would have made him a multimillionaire.[81] Other grafters monitored funeral homes to exploit the families of the recently deceased. By tracking down the heirs, they could purchase inherited, and hence unrestricted, lands for a pittance.[82]

Grafters became more brazen and ruthless in 1901, when a group of white oilmen began drilling in Red Fork, just south of Tulsa. After six weeks of dry drilling, the rig broached a layer of "stray gritty lime" 534 feet below ground. A geyser of oil and natural gas exploded into the sky. Within days, Red Fork was swarming with speculators.[83] They were "fairly tumbling over one another," one witness recalled, "in their undignified but eager scramble for anticipated wealth."[84] Creek chief Pleasant Porter stated laconically, "I think it unfortunate that oil, in apparent commercial quantities has been found."[85] Red Fork was soon dwarfed by Glenn Pool, a small tract of land south of Tulsa that became one of the most profitable oil fields in the world after its discovery in 1905. Two years after the first well was sunk, it generated twenty million barrels of oil, 12 percent of the entire production in the United States.[86]

Though the vast majority of allotments did not have any oil, a few sat atop millions of dollars' worth of crude. Grafters poisoned, shot, and even dynamited Creeks to obtain their oil-rich allotments.[87] Just north of Creek lands in the Osage Nation, the FBI had to be called in to halt a string of murders.[88] More commonly, however, Creeks were dispossessed through a combination of coercion and legal maneuverings. Business partners J. W. Steen and Edwin M. Arnold tried such an approach with Wiley Grayson, presumably a distant relative of Wash and Emma's. Between 1900 and 1906, Wiley, who was deaf and dumb, inherited unrestricted allotments from his father, sister, and half brother. In 1908, Steen and Arnold approached the sixteen-year-old boy to purchase his land. Wiley was living with his stepmother, Mary, "an old Indian woman." Steen snatched the boy away, saying only that he would return him in five days. Steen then went before a local judge and had his attorney, Charles Buford, appointed as Wiley's legal guardian. Buford now had the right to sell Wiley's lands with court approval.[89]

Five months after Steen's visit, Wiley still had not reappeared, and Mary went to the district agent for help. The agent seemed only mildly concerned. "I went personally to see this boy at the home of Mr. Buford here in Checotah," he reported. "He was being well treated and was living with a nice family." Shortly after the agent's visit, Wiley ran away, turning up in the agent's office nine days later. In light of these developments, Steen's partner Arnold admitted to the agent "that there were phases that looked bad but in the light of all the circumstances he thought it would not appear as bad as it seemed to be." Although the partners had paid $250 for 160 acres of Wiley's land ($1.56 per acre), Arnold now offered $800, "in order to show that he desires to do the right thing." Astonishingly, the agent decided to err on the side of caution, by which he meant finding another guardian but approving the land sale if it seemed "reasonable." Wiley fortunately ran into a cousin and made signs that he wished to return to his stepmother. His cousin took him home a few days later, and a county judge disapproved the land sale. The agent concluded, "I cannot believe that Steen & Buford are endeavoring to do anything that is unfair in this matter but sometimes from personal observation it appears that such might be the case."[90] He was either foolish or disingenuous.

Across the road from Eli's Creek-style log house, someone erected a drilling rig, but there was no fortune hidden beneath the pasture- and timberland surrounding Oktaha and Summit.[91] The region's hopes lay in the soil and the Katy Railroad, which received freight and passengers at Oktaha.[92] In spring 1902, the town was surveyed, and businesses began to go up on the east side of the tracks, not far from Eli's land.[93] The *Oktaha American* perhaps too enthusiastically called the area the "Creek 'Valley of the Nile,' " citing as evidence a local apple measuring fifteen inches in circumference. "Three cheers and a tiger for Oktaha," it exclaimed, the "resting place of the God of Nature."[94] In 1907, Eli harvested a newsworthy crop of corn from his thirty acres, and his cousin Julia brought in five gallons of "the finest tame blackberries."[95] But their produce, no matter the size of the corn or the sweetness of the berries, was hardly worth the attention of grafters, and speculation in the area remained negligible. Although Eli and Jeanetta both leased their children's allotments to a local cattle rancher, and Julia (Emma's niece) leased her daughter Nelly's land to Oktaha's leading businessman, there is no evidence that these contracts were exploitative, at least compared with the leases Creeks signed elsewhere.[96]

By contrast to his cousins, Wash lost much more during allotment but did his best to capitalize on the opportunities offered during the period immediately following the division of Creek lands. He purchased lots in Broken Arrow and Coweta, town sites that developers were actively promoting. His Coweta lands, he smartly observed, would be close to the railroad depot when built.[97] He even looked into purchasing lots in Muskogee, where some of the most corrupt speculation was occurring.[98] Wash also befriended a businessman and speculator named A. P. McBride, from Independence, Kansas.[99] McBride wished to develop oil wells around Wash's hometown of Eufaula, and Wash offered to help him secure the necessary leases. In March 1904, he negotiated at least fifteen leases, including one with his brother Sam and with a "negro" also named Sam Grayson, probably a former slave of his family's.[100] By the end of the month, with Wash's assistance, McBride had obtained leases on more than two thousand acres of land.[101]

Yet Wash's finances were deteriorating rapidly. Short of cash, he survived by repeatedly taking out short-term loans from local banks to pay his bills.[102] Wash was even unable to meet his responsibilities toward his church.[103] In December 1904, he confided in his diary that, by "absolutely begging," he induced a local merchant to pay him ten dollars toward five hundred dollars in back rent. "This inability of La Fayette & Bro. to pay me anymore money places me in a pretty bad 'box,' " he wrote. "Greatly troubled" by his financial difficulties and depressed by chronic stomach pain, Wash admitted, "I am despondent and think myself about in that mental condition which drives some people to suicide or drink."[104] The confession stands out in a diary dedicated almost entirely to recording quotidian activities. The next day Wash borrowed another one hundred dollars from the local bank and later went to a minstrel show with his white son-in-law, John Smock.[105]

Wash continued trying to profit from the opportunities opened up by allotment. In June 1905, after watching Smock purchase the surplus lands of "an old negro" named Dick Grayson, Wash wrote to McBride to offer to "buy him some lands from negro citizens if he so desired."[106] But none of his ventures seemed successful. In August, oil drillers in Eufaula reached three thousand feet and found nothing. "This is a complete failure," Wash noted morosely.[107] Later he proposed to McBride that they go into the land business together and was apparently rebuffed.[108] Undaunted, in May 1907 Wash spent fifty dollars on stock in a new Eufaula oil and gas company, but four months later, the enterprise was liquidated.[109] One deal seems to have met with some success. In 1908, Wash's son-in-law John Smock sent a circular letter offering to buy the inherited lands of full-blood Indians. According to Wash, "quite a number" of Indians responded, and he and Smock conducted them to Holdenville to meet the county judge to complete a land deal in Wash's name.[110] Wash failed to spell out the precise details of the transaction in his diary.

Even if Wash was scrupulous in his business dealings, it is clear that he took advantage of other Indians. Nevertheless, he may have felt that he had a right to benefit from the situation—better Creek than white speculators.[111] After all, Wash had once controlled thousands of acres of Muscogee land. Federal laws, imposed unilaterally, reduced his holdings to 160 acres, and now whites were greedily and rapidly dispossessing Creeks of their remaining lands.

Though no Grayson fared well during the postallotment land theft, Wash and his black-Indian cousins stood on opposite sides: Wash was a buyer and leaser; his cousins were sellers and lessees. The contrast is nowhere clearer than in Wash's business dealings in 1909 with William and Judah's grandson, Robert.[112] Born in 1859, perhaps just before Wash visited William and Judah on his way to college, Robert eventually settled with his wife, Louisa, in Brush Hill, just across the North Fork River from Wash's home in Eufaula.[113]

Before 1909, Wash had had only limited contact with this side of the family. One encounter occurred in March 1905, when Wash and his wife, Annie, traveled north to Oktaha to attend the funeral of Stella Tiger, an orphan whom Wash and Annie had taken in and raised.[114] In 1900, Stella had married James Evans, an eighteen-year-old who worked in the butcher business in Checotah.[115] Evans grew up in Oktaha, and he claimed Creek citizenship through his mother, Lettie Escoe, who was from a large family of European, African, and possibly Native American descent.[116] The Escoes were notorious in the Creek Nation for purchasing citizenship, or at least so charged numerous people. The Creek national attorney suggested that Lettie's mother was the daughter of a white planter and his black slave.[117] Wash had greeted news of Stella's marriage to Lettie's son James coldly: "I think this boy is part negro although he is of very fair complexion, besides I don't much believe he is justly entitled to the rights of a citizen of the Creek nation."[118]

At Stella's funeral, Wash and Annie surely met William and Judah's descendants, for only two weeks later the Evans and Grayson families of Oktaha would be joined by a marriage.[119] Wash never wrote about the encounter, but two months afterward, he sat down to write his autobiography. William and Judah's children, he noted, were "the most humble and withal rather worthless citizens" and "unmitigated liars." "Fortunately," he added, "these people, the immediate offspring of this miscegination, were short lived, and are now nearly all dead." "Two or three representatives of that family I think may be living southward of the present town of Muscogee under the names perhaps of Casey and Witherspoon," he added. Had he met John Casey, William and Judah's great-grandson, in Oktaha? (It was John who, two weeks after the funeral, had married into the Evans family.) Had he recognized Vicey Witherspoon, William and Judah's daughter whom he had last seen in 1859, when Vicey and Wash were both teenagers? If so, Wash kept a distance, even in his writing. "I think," "may be living," "perhaps"—these words hardly conveyed a sense of familiarity with the subject. The "hundreds of fullblood negroes" bearing the Grayson surname, Wash felt obliged to add in his autobiography, "are not Graysons by blood at all, but are the former slaves and their numerous descendants of negroes who formerly belonged to the Graysons." "The hundreds of negroes bearing that name," he concluded with certainty, "only show how wealthy in negro slaves would the Graysons be today, had the negro not been emancipated."[120]

Wash's prose reveals his discomfort at facing the African side of the family. Yet occasional encounters could not be avoided. In early 1909, Wash sent a letter to his second cousin Robert, William and Judah's grandson, asking that he deliver votes to make Eufaula the seat of McIntosh County. Soon afterward, Robert appeared in Eufaula drunk, where he tracked down Wash to tell him that he preferred to vote for Checotah, his hometown. Meanwhile, Robert's horse disappeared, and Wash kindly let him spend the night in his house. Robert spent a second night at Wash's before returning home horseless.[121] Perhaps the encounter, despite its certain awkwardness, alerted Wash to a possible opportunity. Two months after Robert's visit, E. E. Shock, the treasurer of McIntosh County, asked Wash to negotiate an oil lease with Robert. Wash traveled to Robert's in mid-April, and after several hours of negotiations, followed by dinner and yet more negotiations, they reached an agreement. A few days later, Robert traveled to Eufaula to sign the lease. Wash received $50 for his services, and Robert's family $320 for the lease of several hundred acres.[122]

A month later, Robert was back at Wash's house, this time because he feared that his daughter's allotment was about to be condemned for use as an oil-pumping station. Wash received a call from Gulf Pipeline Company a day later, asking if he would negotiate a proper lease with Robert. Robert proved a keen bargainer and waited until an initial offer of $1,200 per year for forty acres rose to $2,000 per year. Wash again received $50 for his service. When Gulf Pipeline underpaid Robert by $200 a few months later, he went to Wash for assistance. "This is wrong," Wash recorded in his diary, after reporting the matter to the district Indian agent.[123]

Throughout these extended negotiations, Wash gave no indication in his diary that he was related to Robert. Perhaps he did not know; more likely, he suspected but never acknowledged the relationship. In the small communities of the Creek Nation, family could not be avoided, but they could be repudiated. Midway through the negotiations with Robert, Wash recorded a terse entry in his diary: "A woman claiming to be the wife of Tommy McIntosh of near Oktaha, whose maiden name was Casey, called. She is related to the family of old Billy Grayson who previous to the civil war lived near that portion of the Creek Nation."[124] Again, Wash kept his distance, expressing a good deal of suspicion about his visitor, William and Judah's great-granddaughter Kate. A few months later, Wash bumped into Robert in Eufaula. Robert recounted the recent death of Lucy Bruner, the granddaughter of old John Grayson, Katy's son by her African husband.[125] No matter how hard Wash tried, he could not forget his family history.

Wash may have entered allotment with slightly higher hopes than his relatives, but in the end, whites stole land from Creeks indiscriminately. Neither side of the family fared well. This fact is brought home by a brief encounter between Wash and Robert in July 1910. Robert offered his cousin ten dollars for helping him negotiate with the Gulf Pipeline Company. This small amount was "quite an agreeable windfall," Wash wrote.[126] In 1900, before allotment, Wash possessed two and a half square miles of land. At that time, the meager sum of ten dollars would hardly have appeared as a pleasing windfall.

Profile

Bob Littlejohn, July 1999 and June 2000

The Rudisill Library, a single-story brick building resembling thousands of other low-slung schools and libraries constructed in the early 1970s, sits in the Greenwood District, Tulsa's traditionally black neighborhood. It is the city's resource center for African American history. I met Bob Littlejohn there in July 1999. He had contacted me after I wrote an article about the Graysons for the *Tulsa Eagle*, the city's black-owned newspaper. Over the telephone, he had explained that he is descended from William and Judah through their daughter, Lucy. Dressed in a casual shirt and tie, Littlejohn greeted me warmly in the Rudisill lobby and showed me to a small meeting room.

He opened up a five-inch-thick binder, stuffed with handwritten notes, photocopies, and genealogical trees. The binder documented numerous errors, obfuscations, and lies that he had uncovered in history books. This is Littlejohn's passion, and he explained that he cofounded the North Tulsa Historical Society to rectify the situation.

One family tree, unfolded, stretched several feet across the table. As I peered at the dozens of names, Littlejohn described the ties between Indians and African Americans with excitement and conviction. Then he handed me a set of photocopies from Wash Grayson's autobiography, *A Creek Warrior for the Confederacy*. Littlejohn had highlighted the passages in bright yellow that contained ellipses, rightly suspecting that they hid information about the family's African ancestors. He pointed to the book's introduction, where it explains that certain passages were deleted for "family considerations." "Whose family?" Littlejohn asked rhetorically. This was his family, after all, but no one had consulted him.

I was already aware of the edits made to Wash's autobiography, but I was surprised by Littlejohn's next revelation. He passed me a photocopied page from the published diary of naturalist S. W. Woodhouse, who traveled through Indian Territory in 1849 and 1850. On August 19, the version published by the Uni-

versity of Oklahoma Press tells us, Woodhouse met Lewis Perryman, a prominent Creek politician: "we found him seated in a rocking chair on the piaza he
was a tall man about 6 feet high very dark with a long straight nose and black
mustachoe. . . ."[1] The ellipsis is not explained in the book, but Littlejohn pulled
out a copy of the original handwritten diary. This is what the missing passage
says: "he showed evidently that he had considerable negro blood in him." Littlejohn had recently published his findings about Perryman in the *Tulsa Free
Press*. Perryman is the reputed founder of the city, and many white residents
were horrified. "I don't want to read what historians write, just show me the
original sources," Littlejohn concluded.

Littlejohn's great-grandfather Cornelius was a story-teller, and Littlejohn listened closely. He told Littlejohn about his cousins, second cousins, uncles, great
aunts, and great-great-grandfathers. Littlejohn saw many of them around town,
at church, and at other social gatherings. Some had blue eyes and ruddy com-
plexions; others had skin the color of chocolate. At a recent family reunion,
Littlejohn had to explain to a concerned hotel clerk that the sixteen "white"
people who entered the ballroom were indeed his relatives. Some of them, such
as the Witherspoons of Sapulpa, now are recognized as white, he said.

With his learned distrust of professional historians, Littlejohn has developed
his own elaborate theories about the past. He explained that Indians came from
Africa, that Muskogulge means black people (linguists today still puzzle over the
derivation of this word for the Creek people), and that the Muscogee or Creek
language is related to Mandingo. I began to doubt everything he had told me. I
sparred gently with him, said that he would have a difficult time convincing
people of these theories, queried why Mandingos and Creeks cannot speak to
each other in their native languages. Sometimes I just nodded a dismayed assent,
for fear of offending. We eventually dropped the subject.

A year later, I again met Littlejohn at the Rudisill Library. Soon after we sat
down in the main reading room, a large man sporting a red Langston University
baseball cap approached. He was Curtis Lawson, a divorce lawyer whom Littlejohn introduced as his "business associate." Lawson was initially hostile and
refused to drop his guard unless I conceded his point that there are no such
people as Indians. "No Indians?" I asked in confusion. "Look around the room,"
he replied, scanning the library. "Look at Bob, look at those kids in front of the
computers. This is what Columbus saw."

Lawson also maintains that all Indians are from Africa. When Columbus got
off the boat, he said, the explorer found people eating watermelons and peanuts
and smoking tobacco (and swearing, he joked). These people were all from West
Africa. Littlejohn jumped into the conversation with a list of books I should
consult, including Ivan Van Sertima's *They Came before Columbus* and Leo Wie-

ner's *Africa and the Discovery of America*. Van Sertima, a professor of Africana studies at Rutgers University, uses the physiognomy of ancient Toltec statues in Mexico to argue that Africans settled in the Americas long before Europeans. His evidence is impressionistic and has failed to win over many adherents. Leo Wiener has even fewer followers. A professor at Harvard University in the early twentieth century, Wiener claimed in *Africa and the Discovery of America* (1922) that the majority of root words in American Indian languages come from the Mandekan language group of West Africa. To this day, linguists dispute the origins of Native American languages. No one traces them to Africa; most admit that they can neither draw an accurate family tree of Indian languages nor determine their deepest roots.

Littlejohn summed up his point: "Anything to avoid giving the African people credit. Africans never made a contribution to America except in slavery—this is what they want you to believe. But every one of Oklahoma's leaders was of African descent." "The first so-called Indians who came here [to Oklahoma] were of African descent," he concluded.

On that note, Littlejohn and I headed off to a local diner, where, fortified by fried catfish and two 99-cent martinis, he talked for five hours straight about the Graysons, Creek history, and race. Among other subjects, he spoke about his white relatives. They are not passing, he stated. "I'm just as much Scottish as Negro or Indian," he pointed out. "It depends what you want to be called." He also returned to the subject of Wash Grayson and the publication of his autobiography. "There was always someone in the community who catered to the whites," he explained. " 'Here comes that bastard,' they'd say."

A few weeks later, I was on a bus tour of Oklahoma's historically black towns, organized by Littlejohn for Juneteenth, the annual celebration marking June 19, the day that word of emancipation reached Texas slaves. An insatiable storyteller, Littlejohn grabbed the bus microphone soon after our departure and began talking about history. With Tulsa in the rearview mirror, Littlejohn announced, "We just left a black town." "This is one of the things that has been repressed by historians," he asserted, before recounting his discovery of Lewis Perryman's African ancestry. We sped past Oral Roberts University; it is on the allotment of Legus C. Perryman, a person of African descent, Littlejohn pointedly commented. "We've been stereotyped into believing what an Indian looks like. A lot of you on the bus look like me. You may not know it, but I am an Indian. So when you think of an Indian, don't think of the kind that John Wayne kills." "How many of you have Indian ancestry?" he asked. Three-quarters of the passengers raised their hands. We drove past a burial ground. "There's the Booker T. Washington Cemetery," Littlejohn announced, pointing out the window. "They changed the name last year to Rolling Oaks. I'm sure its obvious why."

On Highway 64, just north of Leonard and a few miles southeast of Tulsa, Littlejohn gestured to the surrounding countryside and asked, "Do you all know where T's barbershop is on Greenwood? All this was on his auntie's allotment, on both sides of the road." Over the course of the day, we visited Taft, Rentiesville, and Clearview. Throughout the trip, Littlejohn shared his astoundingly rich knowledge of local history.

William and Judah could have no more appropriate descendant, I decided. The Graysons' family history neatly culminated in Littlejohn's deep distrust of received history and his absolute refusal to accept the validity of racial categories. So I thought, before making a surprising discovery.

9 ▦ ▦

Wash in the Age of Progress

As imagined by whites, the end of the nineteenth century was an age of progress, epitomized by the relentless and glorious march of democracy and technology across the Great Plains, over the Rockies, and to the shores of the Pacific coast. Progress was inextricably linked to the triumph of Anglo-Saxon Americans and to the demise, subjection, or absorption of "less-favored races," a relationship made clear in two of the more popular Currier and Ives lithographs of the day, Fanny Palmer's *Across the Continent: Westward the Course of Empire Takes Its Way*, and John Gast's *American Progress*. Found in homes, stores, taverns, and bars throughout the United States, Currier and Ives lithographs were the dominant visual medium for conveying information, akin to today's television.[1] *Across the Continent: Westward the Course of Empire Takes Its Way* drew its subtitle from a well-known painting in the U.S. Capitol. Finished in 1868, a year before the completion of the transcontinental railroad, the lithograph shows a train—a particularly beloved emblem of technological progress in the nineteenth century—steaming westward to the limitless horizon. In the foreground, the tracks divide past and present. On one side, a pioneer community brings civilization to the wilderness. Amid the small settlement sit a schoolhouse and church, the twin pillars of liberty. On the other side, black soot spewed by the speeding locomotive engulfs two hapless Indians.[2]

John Gast spelled out the theme with even less subtlety in his lithograph *American Progress*, (1872), commissioned by George Crofutt, who spent his career promoting the West to prospective settlers. In Crofutt's words, *American Progress* pictures a "beautiful and charming female . . . floating westward through the air" and bearing on her forehead the "Star of Empire." "In her right hand," explained Crofutt, she carries a schoolbook, "the emblem of education and the testimonial of our national enlightenment." In the left, "she unfolds and stretches the slender wires of the telegraph, that are to flash intelligence throughout the land." Speeding trains follow closely behind her, joined by a stagecoach and covered wagon. Before her, buffalo, bear, and Indians flee for their lives. *American Progress* became the frontispiece of *Crofutt's Trans-continental Tourist's Guide*, which went through nine editions between 1869 and 1876 and sold 344,000 copies. Crofutt claimed his guide had an annual readership of two million.[3]

Progress, white Americans believed, was divinely ordained, and the star of empire would move west relentlessly, passing beyond the Pacific shore and hovering over the Philippines by the end of the century. Indians might find a place in the empire as manual laborers and servants, or, as was more frequently predicted, they might succumb to the American juggernaut. In its worst manifestation, as in Theodore Roosevelt's heroic narrative *The Winning of the West* (1889), the faith in America's westward expansion was framed as "race-history," the inevitable march of the Anglo-Saxons, whose superior bloodline produced men of unrivaled industry and action. Savagery would inevitably recede before the advance of civilization.[4]

Many Indians, for obvious reasons, had long looked skeptically at the purported achievements of forward-looking, civilized America. In 1876, readers of the *Indian Journal*, a newspaper chartered by the Creek Council, came across this biting comment: "Killing 'Ingins' in the West, and 'niggers' in the South, affords Sunday recreation for one caste of modern civilization."[5] Three years later, the newspaper asked, "How does it happen that nearly half a century of humanizing, Christianizing, civilizing influences have swept over the continent and missed the Mississippian?" It acidly suggested that the state be subjected to a territorial government, precisely the proposal that supposedly civilized Mississippians (and other Americans) put forward to reclaim Indians from "barbarism."[6] Yet, if Creeks did not have a faith in progress, many, including Wash Grayson, were nevertheless resigned to its inevitability. Best to jump aboard rather than be left behind.[7]

In some ways, Emma Grayson's lack of education proved beneficial, for she was spared the lessons of *Morse's Geography* and *Goodrich's Second Reader*, textbooks that helped shape Wash in his youth.[8] Geographies were dense works laden with facts about the world, precursors to almanacs. Morse's *Geography Made Easy: Being an Abridgement of the American Universal Geography* was adapted for use in schools so that students, "at the same time that they are learning to read, might imbibe an acquaintance with their country, and an attachment to its interests."[9] In this case, the country of affection was the United States, and although Wash retained a lifelong dedication to the Creek Nation, books such as *Morse's Geography* shaped his view of the present and future, a point driven home by Wash's decision as a schoolboy to add "George" to his birth name, "Washington Grayson."[10] *Morse's Geography* was structured on the premise that the world was composed of nation-states that administer discrete territories readily described by statistics, a word whose original meaning was tied directly to the state and to statecraft. The future rested with the nation-state, suggested the text. Indians were relics of a past era.

Along the same lines, *Goodrich's Second Reader* presented a series of fables that delivered bourgeois moralistic lessons, all aimed toward forming the modern citizen. The stories illustrated, among other things, the dire consequences of lying and stealing and the rewards of honesty and frugality. Two pages of verse instructed students on the "Pleasure of Industry." The last lesson, a catalog of ten things to be shunned every day, listed as number nine, "Avoid the idle." For good measure, number ten advised, "Avoid idleness."[11]

His early education made Wash a believer in progress, but he revealed less an optimism about modernization than a firm conviction in its inevitability.[12] In 1885, he exposed his sober, even dark, assessment of the future in a letter to John Wesley Powell, the first director of the Smithsonian's American Bureau of Ethnology. "I should like to see somewhere in the scientific literature of your nation," he wrote, "some record or trace showing after we are gone that such a nation of Indians as Creeks or Maskokees did at one time live."[13] After Powell accepted Grayson's generous offer of assistance, Grayson gently prodded the Smithsonian ethnologist. "Respecting our primitive governmental arrangements," he wrote, "I have to state that I regard them as intensely interesting, discovering a wonderful amount of political good sense and acumen when it is remembered that it was planned and perfected by a people in the stage usually denominated savage."[14]

Wash occasionally voiced bitterly cynical opinions about the progress of civilization. When a number of Western ambassadors and missionaries were murdered in Beijing in 1900, Wash noted:

> I rather incline to the view that where persons go uninvited many thousands of miles across the great oceans to hunt up and worry an unoffending, quiet and peaceable people and work to break down their religion and other institutions that are quite as dear to them as such things are to so-called civilized peoples, and persist in their iconoclasm

to the exasperation of that people; if they by the clumsiness of their efforts, bring disaster upon themselves, I don't feel like wasting any great amount of sympathy upon them.[15]

On Thanksgiving Day, 1902, he suggested that people in the United States had reason to celebrate. As for the Creeks, he wrote, "I suspect that in reality there are exceedingly few if any good causes for thanksgiving."[16] Eight years later, he would repeat this sentiment: "Thanksgiving day this: so the people, i.e. the white people say. I don't see much for the common full blood Indian to give thanks for."[17]

Yet progress could not be halted. Beginning in 1898, Wash's diaries offer rare insight into his reading tastes; the books he favored uniformly suggested that Indians were people of the past.[18] In 1899, for instance, Wash read *Civilization and Progress* by John Beattie Crozier and liked it so much that he recommended it to his old friend Pleasant Porter, who would be elected principal chief of the Creek Nation that year.[19] Crozier explained that the first condition of progress was the abandonment of brute force so that weak as well as powerful individuals and small as well as large nation-states could enjoy "the blessings of liberty."[20] The book in some ways addressed the dilemma of the Creek Nation in its relationship with the United States.

A year later, Wash turned to a book by Bernard Moses, *Democracy and Social Growth in America*.[21] Moses opened his work with a description of the "subjection" of America to "civilized peoples." "Our English ancestors" moved "steadily and irresistibly forward," wrote Moses, "and their advance was marked by the disappearance of the uncultivated aborigines."[22] The gist of the book could not have been comforting to Wash. "That community which is descended from a union of Europeans and Indians has naturally more or less of an inclination towards the thoughts and life of its Indian ancestors," Moses asserted.

It is obliged, by a slow and laborious process of cultivation, to eliminate or overcome the influence of the element that makes for degeneracy; and, until this is accomplished, its facility of movement along the way of civilization is impeded, and it is consequently outrun by communities that have been careful to withhold themselves from barbarian contamination.[23]

Wash did not record his response to the book. Perhaps he distanced himself from Moses's offensive conclusions by telling himself that Indians were not degenerate, or that people of Native American and European descent, like himself, did not hew to the thought of their Indian ancestors, or that, if Moses's assertions were true, at least *his* family had withheld itself rather successfully from barbarian contamination.

Whatever his particular reaction to *Democracy and Social Growth in America*, Wash, as an educated and literate American, was bombarded with stories about the inevitability of progress. In 1905, he and his family visited the National Museum in Washington, D.C., the precursor to the Smithsonian's National Museum of American History.[24] The museum made visible a narrative of progress. "In the inevitable course of human history," wrote the chief curator of the ethnographic displays, "the individual races will probably fade out and disappear, and the world will be filled to overflowing with a generalized race in which the dominating blood will be that of the race that today has the strongest claim, physically and intellectually, to take possession of all the resources of the land and sea." Needless to say, the curator predicted that the "resultant race" would not be even one three-hundredth part Native American.[25]

Wash saw other narratives of progress in Wild West shows, which he attended on at least three occasions.[26] In celebrating the American conquest of the West, these shows presented Indians as people of the past, worthy but doomed opponents.[27] In Wash's words, Buffalo Bill's Wild West Show presented "naked and painted Indians fantastically and characteristically adorned with eagle's and other bird's feathers."[28] Wash judged another show called "The Flaming Arrow" to be "sensational," noting that he and his family "enjoyed" it "very much."[29] He seems to have enjoyed Buffalo Bill's show as well, although he revealed his misgivings about the celebratory nature of such performances. With a brilliantly ironic use of words, Wash observed that the spectacle portrayed the West "before that country was invaded by civilization."[30]

Wash saw another representation of the vanishing Indian in January 1912, when he attended Edward S. Curtis's "Indian Picture-Opera" at the Belasco Theater in Washington.[31] Curtis had organized the musicale, as he called it, to raise money for his life's work, *The American Indian*, a twenty-volume set of photogravures and text that he would finally complete in 1930. His photogravures, of stoic warriors, striking maidens, and picturesque dancers, have permeated popular consciousness; when most Americans think of Indians, they unknowingly think of Curtis's images. The musicale presented lantern slides narrated by Curtis and accompanied by a theater orchestra playing "truly primitive" music. "My great desire tonight is that each and every person here enter into the spirit of our evening with the Indians," Curtis announced in one performance. "Toward that end let us close our eyes for an instant, and in that flash of time span the gulf between today's turmoil and the far-away enchanted realm of primitive man."[32] Among the slides Wash likely saw at the Belasco was "The Vanishing Race," a dark, unfocused image of a line of mounted Navajos, riding slowly toward a blackened background. Their long, ghostly shadows suggest that the sun is setting on these unfortunate Americans.[33]

Popular fiction also confirmed the narrative of progress and the inevitable disappearance of American Indians. In 1914, Wash purchased *The Man of Yesterday: A Romance of a Vanishing Race*, a potboiler written by Mary Holland Kinkaid.[34] Across from the title page, a color print showed a Chickasaw woman, Pakali, dressed in "picturesque Indian costume," her jacket open at the neck to reveal, as the author wrote, her "smooth, dark skin."[35] The plot is simple. Pakali is torn between her love for Hattakowa and Arnold, an Indian and a white man who clearly represent the broader cultural choices that Pakali faces in her life. Hattakowa, accused by Pakali of rebelling against the "progress" of the race, sums up the dilemma: "You and I, who mingle in our veins the blood of the white man and the red man, must give allegiance to one race or the other. You have risen to the white man's standard, and I have answered to the backward call. You are an American, I am an Indian."[36] Pakali is betrayed by her white lover, and Hattakowa murders him in revenge.

Hattakowa and Pakali are the Indian versions of the "tragic mulatto," a stock character of the late nineteenth and early twentieth centuries whose always unfortunate fate reflected the perceived impossibility of being mixed-race. The difficulty of being native and American was (and is) very real.[37] Yet if so-called mixed-bloods faced the tragic choice of vanishing with other Indians or surviving with their white enemies, that very choice was in fact an opportunity not available to "full-bloods" and "mixed-bloods" who were part African. Kinkaid's novel concludes with a dramatic speech by Hattakowa, who immediately before his execution urges Indians to abide by the policies of the United States as best they can: "I will counsel you to conform to the changes which are inevitable. It is useless to fight against what is called progress; take what is best of the white man's civilisation and do not waste strength in combating powers that must conquer you."[38] Unlike his cousin Emma, whose recognized ancestry was entirely a liability, Wash could strive to be one of the "good citizens of the United States," as Hattakowa encourages.[39] He might, like Pakali, risk being betrayed by whites but he would not face extinction.

Analyzed in political tracts, demonstrated in museums, dramatized in the theater, and fictionalized in novels, progress found its most powerful illustration in the multitude of marvelous technological inventions and scientific breakthroughs, from the motor car to the airplane, that marked the early twentieth century. On this subject, Wash read Carl Snyder's *New Conceptions in Science with a Foreword on the Relations of Science and Progress*, which included chapters on atomic physics, synthetic chemistry, medicine, technology, and other scientific fields. Snyder concluded, "Modern progress, planted firmly upon machinery, upon the steam-engine, the steam-ship, the dynamo, the telegraph, the printing-press, and all manner of mechanical contrivances, will suffer no serious check."[40] Snyder's enthusiasm extended into the realm of eugenics: "The deformed, the defective, and disease must be incessantly weeded out."[41] Wash noted that he liked the book "quite well."[42]

Each new mechanical contrivance seemed a confirmation of the narrative of progress. Wash's diaries are full of "firsts." In May 1901, the day that the Creeks formally ratified their agreement with the Dawes Commission providing for the dissolution of their nation, Wash used a telephone for the first time to relay the news to his hometown, Eufaula. He recalled the conditions of yesteryear, when he sat under an oak tree, taking notes for the Creek government on paper balanced on his knee. Now, by contrast, the railroad and telegraph were "ready to do our bidding," and the telephone allowed him to speak to his family. "Wonderful, wonderful!" he exclaimed.[43] It was mostly by chance that Wash relayed the news of the Creek Nation's demise by using a telephone for the first time, but the timing of the two events was not entirely coincidental. The enormous technological gap between native peoples and American industry seemed to confirm Indians' savagery and justify the civilizing mission of white Americans. As the speed of laying iron rails and copper cables increased, so too did U.S. efforts to dismantle Indian nations.[44] The irony of Wash's phone call reporting the Creeks' demise appears to have been lost on him.

A little over a year later, Wash noted seeing his first automobile, belonging to the mayor of Muskogee, although Wash had to wait until 1908 to ride in one himself.[45] In 1909, Wash had running water installed in his home for the first time.[46] Of course, not all technologies performed as expected. Wash's water pipes froze and burst that winter, knocking the wash basin off the wall. Unaware of the potential consequences when the water thawed, Wash foolishly left for dinner. When he returned home, water had flooded his house and was streaming into the neighbor's yard. Wash "hurriedly laid hold of two small wheel like attachments" found on the broken pipes, turning them until the water stopped.[47]

The flood did not dampen his enthusiasm for new technology. In 1911, Wash purchased the first gas range ever sold in Eufaula.[48] That same year, he described seeing a "flying machine" for the first time. Eufaula residents stood on cars and rooftops to catch a glimpse of the marvel.[49] Even digging sewers could be breathtaking. In 1913, contractors in Eufaula unloaded a steam-powered ditch-digging machine.[50] "To me who has never seen such a contrivance," wrote Wash, "it appears most marvelous in its execution of the work it was made to do."[51] Alas, technology rarely fulfills its utopian promises. A day later, Wash noted, the machine was "mired down in the middle of the street in front of the Baptist Church which checked their progress."[52]

Nevertheless, Wash confessed that he had to agree with a political speech he heard in Eufaula in 1908: "The great wheel of progress in the case of the Indians had been put in motion and no power short of Omnipotence could turn it back."[53] Wash's sense of disempowerment before the wheel of progress perhaps explains why by 1908 he had begun studying parapsychology. The study of the supernormal powers of the human mind, parapsychology became a popular pursuit in the early twentieth century, attracting luminaries such as William James, C. S. Peirce, and Francis Parkman. Like its contemporary, Freudian psychology, it rejected the mechanistic view of the world propounded by turn-of-the-century scientists, who dismissed everything that was not material as mere fantasy. Yet, by conducting experiments and speaking in the language of the laboratory, psychical researchers wrapped themselves in the cloak of the scientific method, thereby appropriating the tools of their opponents.[54]

When in Washington, Wash attended lectures on "New Thought" by Dr. Bethella Northington, listened to an address by Swami Paramanda on "self-control," and read *The Law of Correspondences Applied to Healing* by W. J. Colville.[55] He also began reading *Eternal Progress*, a monthly magazine whose stated purpose was "to make true idealism practical in everyday life, to bind the common to the superior, to weld together business and scientific living."[56] One issue promised to assist the reader in transforming himself into "an Edition de Luxe of man" who will have "the finest, the strongest, the most perfect, the most beautiful and the most inspiring personality in the world." Material wealth did not matter. "When there is something that you want, never say, 'I hope to get it,' " counseled one issue of *Eternal Progress*; "say that you will get it, and thoroughly believe what you say."[57] "Success becomes inevitable when you *feel* that success is in you," advised another issue; "and success is in you when you arouse to action *all* that is in you."[58]

The serial, renamed the *Progress Magazine* in June 1909, also included encomiums to progress. "The Phenomenal Growth of a Modern City, and Its Future Possibilities" profiled Gary, Indiana, of all places. Poverty and unemployment were not among the future possibilities imagined by the author. "The Conquest of the Air" and "Electric Railways vs. Steam" illustrated the power of new technologies; "Modern Development in the Art of Colonization" described how prefabricated homes facilitated the colonization of western Canada.[59] The October 1910 issue featured a cover story titled "The Indian in Practical Arts," which documented Native Americans at Carlisle and Hampton Institutes making harnesses and baskets and doing the laundry.[60] The following month, the *Progress Magazine* investigated "Scientific Race Culture," informing the reader that eugenics "means simply *judicial mating*."[61]

Parapsychology allowed Wash to be progressive even as the narrative of progress foretold his demise. Science determined he was inferior, technology regarded him as primitive, and business deemed him an obstacle to development. Yet *Progress Magazine* said that by focusing his energies, he could become a success. Some of his more esoteric readings, such as one on Hindu magic, offered even greater hope. This "curious volume," Wash wrote, insisted on an "unwavering faith in the final triumph of right."[62] Its teachings must have seemed revitalizing at a difficult and depressing time.[63]

In the turn-of-the-century narrative of progress, race played a central, indispensable role. In every story, the native, whether African, American, Australian, or Asian, stood as a representative of the past, an obstacle to the future, or a childlike ward in the present. [64] The native was the measure and confirmation of Anglo-Saxon superiority, as any reader of H. N. Hutchinson's *Living Races of Mankind* would learn. Published in England, this book billed itself as *A Popular Illustrated Account of the Customs, Habits, Pursuits, Feasts and Ceremonies of the Races of Mankind throughout the World*. Wash would purchase a copy in 1910.[65] This massive compendium of the world's races must have titillated armchair imperialists, for it included several photographs of bare-breasted, dark-skinned women among its 648 illustrations. Its stated purpose, however, was to educate colonialists: "It is now perceived that, if we are to maintain a great Imperial Policy and a lasting supremacy in trade," wrote Hutchinson, "it must be through a better understanding of the needs and characteristics of the various peoples with whom we are brought in contact."[66]

Not surprisingly, Hutchinson deemed the English "among the finest of the civilized races," noting their "remarkable . . . vigour of body and power of endurance," "love of fair play," "common sense," "practical ability," and their "fondness for outdoor life."[67] As for Africans, "in anything requiring judgment they are easily beaten," Hutchinson opined. They were "indolent" and "avaricious," even if occasionally given to "great feats of sacrifice and devotion." Their alleged insensitivity to pain led Hutchinson to this remarkable conclusion: "Operations can be conducted without anaesthetics which would be fatal to Europeans even with their aid."[68] "Aborigines" fared no better. The Indian was "unsuited to the restraints and trammels of civilised life" and therefore "steadily diminishing in numbers." Hutchinson dispassionately forecast, "There is every prospect of his ultimate disappearance."[69]

According to the narrative of progress, Indians were despondent over their imminent extinction, as numerous white artists imagined in their work. James Earl Fraser famously captured this sentiment in his sculpture, *The End of the Trail* (1915), which pictured a dejected warrior slumped over a dispirited horse.[70] Wash himself identified a despondency among the Creek Nation's leg-islators:

> I suppose when one can see nothing in the future to inspire and animate one's love of the identity of his people as a nation, which has heretofore buoyed him up to patriotic thought and action; when he can see nothing ahead but the extinction of his people as well as himself in the great maelstrom of white population flowing in and surging about the country; in short when he fully compasses the idea that the days of comfort and happiness for the fullblood Indian which were his only a little while ago are fast vanishing from him never again to return, it is natural for one so circumstanced to lose interest and become careless and listless as to the disposition made of public interests.[71]

But Wash spoke speculatively ("I suppose") and in the third person ("one"). He distanced himself from demoralized "full-blood" politicians.

Rather than feeling despondent, he found it also possible to identify with the rising American empire. In 1899, Wash's close friend and intellectual com-panion Alexander Posey, a renowned Creek poet and humorist, penned these lines in honor of recent American conquests:

> Move on, world of the Occident,
>   Move on! Thy footfalls thro' the globe
> Are heard as thou marchest
>   Into that larger day
> Whose dawn lights up the armored front
>   In Cuba and the Philippines.[72]

Elsewhere, Posey referred to "the grand march of our westward civilization," using an inclusive "our" that gave no hint of irony—not unlike Wash's reference to railroads and telegraphs ready to do "our" bidding.[73]

Wash similarly associated himself with progress. In 1900, some Creeks or-ganized an armed resistance to allotment and sought the assistance of other-worldly forces by performing ceremonial dances. "Poor deluded people!" Wash said of them.[74] "Full-bloods" had his "deepest sympathy" and "pity," he wrote, "but their ideas as to the course best to be pursued are so crude and out of harmony with the spirit of progress and advancement that I have long since decided that I am powerless to do them any good."[75] In his autobiography, he asserted that his great-great-grandfather, Robert Grierson, the Scottish progen-itor of the family, was no mere "savage." Rather, Robert was "indued with the true spirit of commerce and was a trader belonging to that class of useful pioneers ever found in the van of progress, boldly and openly blazing the way for advancing civilization and empire."[76] Intended only for the eyes of his family and descendants, the description of Robert was private and heartfelt.[77]

This act of identifying with advancing civilization and dissociating from Indians who were perceived to be in the rear guard demanded extraordinary denials. In 1903, after Wash's son Washington (known as Washie) graduated from West Texas Military Academy in San Antonio, he received an appointment from the U.S. Army in the Philippine Constabulary, a police force created to patrol America's newest colony.[78] Washie, reported the *St. Louis Globe*, "is perhaps the only member of the five civilized tribes of the Indian Territory whose worth and fitness has been recognized by the government by such an appointment."[79] There was an irony in the appointment: just as the United States had colonized Indian country, it was now doing so in the Philippines, and Washie was assisting in the task.[80] Moreover, Washie's very appointment was probably dependent on the connection that U.S. Army officers drew between Native Americans and native Filipinos.[81] Not long before his appointment, the Constabulary had begun enlisting Igorots, the local native peoples, in its ranks.[82] What better place for an Indian officer than in an army of native peoples? "In many respects these mountain people are like our American Indians," wrote one officer, who noted one difference: "Unlike the Indians, however, they never have been converted to wearing trousers."[83]

Wash, too, recognized a connection between the Igorots and Creeks. Shortly after his son's appointment, Wash received word that a Creek women he knew had conversed in the Muscogee language with one of the Igorots then on display at the Philippine Reservation in the St. Louis World's Fair. Wash began to suspect that these Filipinos might be related to the Creeks. "She now knows the no. of his bamboo hut, and his name," he wrote to the American Bureau of Ethnology, urging its anthropologists to investigate, but ultimately it was up to Wash to pursue the lead.[84]

In August 1904, he traveled to St. Louis to visit the fair. Officially titled the Louisiana Purchase Exposition, the fair was a monument to progress and colonization.[85] Inside the Palace of Electricity and Machinery, visitors could watch the manufacture of lightbulbs, study an exhibit on wireless transmission, and marvel at a three-thousand-horsepower steam engine. In the United States Government Building, they could touch a twelve-inch coastal defense rifle and explore a cutaway full-scale section of a warship.[86] Exiting the building, they might have noticed that the massive facade towered over a statue of a fleeing Indian and buffalo. According to an official guidebook, *The Destiny of the Red Man* illustrated the fate of "the aboriginal inhabitants of America." "The Indian with

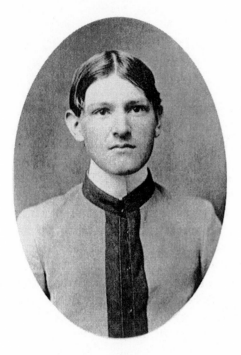

Washie Grayson in school uniform.
Courtesy of the Research Division
of the Oklahoma Historical Society.

all his trappings and superstitions is departing, along with the bison of the plains," the book relayed. "The group expresses the departure of barbarism driven out by civilizing institutions and influences that are making the Indian self-supporting and fitting him for citizenship."[87]

The Philippine Reservation stood within the anthropology exhibit—"47 acres, 1200 Natives," who, according to the chief of the exposition's Department of Anthropology, illustrated the "upward course of human development."[88] (One photogravure from an official publication placed the Indian four spots above prehistoric man but a full seven spots below the crowning "Americo-European," with Arabs, Turks, Japanese, and others intervening.)[89] The exhibit featured Cheyenne, Pueblo, Navajo, Wichita, Sioux, Pawnees, Pima, Kickapoo, Pomo, Ojibwa, Osages, Apaches, Kwakiutl, and Kloakwaht Indians, but it was the Filipinos, especially the "dog-eating human-head hunters," the Igorots, who attracted most viewers.[90] Their culinary practices earned the condemnation of the St. Louis Humane Society, and their scanty clothing drew an alarmed telegram from the White House demanding that they be "more fully clad." Where an Igorot wore a "mere G string," proposed the secretary of war, "it might be well to add a short trunk to cover the buttocks and the front."[91] The suggestion was rejected, and the public continued to flock to the alluring display.[92]

As its name suggested, the Philippine Reservation was intended to draw parallels between the U.S. guardianship of native Filipinos and Native Americans, an association that politicians frequently made in the halls of Congress.[93] The ability, if not obligation, of the United States to civilize the native inhabitants of its most recent conquest was reinforced by the juxtapositions between primitivism and civilization that were everywhere on the fairgrounds: grass dwellings and exhibition palaces, spear-wielding natives and Philippine Constabulary troops, bare-breasted Igorots and St. Louis ladies clothed head to toe.[94] In short, the Louisiana Purchase Exposition celebrated imperialism, both old and new.

Wash's visit with the Igorots ended in mild disappointment, for he "could not alone make out that these people understood any of our language," yet he continued to urge scholars to investigate the linguistic relationship.[95] Despite his insistence on finding common Creek and Igorot heritage, he failed to admit any connection between U.S. colonial policies in the Philippines and in North America. A year after returning from the world's fair, Wash proudly reported that his son had "supreme control" over a population of eight thousand people who had been forced from their homes and concentrated in new settlements.[96] In 1906, Wash learned that Washie "had succeeded in breaking up more bands of ladrones [thieves] and killing off more of them than almost any other young officer." What was remarkable in his case, wrote Wash, was that "after all his deadly work against the natives of the lawless class, he still retained the friendship of the pacified natives, something very few have been able to do."[97] His son's achievements filled him with "pride and satisfaction," Wash confessed when as a Creek diplomat he met President Roosevelt in 1907.[98]

One Constabulary officer, Lieutenant-Colonel Harold Elarth, observed that with the "Indian wars . . . long since over," the "pioneering instinct now found outlet in the new American possessions in the Far Pacific."[99] In some sense, Washie was playing the role of his family's progenitor, Robert Grierson, and Wash himself may have seen the connection when he described his great-great-grandfather "boldly and openly blazing the way for advancing civilization and empire." The experience may not have sat so well with Washie. Although he voluntarily enlisted in a second tour of duty in the Philippines, he returned home in 1913 with a serious drinking problem and soon married a woman reputed to be a prostitute.[100] "Such, and even more disagreeable things have occurred in families before," Wash wrote cryptically, "and we possibly may not expect to be any exception."[101] One wonders to what degree Washie and his father identified with Lieutenant-Colonel Elarth's assessment of the U.S. conquest of the Philippines: "We began to live Kipling for ourselves."[102]

The ideology that justified the conquest of the Philippines also justified white rule at home, specifically the exclusion of southern European immigrants from the United States and the oppression of African Americans.[103] When whites looked forward to Indian Territory's statehood, they imagined not only railroads, steam engines, and the wireless telegraph but also Jim Crow, the segregation of public spaces by race.[104] Yet most whites, though anxious to avoid contact with black Americans, were comparatively tolerant of civilized Indians, and in fact some, including commissioner of Indian affairs Francis Leupp (1904–1909), positively encouraged marriages between the two groups.[105] The children of these unions, Leupp observed, inherited from their Indian blood a "keenness of observation, stoicism under suffering, love of freedom," and "a contempt for petty things"; from their white blood, they acquired "the competitive instinct, individual initiative, resourcefulness in the face of novel obstacles, and a constitution" suited to "the artificialities of modern life."[106] The contrasting white attitudes toward black and Native Americans placed Emma and Wash on opposites sides of the color line.

From Oktaha, Emma and her family watched as Jim Crow spread throughout the region. It started first in Oklahoma Territory, the western half of present-day Oklahoma, and then spread to Indian Territory. Using violence, intimidation, and the sanctions of the law, whites expelled blacks from a long list of places: Lexington (1892), Norman (1896), Tecumseh (1897), Pottawatomie County (1898), Billings (1899), Stroud (1901), Sapulpa (1901), Waurika (1902), Lawton (1902), Shawnee (1902), Marshall (1904), Claremore (1905), and Henryetta (1907).[107]

This grim and violent process had become known across the country as "whitecapping," and local expulsions of blacks became a way of life in Indian Territory. "The ones who wouldn't leave were beaten until they were glad to leave," said one white resident who lived in Henryetta, about thirty miles from Emma's farm in Oktaha. "There were three or four beaten with shinny clubs until they were almost dead."[108] (Henryetta was named after Hugh Henry, Wash's old partner in the cattle industry.) Another Henryetta resident, whose husband was reportedly shot by a black man, recalled unashamedly that she "wanted them to hang him and shoot him full of holes," which is exactly what whites did after stringing the victim up on a telephone pole. That same December night in 1907, they ordered all blacks to leave town by sunrise.[109]

When black Oklahomans recalled these events some seventy-five years later, the sense of fear and anger was still palpable. "When we went through Pryor," just northeast of Tulsa, recalled one elderly couple in 1969, "they waved at us to keep on going." Residents of nearby Adair were similarly hostile. Jenks Ross remembered returning from work at night. When he got off the train at Adair, he would sprint until he got out of town. "This isn't Kansas," a white man warned him. Alice, Jenks's wife, stated simply, "It was a place of horror. I never saw people like that."[110]

Her recollections were matched by those of some whites and Indians who remembered Jim Crow merely as an inconvenience or a source of humor. Nora Eades, a white woman who lived just west of Oklahoma City, recounted how her school had one "negro boy." When drinking water was passed around, she would go without if the bucket and tin cup had reached the black student first.[111] Another, a boardinghouse owner, complained about a white woman who arrived "with a colored man in tow," expecting a room for her companion. The board-inghouse owner compromised by letting the man sleep in the barn. The woman "was some sort of evangelist," the innkeeper recalled, "and got the notion that there should be no color line."[112] Tom Hawkins, an elderly Cherokee, saw only humor in the oppression of African Americans. In 1969, he fondly remembered when one sheriff confronted a suspected bootlegger. The "nigger" complained that he was left standing in freezing weather, while even the sheriff's horse had a blanket. "Sheriff said, why you black son-of-a-bitch, you don't call yourself a man, do you?" The sheriff made the shivering victim wait outside until he had ridden over a distant ridge. Hawkins then recounted another story he found amusing about how his friend crudely directed a "nigger lawyer" to the "nigger hotel." "We never had trouble when we owned niggers," Hawkins concluded.[113]

By 1904, Jim Crow had reached Emma's doorstep. In Oktaha, numbering barely three hundred people, black residents lived almost exclusively on the west side of the tracks, an area soon known as "nigger town."[114] Muskogee, the major city just up the road from Oktaha, also had white and black neighbor-hoods. Separate barrels of drinking water for whites and blacks were placed on Muskogee streets, public toilets were segregated, and a new steam-powered merry-go-round was prohibited to blacks.[115] African Americans who violated the segregated seating policy at Muskogee's only theater were promptly removed by the U.S. marshal.[116] Although there were not yet separate railcars on the train from Oktaha to Muskogee, African Americans sometimes had to defend their equal rights with fists.[117]

The segregation of public space placed race at the center of Creek politics. In 1899, when Wash was being mentioned as a candidate for principal chief, a Tulsa newspaper stated that his opponent, Pleasant Porter, was "intelligent, pro-gressive and an Indian, which cannot be said of Grayson." The comment implied that Indian identity was necessarily a product of blood, but Wash embraced rather than challenged its logic. "This my friends are enjoying as a good joke on me," he wrote, for Porter was "more negro and white than Indian, while I am only Indian and white whatever my general intelligence may be." He concluded, "Porter's friends can ill afford to bring into discussion his blood."[118] When Porter won the election, the opposition moved to disqualify him on account of his being a "Boloxi" Indian rather than Creek.[119] "Having never known of any possible bar to Porter's exercise of all the rights of a Creek citizen save his negro blood," wrote Wash, "all this talk sounds ludicrous to me."[120]

Yet Wash took note of every violation of the color line. He condemned one Creek politician whose wife was of African descent for being "very loose and careless in his marital relations."[121] In December 1903, he found that a hotel he visited in Okmulgee had recently been purchased by "a negro." "Stopping at negro hotels being entirely outside of my way of doing, I excused myself," he wrote.[122] That same month, he declined to join a Creek delegation to attend a constitutional convention called by the Five Tribes because there were two Afro-Creeks in the group.[123] A few years later, he agreed to serve in such a delegation but noted that there was only one "real Indian" in the party. The others were "mixed with negro blood" or "full negroes and of the blackest sort."[124] He recounted an "amusing" incident when one delegate, an "intensely black negro," was asked by a member of Congress to stand at the far end of the table. Wash wrote, "I at once thought that the suggestion might have come from his fear that so fat, sleek and densely black negro would, as such negroes commonly do, emit an odor that would be offensive to his olfactories."[125]

Wash's intellectual companion Alexander Posey made a point of voicing his racist opinions in public. The public forum turned private sentiment into political strategy; no matter how reprehensible, it was an effective means of distancing Indians from their African ancestry and thereby of improving their opportunities in the United States.[126] Posey's public comments, printed in local newspapers, were caustic: when an Indianapolis chambermaid refused to make a bed that Booker T. Washington had slept on, Posey deemed her "too intelligent" for her work and invited her to "come south and live with her friends"; Republicans, he charged, could take Missouri only by importing voters from Haiti; and the Republican *Checotah Times*, he wrote, had "appreciative" readers in Africa.[127] His humor was barbed: sweet potatoes were "nigger chokers"; in Muskogee, "Niggers was thick like blackbirds behind a plow"; a Eufaula train station had "nothing but lots of niggers" who were "fixing to go to Africa, or maybe so to Muskogee or Wildcat."[128]

By 1903, Creek political discourse had degenerated even further. When Wash lost the nomination for principal chief that year, he consoled himself that everyone who voted for him "was a man of good appearance and was a good citizen." His opponents, he alleged, were "largely negroes and very common Indians."[129] (Two years later, he would take similar satisfaction in finding that "the negro votes" went solidly against him in his successful election as a delegate to Washington, D.C.)[130] With Wash out of the running, Legus Perryman and Pleasant Porter faced off in the 1903 contest for principal chief, inspiring Alexander Posey to fill his newspaper columns with racist slurs. Perryman received most of the vitriol. "All that we are able to say is that he is a nigger and a bad one at that," Posey wrote in June 1903.[131] "He hasn't changed a bit," Posey wrote a few months later; "he has the same kind of pigment under his skin that doesn't fade." At a Porter barbecue, wrote Posey, there was "a nigger doll rack for the benefit of those that desire to throw it into Legus." In fact, joked Posey, Perryman was only running for office to seek "a little free advertising" for his invention, "a potient to take the kinks out of wool."[132] Porter did not entirely escape Posey's wrath. When Porter won the election, Posey wrote that Indians voted for other candidates such as Wash, leaving nothing for Porter and Perryman "but niggers to vote for them and maybe so a few half breed that was hungry for pie."[133]

As the political climate turned uglier, Wash became the vice president of the Democratic Club in Eufaula in 1904 and therefore a public proponent of segregation.[134] That same year, he joined with Pleasant Porter and a few others to create a Creek political party that explicitly excluded blacks.[135] Creek freedmen and "nigger" meant the "same thing," wrote Wash's friend Posey.[136] Wash and his allies were on the leading edge of the region's politics, anticipating the policies of the national Democratic and Republican parties, which were battling for control of Oklahoma and Indian Territory in anticipation of statehood. Democrats leveled charges that the Republicans were "nigger lovers" and circulated cartoons of black men marrying white women. In Muskogee, the racist appeals successfully secured the 1905 election for Democrats, who garnered the support of many Indians as well as whites. In response, a faction of the Republican Party rejected its black constituents and began calling itself "lily-white."[137]

Racist politicking reached a fever pitch in 1906 with the election of delegates to the Oklahoma constitutional convention. "Are you, Mr. Voter, going to support a party that openly and brazenly seeks to send a negro to the constitutional convention to write the laws under which we white people are to live?" asked the *Oktaha Democrat* in Emma's hometown.[138] "It is principally a race campaign," concluded the newspaper.[139] In Eufaula, Wash considered running as a Democratic candidate to the convention.[140] When the Democrats took 100 out of 112 seats, whites declared that the new state would be a "white man's country." "The Negro," proclaimed William "Alfalfa Bill" Murray, the convention's president and the state's future governor, "must be taught in the line of his own sphere, as porters, boot-blacks, and barbers, and many lines of agriculture, horticulture and mechanics in which he is adept, but it is an entirely false notion that the negro can rise to the equal of a man in the professions or become an equal citizen to grapple with public questions."[141] Wash would later declare that he was "quite well pleased" with Murray's position on "public questions."[142]

In March 1907, with these dark clouds looming on the horizon, Emma died. In her obituary, the *Checotah Times* mistakenly reported that she had been born two centuries earlier, in 1799, making her 108 at the time of her death. The newspaper suggested that the demise of this ancient woman, whose advanced age seemed to approach biblical proportions, marked the final passing of the premodern era. "She has been an eye witness to a country that knew no agricultural resources and then of its unfolding to one of the most appreciated farming countries known to man," it observed. To "a certainty," the newspaper wistfully concluded, "no child who claims 1907 as the starting point in life will be able to give the undeveloped history of any country as Annie [or Emma] Grayson has given of the Indian Territory."[143] She was buried on her allotment in a small graveyard that also contains the remains of her nephew and niece.

Eight months later, on the day of Oklahoma's statehood, the *Muskogee Phoenix* proclaimed, "There is a new light in the East." "The brightest day in all the history of the Red Man's land has dawned," the elated writer continued. The

Emma Grayson's tombstone, June 2002. Following Creek pronunciation, the stone names her as "Emmer." Photograph by the author.

promise of advancement, the potential of the future, seemed unlimited, at least to white Oklahomans:

> Looking down the darkening shadows of the past, its obstacles to over-come, its disappointments outlived, its obstructions to advancement swept aside by the energy, determination, and ambition of our people, we turn with confidence to the future, proud in the record of yesterday, masterful in the strength of today, and meet the future, secure in the belief that tomorrow will bring to us but additional triumphs in life's battle.[144]

But even this jingoistic writer was careful to note that the bright light from the east shone on the Indian's land, not on the Indian. In fact, white Oklahomans rapidly turned from eulogizing the passing of ancient Indians such as Emma to stealing their lands. With energy, determination, and ambition, they would soon dispossess Emma's heirs of their homes.

Profile

Bob Littlejohn, June 2002

In 2002, when I started writing up my interview with Bob Littlejohn, I looked over my notes for references to his great-great-grandfather Aaron Hall, who had married Lucy, William and Judah's daughter. I found none and asked Tressie Nealy, a friend of mine and an expert genealogist who volunteers at the Oklahoma Historical Society, to check the census records. What she found was surprising. Littlejohn had said he was related to the Graysons through his mother, Maple. In fact, according to the U.S. census, Maple's parents were Joe and Lizzie Hall, both born and raised in Georgia. They were married in southern Georgia in 1908 and moved west to Oklahoma with Joe's parents, Cornelius and Mary, in 1911 or 1912. Joe and Lizzie settled just north of Oktaha.[1] Littlejohn could not have been descended from the Graysons through his mother, according to these records.

Soon after tracing Littlejohn's relatives back to Georgia, I called him to ask again how he was related to the Graysons. This time, he made no mention of Aaron Hall and Lucy. Instead, he stated that Sarah, a daughter of William and Judah's, had remained in Georgia after the family moved to Indian Territory in 1834. Sarah's daughter Mary was Littlejohn's great-great-grandmother. Although it cannot be disproved, this story seems unlikely on several accounts. Mary was born in 1862, meaning that her mother, Sarah, could not have been born much before 1822. Sarah therefore would have been twelve years old when she was left behind by William and Judah. Moreover, it is doubtful that William and Judah would have left behind any daughter, no matter what her age. It is even more doubtful that that daughter would have then moved from Alabama to Georgia, and that the family would have been reunited in Oklahoma two generations and seventy-five years later.

In June 2002, I met Littlejohn at Furr's, a cafeteria-style restaurant in southeastern Tulsa. He immediately warmed to the subject of African and Indian relations and recounted some of his favorite stories. Indians came from West Africa and settled in Mesoamerica, he explained to me once again, this time adding that he himself is related to the Chitimacha Indians of northern Mexico. "Our ancestors did not come on the slave ship," Littlejohn stated. "They were here when Columbus arrived." After dinner, we drove up Memorial Drive to Fifteenth Street, which dead-ends on a small cemetery where a number of Graysons are buried. It is located on the former allotment of Julia Grayson, the descendant of Venus and Jim, Grayson slaves.

It is difficult to reconcile Littlejohn's vast and intimate knowledge of the Graysons with the fact that he is not related to the family. How had he known about William and Judah and their children? Why had he suspected that Wash's autobiography was bastardized, that Katy had in fact borne two children by a man of African descent? Littlejohn undoubtedly spent many hours researching the subject, as had I. But it is also possible that Littlejohn's family stories came from the Graysons themselves, as related through Cornelius, his grandfather the raconteur, who lived near Oktaha and who must have known Eli and Vicey personally.

By including more than it should, Littlejohn's family tree is in some ways the opposite of Wash Grayson's expurgated autobiography. Littlejohn's view of history and family is inclusive to a fault, so that he is related to everyone, and all civilizations are unified by their common origins in Africa. His fictional stories, which undermine racial categories and reinsert Africans into our nation's past, have more truth in them than many histories.

When I finally did locate a possible living descendant of William and Judah Grayson, the experience fell far short of my rewarding meetings with Littlejohn. In spring 2002, I sent letters to nearly 250 Graysons living in Oklahoma, explaining my research and enclosing a self-addressed, stamped postcard should they wish to share family stories. One respondent told me that James Grayson in Tulsa was William and Judah's descendant. James, however, did not return a postcard. I wrote a personal letter to him but received no response. Then I telephoned, and he hung up while I was introducing myself. "He's mad at the world," observed one acquaintance, explaining that the Creek Nation refused to recognize his citizenship. Perhaps his response is as understandable as Littlejohn's. The Graysons' story might culminate in a distrust of received history and a refusal to accept the validity of racial categories. It also might culminate more simply in distrust and anger.

10 ■■

The Graysons in a Black and White World

In the early twentieth century—the era of segregated schools, Jim Crow train coaches, and redlined neighborhoods—Americans believed they were merely enforcing biological prescriptions, the self-evident divisions between black and white. But in fact they were using the force of law and the threat of violence to create the very racial categories they pretended were natural.[1] In this black and white world, Americans made no accommodation for Indians, instead attempting to conceptualize Indian difference in familiar terms. "Prairie nigger," used by whites to describe Plains Indians, reflected just such an effort to place native peoples on one side of the black-white divide that ran through America.[2] Language alone, however, had only limited effectiveness in classifying and segregating Indians. In Oklahoma, with its large native population, the Indian's anomalous status on the color line demanded a legal solution. At the state's constitutional convention, delegates cynically addressed the matter simply by declaring that all Oklahomans were either black or white. Section 3, Article 13, of the state's constitution stipulated that, for purposes of segregating schoolchildren, individuals with even the remotest African ancestry were black; all others, including Indians, were white.[3]

Delegates might have instead defined Indians as black rather than white, but at least a few prominent politicians in the state claimed to have an Indian ancestor in the distant past. Eleven of the 112 delegates were known to be Native American, and many others had close ties to leading native families.[4] The convention's president, William Murray, for example, traced his ancestors to Pocahontas and John Rolfe.[5] (In Virginia in 1924, the number of eminent individuals claiming descent from this marriage gave rise to the "Pocahontas exception": persons who had "less than one sixty-fourth of the blood of an American Indian" and no other "non-Caucasic blood" were defined as white.)[6] Murray could claim more recent Indian ties, as well. He had served as general counsel to the Chick-asaw Nation, and his wife was related to leaders of both the Choctaw and Chick-asaw nations. Although Murray could tolerate and even respect civilized Indians, he "had no use for Negroes," according to one freedman, "especially those who claimed they were not Negroes."[7] The "worst Negroes," Murray once observed, "were those in the Creek Nation who had been partially assimilated."[8] The state constitution may have exposed to everyone that race was man's, not nature's, creation, but the delegates' discomfort at such a revealing act of legislation was outweighed by their relief that the state's Indian population could no longer legally harbor people of African descent.

Legislators soon extended the color line from schools to other public spaces. The first law adopted by the new state segregated public transportation.[9] Other Jim Crow laws followed, each one using the "one-drop" rule to define Oklaho-mans as either black or white. In 1908, the legislature forbade people of African descent from marrying people not of African descent. Two years later, it enacted a law that required voters to pass a literacy test. The law included a grandfather clause that excepted citizens who had been permitted to vote anywhere on Jan-uary 1, 1866. The literacy test, judged arbitrarily, effectively disenfranchised most African Americans, while the grandfather clause automatically enfranchised whites. By shrewdly placing the cutoff date of the grandfather clause on the first day of 1866, just six months before the signing of the treaties that had enfran-chised freed people in the Five Tribes, it also gave Indians but not their ex-slaves the right to vote.[10]

Despite laws making them white, dark-skinned Indians frequently lived "across the tracks" in "Negro Town," as did one Indian resident of Sapulpa.[11] A few, however, crossed over to the white side of town, as was evident in Eufaula, during the first election held after the passage of the voting act. When black Oklahomans approached the ballot boxes, they encountered an election judge, one of the town's leading figures, who administered the literacy test and deter-mined the competency of dark-skinned voters. He was Wash Grayson. "The subjection of the negro voters to the educational test," Wash wrote, "rendered the voting by the negroes a very slow process."[12] Wash and his cousins Eli and Jeanetta now could not legally send their children to the same schools or ride in the same railcars. In black and white Oklahoma, the Graysons lived on op-posite sides of the tracks.

Wash had lost a fortune from allotment and the dissolution of the Creek Nation, but in Oklahoma he was legally white and recognized as a leading citizen.[13] His place along the color line is immediately evident in daily diary entries: "Hired negro . . . and worked him 7 hours"; "a very black negro boy . . . carried in for me about a ton of coal and piled it up in the basement"; "Our Cook man has gone to a negro picnic"; "I got a small and very black negro this morning to cut and split some stove wood for me"; "Wallace my tramp negro began this morning the work of building, or rather, renovating the old paling fence."[14] Wash practiced what he preached: "I don't favor calling negroes up to serve Indians or whites in any capacity other than menials."[15]

In his daily life, he paid careful attention to the rules of Jim Crow. While traveling through Boley, an all-black town, Wash worried that he might have to stay overnight. To his relief, he learned that proprietors of "the 'nigger' hotel," as he called it, "understood and respected" the "preferences and prejudices of whites" and knew "how to treat white customers acceptably."[16] On another occasion, he attended services at an Indian church and found himself placed at a lunch table with "an old negro woman." Although she was at the opposite end, Wash commented that the experience was "something quite out of the usual for me." He made his displeasure known, and the next day, the minister apologized to him for the seating arrangement. "He was quite profuse in his disavowal of the action," wrote Wash, "and was free to promise unsolicited that such action

Wash Grayson's home, photographed from the back. Courtesy of the Western History Collections, University of Oklahoma Libraries.

should not be repeated."[17] These small acts of racism led to a more disturbing disregard for African Americans. On August 1, 1914, Crocket Williams, a black man, was lynched in Wash's hometown. "The mob appears to have been very quiet and orderly in its work," Wash noted, "and the residents of the city were not in the least disturbed in their slumbers." The "consensus of opinion appears to be that the riddance is a good one," he concluded.[18]

Wash's uncompromising attitude toward African Americans was part of a larger effort to identify with selective chapters in his history. Beginning in 1900, he was a brigadier general in the Creek Division of the United Confederate Veterans (UCV).[19] He and his wife, Annie, participated in yearly UCV reunions held on Jefferson Davis's birthday. Some years, the events were close to home, but other years demanded travel to Dallas, Texas (where Wash's daughter Tsianina was appointed "chief maid of honor" to the UCV of Indian Territory); Memphis, Tennessee; and Little Rock, Arkansas.[20] On Jefferson Davis's birthday in 1905, Wash received the "cross of honor" from the Daughters of the Confederacy.[21] In 1912, in Washington, he visited Confederate graves at Arlington National Cemetery.[22] On another visit to Arlington four years later, Wash was moved by a monument to Confederate dead, "a grandly beautiful structure" erected by the United Daughters of the Confederacy. Wash copied into his diary the two inscriptions on the pedestal, a reflection of his conscious identification with the defeated South.[23]

Wash Grayson, a few years before his death. Courtesy of the Western History Collections, University of Oklahoma Libraries.

The UCV parades, reunions, and meetings were public events that drew leading citizens from Wash's hometown and state. His sister-in-law threw a party to raise funds for a memorial in Eufaula; his wife hosted a meeting in their parlor; on the occasion of receiving the cross of honor, he sent a copy of his speech to the local newspaper for publication.[24] In McAlester, Oklahoma, during one reunion, he marched through the center of town while young ladies sang "Dixie."[25] In Muskogee, just north of the residence of old William and Judah, he posed before a camera with one hundred other veterans and then paraded through the streets to "Dixie" and other "martial music."[26] In short, by publicly participating in memorials to the Lost Cause, Wash broadcast his respectability, validated his heritage, and distanced himself from the state's African Americans, who were being kicked off streetcars, run out of towns, and even lynched.

Heritage seems to have become of increasing concern for Wash after statehood. In fact, it is clear from his autobiography, which he began in 1905 and completed in 1913, that the presence of black Graysons in Oklahoma was weighing especially heavily on him at this time. Not meant for the public eye, the autobiography accounted for the existence of black Graysons (they were ex-slaves or William and Katy's children), but it also mounted a spirited defense of the purity of own "lineal descent." "For be it understood," Wash wrote, "that while there have been a number of persons bearing the name Grayson, of whose acts we cannot speak or conceive of with any measure of approval or toleration, the original Scotsman of that name to whom we trace our origin was in all respects a worthy gentleman of whom his descendants may well be proud."[27] After recounting the family's genealogy, he added that "no descendant need ever be ashamed to trace his relationship" to Robert Grierson.[28] Wash assured on numerous occasions that the Graysons were historically the "wealthiest" and "most influential" family in their surrounding country.[29]

Wash not only mounted a vigorous defense of his ancestry but also showed a growing interest in his Scottish heritage. In late March 1908, he visited the Library of Congress in search of information on his "old Scottish ancestors."[30] A week later, he and his son-in-law attended a performance of Thomas Dixon's malevolent play, The Clansman, which purported to dramatize how "the reincarnated souls of the Clansmen of Old Scotland," more prosaically known as the Ku Klux Klan, restored white supremacy to the South after a period of black misrule [31] All the action was filtered through Dixon's central obsession, the violation of white women by black men. The African American intellectual and activist W. E. B. DuBois sarcastically summarized Dixon's theme: "There's a black man who thinks himself a man and is a man; kill him before he marries your daughter!"[32] The play, based closely on Dixon's inflammatory 1905 novel of the same name, was hugely controversial, even among white southerners, but it was also a great commercial success.[33] Wash was well aware of its notoriety. In 1907, African Americans in Muskogee had successfully lobbied against its performance in town.[34]

Wash did not comment on the *The Clansman* in his diary, but it seems only to have encouraged his interest in his Scottish ancestry. In May 1909, he sent away to Cleveland for *The Laird of Lag*, a book about Sir Robert Grierson of Scotland, whom Wash mistakenly suspected to be the progenitor of his family.[35] That same month, he took out a subscription to the *Weekly Scotsman*. He later placed an advertisement in the Edinburgh newspaper asking fellow readers to send him genealogical information on the Griersons.[36] Toward the end of 1909, he purchased *The Scottish Clans and Their Tartans* from a bookseller in New York. The following year, he posted letters to seven different Griersons in Edinburgh, hoping that one of them was his distant relative.[37]

Wash's pursuit of his Scottish ancestry was part of a larger burgeoning of interest in popular genealogy at the end of the nineteenth century. Across the country, newspapers began carrying genealogical columns, and in New York, the Astor Library (the predecessor of the New York Public Library) even installed a separate room to accommodate the large numbers of researchers. Between 1890 and 1900, no fewer than thirty-five hereditary societies, such as the Daughters of the American Revolution, were established. The upsurge in genealogical research had two related sources. First, many white Americans were unsettled by the large numbers of Italian and Jewish immigrants who began flooding East Coast cities in the 1890s. To distance themselves from this "foreign element" and to claim power as guardians of American tradition, nonimmigrants of British descent began tracing their lineal ancestors. Second, with the rise of eugenics, genealogy offered important evidence of one's fitness and worth. It was not by chance that the Daughters of the American Revolution, the National Genealogical Society, the Immigration Restriction League, the American Breeders' Association, and the Eugenics Record Office were all established in the two decades following 1890.[38]

Of course for Indians, American identity was more complicated. Perhaps Wash took the position of Cherokee William Eubanks, like himself a former captain in the Confederate army. Eubanks's brand of nativism rejected not just the "nihilist, the anarchist, the striker," and the "foreign pauper" who invaded the United States but also the "unnumerable long haired, dirty, greasy and black skinned white men" who overran Indian country.[39] From this perspective, Indians were more American than even the Anglo-Saxon bluebloods who looked down on Italians and Jews. Such views were not limited to native peoples. President Theodore Roosevelt once told Wash during a meeting with Creek delegates that he "half wished that he could by tracing back develop an Indian ancestry for himself," for then he "would be a true American."[40]

The equation between Americanness and racial ancestry took its most virulent and influential form in *The Birth of a Nation*, D. W. Griffith's infamous movie based on *The Clansman*. Wash saw it in December 1915 in Muskogee and noted afterward that it was "well worth seeing."[41] Like Dixon's novel and play, *The Birth of a Nation* drew on a prominent school of historical thought that held that Reconstruction—when black Americans were briefly granted civil and political rights after the Civil War—was manifestly unjust to the white South.[42] *The Birth of a Nation* powerfully dramatized this interpretation of the past and suggested that, after the failure of Reconstruction, the United States was triumphantly born as a white man's country.[43] In one memorable scene in the South Carolina House of Representatives in 1871, Griffith shows black representatives boozing, grinning, and eating chicken. After passing a bill providing for the intermarriage of blacks and whites, they leer at the "helpless" white women (as the intertitle describes them) observing from the gallery. "Much of it is distinctly thrilling, while other scenes were pathetic," Wash commented. The film reproduced "the horrors of reconstruction," he wrote, revealing his personal views about race and equality. It showed how "the people of the overpowered South" were "forced" into the Ku Klux Klan "for self-protection," he concluded.[44]

Like Dixon's play, *The Birth of a Nation* centered on the violation of white women by black men. Griffith reportedly cast Lillian Gish as Elsie Stoneman, one of the film's central characters, because, said Gish, she was "blonde and fragile-looking." "The contrast with the dark man evidently pleased Mr. Griffith," she recalled.[45] In the film's climax, the Klan narrowly saves Elsie from being raped by Silas Lynch, "mulatto leader of the blacks."[46] What Wash made of these scenes is impossible to say, although it seems likely that they brought to mind his family's own complicated and reimagined history.

On two occasions, Wash's actions encapsulated the contradictions, ironies, and tragedies of his family's and his nation's history. In 1907, he was asked to write an entry on Pleasant Porter for the Smithsonian's *Handbook of American Indians*. Porter, who died that same year, was his old friend from Confederate war days and a fellow member of the United Confederate Veterans.[47] They had joined together to reconstruct the nation along racial lines after the Civil War, and in 1904 they had cooperated to form a political party that excluded Creek freed people. Wash wrote in the *Handbook*, "His father was a white man, and Pleasant Porter inherited his Indian blood from his mother who through her father Tul-o-pe Tustun-ug-gee was of the Big Springs town of Creeks, but with a decided streak of negro blood in his veins." Porter was "ever true to his people,"

Wash wrote. At Wash's request, his name is not attached to the biographical entry.[48]

Wash similarly exposed Alexander Posey, his close friend and intellectual companion who delighted in maligning Creek politicians of African ancestry. Two years after Posey drowned in 1908, Wash came across a newly published volume of his friend's poems in which the introduction stated the poet was the child of a white man and a Creek woman of "full and pure blood," as Posey himself had maintained.[49] Wash suspected otherwise and broached the subject with a friend. "I asked him for the exact truth concerning Posey's progenitors in order that I might record the fact here for the information of such as may find this page in the future," Wash wrote in his diary. He learned that Posey's maternal grandmother was "so much mixed with negro blood as to appear very much like a full blood negress." Wash repeated the information for emphasis: "Alex. Posey therefore was of Indian, white and negro extraction." Wash, who had written that real Indians did not have "negro blood," who objected to sitting at tables with Negroes, who believed that Negroes should serve Indians and whites as "menials" only, added, "Whatever his lineage, however, he was a bright and most estimable gentleman, and one whom it was my pleasure and pride to number as one of my friends."[50]

Were these acts of unveiling meant to be tentative apologies for excluding people of African descent from the nation? Were they self-confessions, made through a third person? Or were they mean-spirited attacks, serving to draw attention away from his own past?

Across the tracks, Wash's relatives struggled to come to terms with Jim Crow. With Emma's death in 1907, it was left to her sister Vicey and her children, Eli and Jeanetta, to guide the family in the new state of Oklahoma. The color line appeared everywhere, imposed by public pressure and by force of law. Vicey amazingly found herself in the middle of a mean-spirited rumor campaign that upended the mayoral election in Muskogee in 1909. Word began spreading that Ira Reeves, a Republican candidate and veteran of the Spanish-American War, had African ancestry. Reeves's family had applied for Creek citizenship years earlier, wrote one prominent Muskogee resident in a private letter. Although the family "looked like white folks," she continued, "they claimed through a family mixed with negro blood." The rumor seemed substantiated, she suggested, because of the family's "intimacy with old Aunt Vicey Grayson."[51] Reeves quietly moved to Pennsylvania shortly after losing the election.[52]

It was a struggle for the Graysons to remain free from the stigma of African ancestry. Although Vicey, Eli, and Jeanetta were barely literate and left no diaries

Eli Grayson. James M. Etter, *Oktaha, a Track in the Sand* (Oktaha, OK: Oktaha Historical Society, 1982), 60.

or journals documenting their lives, their struggles can be traced in the records of the Oktaha public schools. After statehood, whites fought tirelessly to eliminate people of African descent from their schools. Two well-publicized court cases alerted Vicey, Eli, and Jeanetta to the dangers of living in Oklahoma. In the first, a number of students "forcibly prevented" Louis Hall from joining a literary society that met in a Muskogee public school, charging that Hall "was and is of African descent and negro blood." Hall sued for $10,000 in damages, arguing that he was not of African descent. He lost.[53] The Graysons' local newspaper, the *Oktaha Leader*, reported, "Hall claimed Portuguese blood and that he was a white man, but the jury evidently thought he was like 'Othello the Moore' that there must be negro blood in Hall."[54] It was hardly comforting that the newspaper disapproved of the verdict. Closer to home was a case heard several years later in Eufaula. Lewis Pitman's two daughters, ages nine and seven, were thrown out of school. Although Pitman was a Creek citizen by blood, the school board charged that he was of African descent. Pitman countered that he was "one-eighth pure Creek Indian blood, without a strain of African blood in his veins."[55] Pitman won this case, but the Graysons must have realized that they might at any time come under the attack of their racist neighbors.

A remarkable series of school enumeration reports, preserved because of the initiative of Wally Waits, the genealogy librarian at the Muskogee County Library, illustrates both the growing prominence of the color line and its effect on the Graysons. The booklets list and categorize each student in Muskogee County, including Oktaha. The recording of race became more strict over time, reflecting the growing concern of school clerks to segregate students. In 1912, for instance, the cards do not include an entry for race, although clerks informally placed black children at the back of the index. A year later, an Oktaha clerk clarified in longhand, "From Page 1 to Page 14 you will find the whites"; "From page 40 to page 58 you will find the Negro." Although there was still no entry for race, the solicitous clerk jotted down the race of each student in the lower left corner of the index cards.[56] In 1915 for the first time, the index cards included formal entries for "color" and "tribe."[57]

The Graysons had three sets of children in Oktaha schools, belonging to Eli, Onie Finniegan (Onie was Jeanetta's son), and John Casey (John was William and Judah's great-grandson, the grandson of their daughter Katie Grayson). These children were categorized and recategorized after 1910. John Casey's children were listed along with white students in 1912.[58] John's father was Irish, and there was probably little social pressure to define the family as black. In 1915, when the cards first required an entry for "tribe" and "color," the children were described as belonging to the tribe of "Creeks" and as "Creek" color, perhaps an underhanded way of avoiding listing the children as white.[59] In subsequent years, however, they were enumerated as white Creeks.[60]

The other Graysons, without a white parent or grandparent, were soon stigmatized as black. Onie Finniegan's children had an African American mother. They were listed with white students in 1912.[61] A year later, they were ambiguously described as "citizens," but listed at the back of the index, along with Negroes.[62] By 1915, they were enumerated as "colored" Creek Indians.[63] In 1917, they were listed simply as "colored," with no tribe.[64] Perhaps not coincidentally, the following year, Onie refused to enroll his children in school.[65] With every passing year, it seemed, his children were being stripped of their Indian identity. By 1920, they were back in school, still listed as "colored," but with the following tribal designation: "½ Creek Indian ½ c."[66]

Eli's son Henry was enumerated with white students in 1912 and 1913, the last two years of his schooling.[67] (Later, Henry fought and died in World War I, where, along with other Indians, he was enlisted with white troops.) Eli's other son, Edmond, was too old to attend school, but Edmond's daughter, son, and stepson all appear on the school enumeration reports. Edmond's wife, Maria, was his second cousin, the great-granddaughter of William and Judah. Maria's father was a freedman, a fact that made Edmond uncomfortable. When Edmond initiated divorce proceedings in 1920, he charged that Maria was frequently spending the night in Muskogee at the house of "a colored woman of very bad repute," much to his "chagrin and humiliation." After all, he reminded the court, he was "seven-eighths," and his wife "one-fourth Creek Indian blood."[68] He overlooked the fact that Maria was also at least five-eighths black in the eyes of the court.

Edmond's and Maria's African ancestry as well as Maria's black friends led school officials to single out their children as colored Creeks and colored freedmen.[69] By 1920, their children were described merely as colored, with no tribal affiliation.[70] In 1925, in the last enumeration report available, their daughter was described as a colored member of the Creek Nation and placed in a separate booklet with other "colored" children.[71] These enumeration reports, routine and trivial for the bureaucrats who produced them, in fact reflected the tremendous power that the state had in segregating and oppressing people of African descent. By 1920, both Eli's and Jeanetta's descendants were classified as black, subject to punishing legislation passed by lawmakers, to humiliating daily slights, and to impoverishing economic discrimination that African Americans face in the United States.

The cost of being black became clear to everyone on June 1, 1921, when word reached Oktaha that Tulsa was burning. After rumors swept white Tulsa that a young African American bootblack, Dick Rowland, had molested a white woman, armed whites stormed the black side of town. The mob destroyed one thousand homes and businesses, burning down several city blocks, including "Negro Wall Street," an area renowned for its thriving businesses. No records exist to verify the precise death toll, but white rioters undoubtedly murdered dozens of black Tulsans that day.[72] Photographs attest to the violent deaths of many. In the aftermath, white authorities held four thousand African Americans, one half of the city's black population, under armed guard in internment camps for days. Later a grand jury, charged with investigating the riot's causes, found that the city's black residents were responsible for the actions of the white mob. "Certain propaganda and more or less agitation had been going on among the colored population for some time," the grand jury concluded, and "the negro" began "to believe in equal rights, social equality, and their ability to demand the same."[73]

While Eli's and Jeanetta's descendants struggled to live with Jim Crow, Wash's fate was far different. In 1917, he was appointed by President Woodrow Wilson to serve as the principal chief of the largely defunct Creek Nation.[74] Under Wilson, the Bureau of Indian Affairs sought to cease its minimal protection of Native Americans and to expropriate remaining Indian resources for the benefit of whites. It granted fee-simple title to thousands of allottees, determining competency by calculating blood quantum and years of schooling, and it liberalized regulations permitting the exploitation of Native American lands. In the view of policy makers, most Indians would work as menials; more capable Indians, assumed to be those with a greater degree of European ancestry, would thrive. Such were the inevitable results of the collision between civilization and backwardness, they believed. Wash, as a forward-looking, light-skinned Indian, was therefore a suitable figurehead for the Creek Nation.[75]

The destructive century that followed Katy's and William's decisions came to a fitting close in 1924, when a Creek Indian named Myrtle McNac was called before an Oklahoma state judge. Like Katy more than one hundred years before her, McNac married a man of African descent. When Katy established her relationship with her unnamed partner in 1813, no one knew what their future would hold. Now, the fate of her twentieth-century counterpart made that future clear to all. McNac had to defend herself in court. If her husband had any African ancestry at all, then their marriage would violate the state's 1910 law against miscegenation. Fittingly, McNac's husband, James Grayson, may have been Katy's great-great-great-grandson by her first daughter, Annie.[76]

Myrtle and James met in 1910, but they did not begin seeing each other seriously until 1916.[77] In that year, they decided to live together, after "getting consent" from Myrtle's parents. James had recently signed an oil and gas mining lease on his allotment, located just west of Henryetta. For a single dollar, he had ceded all rights to crude oil extracted from his land for ten full years, and although he was to receive 12.5 percent of gross proceeds, he appears not to have collected any royalties. Because his allotment was either polluted with crude waste or simply poor farming land, James and Myrtle rented out a twelve-acre plot nearby, purchased a team of horses on borrowed money, and began growing cotton. Although James let some of the crop "get away" from him, according to one acquaintance, he "tended what he did pretty well." Desperately poor, they barely scraped together fifteen or twenty dollars every month to purchase needed groceries from the local store. On more than one occasion, they were forced to borrow money to buy food. In September 1917, James died at age thirty.

James had several heirs to his allotment, and some of them urgently needed cash. In 1915, his sister Caroline, for example, had written to the BIA requesting money due her. "I need it so very Bad I have ever thing ready to put up my fence only the wire and times are so hard that I cant feed my hogs," she explained.[78] Within a year of James's death, his siblings, nephews, and nieces had sold their combined interests in his land for $934 to W. R. Blake and several other white investors. A month later, Blake and his friends turned around and sold the allotment for $15,000.

This immense sum, gained by fleecing poor Creeks, would have passed unnoticed in Oklahoma had it not been for a lawsuit, soon entered in Muskogee District Court. The suit eventually made its way to the Oklahoma Supreme Court. William Sessions, a white speculator, claimed a half interest in the allotment because he had purchased Myrtle's rights to the estate of her husband for $100. Although the exploitation of poor, barely literate Creeks was perfectly legal under Oklahoma state law, Blake and his friends recognized that black-white marriages were not. As an Indian without African ancestry, Myrtle was legally white. Therefore, if it could be established that James had African ancestry, their common-law marriage would violate the 1910 miscegenation law, and Blake and his friends would retain their $15,000 profit.[79] Otherwise, the marriage would stand, and Sessions would be entitled to a half share of the allotment.

Blake's lawyers pursued two strategies. First, they tried to undermine the status of the common-law marriage by suggesting that Myrtle had a long history of moving from man to man. In particular, the lawyers sought to tarnish her reputation by insinuating that she slept with black men. "Now Myrtle ran away with a Negro didn't she?" they asked one witness. With Myrtle herself on the stand, they implied that she had "taken up" with several different men and that, in 1913 and 1914, she had run off to Kansas City "in company with a negro."[80] Myrtle denied the charges.

Second, Blake's lawyers attempted to establish that James had African ancestry and was therefore black by state law. Although James appeared on the Creek by-blood roll as three-fourths Indian, many of his close relatives were listed as freed people. Wash Edwards, a local farmer and stockman, took the stand and was questioned by Blake's lawyers:

Q. Everybody in the whole country talking about a nigger man and woman being man and wife?
A. I heard them say they were married.
Q. Were they niggers?

A. I do not know.

Q. Were they white people?

A. They called themselves Creek Indians.

Q. Pretty dark Indians, were they not?

A. Lots of these Creek Indians are dark.

Q. Were these dark?

A. Jim was darker than Myrtle.[81]

Joe Barnwell, a Creek Indian, offered equally damning testimony:

Q. Did you know a mixed blood Indian named James Grayson?

A. Yes.

Q. About what blood was he, if you know?

A. I do not know.

Q. Did he look like a negro or Indian?

A. Looked like he was mixed.

A. Negro and Indian.

A. Yes.[82]

Finally, Robert Grayson, James's brother, explained that their mother Lizzie was a "full-blood" but their father Austin "was three fourths and the other fourth colored."[83]

It only remained to confirm that Myrtle had no African ancestry. She was questioned directly:

Q. Myrtle are you a white person or an Indian?

A. Indian.

Q. Have you got negro blood in you? [objected and sustained]

Q. Are you a full-blood?

A. No, sir.

Q. How much?

A. Three-fourths.

Q. What is the other fourth, white?

A. I guess so.

Q. And three-fourths Indian.

A. Yes, sir.[84]

The district court found that, although James Grayson was enrolled on the by-blood rolls, he was "in truth and in fact a negro or person of african descent as defined by the Constitution and laws of the State."[85] Yet the court unexpectedly went on to rule against Blake. Miscegenation laws did not apply, it decided, since both James and Myrtle were Creek Indians. James and Myrtle had in fact been legally married.

Blake appealed to the state supreme court to determine whether or not the miscegenation statutes applied to persons "of part Indian blood."[86] Sessions's lawyers countered that neither Congress nor the Oklahoma Constitution intended "to make an Indian a white or colored person."[87] But Blake won the appeal, and James and Myrtle's marriage was declared illegal. The supreme court determined that, for purposes of law, all Indians were either black or white.

As is frequently the case, the decision merely followed social practice. In small, traditional Indian communities throughout the state, some people may have still disregarded racial categories. But in towns such as Eufaula and Oktaha, on segregated trains, in public bathrooms, in theaters and schools, there were black Indians and white Indians. Wash used coaches reserved for whites; his cousin Eli did not.

One hundred years after Katy had borne John and Annie by a man of African descent, the social world of the Graysons was pervaded by racism: "nigger," "negro blood," "full blood"—these terms were used casually in a court of law to determine findings of fact. Racist language established which group of white speculators had the right to exploit James's lands. The court showed no interest in the rights of his heirs, except to determine if they had African ancestry. In fact, C. T. Huddleston, Blake's lawyer, made light of James's desperate financial situation. James once had approached Adam Pence, a local banker, to borrow $125 for his farm. Pence turned him away. "And then he wanted $25.00," Pence told Sessions's lawyer, "but I did not let him have it." Huddleston launched his cross-examination. "You say you are a banker and you say this nigger talked you out of $25.00?" he mocked. Pence responded curtly, "No sir, he did not."[88] Swindling an Indian or "nigger" out of $15,000 was routine; loaning $25 to a hardworking black Indian farmer was preposterous.

Between 1918 and 1932, the older generation of Graysons passed away. With their deaths, the African heritage of the Graysons' family history began to fade from the memory of all but the direct descendants of William and Judah. At the same time, memories of what the South and Indian Territory looked like before the construction of a racial hierarchy also began to disappear. Emma Grayson, before her death in 1907, reportedly regaled her friends with stories of the past and "gave the hearers a real history of the Indian of the Creek nation."[89] But as the twentieth century progressed, only more recent memories survived of the stark divide between Indians and blacks, masters and slaves.

Emma's sister Jeanetta died in 1918. She owned 120 acres of land in Oktaha, appraised at $5,000. Because Jeanetta was enrolled as three-fourths blood and could not legally sell her restricted allotment, this impressive sum was meaningless during her lifetime. Her real worth was reflected more accurately in her livestock and personal property, which amounted to $600, after accounting for debt.[90] Wash died two years later, in 1920. He was significantly better-off. He owned thirteen unrestricted lots in Eufala, valued at $2,230, and possessed personal property and cash totaling $6,000.[91] His brother Sam had done even better. He owned unrestricted land worth $39,000 in Texas and Oklahoma.[92]

Vicey died in August 1930, possessing a restricted allotment of 120 acres but no personal property. In her last years, she depended on her neighbor, Alex Robinson, a black farmer, for food and medicine. She left behind a will, reflecting bitterness at being abandoned by her relatives. "My distant relatives have during the past 25 years paid me scant attention, and have left me alone," she stated. "I wish to say," she repeated,

> that while I have some distant relatives, and the same being nieces and nephews, and even more distant relatives, that they or none of them have ever at any time befriended me in my old age, nor have they taken the slightest interest in my wellfare, nor have they administered to me when ill, nor have they attended to my wants when storms kept me housed in.[93]

None fared worse than Eli and his son Edmond. In September 1931, seventy-two-year-old Eli Grayson was charged with first-degree murder. There is no record of the specifics of the case, and it may in fact never have gone to trial. Nevertheless, it put Eli deeply in debt to an attorney, for Eli agreed to pay him $500 for his services, even though his annual income averaged only $100. Eli died in December of that year. At his death, he owned 120 acres of land, a Jersey cow, three mules, eight hogs, a few farming tools, and an old Studebaker automobile, which was worth a mere $10. Medical and legal bills and funeral expenses amounted to a claim of $400 against his estate. The result was that all of Eli's personal belongings were auctioned off for $125 and the proceeds distributed to his creditors. Edmond received nothing but his father's allotment land, which was restricted and therefore not subject to seizure for debt.[94]

The land became unrestricted and alienable immediately upon the transfer of title from father to son, however, and Edmond, like thousands of other Indians in Oklahoma, was rapidly dispossessed of his inheritance. Semiliterate and desperately poor, Edmond was no match for the bankers and merchants who descended on his property. Whether illegally or merely unethically, they took possession of his valuable lands for a pittance. A week after his father's death, Edmond sold forty acres for $300 to J. R. Reinhart, a local merchant who kept many Oktaha residents in constant debt.[95] That same day, he sold another forty acres to R. S. Williams, director of the Oktaha State Bank, for a single dollar and "other considerations," and he mortgaged the remaining land to the Commercial National Bank. Two years later, he sold this mortgaged land for a dollar and "other considerations."[96] "I have got beat out of it," Edmond said of his father's allotment in 1935.[97]

By the mid-1930s, Edmond still possessed his own allotment, but he was in dire straits, having mortgaged both his livestock and his land. In July 1935, creditors threatened to seize Edmond's farm for an outstanding debt of $175, a sum that equaled his annual income. It is not clear how his farm, which was presumably on restricted land, could have legally been seized for debt. Yet the threat was real, and Edmond wrote directly to the commissioner of Indian affairs to request that he direct the BIA to remove the restrictions on four acres of his land that lay fallow across the Katy train tracks. "I have try to have it remove selvel time, but thay wont not do it for me," he wrote. "Now I wont it bad. So I can sell it and paid on my account." He was desperate. "Thay wont do what we ask them if I had money thay would do some things for me but Im just a poor boy and farm all my life."[98] Two weeks later, he received a letter from the BIA, enclosing a copy of the secretary of the interior's order number 420, prohibiting the removal of restrictions except in cases of emergency. The BIA agreed to initiate an inquiry to determine whether or not Edmond's case qualified.[99]

The inquiry came too late. By September, Edmond had lost his livestock and land. He rented back thirty-five acres of his former homestead, but Harrison Hunt, the new owner, threatened to evict him. Hunt had recently purchased the property for $650 from Harry Smith. Only three years earlier, Smith himself had been leasing the land from Edmond. At that time, Edmond claimed that Smith owed him five years of back rent; Smith in turn charged that he had lent Edmond at least twice as much. "If you do not know Edmond Grayson," Smith wrote in his defense, any of the BIA field clerks "can give you his reputation."[100] Edmond once again asked the BIA to remove restrictions on the final 2.55 acres in his name. He needed cash to pay for the hospital bills and funeral expenses of his daughter, Katie, who had recently died at age twenty-three. This time, the BIA approved his request.[101]

While Wash's descendants carried the stigma of being white and Indian in the United States, his relatives bore the heavier burden of being black and Indian.[102] It is ironic that Washie, who spent many years abroad fighting for the United States in the Philippines and in France during World War I, was chosen by the BIA to succeed his father as principal chief of the Creek Nation. He did not speak the Muscogee language.[103] Edmond, by contrast, lived his entire life in Oktaha and did speak Muscogee, yet his family was increasingly identified as black.[104] Washie died in 1962; his third cousin Edmond followed him a year later.[105]

Poverty and Jim Crow defined the lives of dark-skinned Indians in America. The Graysons' story unfortunately validates Katy's determination a century earlier to enslave rather than bear the children of Africans. If William's decision was the more admirable, Katy's was the more prescient.

Afterword

In March 2004, several years after I posted a query about Katy and her unnamed black husband on a Web site entitled the "African-Native American Genealogy Forum," someone identified only as Willie responded. Willie explained that though one of Robert Grierson's daughters and one of his sons did marry "negroes," Katy most certainly did not. Moreover, Willie stated with confidence, neither Katy nor Tulwa Tustanagee had "negro blood."[1] By searching on other genealogy Web sites, I later discovered that "Willie" was a pseudonym for Katy and Tulwa Tustanagee's great-great-granddaughter.

Willie's posting drew a reply from Eli Grayson. Eli, an interior decorator who divides his time between New York and Los Angeles, grew up thinking that he was simply white and Jewish. Then, in 1999, his father, who was born and raised in Oklahoma, revealed his Creek and African roots to his children. Katy indeed "was the daughter that had two children by a black man," Eli explained. "Nice to meet you cousin," he wrote to Willie, adding a postscript, "I find it fascinating that there was a time in Creek history when race was not a big deal."[2]

"That is B.S." replied Willie. She offered a different account of the Graysons' family tree that made no mention of Katy's children by her black husband. "The above is recorded as fact," she asserted, adding, "Not that I care who married what—but let's keep the facts straight." Her grandmother, she noted, had told her that "no one in our lineal background married or had children by negroes."[3] Five hours later, Willie addressed Eli Grayson directly in another posting: "we are not interesting in griding [sic] axes or argument. . . . The first thing we'd like to assert is that if someone is going to complain or get passive aggressive about their lineage, please cough up your role [sic] number . . . or don't claim to be an Indian.' " The Graysons owned a number of slaves, Willie conceded: "This did not imply blood relationship . . . though of course, who knows? Furthermore I won't beat myself up over it, as my ancestors did it, not me!" She concluded on a conciliatory note: "Take care, and I'd enjoy meeting any cousins I don't know about!"[4]

"Hensci ena-hvmke," Eli wrote back, using the Creek phrase for "Hello cousins": "You want me to post my roll number and you have stated nothing but quotes from *A Creek Warrior for the Confederacy*. A nice read, but GW's perspective of the nation was from his own low self esteem (you know cuz, most racist have very low self-esteem)." He added a postscript, what turned out to be the last word in this increasingly acrimonious exchange: "There was a time in Creek history when race was not a factor, but when the Crackers drop only crumbs from their tables, we tore each other apart. Stop the Madness!"[5]

Katy and William's legacy shows no sign of vanishing. In fact, at the close of the twentieth century, a series of political decisions made by the Five Tribes reinforced racial boundaries within the nations and instigated a new round of heated and divisive debates. In 1979, the Creek Nation replaced its 1867 constitution, which had enfranchised ex-slaves. Article II, section 1, of the new constitution reads, "Each Muscogee (Creek) Indian by blood shall have the opportunity for citizenship in the Muscogee (Creek) Nation."[6] By restricting citizenship to people whose ancestors were on the Dawes by-blood census, Creeks excluded the descendants of their slaves. One close relative of the principal chief at the time frankly recalls that the motives for the modern-day disenfranchisement were racist. Creek politicians feared that the descendants of their ex-slaves would wield too much political power within the nation.[7]

In the 1970s and 1980s, the Cherokees, led by Principal Chief Ross Swimmer, similarly disenfranchised the descendants of their slaves, and the Choctaws followed suit in 1983.[8] When Bernice Riggs, whose ancestors appear on the Cherokee freedmen rolls, challenged the disenfranchisement in the Cherokee Supreme Court, the justices ruled against her in a 2002 decision.[9] The following year, descendants of Cherokee slaves asked the BIA to invalidate a Cherokee election because they were not allowed to participate. A regional BIA officer initially seemed prepared to consider the petition favorably and requested a response from the Cherokee Nation. "In this age of self-determination and self governance," replied Principal Chief Chad Smith, "I am shocked to find the contents and tone of your letter to be both patronizing and very paternalistic." After Cherokee leaders urgently requested a personal meeting with top officials from the U.S. Department of the Interior, the BIA summarily dismissed the election challenge.[10] At the time of the dismissal, Ross Swimmer was a high-level Bush appointee in the Department of the Interior, second only to Secretary Gale Norton.[11]

Between 2000 and 2003, a faction of Seminoles also disenfranchised their citizens descended from slaves. The story was followed closely by the *New York Times*, and on this occasion the BIA refused to recognize any government elected under such conditions. Although the Seminole Nation therefore had to restore

the voting rights of the disenfranchised, it did succeed in excluding these mar-
ginalized citizens from educational and social service programs and from a $56
million payout due from the federal government.[12] Of the Five Tribes, only the
Chickasaw Nation did not participate in these modern-day disenfranchisements;
it had never adopted its ex-slaves in the first place.[13]

The U.S. government is equally discriminatory in its definitions of who is
an Indian. Many programs offering federal assistance depend on blood quantum
to determine eligibility. Though the federal government began opening programs
in the 1970s to all citizens of federally recognized tribes regardless of blood
quantum, its Indian policies are suffused by questions of race.[14] Federal recognition itself requires that Indian nations "consist of individuals who descend
from a historical Indian tribe."[15] The stipulation makes past racism a part of
current policy. Abiding by the one-drop rule, nineteenth-century Americans
identified some native communities as black or mulatto and therefore not Indian.
The descendants of these communities are thus unable to document their relationship to a historical Indian tribe and cannot secure federal recognition.[16]

The Department of the Interior, contrary to rulings by the federal courts,
maintains that it has control over how federally recognized tribes determine
citizenship.[17] Yet it has generally ignored the modern-day disenfranchisement
of descendants of slaves, thus both reducing entitlements without political cost
and avoiding a courtroom challenge to its power.[18] Only when these issues drew
the attention of the national media, as in the case of the Seminoles, did the
department act. At the same time, the department has ignored the enfranchisement of tens of thousands of people who trace their ancestry to the Dawes by-
blood census but who neither live in Oklahoma nor maintain any relations with
tribal governments. By so doing, it violates its own stated policy. Indian nations,
wrote one lawyer from the Department of the Interior in 1988, may not grant
citizenship to "persons who are not maintaining some meaningful sort of political
relationship with the tribal government."[19]

While the federal government pretends to leave the question of who is an
Indian to sovereign Indian nations, and while Indian nations assert the sovereign
right to determine their own citizenship, both positions ignore the historical
relationship between race, slavery, and Indian survival in the American South.
Southern Indians weathered the rapid expansion of plantations onto their lands
in the early 1800s, endured Andrew Jackson's removal policies in the 1830s,
withstood the dangerous racial politics of the antebellum era, suffered through
the Civil War, rebuilt their nations in the era of Reconstruction, and watched
them being dismantled again during allotment in the 1890s. Through all these
experiences, survival depended on carefully negotiating the racial hierarchy that
formed U.S. policies and shaped American communities.

In the native South and in Indian Territory, race pervaded everyday social interactions, local economies, and community politics.[20] In the shadow of the United States, Indian survival sometimes demanded the strength not only to walk the trail of tears but also to disown family members, disenfranchise relatives, and deny the past. These are difficult facts to face, but until we fill in the ellipses, present literally in Wash Grayson's autobiography and metaphorically in our national narrative of America's origins, the missing text will continue to haunt our history books and our lives.

A Note on Sources and Historiography

Tracing a single Native American family from the 1780s through the 1920s posed a number of challenges. One was simply the difficulty of reconstructing five generations of the Graysons' family tree. It is a sad commentary on the intrusiveness of the U.S. government in the affairs of a separate and sovereign nation that the task was possible largely using federal records. Creek censuses, payrolls, probate records, Civil War claims, BIA individual Indian files, and the records of the Dawes Commission all proved invaluable. After months of collecting and entering data into a computer, I had compiled a genealogical database of 972 people. Nearly 300 of them were direct descendants of Robert Grierson and his wife, Sinnugee, the progenitors of the Grayson family.

Of course, a skeletal family tree hardly makes for a compelling story. Fortunately, the Grayson family included one highly articulate and prolific writer, George Washington Grayson, who left behind an autobiography as well as diaries. The autobiography has been published, at least in part, as G. W. Grayson, *A Creek Warrior for the Confederacy: The Autobiography of Chief G. W. Grayson,* ed. W. David Baird (Norman: University of Oklahoma Press, 1988). It should be supplemented by Mary Jane Warde's fine biography of Wash Grayson, *George Washington Grayson and the Creek Nation, 1843–1920* (Norman: University of Oklahoma Press, 1999). Warde's book does not discuss the racial divisions within the family.

Unlike the autobiography, Wash's diaries have not been published and remain in the hands of family members. They fill forty-four volumes, encompass more than 6,700 days between 1898 and 1917, and number 840,000 words. With the permission of his aunts who owned the diaries, Harold Osa Hoppe, a descendant of Robert Grierson and Sinnugee, spent the last years of his life preserving Creek history by producing a massive 2,700-page typescript of the volumes. His two children, Karen Crook and Harold Hoppe, were extraordinarily generous and permitted me to read their father's copy. The diaries are a treasure, an unparalleled source for American and American Indian history.[1]

Although invaluable, George Washington Grayson's writings represent the views of one family member, and they cover only a limited period. To re-create the story of the Graysons, I also used numerous documents collected by the Department of War (which managed the government's Indian policy until 1849) and the Department of the Interior, as well as collections housed at the Oklahoma Historical Society, the National Anthropological Archives, the University of Tulsa, and elsewhere. I also relied on the correspondence of Presbyterian and Baptist missionaries in the antebellum era and on the interviews of Indians and ex-slaves conducted by the Works Progress Administration in the 1930s. In addition to these sources, I found the records of the Creek Nation, housed at the Oklahoma Historical Society, especially useful. The equivalent of the National Archives of the United States, the Creek National Records include all manner of documents produced and collected by the Creek Nation. The bulk of the material covers the period between 1866 and 1900. From these sources, the Graysons' past came alive.

There is a substantial and rapidly growing genre of books on race and family, though *Black, White, and Indian* is the first to focus specifically on Indians. Two multigenerational family histories that treat race are Edward Ball, *Slaves in the Family* (New York: Farrar, Straus and Giroux, 1998); and Henry Wiencek, *The Hairstons: An American Family in Black and White* (New York: St. Martin's Press, 1999). They are especially powerful for linking past generations with their present-day descendants. Other narratives of the discovery of black or white ancestors in one's family include Neil Henry, *Pearl's Secret: A Black Man's Search for His White Family* (Berkeley and Los Angeles: University of California Press, 2001); and Gregory Howard Williams, *Life on the Color Line: The True Story of a White Boy Who Discovered He Was Black* (New York: Dutton, 1995). They are less historical than Ball's and Wiencek's works.

In Native American history, numerous books—more than six hundred, by one count—narrate the oral history of a single individual.[2] The vast majority of these works, which mostly recount the lives of Indians in the late nineteenth and early twentieth centuries, are "as-told-to" autobiographies.[3] Multigenerational family histories such as that of the Graysons are rarer. Three notable ones are Dennis McAuliffe, *The Deaths of Sybil Bolton: An American History* (New York: Times Books, 1994); Joe Starita, *The Dull Knifes of Pine Ridge: A Lakota Odyssey* (New York: Putnam, 1995); and Carolyn Gilman and Mary Jane Schneider, *The Way to Independence: Memories of a Hidatsa Indian Family, 1840–1920* (St. Paul: Minnesota Historical Society Press, 1987). Gilman and Schneider's book offers an innovative exploration of family history through material culture. Also see Joel Spring, *The Cultural Transformation of a Native American Family and Its Tribe 1763–1995: A Basket of Apples* (Mahwah, NJ: Erlbaum, 1996), in which the au-

thor traces his own family's history and its participation in the cultural transformation of the Choctaws.

For further explorations on race and Native American history, readers may
wish to consult a number of works. There is a small but important body of
essays on the origins of racism among southeastern Indians. See especially William S. Willis, "Divide and Rule: Red, White, and Black in the Southeast," *Journal
of Negro History* 48 (July 1963): 157–176; William G. McLoughlin, "Red Indians,
Black Slavery and White Racism: America's Slaveholding Indians," *American
Quarterly* 26 (October 1974): 366–383; James H. Merrell, "The Racial Education
of the Catawba Indians," *Journal of Southern History* 50 (August 1984): 363–384;
Kathryn E. Holland Braund, "The Creek Indians, Blacks, and Slavery," *Journal
of Southern History* 57 (November 1991): 601–637; and Nancy Shoemaker, "How
Indians Got to Be Red," *American Historical Review* 102 (June 1997): 625–644.
Shoemaker's article might be set against Theda Perdue, *"Mixed Blood" Indians:
Racial Construction in the Early South* (Athens: University of Georgia Press, 2003).

The historiography on slaves owned by Indians is scattered and undeveloped. Early twentieth-century works on the subject include Annie Heloise Abel's
three volumes, *The American Indian as Slaveholder and Secessionist* (Cleveland:
Arthur H. Clark, 1915); *The American Indian as Participant in the Civil War* (Cleveland: Arthur H. Clark, 1919); and *The American Indian under Reconstruction*
(Cleveland: Arthur H. Clark, 1925). Abel is not particularly sympathetic to the
plight of ex-slaves. By contrast, Kenneth Wiggins Porter wrote a series of essays
in the 1940s and 1950s that paid tribute to the contributions of black Americans
to Indian nations. These essays, which were pioneering but methodologically
unsophisticated, have been collected in Porter, *The Negro on the American Frontier*
(New York: Arno Press, 1971). Porter also worked on a book-length manuscript
between 1947 and his death in 1981, and it has been published posthumously
as Porter, *The Black Seminoles: History of a Freedom-Seeking People* (Gainesville:
University Press of Florida, 1996). One older work that has aged extremely well
is Sigmund Sameth, "Creek Negroes: A Study of Race Relations" (M.A. thesis,
University of Oklahoma, 1940), an extraordinary manuscript based on the author's oral interviews.

Newer offerings include Rudy Halliburton, *Red over Black: Black Slavery
among the Cherokee Indians* (Westport, CT: Greenwood Press, 1977); Theda Perdue, *Slavery and the Evolution of Cherokee Society, 1540–1866* (Knoxville: University of Tennessee Press, 1979); Jack D. Forbes, *Africans and Native Americans:
The Language of Race and the Evolution of Red-Black Peoples* (Urbana: University
of Illinois Press, 1993); and Kevin Mulroy, *Freedom on the Border: The Seminole
Maroons in Florida, the Indian Territory, Coahuila, and Texas* (Lubbock: Texas
Tech University Press, 1993). Four volumes by Daniel F. Littlefield, Jr. show

their age but still provide indispensable background: *Africans and Seminoles: From Removal to Emancipation* (Westport, CT: Greenwood Press, 1977); *Cherokee Freedmen: From Emancipation to American Citizenship* (Westport, CT: Greenwood Press, 1978); *Africans and Creeks: From the Colonial Period to the Civil War* (Westport, CT: Greenwood Press, 1979); and *Chickasaw Freedmen: A People without a Country* (Westport, CT: Greenwood Press, 1980).

More recently, a younger generation of scholars has paid closer attention to culture and gender. See the collection of essays edited by James F. Brooks, *Confounding the Color Line: The Indian-Black Experience in North America* (Lincoln: University of Nebraska Press, 2002); and Tiya Miles, *Ties That Bind: The Story of an Afro-Cherokee Family in Slavery and Freedom* (Berkeley and Los Angeles: University of California Press, 2005). See also the dissertations of Barbara Krauthamer, "Blacks on the Borders: African-Americans' Transition from Slavery to Freedom in Texas and the Indian Territory, 1836–1907" (Ph.D. diss., Princeton University, 2000); and Celia Naylor-Ojurongbe, " 'More at Home with the Indians': African-American Slaves and Freedpeople in the Cherokee Nation, Indian Territory, 1838–1907" (Ph.D. diss., Duke University, 2001).

Despite this literature on slavery and racism, histories of the Five Tribes do not incorporate the experiences of Native American slaves, nor do they recognize the impact of race on everyday social interactions, local economies, and community politics in the native South. One exception is Claudio Saunt, *A New Order of Things: Property, Power, and the Transformation of the Creek Indians, 1733–1816* (New York: Cambridge University Press, 1999). For further background on the Creeks before their removal to Indian Territory, see Michael D. Green, *The Politics of Indian Removal: Creek Government and Society in Crisis* (Lincoln: University of Nebraska Press, 1982); Florette Henri, *Southern Indians and Benjamin Hawkins, 1796–1816* (Norman: University of Oklahoma Press, 1986); Steven C. Hahn, *The Invention of the Creek Nation, 1670–1763* (Lincoln: University of Nebraska Press, 2004); Joshua Piker, *Okfuskee: A Creek Indian Town in Colonial America* (Cambridge, MA: Harvard University Press, 2004); and the dated but still useful David H. Corkran, *The Creek Frontier, 1540–1783* (Norman: University of Oklahoma Press, 1967).

Books on the other southeastern Indian nations include James Carson, *Searching for the Bright Path: The Mississippi Choctaws from Prehistory to Removal* (Lincoln: University of Nebraska Press, 1999); Greg O'Brien, *Choctaws in a Revolutionary Age* (Lincoln: University of Nebraska Press, 2002); William G. McLoughlin, *Cherokee Renascence in the New Republic* (Princeton, NJ: Princeton University Press, 1986); Theda Perdue, *Cherokee Women: Gender and Culture Change, 1700–1835* (Lincoln: University of Nebraska Press, 1998); James W. Covingtoin, *The Seminoles of Florida* (Gainesville: University of Florida Press, 1993); and

James Atkinson, *Splendid Land, Splendid People: The Chickasaw Indians to Removal* (Tuscaloosa: University of Alabama Press, 2004). On U.S. Indian policy in the early years of the Republic, see Bernard W. Sheehan, *The Seeds Extinction: Jeffersonian Philanthropy and the American Indian* (Chapel Hill: University of North Carolina Press, 1973); and Anthony F. C. Wallace, *Jefferson and the Indians: The Tragic Fate of the First Americans* (Cambridge, MA: Harvard University Press, 1999).

There are numerous popular histories on removal, but most cast the experience as a maudlin drama and forgo any deeper historical analysis. One old but valuable account, written by a former member of the Dawes Commission, is Grant Foreman, *Indian Removal: The Emigration of the Five Civilized Tribes of Indians* (Norman: University of Oklahoma Press, 1932). On the development and context of U.S. Indian policy during this period, see Reginald Horsman, *Race and Manifest Destiny: The Origins of American Racial Anglo-Saxonism* (Cambridge, MA: Harvard University Press, 1981); Robert E. Bieder, *Science Encounters the Indian, 1820–1880: The Early Years of American Ethnology* (Norman: University of Oklahoma Press, 1986); and Ronald N. Satz, *American Indian Policy in the Jacksonian Era* (Norman: University of Oklahoma Press, 2002). Andrew Jackson's biographer, Robert Remini, has also produced a useful treatment of Jackson's relationship with Indians, *Andrew Jackson and His Indian Wars* (New York: Viking, 2001).

Work on the postremoval period is remarkably scant. On the Creeks, see the dated but still valuable book by Angie Debo, *The Road to Disappearance* (Norman: University of Oklahoma Press, 1941); and J. Leitch Wright Jr., *Creeks and Seminoles: The Destruction and Regeneration of the Muscogulge People* (Lincoln: University of Nebraska Press, 1986). On the Cherokees, see William G. McLoughlin, *After the Trail of Tears: The Cherokees' Struggle for Sovereignty, 1839–1880* (Chapel Hill: University of North Carolina Press, 1993). More generally, see H. Craig Minor, *The Corporation and the Indian: Tribal Sovereignty and Industrial Civilization in Indian Territory, 1865–1907* (Columbia: University of Missouri Press, 1976); and M. Thomas Bailey, *Reconstruction in Indian Territory: A Story of Avarice, Discrimination, and Opportunism* (Port Washington, NY: Kennikat Press, 1972), although the value of Bailey's otherwise excellent book is diminished by the absence of source citations.

Anyone interested in the destruction of the Five Tribes in the late nineteenth century and the appalling theft of Indian lands that followed should consult Angie Debo, *And Still the Waters Run: The Betrayal of the Five Civilized Tribes* (Norman: University of Oklahoma Press, 1940). This classic and pathbreaking work may be supplemented by Frederick E. Hoxie, *A Final Promise: The Campaign to Assimilate the Indians, 1880–1920* (Lincoln: University of Nebraska Press,

1984), which masterfully investigates the development of U.S. policy during the same period. Accounts of this era and its aftermath also include two biographies exploring the oil fortunes of a Creek freedman, Jake Simmons, and a Creek Indian with African ancestry, Jackson Barnett: Jonathan D. Greenberg, *Staking a Claim: Jake Simmons and the Making of an African-American Oil Dynasty* (New York: Atheneum, 1990); and Tanis C. Thorne, *The World's Richest Indian: The Scandal over Jackson Barnett's Oil Fortune* (New York: Oxford University Press, 2003). Also see the fictionalized account of the Osages during allotment, Linda Hogan, *Mean Spirit: A Novel* (New York: Atheneum, 1990).

On race and Oklahoma statehood, see Arthur Tolson, "The Negro in Oklahoma Territory, 1889–1907: A Study in Racial Discrimination" (Ph.D. diss., University of Oklahoma, 1966); Philip Mellinger, "Discrimination and Statehood in Oklahoma," *Chronicles of Oklahoma* 49 (1971): 340–378; Danney Goble, *Progressive Oklahoma: The Making of a New Kind of State* (Norman: University of Oklahoma Press, 1980); Murray R. Wickett, *Contested Territory: Whites, Native Americans, and African Americans in Oklahoma, 1865–1907* (Baton Rouge: Louisiana State University Press, 2000); and David A. Y. O. Chang, "From Indian Territory to White Man's Country: Race, Nation, and the Politics of Land Ownership in Eastern Oklahoma, 1889–1940" (Ph.D. diss., University of Wisconsin–Madison, 2002). In addition, the *Chronicles of Oklahoma*, the state's historical journal, remains an indispensable source for articles on specific topics.

On politics and race in Native America at the end of the twentieth century, see Circe Sturm, *Blood Politics: Race, Culture, and Identity in the Cherokee Nation of Oklahoma* (Berkeley and Los Angeles: University of California Press, 2002); and the relevant chapters in the highly readable Fergus M. Bordewich, *Killing the White Man's Indian: Reinventing Native Americans at the End of the Twentieth Century* (New York: Anchor Books, 1996). Readers interested in exploring the complicated legal questions surrounding Indian identity should consult Margo S. Brownell, "Who Is an Indian? Searching for an Answer to the Question at the Core of Federal Indian Law," *University of Michigan Journal of Law Reform* 34 (2000–2001): 275–320. Finally, those who wish to follow the still unfolding story of race in Native America should consult the following online news sources: Indianz.com, Indiancountry.com, and Nativetimes.com.

Notes

Abbreviations

ABCFM   American Board of Commissioners for Foreign Missions. Microfilm collection.

ABHS   American Baptist Historical Society. Microfilm of American Indian Correspondence, Foreign Mission Society Records, 1817–1959.

ADAH   Alabama Department of Archives and History, Montgomery.

AGWG G. W. Grayson, *A Creek Warrior for the Confederacy: The Autobiography of Chief G. W. Grayson*, ed. W. David Baird. Norman: University of Oklahoma Press, 1988.

ASPIA *American State Papers, Class II: Indian Affairs*. 2 vols. Washington, DC, 1832.

CIMA   Creek Indian Memorial Association

CO   Colonial Office

CRN   Creek National Records

DGWG   Diaries of George Washington Grayson. Transcripts of the diaries of George Washington Grayson, prepared by Harold Osa Hoppe, are used with the permission of Karen Elaine Crook and Harold Grayson Hoppe.

DU   Doris Duke American Indian Oral History Collection, on microfiche.

GDAH   Georgia Department of Archives and History, Atlanta.

HAR   Hargrett Rare Book and Manuscript Library, University of Georgia, Athens.

IPP   Indian-Pioneer Papers, originals in the Oklahoma Historical Society, Oklahoma City.

LBH   *Letters, Journals, and Writings of Benjamin Hawkins*, ed. C. L. Grant. 2 vols. Savannah, GA: Beehive Press, 1980.

LR   Letters received

NA   National Archives, Washington, DC.

NAFW   National Archives, Fort Worth, Texas.

NASP *The New American State Papers, Indian Affairs*. Wilmington, DE: Scholarly Resources, 1972.

NWR   *Niles' Weekly Register*

OHS   Oklahoma Historical Society, Oklahoma City.

OIA   Office of Indian Affairs

PHS   American Indian Correspondence: The Presbyterian Historical Society Collection of Missionaries' Letters, 1833–1893. Microfilm collection.

PKY   P. K. Yonge Library of Florida History, Gainesville, FL.

PRO   Public Records Office

RG   Record Group

USS   *United States Serials Set.* These citations refer to congressional documents published under directive of the United States Congress. They are given in the standard bibliographic form as used by the Congressional Information Service.

WHC   Western History Collections, University of Oklahoma, Norman.

WRB   *The War of the Rebellion: A Compilation of the Official Records of the Union and Confederate Armies.* Washington, DC: Government Printing Office, 1880–1901.

Prologue

1. May 12, 1905, book 15, DGWG.

2. *AGWG*, 71.

3. March 9, 1912, book 34, DGWG.

4. January 21, 1913, book 36, DGWG.

5. J. Leitch Wright, *Creeks and Seminoles: The Destruction and Regeneration of the Muscogulge People* (Lincoln: University of Nebraska Press, 1986), 78–79.

6. *AGWG*.

7. David Baird to Claudio Saunt, January 7, 1997.

8. *AGWG*, 21.

9. E. E. Dale to Eloise Smock, September 28, 1934, box 63, folder 17, E. E. Dale Collection, WHC.

10. Eloise Smock to E. E. Dale, October 5, 1934, box 63, folder 17, E. E. Dale Collection, WHC.

11. E. E. Dale to Eloise Smock, October 11, 1934, box 63, folder 17, E. E. Dale Collection, WHC; E. E. Dale to Eloise Smock, October 23, 1934, box 63, folder 17, E. E. Dale Collection, WHC; E. E. Dale to Eloise Smock, January 9, 1936, box 63, folder 17, E. E. Dale Collection, WHC.

12. E. E. Dale to Eloise Smock, April 10, 1935, box 63, folder 17, E. E. Dale Collection, WHC.

13. E. E. Dale to Eloise Smock, February 9, 1938, box 63, folder 17, E. E. Dale Collection, WHC.

14. Eloise Smock to E. E. Dale, February 24, 1938, box 63, folder 17, E. E. Dale Collection, WHC.

15. E. E. Dale to Eloise Smock, February 28, 1938, box 63, folder 17, E. E. Dale Collection, WHC.

16. E. E. Dale to Eloise Smock, March 23, 1938, box 63, folder 17, E. E. Dale Collection, WHC; Eloise Smock to E. E. Dale, May 14, 1938, box 63, folder 17, E. E. Dale Collection, WHC; E. E. Dale to Eloise Smock, May 17, 1938, box 63, folder 17, E. E. Dale Collection, WHC.

17. *AGWG*, 25.

18. Ibid., 49.

Introduction

1. Charles Hudson, *Knights of Spain, Warriors of the Sun: Hernando de Soto and the South's Ancient Chiefdoms* (Athens: University of Georgia Press, 1997); Vernon J. Knight Jr., "The Formation of the Creeks," in *The Forgotten Centuries: Indians and Europeans in the American South, 1521–1704*, ed. Charles Hudson and Carmen Chaves Tesser (Athens: University of Georgia Press, 1994), 373–392; Marvin T. Smith, *Archaeology of Aboriginal Culture Change in the Interior Southeast: Depopulation during the Early Historic Period* (Gainesville: University Press of Florida, 1987); and Smith, *Coosa: The Rise and Fall of a Southeastern Mississippian Chiefdom* (Gainesville: University Press of Florida, 2000).

2. For the Creeks' manipulation of imperial rivalries, see David Corkran, *The Creek Frontier, 1540–1783* (Norman: University of Oklahoma Press, 1962); and Steven C. Hahn, *The Invention of the Creek Nation, 1670–1763* (Lincoln: University of Nebraska Press, 2004). On trade, see Kathryn E. Holland Braund, *Deerskins and Duffels: The Creek Indian Trade with Anglo-America, 1685–1815* (Lincoln: University of Nebraska Press, 1993); and the still valuable Verner W. Crane, *The Southern Frontier* (Durham, NC: Duke University Press, 1928).

3. On American states as colonies, see D. W. Meinig, *The Shaping of America: Continental America, 1800–1867* (New Haven, CT: Yale University Press, 1993), vol. 2. For a thoughtful essay on the integration of U.S. history and colonial studies, see Ann Laura Stoler, "Tense and Tender Ties: The Politics of Comparison in North American History and (Post) Colonial Studies," *Journal of American History* 88 (2001): 829–865.

4. This period is ably covered by Michael D. Green, *The Politics of Indian Removal: Creek Government and Society in Crisis* (Lincoln: University of Nebraska Press, 1982).

5. The classic work on the dissolution of the Creeks, Cherokees, Choctaws, Chickasaws, and Seminoles is Angie Debo, *And Still the Waters Run: The Betrayal of the Five Civilized Tribes* (Princeton, NJ: Princeton University Press, 1940).

6. On the need to link the larger social context of race to the everyday life of individuals, see Thomas C. Holt, "Marking: Race, Race-making, and the Writing of History," *American Historical Review* 100 (1995): 1–20; and Martha Hodes, "The Mercurial Nature and Abiding Power of Race: A Transnational Family Story," *American Historical Review* 108 (2003): 84–118.

7. Several articles investigate the origins of racism among southeastern Indians, but book-length studies on the South's native peoples rarely integrate race into their narratives. Two exceptions are Theda Perdue, *Slavery and the Evolution of Cherokee Society, 1540–1866* (Knoxville: University of Tennessee Press, 1979); and Claudio Saunt, *A New Order of Things: Property, Power, and the Transformation of the Creek Indians, 1733–1816* (New York: Cambridge University Press, 1999). For a recent statement on the unimportance of race in southeastern Indian societies, see Theda Perdue, "Mixed

Blood" Indians: Racial Construction in the Early South (Athens: University of Georgia Press, 2003).

8. Whiteness studies, a field of scholarship that exploded in the 1990s, might suggest superficial parallels between the experiences of Indians and other minority groups in the United States. As Neil Foley points out, for example, Mexican Americans made "Faustian bargains that offered them inclusion within whiteness provided that they subsumed their ethnic identities under their newly acquired White racial identity and its core value of White supremacy." Mexican Americans, as well as Irish Catholics and working-class Americans more generally, made those bargains to secure for themselves the rights of U.S. citizenship. Whiteness, entangled in a complex relationship between republicanism and class formation, therefore has little relevance to Native American history. Indians abided by America's racial hierarchy not in quest of citizenship, not to lend dignity to wage labor or, in David Roediger's assessment of white workers, to "displace anxieties" about "working class formation" onto blacks. Rather, Indians did so to save their distinct communities and defend their sovereign rights. Foley, "Becoming Hispanic: Mexican Americans and the Faustian Pact with Whiteness," in *Reflexiones 1997: New Directions in Mexican American Studies*, ed. Neil Foley (Austin: University of Texas Press, 1998), 63; David R. Roediger, *The Wages of Whiteness: Race and the Making of the American Working Class*, rev. ed. (London: Verso, 1999), 100. Useful assessments of the substantial literature on whiteness include Eric Arnesen, "Whiteness and the Historians' Imagination," *International Labor and Working-Class History* 69 (2001): 3–32; and Peter Kolchin, "Whiteness Studies: The New History of Race in America," *Journal of American History* 89 (2002): 154–173.

A Symposium of Dartmouth College

1. Reinventing the enemy's language has been the primary goal of Native American as well as third world writers, as Louis Owens points out in *Mixed Blood Messages: Literature, Film, Family, Place* (Norman: University of Oklahoma Press, 1998), xi–11. More generally, on postcolonial writers and the reinvention of the colonists' language, see Bill Ashcroft, *The Empire Writes Back: Theory and Practice in Post-colonial Literatures* (London: Routledge, 1989). As the story of the Graysons illustrates, many Indians were forced as a matter of survival to adopt certain aspects of the language of their enemies.

Chapter 1

1. Indian agent Benjamin Hawkins recorded Sinnugee's clan in Journal of Benjamin Hawkins, December 11, 1796, *LBH*, 1:15. Linguist Jack Martin notes that Spanalgee is Creek for Spanish and that the term was used for women from Spanish Florida who were adopted into Creek communities. Jack Martin to the author, August 4, 1999. On Florida's early black history, see Jane Landers, *Black Society in Spanish Florida* (Urbana: University of Illinois Press, 1999).

2. This description of Hilabi is heavily indebted to Gregory A. Waselkov and Marvin T. Smith, "Upper Creek Archaeology," in *Indians of the Greater Southeast: Historical Archaeology and Ethnohistory*, ed. Bonnie G. McEwan (Gainesville: University Press of Florida, 2000), 242–264.

3. Caleb Swan, "Position and State of Manners and Arts in the Creek, or Muscogee

Nation in 1791," in *Information Respecting the History, Condition and Prospects of the Indian Tribes of the United States*, 6 vols., ed. Henry Rowe Schoolcraft (New York: Paladin Press, 1855), 5:264–265.

4. "The Muskogees and Seminoles," in *The Monthly Magazine of Religion and Literature*, ed. W. M. Reynolds (Gettysburg: H. C. Neinstedt, 1840) 1:142–143.

5. William Bartram, "Observations on the Creek and Cherokee Indians, 1789, with Prefatory and Supplementary Notes by E. G. Squier," *Transactions of the American Ethnological Society* (New York: American Ethnological Society, 1853), vol. 3, 1:34–35; reprinted in Gregory A. Waselkov and Kathryn E. Holland Braund, eds., *William Bartram and the Southeastern Indians* (Lincoln: University of Nebraska Press, 1995), 133–186.

6. James White to John Cocke, November 24, 1813, *NWR*, December 25, 1813, 282–283.

7. Journal of Benjamin Hawkins, December 9–10, 1796, *Letters of Benjamin Hawkins, 1796–1806: Collections of the Georgia Historical Society*, vol. 9 (Savannah: Georgia Historical Society, 1916), 29–30.

8. Journal of Benjamin Hawkins, December 9–10, 1796, *Letters of Benjamin Hawkins, 1796–1806*, 29–30.

9. Benjamin Hawkins, "A Sketch of the Creek Country in the Years 1798 and 1799," *LBH*, 1:301.

10. "At a Congress of the Principal Chiefs and Warriors of the Upper Creek Nation," October 29, 1771, Lockey Collection, PRO, CO 5/589, PKY; Journal of Benjamin Hawkins, December 9–10, 1796, *Letters of Benjamin Hawkins, 1796–1806*, 29–30; Benjamin Hawkins, "A sketch of the Creek Country in the years 1798 and 1799," *LBH*, 1: 301.

11. "An Assortment of Goods Proper for Indian Presents for West Florida," enclosed in George Johnstone to the Secretary of the Board of Trade, January 29, 1764, PRO 5/574, p. 11, reel 66-K, PKY.

12. "At a Congress of the Principal Chiefs and Warriors of the Upper Creek Nation," October 29, 1771, Lockey Collection, PRO, CO 5/589.

13. Arturo O'Neill to Estevan Miró, October 28, 1788, leg. 38, 555, reel 191, Papeles Procedentes de Cuba, PKY; Martin Palao and Josef Monroy to Arturo O'Neill, November 23, 1788, leg. 38, 600, reel 191, Papeles Procedentes de Cuba, PKY.

14. Benjamin Hawkins, "A Sketch of the Creek Country in the Years 1798 and 1799," *LBH*, 1:301.

15. Journal of Benjamin Hawkins, December 11, 1796, *LBH*, 1:15. Hawkins stated that Sinnugee was of the "Spanalgee" family. Linguist Jack Martin explains that "Spanalgee" refers to someone of Spanish or Mexican descent, or, in the case of the Southeast, to someone from Spanish Florida. Jack Martin to the author, August 4, 1999.

16. Benjamin Hawkins, "A Sketch of the Creek Country in the Years 1798 and 1799," *LBH*, 1:301.

17. Affidavit of John Eades, October 30, 1793, "Creek Indian Letters, Talks, and Treaties, 1705–1839," ed. J. E. Hays, 1:349, GDAH.

18. For a portrait of one Scottish trader, see Edward J. Cashin, *Lachlan McGillivray, Indian Trader: The Shaping of the Southern Colonial Frontier* (Athens: University of Georgia

Press, 1992). See also Alan Gallay, *The Formation of a Planter Elite: Jonathan Bryan and the Southern Colonial Frontier* (Athens: University of Georgia Press, 1989).

19. Journal of Benjamin Hawkins, December 9, 1796, *LBH*, 1:14.

20. Saunt, *A New Order of Things: Property, Power, and The Transformation of the Creek Indians, 1733–1811,* (Cambridge University Press, 1999) chap. 6.

21. Richard White describes the tensions between European and Native American trade practices in White, *The Middle Ground: Indians, Empires, and Republics in the Great Lakes Region, 1650–1815* (New York: Cambridge University Press, 1991), 115–119.

22. The role of women in the fur trade is examined in Jennifer S. H. Brown, *Strangers in Blood: Fur Trade Company Families in Indian Country* (Vancouver: University of British Columbia Press, 1980); Sylvia van Kirk, *"Many Tender Ties": Women in Fur-Trade Society in Western Canada, 1670–1870* (Winnipeg, Manitoba: Watson and Dwyer, 1980), and Susan Sleeper-Smith, *Indian Women and French Men: Rethinking Cultural Encounter in the Western Great Lakes* (Amherst: University of Massachusetts Press, 2001). In the Southeast, see Kathryn E. Holland Braund, "Guardians of Tradition and Handmaidens to Change: Women's Roles in Creek Economic and Social Life during the Eighteenth Century," *American Indian Quarterly* 14 (1990): 239–258; and Theda Perdue, *Cherokee Women: Gender and Culture Change, 1700–1835* (Lincoln: University of Nebraska Press, 1998).

23. *South Carolina Gazette*, March 7 to March 14, 1761.

24. Copy of letter from John Stuart to Jeffrey Amherst, October 4, 1763, Thomas Gage Papers, American series, reel 140F, PKY, original in William L. Clements Library. In 1767, Hilabis also murdered a packhorse man working for trader Thomas Scott. John Stuart to General Haldimand, June 7, 1767, Haldimand Papers, MG21/B11, BM 21671, 212/281, reel 59D, PKY.

25. The number of deerskins exported annually declined steadily after the American Revolution, marking the rise of plow agriculture and ranching. Kathyrn E. Holland Braund, *Deerskins and Duffels: The Creek Indian Trade with Anglo-America, 1685–1815* (Lincoln: University of Nebraska Press, 1993), 97–98.

26. John Stuart to Patrick Tonyn, July 21, 1777, enclosed in Tonyn to Germain, September 18, 1777, PRO 5/557, p. 643, reel 66-C, PKY; David Taitt to Patrick Tonyn, August 24, 1777, enclosed in Tonyn to Germain, September 18, 1777, PRO 5/557, p. 699, reel 66-C, PKY; John Stuart to Patrick Tonyn, July 10, 1778, enclosed in Tonyn to Germain, September 25, 1778, PRO 5/558, p. 453, reel 66-C, PKY; Alexander Cameron to Prevost, October 15, 1779, Sir Guy Carleton Papers, reel 58A-9, doc. 2372, PKY.

27. Benjamin Hawkins, "A Sketch of the Creek Country in the Years 1798 and 1799," *LBH*, 1:301; Journal of Benjamin Hawkins, December 9–10, 1796, *Letters of Benjamin Hawkins, 1796–1806*, 29–30; Benjamin Hawkins to Silas Dinsmoor, January 6, 1799, *LBH*, 1:236; Robert Grierson to William Panton, February 8, 1797, Cruzat Papers, PKY; John Pope, *A Tour through the Southern and Western Territories of the United States of North America; the Spanish Dominions on the River Mississippi, and the Floridas; the Countries of the Creek Nations; and Many Uninhabited Parts* (1792; reprint, Gainesville: University Press of Florida, 1979).

28. Robert Grierson to William Panton, July 19, 1797, Papers of Panton, Leslie and Co., reel 11, frames 42–43.

29. Journal of Benjamin Hawkins, December 9–10, 1796, *Letters of Benjamin Hawkins, 1796–1806*, 29–30.

30. Even within the British colonies and the United States, chattel slavery varied widely. Ira Berlin, *Many Thousands Gone: The First Two Centuries of Slavery in North America* (Cambridge: Belknap Press, 1998).

31. For a sophisticated investigation of kinship slavery in the American Southwest, see James F. Brooks, *Captives and Cousins: Slavery, Kinship, and Community in the Southwest Borderlands* (Chapel Hill: University of North Carolina Press, 2002). Philip Morgan points out that in the United States, although free and enslaved peoples were always clearly distinguished by law, slavery nevertheless must be understood as one extreme on a spectrum of kinds of forced labor. Morgan, *Slave Counterpoint: Black Culture in the Eighteenth-Century Chesapeake and Lowcountry* (Chapel Hill: University of North Carolina Press, 1998), 270–271.

32. Benjamin Hawkins, "A Sketch of the Creek Country in the Years 1798 and 1799," *LBH*, 1:301.

33. Journal of Benjamin Hawkins, December 9–10, 1796, *Letters of Benjamin Hawkins, 1796–1806*, 29–30; Benjamin Hawkins, "A Sketch of the Creek Country in the Years 1798 and 1799," *LBH*, 1:301; Benjamin Hawkins to James McHenry, January 9, 1799, *LBH*, 1:238.

34. Statement made by John Winslett, April 13, 1832, LR, OIA, frames 337–340, reel 236, M-234, NA. Winslett's statement is confirmed by several documents that list nearly one hundred of Robert's slaves by name: Journal of John Crowell, ADAH; Statement of Robert Grierson, February 10, 1817, Records of Conveyance, book A–D, County Courthouse, Montgomery County, AL; Affidavit of Tustunnuggee Opoie et al., May 22, 1820, LR, OIA, frame 331, reel 236, M-234, NA; *Robert Grierson v. James Black*, 1818, Jasper County Superior Court Case Files, 179-1-1, GDAH.

35. Robert Grierson to David Mitchell, November 29, 1820, box 6, folder 20, doc. 3, Keith Read Collection, HAR.

36. George Washington to James Duane, September 7, 1783, in *George Washington: Writings* (New York: Library of America, 1997), 541.

37. Absalom H. Chappell, *Miscellanies of Georgia* (Atlanta: James F. Meegan, 1874), 67.

38. Bernard W. Sheehan, *Seeds of Extinction: Jeffersonian Philanthropy and the American Indian* (Chapel Hill: University of North Carolina Press, 1973); Anthony F. C. Wallace, *Jefferson and the Indians: The Tragic Fate of the First Americans* (Cambridge: Belknap Press, 1999).

39. Saunt, *New Order of Things*, 271.

40. John Hambly to [Governor of St. Augustine], April 21, 1794, East Florida Papers, bnd. 196A16, doc. 1794-19, reel 83, PKY; "Journal of Benjamin Hawkins," July 15, 1804, *LBH*, 2:476; Benjamin Hawkins to Henry Dearborn, September 16, 1807, *LBH*, 2:524; Benjamin Hawkins to Reverend Christian Benzien, October 7, 1810, *LBH*, 2:569.

41. Report of Commissioners to the Secretary of War, June 1796, *ASPIA*, 1:597–616.

42. Robert Grierson, "by a steady conduct, contributed to mend the manners of these people," commented Indian agent Benjamin Hawkins. Benjamin Hawkins, "A Sketch of the Creek Country in the Years 1798 and 1799," *LBH*, 1:301. Robert also came to the attention of Creeks for failing to pay his debts to Panton, Leslie, and Company, a mercantile firm based in Pensacola. The firm demanded Creek lands to cancel outstanding debt. Upper Creeks to Benjamin Hawkins, April 26, 1813, *ASPIA*, 1:841.

43. Robert Grierson to Andrew Jackson, November 13, 1813, letterbook D, p. 205, reel 61, Andrew Jackson Papers, Library of Congress.

44. Extracts of occurrences in the agency for Indian affairs, August 1813, "Letters of Benjamin Hawkins, 1797–1815," ed., J. E. Hays, 240 GDAH.

45. Benjamin Hawkins to John Armstrong, July 28, 1813, *LBH*, 2:651.

46. Ibid.; extracts of occurrences in the agency for Indian affairs, August 1813, "Letters of Benjamin Hawkins, 1797–1815," ed. J. E. Hays, 238, GDAH; Robert Grierson to Andrew Jackson, November 13, 1813, letterbook D, p. 205, reel 61, Andrew Jackson Papers, Library of Congress.

47. Benjamin Hawkins to Governor Mitchell, August 9, 1815, "Letters of Benjamin Hawkins, 1797–1815," 236.

48. Extracts of occurrences in the agency for Indian affairs, August 1813, "Letters of Benjamin Hawkins, 1797–1815," ed. J. E. Hays 238, GDAH; Benjamin Hawkins to Governor Mitchell, September 13, 1813, "Letters of Benjamin Hawkins, 1797–1815," ed. J. E. Hays 247, GDAH.

49. Margaret Mitchell, *Gone with the Wind* (New York: Macmillan, 1936), 452–453. For more on Fort Mims, see Saunt, *New Order of Things*, chap. 11.

50. Robert Grierson to Benjamin Hawkins, September 23, 1813, "Letters of Benjamin Hawkins, 1797–1815," ed. J. E. Hays 254, GDAH.

51. Robert Grierson to Andrew Jackson, November 13, 1813, letterbook D, p. 205, reel 61, Andrew Jackson Papers, Library of Congress.

52. Ibid.

53. Robert Grierson to Benjamin Hawkins, September 23, 1813, "Letters of Benjamin Hawkins, 1797–1815," ed. J. E. Hays 254, GDAH; Robert Grierson to Andrew Jackson, November 13, 1813, letterbook D, p. 205, reel 61, Andrew Jackson Papers, Library of Congress; Robert Grierson to Andrew Jackson, February 11, 1814, reel 8, Andrew Jackson Papers, Library of Congress.

54. Robert Grierson to Andrew Jackson, February 11, 1814, reel 8, Andrew Jackson Papers, Library of Congress.

55. William Grayson gave conflicting information on his enlistment. On one occasion, he stated that he had enlisted at Turkey Town in the Cherokee Nation in fall 1813 and served through spring 1814; on another, he claimed that he had enlisted at Fort Hawkins in October 1813 and served through January 1814. Although he applied for bounty lands as a veteran of the War of 1812, there are no surviving muster rolls attesting to his service. There are surviving muster rolls for his brother Walter (Watt) Grayson, however. William Grayson, Bounty Land Warrant Application Files, Colonel

Morgan's Regiment of Cherokee Indians, Creek War of 1813, RG 94, NA; Walter Grayson, compiled military records, Colonel Morgan's Regiment of Cherokee Indians, War of 1812, RG 94, NA.

56. Andrew J. Pickett, *History of Alabama and Incidentally of Georgia and Mississippi from the Earliest Period* (1851; reprint, Birmingham: Webb Book Company, 1900), 556–557; Robert Grierson to Andrew Jackson, November 13, 1813, letterbook D, p. 205, reel 61, Andrew Jackson Papers, Library of Congress.

57. James White to John Cocke, November 24, 1813, *NWR*, December 25, 1813, 282–283; Robert Breckinridge McAfee, *History of the Late War in the Western Country* (1816; reprint, Bowling Green, OH: Historical Publications, 1919), 507; Henry Sale Halbert and T. H. Ball, *The Creek War of 1813 and 1814* (Montgomery, AL: White, Woodruff, and Fowler, 1895), 271–272.

58. John Floyd to Thomas Pinckney, December 4, 1813, *NWR*, December 25, 1813, 283–284; Ferdinand L. Claiborne to the Secretary of War, January 1, 1814, *NWR*, February 19, 1814, 412; Andrew Jackson to General Pinckney, January 29, 1814, *NWR*, February 26, 1814, 427–429.

59. Andrew Jackson to Thomas Pinckney, March 28, 1814, *Papers of Andrew Jackson*, ed. Harold D. Moser, Sharon MacPherson, David R. Hoth, and John H. Reinbold (Knoxville: University of Tennessee Press, 1991), vol. 3, 52–53.

60. Andrew Jackson to Thomas Pinckney, March 28, 1814, *The Papers of Andrew Jackson*, 3:52–53; Andrew Jackson to Willie Bount, March 31, 1814, *NWR*, April 30, 1814, 146–148; John Coffee to Andrew Jackson, April 1, 1814, *Papers of Andrew Jackson*, 3:55–57.

61. Statement made by John Winslett, April 13, 1832, LR, OIA, frames 337–340, reel 236, M-234, NA. Winslett stated that Robert left the Creek Nation in 1812, but Grierson clearly remained in Hilabi through November 13, 1813.

62. William Grayson, Bounty Land Warrant Application Files, Colonel Morgan's Regiment of Cherokee Indians, Creek War of 1813, RG 94, NA. The following court case indicates that William was in Jasper County by July 1814. *Henry Walker v. Robert Grierson,* 1817, Jasper County Superior Court Case Files, 179-1-1, GDAH.

63. Saunt, *New Order of Things*, 270.

64. Angie Debo, *The Road to Disappearance: A History of the Creek Indians* (Norman: University of Oklahoma Press, 1941), 83.

65. Chappell, *Miscellanies of Georgia*, 72.

66. Andrew Jackson to Rachel Jackson, August 10, 1814, *Papers of Andrew Jackson*, 3:114.

67. Interview with Rufus "Buddy" Cox, June 14, 2000, Oklahoma City.

68. Autobiography of G. W. Grayson, in possession of the author.

69. The date of John's birth is revealed in Claim no. 1184, John Grayson, Records Relating to Loyal Creek Claims, 1869–1870, box 12, entry 687, RG 75, NA.

70. Autobiography of G. W. Grayson, in possession of the author.

71. Andrew Jackson to Rachel Jackson, August 23, 1814, *Papers of Andrew Jackson*, 3:117–118.

72. W. H. Sparks, *The Memories of Fifty Years*, 4th ed. (Philadelphia: E. Claxton and Company, 1882), 27.

73. *Henry Walker v. Robert Grierson*, 1817, Jasper County Superior Court Case Files, 179-1-1, GDAH; Robert Grierson to David Mitchell, November 29, 1820, box 6, folder 20, doc. 3, Keith Read Collection, HAR; Robert Grierson to Andrew Jackson, November 13, 1813, letterbook D, p. 205, reel 61, Andrew Jackson Papers, Library of Congress.

74. *Philadelphia Journal*, quoted in the Jasper County Historical Foundation, *History of Jasper County, Georgia* (Roswell, GA: W. H. Wolfe Associates, 1976), 113.

75. *History of Jasper County, Georgia*, 281.

76. Ibid., 1–2, 97.

77. Oliver H. Prince, *A Digest of the Laws of the State of Georgia* (Milledgeville, GA: Grantland and Orme, 1822), 446, 461.

78. D. B. Mitchell to James Monroe, October 13, 1812, p. 133, State Department Territorial Papers, Florida Series, 1777–1824, vol. 2, microcopy no. 116/2.

79. William Harris Crawford to Andrew Jackson, March 15, 1816, *Papers of Andrew Jackson*, ed. Harold D. Moser, George H. Hoemann, and David R. Hoth (Knoxville: University of Tennessee Press, 1993), vol. 4, 15–16.

80. *NWR*, July 17, 1815, 347.

81. Hugh M. Thomason, "Governor Peter Early and the Creek Indian Frontier, 1813–1815," *Georgia Historical Quarterly* 45 (1961): 223–232.

82. Chappell, *Miscellanies of Georgia*, 72.

83. Treaty with the Creeks, 1814, in Charles J. Kappler, *Indian Treaties, 1778–1883* (1904; reprint, New York: Interland Publishing, 1972), 107–110.

84. Saunt, *New Order of Things*, chap. 12.

85. Laws of the Creek Nation, June 12, 1818, box 2, folder 50, D. B. Mitchell Papers, Ayer Modern Manuscripts, Special Collections, the Newberry Library, Chicago.

86. For a clear and convincing explanation of why this racial term has no scientific basis, see Luigi-Luca Cavalli-Sforza, *Genes, Peoples, and Languages* (New York: North Point Press, 2000).

87. Frantz Fanon, *Black Skin, White Masks*, trans. Charles Lam Markmann, (1952; New York: Grove, 1967), 112.

88. An 1817 amendment repealed the power of the Georgia governor to commute these executions. Prince, *Digest of the Laws of the State of Georgia*, 461–462.

89. Ibid., 456.

90. Frederick Douglass, *Narrative of the Life of Frederick Douglass, an American Slave: Written by Himself* (1845; reprint, New Haven, CT: Yale University Press, 2001), 25.

91. Laws of the Creek Nation, June 12, 1818, box 2, folder 50, D. B. Mitchell Papers, Ayer Modern Manuscripts, Special Collections, the Newberry Library, Chicago.

92. *AGWG*, 24.

93. Statement of Robert Grierson, February 10, 1817, Records of Conveyance, book A–D, County Courthouse, Montgomery County, AL; Journal of John Crowell, ADAH.

94. *AGWG*, 17.

95. Robert Grierson to David Mitchell, November 29, 1820, box 6, folder 20, doc.

3, Keith Read Collection, HAR. Description of Big Warrior from Chappell, *Miscellanies of Georgia*, 72.

96. Robert Grierson to David Mitchell, November 29, 1820, box 6, folder 20, doc. 3, Keith Read Collection, HAR.

97. William Jr. was born sometime in 1819. Council Minutes of the Creek Nation West, 1831–1835, CIMA roll 1, frame 234/235, OHS.

Native Art, June 2000

1. Christie S. Schultz to the author, March 14, 2000.

2. Pub. L. 101-644. For an in-depth examination of the Indian Arts and Crafts Act of 1990, see Gail K. Sheffield, *The Arbitrary Indian: The Indian Arts and Crafts Act of 1990* (Norman: University of Oklahoma, 1997).

3. David Cornsilk to the author, May 9, 2000.

Chapter 2

1. Lee Compere, Withington Journal, March 1828, FM-98, ABHS.

2. Grant Foreman, *Indian Removal: The Emigration of the Five Civilized Tribes of Indians* (1932; reprint, Norman: University of Oklahoma Press, 1972), quotation on 108n7.

3. Edward J. Harden, *The Life of George M. Troup* (Savannah, GA: E. J. Purse, 1859), 209.

4. Statement made by John Winslett, April 13, 1832, LR, OIA, frames 337–340, reel 236, M-234, NA; Affidavit of Tustunnuggee Opoie et al., May 22, 1820, LR, OIA, frame 331, reel 236, M-234, NA; Robert Grierson to David Mitchell, November 29, 1820, box 6, folder 20, doc. 3, Keith Read Collection, HAR; Kendall Lewis to the United States Commissioners at Fort Gibson, November 30, 1832, box 1, folder 1833, Creek Removal Records, entry 300, RG 75, NA.

5. Michael D. Green, *The Politics of Indian Removal: Creek Government and Society in Crisis* (Lincoln: University of Nebraska Press, 1982), 56; Sherry L. Boatright, *The McIntosh Inn and Its Place in Creek Indian History, Butts County, Georgia* (Atlanta: State of Georgia, Department of Natural Resources, 1976), 42. Georgia's treatment of the Creeks can be followed in these works and in Harden, *Life of George M. Troup.*

6. One genealogist of the McIntosh family states that Robert Grierson's daughter Elizabeth was one of William McIntosh's wives, but circumstantial evidence suggests this not to be the case. Moreover, in 1826, a witness "well acquainted in the Creek Nation" positively stated that Eliza McIntosh, William's wife, was the daughter of Stephen Hawkins, not Robert Grierson. It is certain, however, that Robert's daughter Sarah married Stephen Hawkins. Their son Sam in turn married Jane McIntosh, a daughter of William's. Harriet Turner Corbin, *A History and Genealogy of Chief William McIntosh, Jr., and His Known Descendants* (self-published, 1967), 85; Charles Pendleton Tutt to James Barbour, November 25, 1826, LR, OIA, frames 694–695, reel 220, M-234, NA.

7. *Elizabeth Grierson v. Hillabee Indians*, box 10, 1st series, no. 24, Creek Removal Records, entry 300, RG 75, NA.

8. Ibid.

9. McIntosh Party Claims, frames 808–811, reel 27, OIA Special Files, M-574, NA.

10. Copy of laws of the Creek Nation, January 7, 1825, box 6, folder 22, doc. 1, Keith Read Collection, HAR.

11. McIntosh Party Claims, frames 1121–1122, reel 27, OIA Special Files, M-574, NA; Claimants' accounts, December 1825, LR, OIA, frames 776–777, reel 220, M-234, NA.

12. *Dick Grayson v. the Creek Nation*, box 10, 1st series, no. 20, Creek Removal Records, entry 300, RG 75, NA.

13. Journal of John Crowell, ADAH. One document suggests that William Grayson may have been included in his father's will, but the final disposition of property suggests that he was excluded or at least disfavored by his father. *USS*.H.rpt. 125 (22–1) 236.

14. Copy of laws of the Creek Nation, January 7, 1825, box 6, folder 22, doc. 1, Keith Read Collection, HAR.

15. The date of the raids is established by *Dick Grayson v. the Creek Nation*, box 10, 1st series, no. 20, Creek Removal Records, entry 300, RG 75, NA.

16. Robert Grierson to David Mitchell, November 29, 1820, box 6, folder 20, doc. 3, Keith Read Collection, HAR.

17. Quoted in Harden, *Life of George M. Troup*, 299.

18. Ibid. W. H. Sparks, *The Memories of Fifty Years*, 4th ed. (Philadelphia: E. Claxton and Company, 1882), 140.

19. Harden, *Life of George M. Troup*, 197–198.

20. The classic account of this corrupt treaty is Green, *Politics of Indian Removal*. For a narrative written from the perspective of George M. Troup, see Harden, *Life of George M. Troup*.

21. Quoted in Boatright, *McIntosh Inn*, 62.

22. List of signers to the treaty at Indian Springs, *NASP*, 7:254–256.

23. Troup to the Secretary of War, August 15, 1825, *NASP*, 8:106–108.

24. Quoted in Harden, *Life of George M. Troup*, 269–270.

25. Copy of Affidavit of Samuel Dorsey, September 12, 1825, LR, OIA, frames 1988–1989, reel 220, M-234, NA; Claimants' accounts, December 1825, LR, OIA, frames 752–754, reel 220, M-234, NA; McIntosh Party Claims, frames 827–830, reel 27, OIA Special Files, M-574, NA.

26. Claimants' accounts, December 1825, LR, OIA, frames 763–764, reel 220, M-234, NA.

27. September 15, 1825, Special Files, OIA, frame 1073, reel 27, M-574, NA.

28. A. J. Pickett to George White, September 13, 1853, in George White, *Historical Collections of Georgia* (New York: Pudney and Russell, 1854), 170–173; Benjamin W. Griffith Jr., *McIntosh and Weatherford, Creek Indian Leaders* (Tuscaloosa: University of Alabama Press, 1988), 248–252; Green, *Politics of Indian Removal*, 96–97.

29. Copy of Affidavit of Stephen Hawkins, June 21, 1825, LR, OIA, frames 1944–1945, reel 220, M-234, NA.

30. Statement of chiefs of Creek Nation, 1826, Special Files, OIA, frames 969–971, reel 27, M-574, NA.

31. John C. Webb, assee. of *E. Grierson v. the Creek Nation*, May 23, 1832, box 10, 1st series, no. 36, Creek Removal Records, entry 300, RG 75, NA.

32. Journal of John Crowell, ADAH.

33. George M. Troup to John C. Calhoun, February 28, 1824, *ASPIA*, 2:475–476; William G. McLoughlin, "Red Indians, Black Slavery and White Racism: America's Slaveholding Indians," *American Quarterly* 26 (1974): 376–377.

34. Slavery was prohibited in Georgia until 1751, when transplanted slaveholders from South Carolina successfully lobbied to overturn the ban. Although many Georgians in the Revolutionary generation remained opposed to the institution, their opposition was eclipsed by powerful planters. For a survey of slavery in colonial Georgia, see Betty Wood, *Slavery in Colonial Georgia, 1730–1775* (Athens: University of Georgia Press, 1984).

35. Lee Compere to Dr. Bolles, September 31, 1826, FM-98, ABHS.

36. Lee Compere, Withington Journal, September 1, 1827, to February 28, 1828, FM-98, ABHS.

37. Lee Compere to Lucius Bolles, May 19, 1828, FM-98, ABHS.

38. Lee Compere to Thomas McKenney, May 20, 1828, LR, OIA, frames 703–707, reel 221, M-234, NA.

39. Lee Compere, Withington Journal, March 1828, FM-98, ABHS.

40. Ibid.

41. B. S. Parsons to Lewis Cass, October 16, 1832, LR, OIA, frames 281–282, reel 223, M-234, NA. See also B. S. Parsons to Lewis Cass, October 21, 1832, LR, OIA, frames 283–285, reel 223, M-234, NA.

42. 1832 Census of Creek Indians, pp. 58, 60, T-275, NA.

43. B. S. Parsons to Lewis Cass, October 21, 1832, LR, OIA, frames 283–285, reel 223, M-234, NA.

44. Lee Compere, Withington Journal, September 1, 1827, to February 28, 1828, FM-98, ABHS.

45. Sparks, *Memories of Fifty Years*, 133, 139.

46. Green, *Politics of Indian Removal*, 98–125; Harden, *Life of George M. Troup*, 425–493.

47. D. Brearly to James Barbour, December 1, 1827, LR, OIA, frame 73, reel 237, M-234, NA; Matthew Arbuckle to John Campbell, October 23, 1831, LR, OIA, frames 210–212, reel 236, M-234, NA.

48. Harden, *Life of George M. Troup*, 492.

49. Copy of an Act to extend the civil and criminal jurisdiction . . . , January 11, 1827, LR, OIA, frames 190–191, reel 221, M-234, NA; Copy of an Act to prevent the Creek Indians from hunting and trapping . . . , January 11, 1827, LR, OIA, frames 192–193, reel 221, M-234, NA.

50. Memorial of the Head Men and Warriors of the Creek Nation of Indians, February 6, 1832, *NASP*, 9:192–196.

51. J. Austill to Lewis Cass, October 26, 1833, LR, OIA, frames 534–536, reel 223, M-234, NA.

52. William Walker to Thomas L. McKenney, December 12, 1828, LR, OIA, frames 181–183, reel 237, M-234, NA.

53. Affidavit of William Hudson, March 8, 1828, LR, OIA, frames 877–880, reel 221, M-234, NA; Affidavit of Pleasant D. Austin, March 8, 1828, LR, OIA, frames 881–

883, reel 221, M-234, NA; Affidavits of John Reed and John Berryhill, May 1, 1828, LR, OIA, frames 751–752, reel 221, M-234, NA; *NASP*, 9:176–178.

54. John Coffee to John H. Eaton, November 16, 1829, LR, OIA, frames 248–250, reel 237, M-234, NA. Later, the Dannelys would marry into the Grayson family. Creek enrollment card 1606, by blood, Enrollment Cards for the Five Civilized Tribes, 1898–1914, M-1186, NA.

55. Affidavit of John McCole, May 29, 1828, LR, OIA, frame 753, reel 221, M-234, NA; Adjutant General to Colonel Clinch, July 3, 1828, LR, OIA, frames 754–755, reel 221, M-234, NA.

56. John Crowell to John H. Eaton, May 7, 1829, LR, OIA, frames 59–61, reel 222, M-234, NA; John Crowell to John Branch, May 11, 1829, LR, OIA, frames 66–72, reel 222, M-234, NA.

57. John Crowell to Thomas McKenney, October 6, 1829, LR, OIA, frames 126–130, reel 222, M-234, NA.

58. Neha Micco et al. to the President, January 21, 1830, LR, OIA, frame 274, reel 222, M-234, NA.

59. List of families enrolled under David Connor, 1830, box 10, 1st series, Creek Removal Records, entry 300, RG 75, NA.

60. Receipt, 1830, box 10, 1st series, Creek Removal Records, entry 300, RG 75, NA.

61. *Phill Grierson v. Sockahpautia*, box 10, 1st series, no. 22, Creek Removal Records, entry 300, RG 75, NA; *Phill Grierson v. the Creek Nation*, box 10, 1st series, no. 28, Creek Removal Records, entry 300, RG 75, NA.

62. *Sandy Grierson v. the Creek Nation*, box 10, 1st series, no. 31, Creek Removal Records, entry 300, RG 75, NA.

63. John Crowell to John H. Eaton, June 30, 1830, LR, OIA, frames 315–316, reel 222, M-234, NA.

64. Stidham Roll, 1886, OHS.

65. John Crowell to John H. Eaton, August 8, 1830, LR, OIA, frames 319–324, reel 222, M-234, NA.

66. P. Wager to John H. Eaton, December 28, 1830, LR, OIA, frame 402, reel 222, M-234, NA; John Crowell to Lewis Cass, December 15, 1831, LR, OIA, frame 545, reel 222, M-234, NA; Foreman, *Indian Removal*; 109.

67. List of white intruders living in the Creek Nation, December 13, 1831, LR, OIA, frames 549–551, reel 222, M-234, NA.

68. John Crowell to John H. Eaton, August 8, 1830, LR, OIA, frames 319–324, reel 222, M-234, NA.

69. Creek chiefs to the President, May 21, 1831, LR, OIA, frames 441–443, reel 222, M-234, NA.

70. Neha Micco et al. to John Crowell, December 13, 1831, LR, OIA, frames 546–547, reel 222, M-234, NA.

71. This treaty and its consequences are discussed in Green, *Politics of Indian Removal*, 170–186; and Mary E. Young, *Redskins, Ruffleshirts, and Rednecks: Indian Allotments in Alabama and Mississippi, 1830–1860* (Norman: University of Oklahoma Press, 1961). The text of the treaty can be found in *NASP*, 9:214–217.

72. Creek Reservations under the Treaty of March 24, 1832, Creek vol. 86, CRN 1, OHS.

73. Report of T. Hartley Crawford, May 11, 1836, *NASP*, 10:19.

74. Ibid., 20–21.

75. Ibid., 21.

76. On the war against squatters, see John Crowell to Lewis Cass, August 3, 1832, LR, OIA, frame 138, reel 223, M-234, NA; Robert Crawford to John Robb, September 15, 1832, LR, OIA, frames 54–58, reel 223, M-234, NA; Robert Crawford to D. Kurty, December 6, 1832, LR, OIA, frames 61–63, reel 223, M-234, NA. On McIntosh and the false promises of emigration agents, see Enoch Parsons to Elbert Herring, February 10, 1833, LR, OIA, frames 1025–1027, reel 223, M-234, NA.

77. Quoted in Foreman, *Indian Removal*, 130.

78. Report of A. Balch, January 14, 1837, *NASP*, 9:505.

79. John Hogan to the Commissioner of Indian Affairs, February 14, 1836, quoted in Report of Alfred Balch, June 2, 1838, *NASP*, 10:113.

80. Elijah Corley to Scott and Cravens, March 25, 1835, *NASP*, 9:513–514.

81. Report of T. Hartley Crawford, May 11, 1838, *NASP*, 10:19.

82. William H. House to J. J. Abert, December 23, 1833, box 1, folder 1834, Creek Removal Records, entry 300, RG 75, NA.

83. J. Austill to Lewis Cass, July 26, 1833, LR, OIA, frames 508–513, reel 223, M-234, NA.

84. Hopoeth-yoholo et al. to Dr. McHenry, March 23, 1835, box 3, correspondence of certifying agents, entry 293, RG 75, NA.

85. *NASP*, 9:510, 514.

86. Report of T. Hartley Crawford, May 11, 1838, *NASP*, 10:23.

87. Deposition of John Taylor, January 16, 1837, *NASP*, 10:58–61.

88. Eli Shorter to John S. Scott and M. M. and N. H. Craven, January 28, 1835, *NASP*, 9:510–511.

89. Elijah Corley to Scott and Craven, March 25, 1835, *NASP*, 9:513–514.

90. Eli Shorter to John S. Scott and E. Corley, and M. M. and N. H. Craven, March 1, 1835, *NASP*, 9:511–513; Deposition of Arnold Seale, February 21, 1837, *NASP*, 10:45–51.

91. Eli Shorter to John S. Scott and E. Corley, and M. M. and N. H. Craven, March 1, 1835, *NASP*, 9:511–513.

92. Benjamin P. Tarver to M. A. Craven, March 1, 1835, *NASP*, 9:513.

93. Creek Reservations under the Treaty of March 24, 1832, Creek vol. 86, CRN 1, OHS; Creek Land Location Register, vol. 4, Creek Lands, Creek Removal Records, entry 287, RG 75, NA.

94. Index of Creek Land Transactions, vol. CM3, CIMA 1, OHS.

95. David Hubbard to Lewis Cass, May 1, 1834, LR, OIA, frames 425–428, reel 237, M-234, NA.

96. Hopoethleyoholo to Thomas Jesup, August 26, 1836, Letters Received during the Creek War, 1836–38, from Camps and Forts, box 15, the Office of the Adjutant General, Generals' Papers and Books, General Jesup, entry 159, RG 94, NA.

97. Muster roll, May 16, 1837, LR, OIA, frames 223–231, reel 238, M-234, NA; Report of A. Balch, January 14, 1837, *NASP*, 9:507.

98. One 1825 receipt signed by a daughter of William McIntosh confirms the delivery of Jeff, Molly, Peggy, two children Diana and Tildy, and "one Sorrel Mare with one Eye out." Like domesticated animals, slaves were considered personal property, and they fell under the same customs and laws. Receipt for slaves, October 6, 1825, William McIntosh Papers, folder 18, the Thomas Gilcrease Institute of American History and Art, Tulsa; Parsons and Cooper to D. B. Mitchell, August 10, 1832, box 1, folder 10, D. B. Mitchell Papers, Ayer Modern Manuscripts, Special Collections, the Newberry Library, Chicago.

99. Journal of John Crowell, ADAH.

100. Statement of Elizabeth Grierson, August 8, 1819, Records of Conveyance, book A–D, Montgomery County Courthouse, Alabama.

101. Passage deleted from *AGWG*, courtesy of W. David Baird.

102. Self Emigration Claims of Creek Indians, February 7, 1874, LR, OIA, frames 243–248, reel 235, M-234, NA.

103. Three Graysons from Lochapoka Town removed to Indian Territory before 1832. They were likely the children of Robert Grayson's brother, Thomas. A Benjamin Grayson from Hilabi did precede William on his journey. Benjamin's ancestry is unknown, and he does not turn up in later Indian Territory documents. Historians have assumed that Katy Grayson moved west before 1832, as well. Her daughter-in-law Jane or Jennie appears on a list of early immigrants, but Jennie came to Indian Territory as a young child. Her place on the Old Settlers Roll is evidently as the heir of her parents, who moved west with the McIntosh party. Katy Grayson emigrated in the winter of 1836 and appears on a January 23, 1837, Muster Roll of Emigrant Creek Indians, 1836–1838, NA. See also Old Settlers Roll, 1858, item 3, entry 906, RG 75, NA; *AGWG*, 27–30.

104. Foreman, *Indian Removal*, 126–128.

105. Quoted in Carolyn Thomas Foreman, "North Fork Town," *Chronicles of Oklahoma* 29 (1951): 98–99.

106. Council Minutes of the Creek Nation West, 1831–1835, CIMA roll 1, frame 234/235, OHS.

107. Alexis de Toqueville, *Democracy in America* (Chicago: University of Chicago Press, 2000), 590.

Rudy Hutton, September 1999 and June 2000

1. Testimony of Joe Grayson, Sr., Letters and Documents Relating to Citizenship in the Creek Nation, 1874–1895, Creek Citizenship, doc. 25415, frame 514, CRN 3, OHS.

2. Journal of John Crowell, ADAH.

3. Testimony of Joe Grayson, Sr., Letters and Documents Relating to Citizenship in the Creek Nation, 1874–1895, Creek Citizenship, doc. 25415, frame 514, CRN 3, OHS; Dawes Commission, Citizenship Commission Record Book, vol. 82-8-12, A-6-86-5, RG 75, NAFW.

4. Joe Grayson, jacket 92, roll 327, Applications for Enrollment of the Commission to the Five Civilized Tribes, 1898–1914, M1301, NA; Testimony of Joseph Grayson,

Jr., Letters and Documents Relating to Citizenship in the Creek Nation, 1874–1895, Creek Citizenship, doc. 25415, frames 509–513, CRN 3, OHS.

5. Joe Grayson, jacket 92, roll 327, Applications for Enrollment of the Commission to the Five Civilized Tribes, 1898–1914, M1301, NA.

6. Creek Census, 1882, roll 7RA43, NAFW.

7. Election Returns, May 1, 1899, Elections, box 19, folder 7, doc. 29629, CRN 34, OHS; Names erased from election returns, October 1, 1877, doc. 35654, frame 247, CRN 23, OHS.

8. Quarterly Report, Coon Creek Day School, September 5 to September 30 1904, Dawes Commission, Creek Correspondence, 67–9, OHS.

9. June 27, 1908, book 22, DGWG.

Chapter 3

1. *AGWG*, 21–25. In 1792, one Georgia resident mentioned a Charlotte Benson, taken prisoner some fifteen years earlier. Charlotte may in fact have been Tulwa Tustanagee's mother. Samuel Alexander to Edward Telfair, 1792, "Creek Indian Letters, Talks, and Treaties, 1705–1839," ed. J. E. Hays, 1:262, GDAH.

2. *AGWG*, 24.

3. Creek Land Location Register, vol. 4, Creek Lands, Creek Removal Records, entry 287, RG 75, NA.

4. There is a small possibility that Annie Grayson is the "unknown woman from Ketchapataka" so identified in a massive Barnett family tree compiled in 1936 by Sim L. Liles of Sapulpa, Oklahoma, and now in archives of the OHS.

5. 1832 Census of Creek Indians, T-275, NA.

6. Charles McLemore to the President of the United States, April 7, 1835, LR, OIA, frames 355–357, reel 242, M-234, NA.

7. George F. Salli to Lewis Cass, May 13, 1836, LR, OIA, frames 151–152, reel 225, M-234, NA.

8. Ibid.

9. William Schley to Alfred Balch and T. Hartley Crawford, October 7, 1836, *NASP*, 9:495–496.

10. Deposition of Arnold Seale, February 21, 1837, *NASP*, 10:45–51.

11. William Schley to Alfred Balch and T. Hartley Crawford, October 7, 1836, *NASP*, 9:495–496.

12. Testimony against Philander R. Broad, 1836, LR, OIA, frames 1336–1339, reel 243, M-234, NA.

13. John Hogan to Thomas Jesup, August 4, 1836, Various Reports, returns and papers, 1836, folder 3, box 40, the Office of the Adjutant General, Generals' Papers and Books, General Jesup, entry 159, RG 94, NA; John Hogan to Thomas Jesup, August 3, 1836, Various Reports, returns and papers, 1836, folder 5, box 40, the Office of the Adjutant General, Generals' Papers and Books, General Jesup, entry 159, RG 94, NA.

14. Lewis Cass to Thomas Jesup, May 19, 1836, LR, OIA, frames 26–30, reel 225, M-234, NA.

15. Tuckabatche Micco et al. to the Secretary of War, May 10, 1836, LR, OIA, frames 46–48, reel 225, M-234, NA; C. C. Clay to Thomas Jesup, June 14, 1836, Letters

Received from the Govs. of Alabama and Georgia, 1836, box 17, the Office of the Adjutant General, Generals' Papers and Books, General Jesup, entry 159, RG 94, NA; John B. Hogan to Thomas Jesup, June 15, 1836, Letters Received Relating to Creek and Seminole Affairs, June 1836, folder 1, box 24, the Office of the Adjutant General, Generals' Papers and Books, General Jesup, entry 159, RG 94, NA.

16. M. P. Lomax to Thomas Jesup, June 19, 1836, box 12, the Office of the Adjutant General, Generals' Papers and Books, General Jesup, entry 159, RG 94, NA; B. Patterson to the governor of Alabama, June 22, 1836, Letters Received during the Creek War, 1836–38, from Camps and Forts, box 15, the Office of the Adjutant General, Generals' Papers and Books, General Jesup, entry 159, RG 94, NA; John B. Hogan to Thomas Jesup, June 24, 1836, Letters Received during the Creek War, 1836–38, from Camps and Forts, box 15, the Office of the Adjutant General, Generals' Papers and Books, General Jesup, entry 159, RG 94, NA.

17. John B. Hogan to Thomas Jesup, June 25, 1836, Letters Received during the Creek War, 1836–38, from Camps and Forts, box 15, the Office of the Adjutant General, Generals' Papers and Books, General Jesup, entry 159, RG 94, NA.

18. Benjamin Young to Thomas Jesup, July 6, 1836, box 12, the Office of the Adjutant General, Generals' Papers and Books, General Jesup, entry 159, RG 94, NA.

19. Wilson to Thomas Jesup, April 22, 1837, Letters and Reports from various individuals pre and after Seminole wars, folder 3, box 36, the Office of the Adjutant General, Generals' Papers and Books, General Jesup, entry 159, RG 94, NA.

20. J. S. McIntosh to Thomas Jesup, August 13, 1836, box 12, the Office of the Adjutant General, Generals' Papers and Books, General Jesup, entry 159, RG 94, NA.

21. Dearborn to Col. Stanton, September 14, 1836, box 11, the Office of the Adjutant General, Generals' Papers and Books, General Jesup, entry 159, RG 94, NA.

22. M. Lomax to Thomas Jesup, July 18, 1836, box 12, the Office of the Adjutant General, Generals' Papers and Books, General Jesup, entry 159, RG 94, NA.

23. Capt. F. S. Betton's journal of occurrences, August–September 1836, LR, OIA, frames 520–526, reel 237, M-234, NA.

24. Index to Compiled Service Records of Volunteer Soldiers Who Served during Indian Wars and Disturbances, 1815–1858, M629, NA.

25. Public meeting, May 28, 1836, LR, OIA, frames 57–59, reel 225, M-234, NA.

26. B. Patterson to the governor of Alabama, June 22, 1836, Letters Received during the Creek War, 1836–38, from Camps and Forts, box 15, the Office of the Adjutant General, Generals' Papers and Books, General Jesup, entry 159, RG 94, NA.

27. John Pagle to [?], July 20, 1836, Letters Received Relating to Creek and Seminole Affairs, July 1836, folder 1, box 24, the Office of the Adjutant General, Generals' Papers and Books, General Jesup, entry 159, RG 94, NA.

28. Thomas Jesup, Order no. 63, August 17, 1836, Orders, August 1836, box 38, the Office of the Adjutant General, Generals' Papers and Books, General Jesup, entry 159, RG 94, NA; A. Q. Nicks to Thomas Jesup, August 23, 1836, box 12, the Office of the Adjutant General, Generals' Papers and Books, General Jesup, entry 159, RG 94, NA.

29. Muster Roll of Emigrant Creek Indians, 1836–1838, NA.

30. Edward Deas to George Gibson, October 26, 1836, LR, OIA, frames 541–544, reel 237, M-234, NA; Edward Deas to George Gibson, November 5, 1836, LR, OIA, frames 546–547, reel 237, M-234, NA; J. T. Sprague to C. A. Harris, April 1, 1837, LR, OIA, frames 739–756, reel 238, M-234, NA; Gaston Litton, "The Journal of a Party of Emigrating Creek Indians, 1835–1836," *Journal of Southern History* 7 (1941): 230.

31. Edward Deas to George Gibson, November 22, 1836, LR, OIA, frames 553–556, reel 237, M-234, NA.

32. Edward Deas to George Gibson, December 19, 1836, LR, OIA, frames 558–560, reel 237, M-234, NA.

33. Muster Roll of Emigrant Creek Indians, 1836–1838, NA.

34. Edward Deas to George Gibson, December 19, 1836, LR, OIA, frames 558–560, reel 237, M-234, NA; Muster Roll of Emigrant Creek Indians, 1836–1838, NA.

35. William Armstrong to C. A. Harris, January 27, 1837, LR, OIA, frames 26–27, reel 238, M-234, NA; frame 222, Muster Roll of Emigrant Creek Indians, 1836–1838, NA; M. W. Bateman to Thomas Jesup, February 10, 1837, Letters Received Relating to Creek and Seminole Affairs, 1837, box 24, the Office of the Adjutant General, Generals' Papers and Books, General Jesup, entry 159, RG 94, NA.

36. John Stuart to R. Jones, February 23, 1837, LR, OIA, frames 19–22, reel 238, M-234, NA.

37. A. J. Raines to the Commissioner of Indian Affairs, June 4, 1838, *NASP*, 10: 542–549; W. W. Lear to E. A Hitchcock, March 8, 1842, *NASP*, 10:557; *USS.*H.rpt. 271 (27–3) 428:114–115.

38. Testimony of Litle Sims, January 25, 1842, *NASP*, 10:524–525.

39. Testimony of George Shirley, January 30, 1842, *NASP*, 10:529–530.

40. Sinnugee may have been still living as late as 1854. Powers of attorney to Neal Smith, April 14, 1854, LR, OIA, frames 142–143, reel 229, M-234, NA.

41. Interview with Elsie Edwards, September 17, 1937, IPP, 27:189–193.

42. Thomas J. Abbot to C. A. Harris, April 30, 1837, LR, OIA, frames 6–8, reel 244, M-234, NA.

43. John C. Greene, "Some Early Speculations on the Origin of Human Races," *American Anthropologist* 56 (1954): 31–41; Reginald Horsman, *Race and Manifest Destiny: The Origins of American Racial Anglo-Saxonism* (Cambridge, MA: Harvard University Press, 1981); William Stanton, *The Leopard's Spots: Scientific Attitudes toward Race in America, 1815–59* (Chicago: University of Chicago Press, 1960); Robert E. Bieder, *Science Encounters the Indian, 1820–1880: The Early Years of American Ethnology* (Norman: University of Oklahoma Press, 1986). For the sixteenth and seventeenth centuries, see Lee Eldgridge Huddleston, *Origins of the American Indians: European Concepts, 1492–1729* (Austin: University of Texas Press, 1967).

44. Horsman, *Race and Manifest Destiny*, 99.

45. Stanton, *Leopard's Spots*, 5–7, 12–13.

46. Quoted in Horsman, *Race and Manifest Destiny*, 108. The classic work on environmentalism and Indian policy is Bernard W. Sheehan, *Seeds of Extinction; Jeffersonian Philanthropy and the American Indian* (Chapel Hill: University of North Carolina Press, 1973).

47. Quoted in Horsman, *Race and Manifest Destiny*, 141.

48. Quoted in Ibid., 117.

49. Charles Caldwell, *Thoughts on the Original Unity of the Human Race*, 2nd ed. (Cincinnati, OH: J. A. and U. P. James, 1852), 100.

50. Ibid., 57–58, 77–78, 82.

51. Horsman, *Race and Manifest Destiny*, 54–59, 120.

52. George Combe, *Notes on the United States of America, during a Phrenological Visit in 1838–39–40* (Edinburgh, 1841), 1:98.

53. Ibid., 1:101.

54. Ibid., 1:141, 181.

55. Samuel George Morton, *Catalogue of Skulls of Man and the Inferior Animals*, 3rd ed. (Philadelphia, PA: Merrihew and Thompson, 1849); Stanton, *Leopard's Spots*, 102.

56. In 1894, the Creek Nation would pass a law against disinterring the dead for the purposes of dissection, theft, or "mere wontonness." D. C. Watson, *Acts and Resolutions of the Creek National Council* (Muskogee, 1894; reprint, Wilmington, DE: Scholarly Resources, 1873), 4–5.

57. Quoted in Bieder, *Science Encounters the Indian*, 65–66.

58. For an examination of Morton's flawed science, see Stephen Jay Gould, *The Mismeasure of Man* (New York: Norton, 1981).

59. Caldwell, *Thoughts on the Original Unity of the Human Race*, 82.

60. T. Hartley Crawford to B. F. Butler, January 9, 1837, *NASP*, 9:550.

61. Samuel George Morton, *Crania Americana* (Philadelphia: J. Dobson, 1839), 170.

62. The five Graysons who served in the Creek War of 1836 are listed in Index to Compiled Service Records of Volunteer Soldiers Who Served during Indian Wars and Disturbances, 1815–1858, M629, NA.

63. Skull no. 441 could possibly have belonged to Athlaha Ficksa, but Morton indicated that it had a different provenance. Morton, *Catalogue of Skulls of Man and the Inferior Animals*.

64. Stanton, *Leopard's Spots*, 66–67.

65. Ibid., 120, 142.

66. Ibid., 194.

67. Talk of Creek leaders, June 11, 1735, *Original Papers, Correspondence to the Trustees, James Oglethorpe, and Others, 1732–1735*, ed. Kenneth Coleman and Milton Ready (Athens: University of Georgia Press, 1982), 381–387.

68. "At a Congress held at the Fort of Picolata in the Province of East Florida . . . ," December 9, 1765, PRO, CO 5/548, p. 113, in Writers' Program. Florida; British Colonial Office Records, 2:574, PKY.

69. Mr. Payne to James Seagrove, May 23, 1793, *ASPIA*, 1:392.

70. A talk from the White Lieutenant of the Ofuskees to his Friend and Brother, and also his Father, the Governor of New Orleans, November 9, 1793, no. 212, in *McGillivray of the Creeks*, ed. John Walton Caughey (Norman: University of Oklahoma Press, 1938).

71. John R. Swanton, *Myths and Tales of the Southeastern Indians* (1929; reprint, Norman: University of Oklahoma Press, 1995), 74–75; Alan Dundes, "Washington

Irving's Version of the Seminole Origin of Races," *Ethnohistory* 9 (1962): 257–264; William C. Sturtevant, "Seminole Myths of the Origin of Races," *Ethnohistory* 10 (1963): 80–86.

72. In 1842, one Creek would recount a similar story to a visitor in Indian Territory. Ethan Allen Hitchcock, *A Traveler in Indian Territory: The Journal of Ethan Allen Hitchcock, Late Major-General in the United States Army*, ed. Grant Foreman (Norman: University of Oklahoma Press, 1996), 125–127. For another version of this origin story, see Augustus W. Loomis, *Scenes in the Indian Country* (Philadelphia: Presbyterian Board of Publication, 1859), 54–57.

73. For an examination of the motives behind Indian recountings of stories about the origins of the races, see William G. McLoughlin and Walter H. Conser Jr., " 'The First Man Was Red'—Cherokee Responses to the Debate over Indian Origins, 1760–1860," *American Quarterly* 41 (1989): 243–264.

74. William G. McLoughlin, "A Note on African Sources of American Racial Myths," *Journal of American Folklore* 89 (1976): 331–335; Alan Dundes, "African Tales among the North American Indians," in *Mother Wit from the Laughing Barrel: Readings in the Interpretation of Afro-American Folklore*, ed. Alan Dundes (1973; reprint, Jackson: University Press of Mississippi, 1990), 114–125.

75. Nancy Shoemaker, "How Indians Got to Be Red," *American Historical Review* 102 (1997): 625–644.

76. James H. Merrell, "The Racial Education of the Catawba Indians," *Journal of Southern History* 50 (1984): 363–384.

77. *AGWG*, 26, 32; U.S. Census of Indian Lands West of Arkansas, free inhabitants in the Choctaw Nation in the Cole District.

78. The well-known Creek poet and journalist Alexander Posey died in 1908 while crossing the floodwaters of the North Canadian River, undertaking the same journey that William would have to visit his relatives. Daniel F. Littlefield Jr., *Alex Posey: Creek Poet, Journalist, and Humorist* (Lincoln: University of Nebraska Press, 1992), 1.

79. Creek Land Location Register, vol. 4, Creek Lands, Creek Removal Records, entry 287, RG 75, NA.

80. Angie Debo, *The Rise and Fall of the Choctaw Republic* (Norman: University of Oklahoma Press, 1934), 59–60.

81. Grant Foreman, *The Five Civilized Tribes: Cherokee, Chickasaw, Choctaw, Creek, Seminole* (Norman: University of Oklahoma Press, 1934), 33.

82. Hitchcock, *Traveler in Indian Territory*, 151–152.

Chapter 4

1. Abraham Redfield to David Greene, August 25, 1834, frames 846–847, reel 779, Unit 6, ABCFM, 18.4.4; *Annual Report of the Commissioner of Indian Affairs*, USS.H.doc. 2 (27-2) 401; *Annual Report of the Commissioner of Indian Affairs*, USS.S.doc. 1 (29-1) 470; *Annual Report of the Commissioner of Indian Affairs*, USS.S.exdoc. 1 (32-1) 613; R. M. Loughridge to Bro. Wilson, May 21, 1855, box 6, vol. 1, no. 24, reel 6, PHS.

2. J. R. Ramsay to J. L. Wilson, December 23, 1858, box 6, vol. 1, no. 197, reel 6, PHS.

3. John Lilley to J. L. Wilson, June 1, 1856, box 6, vol. 1, no. 70, reel 6, PHS.

4. 1832 Census of Creek Indians, T-275, NA; Creek Payment Roll, 1859, reel 7RA 23/1, RG 75, NAFW.

5. 1832 Census of Creek Indians, T-275, NA.

6. Dunn Roll of Freedmen, 1869, 7RA-05, OHS. The slave schedule of the 1860 census enumerates 249 fewer slaves in the Creek Nation. I have used the Dunn Roll because, unlike the 1860 census, it includes slaves belonging to Creek citizens not resident in the nation. Considering that many Creek slaves died during the Civil War and others never returned to the nation after the conflict, the number of freed persons present in 1869 surely is less than the number of slaves in 1860.

7. Interview with Edmond Flint, November 29, 1937, IPP, 30:315–316.

8. Albert Pike to Robert Toombs, May 29, 1861, *WRB*, series 4, 1:359.

9. Lindsay Baker and Julie P. Baker, eds., *The WPA Oklahoma Slave Narratives* (Norman: University of Oklahoma Press, 1996), 171–180.

10. *AGWG*, 27.

11. *Ibid.*, 45.

12. *Ibid.*, 39n5.

13. *Ibid.*, 45.

14. *Ibid.*, 66.

15. *Ibid.*, 52, 53.

16. Quoted in Ethan Allen Hitchcock, *A Traveler in Indian Territory: The Journal of Ethan Allen Hitchcock, Late Major-General in the United States Army*, ed. Grant Foreman (Norman: University of Oklahoma Press, 1996), 95n56.

17. Ibid., 187.

18. Wiley Britton, *The Union Brigade in the Civil War* (Kansas City, MO: Franklin Hudson, 1922), 194–195.

19. Stephen Jay Gould, *The Mismeasure of Man* (New York: Norton, 1981), 82–104.

20. Baker and Baker, *WPA Oklahoma Slave Narratives*, 107–117.

21. These figures were determined using the slave schedule in Indian Territory from the 1860 U.S. census and Michael F. Doran, "Population Statistics of Nineteenth Century Indian Territory," *Chronicles of Oklahoma* 53 (1975–1976): 501. The author wishes to thank Tressie L. Nealy, Sharron Standifer Ashton, and Jack D. Baker of the Oklahoma Historical Society for their assistance.

22. Report of T. P. Andrews, August 1, 1825, LR, OIA, frame 550, reel 219, M-234, NA; slave schedule in Indian Territory from the 1860 U.S. census.

23. Wash Grayson married Annie Stidham, the daughter of slaveholder G. W. Stidham, in 1869. *AGWG*, 127–129.

24. Slave Inhabitants in the Choctaw Nation, Cole County, slave schedule, 1860 U.S. Census.

25. Interview with Ned Thompson, August 20, 1937, IPP, 90:386–398.

26. *Constitution and Laws of the Muskogee Nation, as Compiled and Codified by A. P. McKellop, under Act of October 15, 1892* (Muskogee: F. C. Hubbard, 1893; reprint, Wilmington, DE: Scholarly Resources, 1973), 103–104; Slave Inhabitants in the Choctaw Nation, Cole County, slave schedule, 1860 U.S. Census. The Dunn Roll of Freedmen,

1869, 7RA–05, OHS, suggests that the Graysons may have owned more than thirty-eight slaves.

27. In fact, kinship relations and corporate slavery are not necessarily benign. Igor Kopytoff, "The Cultural Context of African Abolition," in *The End of Slavery in Africa*, ed. Suzanne Miers and Richard Roberts (Madison: University of Wisconsin Press, 1988), 491. There is a heated debate among African historians over the nature of African, or kin-based, slavery. See Igor Kopytoff and Suzanne Miers, "Introduction: African 'Slavery' as an Institution of Marginality," in *Slavery in Africa: Historical and Anthropological Perspectives*, ed. Igor Kopytoff and Suzanne Miers (Madison: University of Wisconsin Press, 1977), 3–84; Claude Meillassoux, *The Anthropology of Slavery: The Womb of Iron and Gold* (London: Athlone Press, 1991); and Miers and Roberts, *End of Slavery in Africa*.

28. Diary of Mrs. John B. Lilley, pp. 13–14, 20, 21–22, Mrs. John B. Lilley Collection, Minor Archives, box L-5, WHC.

29. William Robertson to his parents, October 22, 1849, box 3, file 7, Alice Robertson Collection, OHS.

30. Grayson, *AGWG* 34, 56.

31. Quoted in Sigmund Sameth, "Creek Negroes: A Study of Race Relations" (M.A. thesis, University of Oklahoma, 1940), 20.

32. Joe Grayson, jacket 92, roll 327, Applications for Enrollment of the Commission to the Five Civilized Tribes, 1898–1914, M1301, NA; Annual Report of the Commissioner of Indian Affairs, *USS*.S.exdoc. 1 (30–1) 503: 886–887; Baker and Baker, *WPA Oklahoma Slave Narratives*, 30–34.

33. Interview with John Harrison, n.d., IPP, 39: 324–352, OHS.

34. Hitchcock, *Traveler in Indian Territory*, 174.

35. See, for example, interview with Ed Butler, July 17, 1937, IPP, 14:82–85; and Baker and Baker, *WPA Oklahoma Slave Narratives*, 82–83, 171–181, 224–228.

36. Interview with Alex Haynes, May 21, 1937, IPP, 40:298–299.

37. Interview with Ed Butler, July 17, 1937, IPP, 14:82–85.

38. Interview with Tony Carolina, September 15, 1937, IPP, 16:85–89.

39. Bill of sale, September 30, 1853, LR, OIA, frame 470, reel 229, M-234, NA; Mary A. Lilley to Walter Lowrie, November 30, 1853, box 12, vol. 2, no. 237, reel 16, PHS; William Robertson to his parents, May 22, 1855, box 3, file 10, Alice Robertson Collection, OHS; Statement of the claim of James Logan, n.d., LR, OIA, frames 345–347, reel 230, M-234, NA.

40. Bill of sale, October 26, 1827, LR, OIA, frame 294, reel 236, M-234, NA.

41. Affidavit of Watt Grayson, October 26, 1851, LR, OIA, frame 358, reel 230, M-234, NA.

42. Interview with John Harrison, n.d., IPP, 39:324–352.

43. Baker and Baker, *WPA Oklahoma Slave Narratives*, 107–117.

44. Interview with Jordan D. Folsom, February 17, 1938, IPP, 31:63–74.

45. Interview with Ned Thompson, August 20, 1937, IPP, 90:386–398.

46. Hitchcock, *Traveler in Indian Territory*, 28; William Armstrong to T. Hartley Crawford, October 20, 1845, LR, OIA, frames 396–397, reel 227, M-234, NA; Roly McIntosh et al. to James Logan, September 15, 1845, LR, OIA, frames 405–406, reel

227, M-234, NA; Statement of Jesse Chisholm, September 17, 1845, LR, OIA, frame 408, reel 227, M-234, NA; Statement of George Brinton, September 17, 1845, LR, OIA, frame 412, reel 227, M-234, NA.

47. William F. Vaill to Jeremiah Evarts, April 26, 1831, frames 334–337, reel 779, Unit 6, ABCFM, 18.4.4; William F. Vaill to David Greene, October 20, 1831, frames 383–386, reel 779, Unit 6, ABCFM, 18.4.4; William F. Vaill to David Greene, June 20, 1832, frames 410–416, reel 779, Unit 6, ABCFM, 18.4.4; Report, 1832, frame 801, reel 779, Unit 6, ABCFM, 18.4.4.

48. Isaac McCoy, *History of Baptist Indian Missions: Embracing Remarks on the Former and Present Condition of the Aboriginal Tribes; Their Settlement within the Indian Territory, and Their Future Prospects* (Washington, DC: William M. Morrison, 1840), 451–454; John Fleming to David Green, June 5, 1834, frames 223–229, reel 779, Unit 6, ABCFM, 18.4.4.

49. Washington Irving, *The Western Journals of Washington Irving*, ed. John Francis McDermott (Norman: University of Oklahoma Press, 1944), 108–109.

50. David Rollin to Lucius Bolles, June 6, 1836, FM-101-11, ABHS.

51. Hitchcock, *Traveler in Indian Territory*, 111–112.

52. John Fleming to David Green, October 29, 1833, frames 209–212, reel 779, Unit 6, ABCFM, 18.4.4.

53. David Rollin to Lucius Bolles, January 19, 1835, FM-101-10, ABHS.

54. M. Thomas Bailey, *Reconstruction in Indian Territory: A Story of Avarice, Discrimination, and Opportunism* (Port Washington, NY: Kennikat Press, 1972), 23.

55. Roley McIntosh et al. to Matthew Arbuckle, August 31, 1836, LR, OIA, frames 692–693, reel 236, M-234, NA.

56. McCoy, *History of Baptist Indian Missions*, 507–508.

57. M. Arbuckle to J. R. Poinsett, July 6, 1838, LR, OIA, frames 503–505, reel 225, M-234, NA.

58. Creek leaders as quoted in ibid.

59. Charles Kellam to Lucius Bolles, October 3, 1839, FM-99-17, ABHS.

60. Charles Kellam to Lucius Bolles, March 12, 1838, FM-99-17, ABHS.

61. Charles Kellam to Lucius Bolles, November 20, 1839, FM-99-17, ABHS.

62. Roley McIntosh et al. to Matthew Arbuckle, August 31, 1836, LR, OIA, frames 692-693, reel 236, M-234, NA; McCoy, *History of Baptist Indian Missions*, 507–508.

63. Carl Mauelshagen and Gerald H. Davis, eds., *Partners in the Lord's Work: The Diary of Two Moravian Missionaries in the Creek Indian Country, 1807–1813*, School of Arts and Sciences Research Papers (Atlanta: Georgia State College, 1969), 22, 72; quotation p. 30.

64. James Logan to William Armstrong, February 10, 1840, LR, OIA, frames 145–146, reel 226, M-234, NA; John Fleming to Walter Lowrie, April 6, 1840, box P, vol. 3:31, reel 34, PHS.

65. Newspaper enclosure, in William Armstrong to T. Hartley Crawford, March 30, 1840, LR, OIA, frames 129–133, reel 226, M-234, NA.

66. R. M. Loughridge to the Presbyterian Board of Foreign Missions, February 17, 1842, box 9, vol. 1, no. 2, reel 11, PHS.

67. John D. Lang and Samuel Taylor Jr., *Report of a Visit to Some of the Tribes*

Located West of the Mississippi River (Providence, RI: Knowles and Vose, 1843), 40–41; Alvin Rucker, "The Story of the Uprising in Oklahoma," *Daily Oklahoman*, October 30, 1932.

68. Creek laws, box 13, folder 2, no. 83.229, Grant Foreman Collection, OHS.

69. Calculated from Claim no. 9, Sophy Kennard, Records Relating to Loyal Creek Claims, 1869–1870, box 1, entry 687, RG 75, NA.

70. John M. Cromwell, "The Aftermath of Nat Turner's Insurrection," *Journal of Negro History* 5 (1920): 218–234.

71. Benjamin Marshall et al. to the Commissioner of Indian Affairs, March 29, 1848, LR, OIA, frames 64–66, reel 228, M-234, NA.

72. Creek laws, box 13, folder 2, no. 83.229, Grant Foreman Collection, OHS.

73. Ibid. Other Indian nations passed similar laws against marriage with African Americans. Karen M. Woods, "A 'Wicked and Mischievous Connection': The Origins of Indian-White Miscegenation Law," in *Mixed Race America and the Law: A Reader*, ed. Kevin R. Johnson (New York: New York University Press, 2003), 83–85.

74. Claim no. 1310, Judy Grayson, Records Relating to Loyal Creek Claims, 1869–1870, box 14, entry 687, RG 75, NA.

75. On the clothing of blacks and Creeks, see *Through the Country of the Comanche Indians in the Fall of the Year 1845: The Journal of a U.S. Army Expedition Led by Lieutenant James W. Abert . . .* , ed. John Galvin (San Francisco: John Howell, 1970), 62–64; and Irving, *Tour on the Prairies*, 20, 22, 30.

76. Hitchcock, *Traveler in Indian Territory*, 110.

77. R. M. Loughridge to the Presbyterian Board of Foreign Missions, February 17, 1842, box 9, vol. 1, no. 2, reel 11, PHS; Charles Kellam to Lucius Bolles, August 1, 1842, FM-99-17, ABHS.

78. Lang and Taylor, *Report of a Visit*, 40–41; Charles Kellam to Lucius Bolles, August 1, 1842, FM-99-17, ABHS.

79. R. M. Loughridge to Walter Lowrie, November 2, 1843, box 9, vol. 1, no. 11, reel 11, PHS; Eber Tucker to E. Patterson, November 15, 1843, FM-101-30, ABHS; J. L. Dawson to J. H. Crawford, December 5, 1843, LR, OIA, frames 146–147, reel 227, M-234, NA.

80. Eber Tucker to E. Patterson, March 5, 1843, FM-101-30, ABHS.

81. Carolyn Thomas Foreman, "North Fork Town," *Chronicles of Oklahoma* 29, no. 1 (1951): 82. In 1845, Jesse, "a Negro preacher," was also whipped in the Creek Nation. E. C. Rough, *Chronicles of Oklahoma* 14 (1936): 459–460.

82. Michael A. Morrison, *Slavery and the American West: The Eclipse of Manifest Destiny and the Coming of the Civil War* (Chapel Hill: University of North Carolina Press, 1997).

83. Eric Foner, *Free Soil, Free Labor, Free Men: The Ideology of the Republican Party before the Civil War* (New York: Oxford University Press, 1970).

84. For a collection of pro-slavery writings, see Drew Gilpin Faust, ed., *The Ideology of Slavery: Proslavery Thought in the Antebellum South, 1830–1860* (Baton Rouge: Louisiana State University Press, 1981).

85. Grant Foreman, *The Five Civilized Tribes—Cherokee, Chickasaw, Choctaw, Creek, Seminole* (Norman: University of Oklahoma Press, 1934), 243; T. Hartley Crawford to

Major William Armston, April 10, 1844, box 9, vol. 1, no. 3, reel 11, PHS; Tom Marthlo Micco et al. to J. H. Crawford, July 25, 1843, LR, OIA, frames 121–123, reel 227, M-234, NA; J. L. Dawson to J. H. Crawford, April 4, 1844, LR, OIA, frames 297–304, reel 227, M-234, NA. See also Jane F. Lancaster, *Removal Aftershock: The Seminoles' Struggles to Survive in the West, 1836–1866* (Knoxville: University of Tennessee Press, 1994).

86. James Logan to William Medill, January 12, 1847, LR, OIA, frames 579–580, reel 227, M-234, NA; Benjamin Marshall et al. to the Commissioner of Indian Affairs, March 29, 1848, LR, OIA, frames 64–66, reel 228, M-234, NA.

87. John Lilley to Walter Lowrie, January 29, 1849, box 9, vol. 1, no. 129, reel 11, PHS. See also D. W. Eakins to Walter Lowrie, February 18, 1849, box 9, vol. 1, no. 135, reel 11, PHS.

88. *AGWG*, 36.

89. Hitchcock, *Traveler in Indian Territory*, 110.

90. David Rollin to Lucius Bolles, June 6, 1836, FM-101-11, ABHS.

91. Foreman, *Five Civilized Tribes*, 195.

92. *AGWG*, 37.

93. J. Ross Ramsay to Walter Lowrie, November 13, 1851, box 12, vol. 2, no. 98, reel 16, PHS.

94. M. L. Price to J. Leighton Wilson, November 12, 1855, box 6, vol. 1, no. 44, reel 6, PHS.

95. A list of the scholars of Kowetah boarding school, September 1852, box 12, vol. 2, no. 150, reel 16, PHS.

96. C. Stanislaus to Walter Lowrie, February 25, 1854, box 12, vol. 2, no. 248, reel 16, PHS.

97. Mary A. Lilley to Walter Lowrie, November 30, 1853, box 12, vol. 2, no. 237, reel 16, PHS.

98. *AGWG*, 46–48.

99. Ibid., 49.

100. Frances Woods, *Indian Lands West of Arkansas (Oklahoma): Population Schedule of the United States Census of 1860* (Arrow Printing Company, 1964), 15.

101. *AGWG*, 45.

102. Mary Harrod, nos. 2345–2366, Loyal Creek Claims, 1903, Special Series A, box 15, entry 126, RG 75, NA.

103. *AGWG*, 50.

104. *Through the Country of the Comanche Indians*, 62–64.

105. Claim no. 1311, Thomas Adams (administrator), Records Relating to Loyal Creek Claims, 1869–1870, box 14, entry 687, RG 75, NA.

106. Claim no. 1310, Judy Grayson, Records Relating to Loyal Creek Claims, 1869–1870, box 14, entry 687, RG 75, NA.

107. Vicey Grayson, no. 2618, Loyal Creek Claims, 1903, Special Series A, box 15, entry 126, RG 75, NA.

108. Claim no. 1197, Simpson Grayson, Records Relating to Loyal Creek Claims, 1869–1870, box 12, entry 687, RG 75, NA.

109. Claim no. 1196, Lem Grayson, Records Relating to Loyal Creek Claims,

1869–1870, box 12, entry 687, RG 75, NA; Claim no. 1176, Mary Grayson, Records Relating to Loyal Creek Claims, 1869–1870, box 12, entry 687, RG 75, NA; Claim no. 153, Mary Ann Grayson, Records Relating to Loyal Creek Claims, 1869–1870, box 2, entry 687, RG 75, NA.

110. Calculated from Abstract of Loyal Creek Claims, entry 688, RG 75, NA.

111. A list of the scholars of Kowetah boarding school, September 1852, box 12, vol. 2, no. 150, reel 16, PHS; *AGWG*, 37.

112. Vicey Grayson, no. 2618, Loyal Creek Claims, 1903, Special Series A, box 15, entry 126, RG 75, NA.

113. Judy and Vicey Grayson (later Weatherspoon) signed documents with a simple x. See, for example, Vicey Weatherspoon, no. 2352, by blood, Creek Allotment Records, entry 135, RG 75, NAFW; Claim no. 1310, Judy Grayson, Records Relating to Loyal Creek Claims, 1869–1870, box 14, entry 687, RG 75, NA.

114. *AGWG*, 49.

115. Alice Mary Robertson, "In going from Tullahassee . . . ," series I, box 2, folder 4, Alice Robertson Collection, McFarlin Library, University of Tulsa.

116. *AGWG*, 49.

Napoleon Davis, June 2000

1. Claim no. 15, Aaron Grayson, Records Relating to Loyal Creek Claims, 1869–1870, box 1, entry 687, RG 75, NA; Creek National Records, Pensions, box 41, folder 5, doc. 35150, CRN 42, OHS.

2. Claim no. 22, Hardy Grayson, Records Relating to Loyal Creek Claims, 1869–1870, box 1, entry 687, RG 75, NA.

3. Hardy Grayson to Samuel Checote, October 10, 1882, Creek National Records, Outbreaks, box 37, folder 7, doc. 34186, CRN 40, OHS.

Chapter 5

1. Wiley Britton, *The Civil War on the Border* (New York: Putnam, 1899), 2:24–25.

2. Ibid.

3. See Pleasant Porter's testimony, in Creek Field Jacket 3915, roll 355, M1301, NA.

4. Martha Hodes shows that fears of interracial sex in nineteenth-century America rose strikingly as the color line came under attack in the era of the Civil War and Reconstruction. Martha Hodes, *White Women, Black Men: Illicit Sex in the Nineteenth-Century South* (New Haven, CT: Yale University Press, 1997).

5. Sidney Kaplan, "The Miscegenation Issue in the Election of 1864," in Kaplan, *American Studies in Black and White: Selected Essays, 1949–1989* (Amherst: University of Massachusetts Press, 1991), 47–100.

6. Cherokees also protested the presence of abolitionists in their country. R. M. Loughridge to J. L. Wilson, August 6, 1860, box 6, vol. 3, no. 14, reel 7, PHS.

7. J. Lilley to J. L. Wilson, November 3, 1860, box 6, vol. 3, no. 166, reel 7, PHS.

8. R. M. Loughridge to J. L. Wilson, September 12, 1860, box 6, vol. 3, no. 15,

reel 7, PHS; R. M. Loughridge to Walter Lowrie, November 12, 1860, box 6, vol. 3, no. 18, reel 7, PHS.

9. Creek laws, box 13, folder 2, no. 83.229, Grant Foreman Collection, OHS; Extract of a letter from R. M. Loughridge to J. R. Ramsay, March 1861, box 6, vol. 3, no. 177, reel 7, PHS.

10. Creek laws, box 13, folder 2, no. 83.229, Grant Foreman Collection, OHS.

11. Creek Field Jacket 3915, roll 355, M1301, NA.

12. Frances Woods, *Indian Lands West of Arkansas (Oklahoma): Population Schedule of the United States Census of 1860* (Arrow Printing Company, 1964), 15.

13. William S. Robertson to Nancy Thompson, March 1, 1861, series II, box 19, folder 5, doc. 80, Alice Robertson Collection, McFarlin Library, University of Tulsa.

14. *AGWG*, 54.

15. Ibid., 56.

16. Resolutions of the Chickasaw Legislature, May 25, 1861, *WRB*, series 1, 3:585–587.

17. Michael F. Doran, "Population Statistics of Nineteenth Century Indian Territory," *Chronicles of Oklahoma* 53 (1975–1976): 501.

18. Proclamation by the Principal Chief of the Choctaw Nation, June 14, 1861, *WRB*, series 1, 3:593–594.

19. R. M. Loughridge to Walter Lowrie, March 20, 1861, box 6, vol. 3, no. 35, reel 7, PHS.

20. David Hubbard to John Ross and Benjamin McCulloch, June 12, 1861, *WRB*, series 1, 13:497–498.

21. Annual Report of the Commissioner of Indian Affairs, *USS*.H.exdoc. 1 (38-1) 1182:346. For an exploration of John Ross's motives during the Civil War, see Ari Kelman, "Deadly Currents: John Ross's Decision of 1861," *Chronicles of Oklahoma* 73 (1995): 80–103.

22. Official report of the proceedings of the council with the Indians . . . held at Fort Smith, September 1865, *USS*.H.exdoc.106 (39-1) 1248:512–514.

23. Mrs. G. W. Grayson, "Confederate Treaties," *Indian Journal* (Eufaula and Muskogee), May 9, 1913.Check Foreman, North Fork Town, 8, 103.

24. Proceedings of a general meeting of the Cherokee Nation, August 21, 1861, *WRB*, series 1, 3:673–676.

25. Official report of the proceedings of the council with the Indians . . . held at Fort Smith, September 1865, *USS*.H.exdoc.106 (39-1) 1248:512–514.

26. A Treaty of Friendship, July 10, 1861, *WRB*, series 4, 1:426–443.

27. Ibid.

28. Ben. McCulloch to L. P. Walker, June 22, 1861, *WRB*, series 1, 3:595–596.

29. David Hubbard to John Ross and Benjamin McCulloch, June 12, 1861, *WRB*, series 1, 13:497–498.

30. Wash's wife, Annie Grayson, suggested in 1913 that the Creeks' desire to protect their human property led them to join the Confederacy. Mrs. G. W. Grayson, "Why the Five Civilized Tribes Joined the Confederacy," *Indian Journal* (Eufaula and Muskogee), June 6, 1913. Historians, however, frequently discount the importance of slavery in the Creek Nation. See, for example, Angie Debo, *The Road to Disappearance: A History*

of the Creek Indians (Norman: University of Oklahoma Press, 1941), 142–176; Arrell Morgan Gibson, The Chickasaws (Norman: University of Oklahoma Press, 1971), 227–246; Kenny A. Franks, Stand Watie and the Agony of the Cherokee Nation (Memphis: Memphis State University Press, 1979); W. Craig Gaines, The Confederate Cherokees: John Drew's Regiment of Mounted Rifles (Baton Rouge: Louisiana State University Press, 1989); Christine Schultz White and Benton R. White, Now the Wolf Has Come: The Creek Nation in the Civil War (College Station: Texas A&M University Press, 1996); Mary Jane Warde, George Washington Grayson and the Creek Nation, 1843–1920 (Norman: University of Oklahoma Press, 1999), 58–59; Carolyn Ross Johnston, " 'The Panther's Scream Is Often Heard': Cherokee Women in Indian Territory during the Civil War," Chronicles of Oklahoma 78 (2000): 84–107. Yet as William G. McLoughlin points out, Confederate Indians themselves may be responsible for the origins of the interpretation that slavery had little to do with Indian participation in the Civil War. After the conflict, southern Cherokees promoted the view that long-standing factionalism rather than slavery had divided the nation. Yet, as early as 1859, the Cherokees had formed a pro-slavery organization called the Knights of the Golden Circle. According to its constitution, "No person shall be a member . . . who is not a pro-slavery man." McLoughlin, "Political Polarization and National Unity: The Keetoowah Society, 1860–1871," in The Cherokees and Christianity, 1794–1870 (Athens: University of Georgia Press, 1994), 256–259, 276–278.

31. Interview with Jim Tomm, April 19 and April 20, 1937, IPP, 91:323–352.

32. Interview with J. W. Stephens, March 22, 1938, IPP, 87:190–205.

33. Interview with Jim Tomm, April 19 and April 20, 1937, IPP, 91:323–352; Warde, George Washington Grayson, 89.

34. A Treaty of Friendship, July 10, 1861, WRB, series 4, 1:426–443.

35. William A. Sapulpa, "Sapulpa," Chronicles of Oklahoma 4 (1926): 329–332.

36. Will of Abraham Foster, December 19, 1864, doc. 39508, CRN 51, OHS.

37. Muster roll of a company of Creek Indians, February 14, 1846, LR, OIA, frame 391, reel 240, M-234, NA.

38. Resolutions of the General Council of the Choctaw Nation, February 7, 1861, WRB, series 1, 1:682. The Cherokee and Chickasaw governments made similar statements. Proceedings of a general meeting of the Cherokee Nation, August 21, 1861, WRB, series 1, 3:673–676; Resolutions of the Chickasaw Legislature, May 25, 1861, WRB, series 1, 3:585–587.

39. S. S. Scott to George W. Randolph, October 22, 1862, WRB, series 1, 13:890–891.

40. J. A. Scales to W. P. Adair, April 12, 1863, WRB, series 1, vol. 22, 2:821–822.

41. Report of William Steele, February 15, 1864, WRB, series 1, vol. 22, 1:28–36; Stand Watie to S. S. Scott, August 8, 1863, WRB, series 1, vol. 22, 2:1104–1105; William Steele to S. Cooper, December 19, 1863, WRB, series 1, vol. 22, 2:1100–1101.

42. Petition of Chickasaw Nation to James A. Seddon, October 7, 1863, WRB, series 1, vol. 22, 2:1123–1124.

43. Albert Pike to L. P. Walker, July 31, 1861, WRB, series 1, 3:623–624.

44. Claim no. 33, Joe Fife, Records Relating to Loyal Creek Claims, 1869–1870, box 1, entry 687, RG 75, NA.

45. Claim no. 86, Gilbert Lewis, Records Relating to Loyal Creek Claims, 1869–1870, box 1, entry 687, RG 75, NA.

46. Claim no. 143, Thomas Bruner, Records Relating to Loyal Creek Claims, 1869–1870, box 2, entry 687, RG 75, NA.

47. Opoithleyahola to Abraham Lincoln, August 15, 1861, LR, OIA, frames 595–596, reel 230, M-234, NA.

48. Moty Canard to Douglas H. Cooper, October 31, 1861, Creek Nation Civil War Records, acc. number 84.58, OHS; Douglas H. Cooper to Motey Canard, October 31, 1861, Creek Nation Civil War Records, acc. number 84.58, OHS.

49. M. Thomas Bailey, *Reconstruction in Indian Territory: A Story of Avarice, Discrimination, and Opportunism* (Port Washington, NY: Kennikat Press, 1972), 75–77.

50. Douglas H. Cooper to J. P. Benjamin, January 20, 1862, *WRB*, series 1, 8:5–14.

51. Official report of the proceedings of the council with the Indians . . . held at Fort Smith, September 1865, *USS*.H.exdoc.106 (39-1) 1248:513; Hopoeithleyhohla and Aluktustenuke to the President, January 28, 1862, *WRB*, series 1, 8:534.

52. A. B. Campbell to Joseph K. Barnes, February 5, 1862, *WRB*, series 2, 4:6–7.

53. George W. Collamore to William P. Dole, April 21, 1862, *WRB*, series 2, 4:11–12.

54. William Armstrong to C. A. Harris, August 31, 1836, LR, OIA, frame 675, reel 236, M-234, NA.

55. *AGWG*, 59.

56. Claim no. 55, Joseph Cooney, Records Relating to Loyal Creek Claims, 1869–1870, box 1, entry 687, RG 75, NA.

57. Claim no. 30, Saucer Bradley, Records Relating to Loyal Creek Claims, 1869–1870, box 1, entry 687, RG 75, NA; Saucer Brady, compiled military records, U.S.C.T., 79th Infantry, New Organization, Civil War, RG 94, NA.

58. Claim no. 30, Saucer Bradley, Records Relating to Loyal Creek Claims, 1869–1870, box 1, entry 687, RG 75, NA; Creek Field Jacket 3179, roll 353, M1301, NA.

59. Records Relating to "Unaccounted For" Creeks, 1902–1905, entry 120A, RG 75, NAFW.

60. Record of Events for the First Indian Home Guards, *Supplement to the Official Records of the Union and Confederate Armies: Record of Events* (Wilmington, NC: Broadfoot Publishing, 1998), pt. 2, 80:603–621; Wiley Britton, *The Union Indian Brigade in the Civil War* (Kansas City, MO: Franklin Hudson, 1922), 179. On black soldiers in the First Indian Home Guards, see Gary Zellar, "Occupying the Middle Ground: African Creeks in the First Indian Home Guard, 1862–1865," *Chronicles of Oklahoma* 76 (1998): 48–71.

61. Index of Records of Volunteer Soldiers Who Served with U.S. Colored . . . , reels 9 and 34, M589, NA.

62. William Weer to Charles Doubleday, June 6, 1862, *WRB*, series 1, 13:418–419.

63. William Weer to Thomas Moonlight, June 21, 1862, *WRB*, series 1, 13:441–442; William Weer to Thomas Moonlight, July 6, 1862, *WRB*, series 1, 13:137–138.

64. T. C. Hindman to S. Cooper, June 19, 1863, *WRB*, series 1, 13:29–44.

65. Douglas H. Cooper to T. C. Hindman, August 7, 1862, *WRB*, series 1, 13:977.

66. William Weer to Thomas Moonlight, July 12, 1862, *WRB*, series 1, 13:487–488; "Journal and Letters of Stephen Foreman, Cherokee Minister," July 20, 1862, pp. 34–35, Stephen Foreman Collection, WHC.

67. Claim no. 94, Lewis Marshall, Records Relating to Loyal Creek Claims, 1869–1870, box 1, entry 687, RG 75, NA.

68. Claim no. 2, Harry Island, Records Relating to Loyal Creek Claims, 1869–1870, box 1, entry 687, RG 75, NA.

69. Testimony of Joe Grayson, Sr., Letters and Documents Relating to Citizenship in the Creek Nation, 1874–1895, Creek Citizenship, doc. 25415, frame 514, CRN 3, OHS.

70. Journal of John Crowell, ADAH.

71. Ibid.

72. E. H. Carruth and H. W. Martin to James G. Blunt, July 19, 1862, *WRB*, series 1, 13:478; F. Salomon to James G. Blunt, July 20, 1862, *WRB*, series 1, 13:484–485.

73. R. W. Furnas to James G. Blunt, July 25, 1862, *WRB*, series 1, 13:511–512.

74. William A. Phillips to Colonel R. W. Furnas, August 6, 1862, *WRB*, series 1, 13:183–184.

75. Claim no. 45, Perry McIntosh, Records Relating to Loyal Creek Claims, 1869–1870, box 1, entry 687, RG 75, NA; Claim no. 28, George Marshall, Records Relating to Loyal Creek Claims, 1869–1870, box 1, entry 687, RG 75, NA.

76. Diary of Hannah Hicks, January 4, 1863, series I, box 1, folder 10, Alice Robertson Collection, McFarlin Library, University of Tulsa, original in the Gilcrease Museum, Tulsa, Oklahoma.

77. "Journal and Letters of Stephen Foreman, Cherokee Minister," July 15, 1862, pp. 34–35, and July 29, 1862, p. 48, Stephen Foreman Collection, WHC, University of Oklahoma, Norman, OK.

78. Lindsay Baker and Julie P. Baker, eds., *The WPA Oklahoma Slave Narratives* (Norman: University of Oklahoma Press, 1996), 171–180.

79. Britton, *Civil War on the Border*, 2:16–17.

80. Annual Report of the Commissioner of Indian Affairs, *USS*.H.exdoc. 1 (37-3) 1157:281.

81. H. C. Ketchan to A. J. Coffin, September 15, 1863, enclosed in Annual Report of the Commissioner of Indian Affairs, *USS*.H.exdoc. 1 (38-1) 1182.

82. Albert Pike to the Secretary of War, July 20, 1862, *WRB*, series 1, 13:859–860; William A. Phillips to Samuel R. Curtis, January 19, 1863, *WRB*, series 1, vol. 22, 2:55–56.

83. S. S. Scott to Major-General Holmes, November 2, 1862, *WRB*, series 1, 13:919–921.

84. William A. Phillips to Samuel R. Curtis, January 19, 1863, *WRB*, series 1, vol. 22, 2:61–62; William A. Phillips to Samuel R. Curtis, January 29, 1863, *WRB*, series 1, vol. 22, 2:85.

85. William A. Phillips to Samuel R. Curtis, February 11, 1863, *WRB*, series 1, vol. 22, 2:108–109.

86. William A. Phillips to Major-General Curtis, January 19, 1863, *WRB*, series 1, vol. 22, 2:60–61; William A. Phillips to Samuel R. Curtis, January 19, 1863, *WRB*, series 1, vol. 22, 2:61–62.

87. *AGWG*, 58–61.

88. Albert Pike to [?], May 4, 1862, *WRB*, series 1, 13:819–823.

89. Albert Pike to George W. Randolph, June 30, 1862, *WRB*, series 1, 13:848–849.

90. Albert Pike to T. C. Hindman, July 3, 1862, *WRB*, series 1, 13:954–962.

91. Tustanarkchopko to the President of the United States, May 16, 1863, LR, OIA, frames 712–715, reel 230, M-234, NA.

92. Albert Pike to T. C. Hindman, July 3, 1862, *WRB*, series 1, 13:954–962.

93. W. S. Robertson to Walter Lowrie, December 27, 1861, box 6, vol. 3, no. 82, reel 7, PHS.

94. Copy of an Address . . . by the Friendly Indians, May 18, 1825, LR, OIA, frames 1706–1716, reel 220, M-234, NA.

95. Enoch Parsons to Elbert Herring, February 10, 1833, LR, OIA, frames 1025–1027, reel 223, M-234, NA.

96. Roly McIntosh et al. to John C. Spencer, August 25, 1842, LR, OIA, frames 410–419, reel 226, M-234, NA; Benjamin Marshall et al., February 14, 1856, LR, OIA, frames 497–498, reel 229, M-234, NA; Daniel F. Littlefield Jr., *Africans and Creeks: From the Colonial Period to the Civil War* (Westport, CT: Greenwood Press, 1979), 221–222.

97. Lary C. Rampp and Donald L. Rampp, *The Civil War in the Indian Territory* (Austin, TX: Presidial Press, 1975), 81.

98. William A. Phillips to Major-General Curtis, January 19, 1863, *WRB*, series 1, vol. 22, 2:60–61.

99. *AGWG*, 58–61.

100. William A. Phillips to James Blunt, December 25, 1862, *WRB*, series 1, vol. 22, 1:781–783; Claim no. 23, Warrior Marshall, Records Relating to Loyal Creek Claims, 1869–1870, box 1, entry 687, RG 75, NA.

101. William A. Phillips to Samuel R. Curtis, January 19, 1863, *WRB*, series 1, vol. 22, 2:55–56.

102. Stand Watie to S. S. Scott, August 8, 1863, *WRB*, series 1, vol. 22, 2:1104–1105.

103. Stand Watie to the Governor of the Creek Nation, August 9, 1863, *WRB*, series 1, vol. 22, 2:1105–1106.

104. Wiley Britton, *Memoirs of the Rebellion on the Border, 1863* (1882; reprint, Lincoln: University of Nebraska Press, 1993), 205; William A. Phillips to James G. Blunt, April 12, 1863, *WRB*, series 1, vol. 22, 2:211–212; "Journal and Letters of Stephen Foreman, Cherokee Minister," April 15, 1863, p. 92, Stephen Foreman Collection, WHC.

105. James G. Blunt to William A. Phillips, May 30, 1863, *WRB*, series 1, vol. 22, 2:297–298.

106. James G. Blunt to John A. Scholfield, July 26, 1863, *WRB*, series 1, vol. 22, 1:447–448.

107. In addition to Saucer Brady, Bob Grayson (parents unknown) enlisted before the Battle of Honey Springs. Bob Grayson, compiled military records, U.S.T., 1st Indian Home Guards, Kansas Infantry, Civil War, RG 94, NA.

108. James G. Blunt to John A. Scholfield, July 26, 1863, *WRB*, series 1, vol. 22, 1:447–448.

109. *AGWG*, 61.

110. Ibid., 61–63.

111. Baker and Baker, *WPA Oklahoma Slave Narratives*, 107–117.

112. Sturgis Williams Darling, "Oktaha," 22, sec. X, towns—Oktaha, OHS.

113. Baker and Baker, *WPA Oklahoma Slave Narratives*, 107–117.

114. James G. Blunt to John A. Scholfield, July 26, 1863, *WRB*, series 1, vol. 22, 1:447–448.

115. Baker and Baker, *WPA Oklahoma Slave Narratives*, 107–117.

116. *AGWG*, 62–63.

117. Britton, *Civil War on the Border*, 123; James G. Blunt to John A. Scholfield, July 26, 1863, *WRB*, series 1, vol. 22, 1:447–448.

118. James G. Blunt to John A. Scholfield, July 26, 1863, *WRB*, series 1, vol. 22, 1:447–448; Douglas H. Cooper to William Steele, August 12, 1863, *WRB*, series 1, vol. 22, 1:457–459.

119. Sturgis Williams Darling, "Oktaha," 22, sec. X, towns—Oktaha, OHS. Darling writes that Eli himself remembered finding dead bodies after the Battle of Honey Springs, but Eli was only an infant at the time.

120. See, for example, Claim no. 21, Samuel Barnett, Records Relating to Loyal Creek Claims, 1869–1870, box 1, entry 687, RG 75, NA; Claim no. 22, Hardy Grayson, Records Relating to Loyal Creek Claims, 1869–1870, box 1, entry 687, RG 75, NA; Claim no. 25, Hannah Grayson, Records Relating to Loyal Creek Claims, 1869–1870, box 1, entry 687, RG 75, NA; Claim no. 40, Phoebe Grayson, Records Relating to Loyal Creek Claims, 1869–1870, box 1, entry 687, RG 75, NA.

121. Claim no. 69, William Hawkins, Records Relating to Loyal Creek Claims, 1869–1870, box 1, entry 687, RG 75, NA.

122. Claim no. 15, Aaron Grayson, Records Relating to Loyal Creek Claims, 1869–1870, box 1, entry 687, RG 75, NA.

123. Claim no. 167, Mary Ann Grayson, Records Relating to Loyal Creek Claims, 1869–1870, box 1, entry 687, RG 75, NA.

124. Claim no. 56, Soda Hawkins, Records Relating to Loyal Creek Claims, 1869–1870, box 1, entry 687, RG 75, NA.

125. Claim no. 75, Mory Marshall, Records Relating to Loyal Creek Claims, 1869–1870, box 1, entry 687, RG 75, NA.

126. Claim no. 1184, John Grayson, Records Relating to Loyal Creek Claims, 1869–1870, box 12, entry 687, RG 75, NA.

127. Polly Miller, no. 3240, Loyal Creek Claims, 1903, Special Series A, box 16, entry 126, RG 75, NA.

128. Britton, *Union Indian Brigade*, 257.

129. Annual Report of the Commissioner of Indian Affairs, *USS*.H.exdoc. 1 (38-1) 1182:329.

130. Claim no. 160, Cow Tom, Records Relating to Loyal Creek Claims, 1869–1870, box 2, entry 687, RG 75, NA.

131. Oktarsars Harjo to the Commissioner of Indian Affairs, July 16, 1864, LR, OIA, frames 17–19, reel 231, M-234, NA.

132. Claim no. 1312, Thomas Adams, Records Relating to Loyal Creek Claims, 1869–1870, box 14, entry 687, RG 75, NA.

133. Claim no. 1187, Martha Grayson, Records Relating to Loyal Creek Claims, 1869–1870, box 12, entry 687, RG 75, NA.

134. Claim no. 167, Mary Ann Grayson, Records Relating to Loyal Creek Claims, 1869–1870, box 1, entry 687, RG 75, NA; Claim no. 153, Mary Ann Grayson, Records Relating to Loyal Creek Claims, 1869–1870, box 2, entry 687, RG 75, NA.

135. *AGWG*, 64–73; Joe Grayson, jacket 92, roll 327, Applications for Enrollment of the Commission to the Five Civilized Tribes, 1898–1914, M1301, NA.

136. *AGWG*, 74; Claim no. 1401, Simpson Grayson, Records Relating to Loyal Creek Claims, 1869–1870, box 15, entry 687, RG 75, NA.

137. Claim no. 1401, Simpson Grayson, Records Relating to Loyal Creek Claims, 1869–1870, box 15, entry 687, RG 75, NA.

138. Henderson Grayson, compiled military records, U.S.T., 1st Indian Home Guards, Kansas Infantry, Civil War, RG 94, NA.

139. Treaty of 1863, Creek National Records, Federal Relations, box 20, folder 10, doc. 29690, CRN 34, OHS.

140. Annual Report of the Commissioner of Indian Affairs, *USS*.H.exdoc. 1 (38-1) 1182:145–146, 294.

141. Joseph Perryman to W. S. Robertson, June 1, 1864, box 6, vol. 3, no. 128, reel 7, PHS.

142. Oktarsars Harjo to the Commissioner of Indian Affairs, July 16, 1864, LR, OIA, frames 17–19, reel 231, M-234, NA.

143. *AGWG*, 85, 103.

144. Record of Events for (New) Seventy-ninth United States Colored Infantry (formerly First Kansas Colored Infantry Volunteers), *Supplement to the Official Records of the Union and Confederate Armies*, pt. 2, 78:614–641.

145. Britton, *Union Indian Brigade*, 437–440.

146. *AGWG*, 96; Britton, *Union Indian Brigade*, 437–440; Curtis Johnson to George H. Hoyt, September 25, 1864, *WRB*, series 1, vol. 41, 1:775–776.

147. William A. Phillips to Major-General Curtis, January 19, 1863, *WRB*, series 1, vol. 22, 2:56–58.

148. John W. Noble to Samuel R. Curtis, April 12, 1862, *WRB*, series 1, 8:206.

149. Samuel R. Curtis to B. F. Wade, May 21, 1862, *WRB*, series 1, 8:206.

150. David Tod to E. M. Stanton, September 9, 1862, *WRB*, series 2, 4:499; E. M. Stanton to David Tod, September 9, 1862, *WRB*, series 2, 4:499.

151. Charles de Morse to D. H. Cooper, July 3, 1864, *WRB*, series 1, vol. 34, 4: 699–700; W. C. Schaumburg to W. R. Boggs, October 26, 1863, *WRB*, series 1, vol. 22, 2:1049–1053.

152. Samuel R. Curtis to William A. Phillips, February 11, 1864, *WRB*, series 1, vol. 34, 2:301–302.

153. William A. Phillips to Samuel R. Curtis, February 29, 1864, *WRB*, series 1, vol. 34, 2:467–468.

154. T. M. Scott to S. B. Maxey, April 12, 1864, *WRB*, series 1, vol. 34, 3:762–763.

155. F. J. Herron to C. T. Christensen, November 18, 1864, *WRB*, series 1, vol. 41, 4:605–606.

156. William A. Phillips to Edward R. S. Canby, February 16, 1865, *WRB*, series 1, vol. 48, 1:870–872.

Chester Adams, June 2000

1. Creek Equalization Payments, 2146, entry 548B, RG 75, NAFW.

2. Creek Equalization Payments, 3008, entry 548B, RG 75, NAFW.

Chapter 6

1. *AGWG*, 115.

2. John Bartlett Meserve, "Chief Pleasant Porter," *Chronicles of Oklahoma* 9 (1931): 318–334.

3. [Legus Perryman?] to Mrs. Robertson, May 1, 1864, box 6, vol. 3, no. 129, reel 7, PHS; D. D. Hitchcock to the Robertsons, August 1, 1866, series II, box 18, folder 1, doc. 231, Alice Robertson Collection, McFarlin Library, University of Tulsa; September 17, 1907, book 21, DGWG.

4. Eric Foner, *Reconstruction: America's Unfinished Revolution, 1863–1877* (New York: Harper and Row, 1988).

5. Statement of Mrs. N. B. Moore, Ann Augusta Robertson Moore Papers, OHS; Interview with Ethel Dawes Newton, August 19, 1968, T308-1, fiche 167, vol. 29, Doris Duke Oral History Collection, WHC.

6. *AGWG*, 124.

7. Ibid., 123–124.

8. Politicians in other Indian tribes also conflated nationalism and racism. See, for example, Circe Sturm, *Blood Politics: Race, Culture, and Identity in the Cherokee Nation of Oklahoma* (Berkeley and Los Angeles: University of California Press, 2002), chaps. 3 and 4.

9. Report of D. N. Cooley, October 30, 1865, *USS*.H.exdoc.105 (39-1) 1248:482–483.

10. The proposal for a territory-wide government was contained in Senate bill 459, which provided for the creation of governmental machinery similar to that found in other organized U.S. territories. Annie Heloise Abel, *The American Indian under Reconstruction* (Cleveland: Arthur H. Clark, 1925), 219–267.

11. Quoted in Abel, *The American Indian under Reconstruction*, 255.

12. John B. Sanborn to James Harlan, January 5, 1866, *USS*.H.exdoc.147 (39-2) 1284:285.

13. Monday Durant to W. P. Dole, February 23, 1864, LR, OIA, frame 4, reel 231, M-234, NA.

14. Ibid.

15. Official report of the proceedings of the council with the Indians . . . held at Fort Smith, September 1865, *USS*.H.exdoc.106 (39-1) 1248:497.

16. Ibid., 514–515.

17. Francis Springer to J. W. Sprague, December 4, 1865, enclosed in J. W. Sprague to O. O. Howard, December 18, 1865, Registers and Letters Received by the Commissioner of the Bureau of Refugees, Freedmen, and Abandoned Lands, roll 22, frame 631, M752, NA.

18. Treaty of 1863, Creek National Records, Federal Relations, box 20, folder 10, doc. 29690, CRN 34, OHS.

19. In 1902, a lawyer for ex-slaves later made a compelling case for the application of the Thirteenth Amendment to Indian Territory, but the U.S. Court of Claims rejected it. *The United States v. the Choctaw Nation and the Chickasaw Nation and the Chickasaw Freedmen*, 23115, U.S. Court of Claims, General Jurisdiction Case Files, box 1648, entry 1, RG 123, NA.

20. In U.S. v. D. L. Payne, I. C. Parker, the "hanging judge," suggested that slavery was abolished in Indian Territory by the Emancipation Proclamation and the Thirteenth Amendment. *USS*.S.doc. 157 (55-1) 3563, p. 7.

21. *The United States v. the Choctaw Nation and the Chickasaw Nation and the Chickasaw Freedmen*, 23115, U.S. Court of Claims, General Jurisdiction Case Files, box 1648, entry 1, RG 123, NA.

22. J. H. Leard to O. O. Howard, October 25, 1865, Freedmen's Bureau, roll 21, frame 774, M752, NA; Foner, *Reconstruction*, 119–121.

23. J. H. Leard to O. O. Howard, October 25, 1865, Freedmen's Bureau, roll 21, frame 774, M752, NA.

24. John B. Sanborn to James Harlan, January 5, 1866, *USS*.H.exdoc.147 (39-2) 1284:284.

25. Ibid.

26. Record of Issues to Indigent Refugee Creeks, vol. 53, CRN 6, OHS.

27. *AGWG*, 121.

28. Interview with Sarah Wilson, February 22, 1937, IPP, 99:254–255, OHS.

29. Interview with Ned Thompson, August 20, 1937, IPP, 90:386–398, OHS.

30. Cloey Grayson, widow of George Grayson, Pension file, no. 406050, NA.

31. Alice Mary Robertson, "As the months passed . . . ," series I, box 2, folder 4, Alice Robertson Collection, McFarlin Library, University of Tulsa.

32. Interview with Eloise Grayson Smock, April 9, 1937, IPP, 85:369, OHS.

33. W. A. Phillips to the Commissioner of Indian Affairs, February 27, 1865, LR, OIA, frames 47–48, reel 231, M-234, NA; Cyrus Bussey to John Levering, April 2, 1865, *WRB*, series 1, vol. 48, 2:15; William A. Phillips to J.J. Reynolds, April 4, 1865, *WRB*, series 1, vol. 48, 2:27–28.

34. Citizenship Commission Record Books, no. 82-8-12 (01890) and 100166, roll 7RA68-2, NAFW.

35. A. W. Ballard to J. W. Sprague, November 30, 1865, enclosed in J. W. Sprague to O. O. Howard, December 18, 1865, Freedmen's Bureau, roll 22, frame 614, M752, NA.

36. J. W. Dunn to Elijah Sells, August 10, 1865, LR, OIA, frames 49–54, reel 231, M-234, NA.

37. Francis Springer to J. W. Sprague, December 4, 1865, enclosed in J. W. Sprague to O. O. Howard, December 18, 1865, Freedmen's Bureau, roll 22, frame 631, M752, NA; J. W. Sprague to O. O. Howard, December 18, 1865, Freedmen's Bureau, roll 22, frame 614, M752, NA.

38. M. Thomas Bailey, *Reconstruction in Indian Territory: A Story of Avarice, pch-Discrimination, and Opportunism* (Port Washington, NY: Kennikat Press, 1972), 68–69.

39. Abel, *The American Indian under Reconstruction*, 321, 325, 337, 343, 361.

40. Daniel N. McIntosh and James M. C. Smith to D. N. Cooley, et al., March 18, 1866, LR, OIA, frames 98–108, reel 231, M-234, NA.

41. *Constitution and Laws of the Muskogee Nation, as Compiled and Codified by A. P. McKellop, under Act of October 15, 1892* (Muskogee: F. C. Hubbard, 1893; reprint, Wilmington, DE: Scholarly Resources, 1973), 198.

42. Report from the Committee on Indian Affairs, *USS.S.doc.* 1278 (49-1) 2363: 183.

43. Oktarsars Harjo et al. to Perry Fuller, January 28, 1868, LR, OIA, frames 534–544, reel 231, M-234, NA; Oktarsars Harjo to the Commissioner of Indian Affairs, October 26, 1869, LR, OIA, frames 144–149, reel 232, M-234, NA.

44. Stand Watie to T. B. Heiston, October 3, 1864, *WRB*, series 1, vol. 41, 1:784–788.

45. *Muskogee Daily Phoenix*, February 18, 1911; "Samuel Benton Callahan," *Chronicles of Oklahoma* 33 (1955): 314–315.

46. A Treaty of Friendship, July 10, 1861, *WRB*, series 4, 1:426–443.

47. William Graham to J. C. Lowrie, March 14, 1872, box L, vol. 1, no. 94, reel 29, PHS.

48. S. W. Perryman to William S. Robertson, July 28, 1865, series II, box 18, folder 6, doc. 209, Alice Robertson Collection, McFarlin Library, University of Tulsa.

49. William Graham to J. C. Lowrie, March 14, 1872, box L, vol. 1, no. 94, reel 29, PHS; "Rev. T. Hill, D.D. in the Indian Territory," *Indian Journal* (Eufaula and Muskogee), May 1, 1879.

50. William Graham to General Walker, August 31, 1872, LR, OIA, frames 583–598, reel 233, M-234, NA.

51. William Graham to J. C. Lowrie, March 14, 1872, box L, vol. 1, no. 94, reel 29, PHS.

52. Deposition of Oktarsarsharjo, Coweta Micco, Cotchuteseh, and Harry Island, July 4, 1867, enclosed in J. B. Jones to J. B. Simmons, August 22, 1867, Registers and Letters Received by the Commissioner of the Bureau of Refugees, Freedmen, and Abandoned Lands, roll 49, frame 912, M752, NA.

53. Oktarsars Harjo et al. to Perry Fuller, January 28, 1868, LR, OIA, frames 534–544, reel 231, M-234, NA.

54. Oktarsars Harjo to the Commissioner of Indian Affairs, October 26, 1869, LR, OIA, frames 144–149, reel 232, M-234, NA.

55. Ohland Morton, "The Government of the Creek Indians," *Chronicles of Oklahoma* 8, no. 1 (1930): 42–64.

56. Statement showing the number of votes, September 4, 1871, LR, OIA, frames 536–537, reel 233, M-234, NA.

57. J. W. Dunn to W. Byers, January 1, 1867, enclosed in J. B. Jones to J. B. Simmons, August 22, 1867, Registers and Letters Received by the Commissioner of the Bureau of Refugees, Freedmen, and Abandoned Lands, roll 49, frame 912, M752, NA.

58. J. W. Dunn to Charles E. Mix, June 1, 1868, LR, OIA, frames 495–497, reel 231, M-234, NA.

59. Dunn Roll of Creek Citizens, 1867, 7RA44, OHS.

60. J. B. Jones to J. B. Simmons, August 22, 1867, Registers and Letters Received by the Commissioner of the Bureau of Refugees, Freedmen, and Abandoned Lands, roll 49, frame 912, M752, NA.

61. Oktarsars Harjo to J. D. Cox, April 5, 1869, LR, OIA, frames 171–174, reel 232, M-234, NA.

62. Oktarsars Harjo to the Commissioner of Indian Affairs, October 26, 1869, LR, OIA, frames 144–149, reel 232, M-234, NA.

63. J. W. Dunn to Charles E. Mix, June 1, 1868, LR, OIA, frames 495–497, reel 231, M-234, NA.

64. O. O. Howard to U. S. Grant, September 19, 1867, Registers and Letters Received by the Commissioner of the Bureau of Refugees, Freedmen, and Abandoned Lands, roll 49, frame 909, M752, NA.

65. O. H. Browning to N. G. Taylor, August 12, 1868, LR, OIA, frame 577–578, reel 231, M-234, NA.

66. Micco Hutke to N. G. Taylor, July 19, 1868, LR, OIA, frame 554, reel 231, M-234, NA.

67. G. W. Stidham and S. W. Perryman to C. E. Mix, August 5, 1868, LR, OIA, frame 642, reel 231, M-234, NA.

68. O. H. Browning to N. G. Taylor, August 12, 1868, LR, OIA, frames 577–578, reel 231, M-234, NA.

69. Creeks were not the first Indians to adopt the language of states' rights. William Apess, a Pequot, had done so in the antebellum era. Scott Michaelsen, *The Limits of Multiculturalism: Interrogating the Origins of American Anthropology* (Minneapolis: University of Minnesota Press, 1999), 62.

70. In the years following the Civil War, U.S. policy toward Indians was closely related to the general expansion of federal power in the name of civil rights. Barbara Fields observes, "The Reconstruction amendments asserted the supremacy of the national state and the formal equality under the law of everyone within it. In so doing, they eliminated competing bases of sovereignty (such as the relation of master and slave) and set forth in the organic law that there was one and only one source of citizenship, that citizenship was to be nationally defined, and that the rights, privileges, and immunities deriving from citizenship arose from the federal Constitution." Fields, "Ideology and Race in American History," in *Region, Race, and Reconstruction: Essays in Honor of C. Vann Woodward*, ed. J. Morgan Kousser and James M. McPherson (New York: Oxford University Press, 1982), 163.

71. Dunn Roll of Freedmen, 1869, 7RA-05, OHS.

72. Prissie Carruthers, jacket 638, roll 331, Applications for Enrollment of the Commission to the Five Civilized Tribes, 1898–1914, M1301, NA; Arceny Wofford, jacket 1033, roll 331, Applications for Enrollment of the Commission to the Five Civilized Tribes, 1898–1914, M1301, NA.

73. Arceny Wofford, jacket 1033, roll 331, Applications for Enrollment of the Commission to the Five Civilized Tribes, 1898–1914, M1301, NA.

74. Prissie Carruthers, jacket 638, roll 331, Applications for Enrollment of the Commission to the Five Civilized Tribes, 1898–1914, M1301, NA.

75. Mollie Daniels et al., nos. 1973–1975, by blood, Creek Allotment Records, entry 135, RG 75, NAFW. Saucer Brady is on the Dunn Roll of Freedmen as Saucer Harred. See Dawes freedman card no. 907.

76. Jimpson Grayson, Creek 1727, Individual Indian Case Files, entry 552, RG 75, NAFW. Misplaced in this case file is the proof of heirship for Jeanetta Grayson.

77. *AGWG*, 121–122.

78. Isaac Coleman to General Bussey, March 31, 1865, *WRB*, series 1, vol. 48, 1: 1303.

79. J. W. Dunn to Elijah Sells, January 5, 1866, LR, OIA, frames 159–162, reel 231, M-234, NA.

80. *AGWG*, 123.

81. Claim no. 1311, Thomas Adams, Records Relating to Loyal Creek Claims, 1869–1870, box 14, entry 687, RG 75, NA; Claim no. 1310, Judy Grayson, Records Relating to Loyal Creek Claims, 1869–1870, box 14, entry 687, RG 75, NA.

82. Claim no. 1311, Thomas Adams, Records Relating to Loyal Creek Claims, 1869–1870, box 14, entry 687, RG 75, NA.

83. *AGWG*, 126, 131; Okmulgee District, Estate Book, vol. 47, p. 165, frame 132, CRN 20, OHS.

84. *AGWG*, 127–129.

85. H. F. O'Beirne and E. S. O'Beirne, *The Indian Territory: Its Chiefs, Legislators and Leading Men* (St. Louis: C. B. Woodward, 1892), 131–134.

86. *AGWG*, 128.

87. Joan Severa, *Dressed for the Photographer: Ordinary Americans and Fashion, 1840–1900* (Kent, OH: Kent State University Press, 1995), chap. 3.

88. Oktarsars Harjo et al. to Perry Fuller, January 28, 1868, LR, OIA, frames 534–544, reel 231, M-234, NA.

89. Oktarsars Harjo to the Commissioner of Indian Affairs, October 26, 1869, LR, OIA, frames 144–149, reel 232, M-234, NA.

90. Oktarsars Harjo to J. D. Cox, April 5, 1869, LR, OIA, frames 171–174, reel 232, M-234, NA.

91. Oktarsars Harjo to F. S. Lyon, August 7, 1871, LR, OIA, frames 485–486, reel 233, M-234, NA.

92. F. A. Fields to E. S. Parker, September 5, 1870, LR, OIA, frames 415–417, reel 232, M-234, NA.

93. Oktarsars Harjo to F. A. Field, August 27, 1869, LR, OIA, frames 34–37, reel 232, M-234, NA.

94. F. S. Lyon to E. S. Parker, September 20, 1871, LR, OIA, frames 215–218, reel

233, M-234, NA; F. S. Lyon to the Commissioner of Indian Affairs, October 18, 1871, LR, OIA, frames 234–239, reel 233, M-234, NA; Dixon v. Lyon, July 27, 1872, LR, OIA, frames 459–471, reel 233, M-234, NA.

95. Enoch Hoag and Robert Campbell to F. A. Walker, December 1, 1872, LR, OIA, frame 459, reel 233, M-234, NA.

96. William Graham to General Walker, August 31, 1872, LR, OIA, frames 583–598, reel 233, M-234, NA.

97. North Fork District Court, vol. 40, p. 12, frame 14, CRN 20, OHS; North Fork District Court, vol. 40, p. 9, frame 12, CRN 20, OHS; North Fork District Court, vol. 40, p. 29, frame 22, CRN 20, OHS; North Fork District Court, vol. 40, p. 37, frame 26, CRN 20, OHS.

98. Grant Foreman, *Muskogee: The Biography of an Oklahoma Town* (Norman: University of Oklahoma Press, 1943), 37.

99. Proceedings of the Court of the District of Arkansas, April 12, 1875, Creek Nation, vol. 7, p. 59, CRN 18, OHS.

100. D. N. McIntosh et al. to Louchar Harjo, October 21, 1876, Creek National Records, Pardons, box 40, folder 1, doc. 34571, CRN 42, OHS.

101. Ward Coachman to Coweta Micco, July 19, 1878, Creek Executive Office, vol. 63, p. 67, frame 73, CRN 21, OHS.

102. It should be noted that over the course of the twentieth century, the United States gradually, if not completely, abandoned its racial definition of "Indian." Christopher A. Ford, "Administering Identity: The Determination of 'Race' in Race-Conscious Law," in *Mixed Race America and the Law: A Reader*, ed. Kevin R. Johnson (New York: New York University Press, 2003), 141–143.

103. Walter Smith to the Commissioner of Indian Affairs, April 4, 1871, LR, OIA, frames 74–75, reel 233, M-234, NA. The decision of the secretary of the interior conformed to the legal framework established by *United States v. Rogers* (1846), in which Chief Justice Roger Taney determined that Indian nations only have authority over Indians. Sidney Harring, *Crow Dog's Case: American Indian Sovereignty, Tribal Law, and the U.S. Law in the Nineteenth Century* (New York: Cambridge University Press, 1994), 60–61.

104. Karen M. Woods observes that Indians long recognized that their sovereignty depended on maintaining a "sense of separate 'Indianness.' " Woods, "A 'Wicked and Mischievous Connection': The Origins of Indian-White Miscegenation Law," in *Mixed Race America and the Law: A Reader*, ed. Kevin R. Johnson (New York: New York University Press, 2003), 81.

105. Sam Checote to F. S. Lyon, May 1, 1871, LR, OIA, frames 89–90, reel 233, M-234, NA.

106. C. Delany to the Commissioner of Indian Affairs, May 20, 1871, LR, OIA, frames 75–76, reel 233, M-234, NA; C. Delano to Francis A. Walker, February 2, 1872, LR, OIA, frames 667–670, reel 233, M-234, NA.

107. Carolyn Thomas Foreman, "North Fork Town," *Chronicles of Oklahoma* 29, no. 1 (1951): 91.

108. Ethan Allen Hitchcock, *A Traveler in Indian Territory: The Journal of Ethan Allen Hitchcock, Late Major-General in the United States Army*, ed. Grant Foreman (Cedar

Rapids, IA: Torch Press, 1930), 110; Jimmie Lewis Franklin, *Journey toward Hope: A History of Blacks in Oklahoma* (Norman: University of Oklahoma Press, 1982), 154. Until 1848, Baptist churches in Indian Territory were run in part by "a Negro preacher named Jacobs." Grant Foreman, *The Five Civilized Tribes: Cherokee, Chickasaw, Choctaw, Creek, Seminole* (Norman: University of Oklahoma Press, 1934), 195.

109. Foner, *Reconstruction*, 88–91.

110. Ward Coachman to E. A. Hayt, May 1879, Creek National Records, Intruders, box 24, folder 6, doc. 30953, CRN 37, OHS; R. A. Leslie to Ward Coachman, May 3, 1879, Creek National Records, Intruders, box 24, folder 6, doc. 30950, CRN 37, OHS; A. B. Meacham to E. A. Hayt, July 31, 1879, Creek National Records, Intruders, box 24, folder 6, doc. 30955, CRN 37, OHS; E. A. Hayt to Ward Coachman, August 9, 1879, Creek National Records, Intruders, box 24, folder 6, doc. 30956, CRN 37, OHS.

111. *Indian Journal* (Eufaula and Muskogee), May 15, 1879.

112. John Kernal to Ward Coachman, May 23, 1879, Creek National Records, Foreign Relations, box 23, folder 7, doc. 30444, CRN 36, OHS.

113. Lindsay Baker and Julie P. Baker, eds., *The WPA Oklahoma Slave Narratives* (Norman: University of Oklahoma Press, 1996), 194–197, 355–358, 435–443; Daniel F. Littlefield, *Cherokee Freedmen: From Emancipation to American Citizenship* (Westport, CT: Greenwood Press, 1978), 78; *Indian Journal* (Eufaula and Muskogee), August 7, 1879.

114. Med Roling et al. to the Houses of Kings and Warriors, December 5, 1879, Creek National Records, Foreign Relations, box 23, folder 7, doc. 30508, CRN 36, OHS.

115. Scipio Sango et al. to Samuel Checote, February 23, 1880, Creek National Records, Foreign Relations, box 23, folder 7, doc. 30449, CRN 36, OHS. Angie Debo recounts the story of hostilities between black Creeks and Cherokees with little sympathy for the former. Angie Debo, *The Road to Disappearance: A History of the Creek Indians* (Norman: University of Oklahoma Press, 1941), 253–257. She rightly concludes that "if the trouble had occurred in one of the neighboring states the negroes would not have received greater justice" (257).

116. William Cobb murder, Creek National Records, Foreign Relations, box 23, folder 8, docs. 30539–30596, CRN 36, OHS.

117. Trial of Daniel Luckey, April 3, 1882, Creek National Records, Foreign Relations, box 23, folder 8, doc. 30556, CRN 36, OHS.

118. [Snow Sells] to Samuel Checote, April 9, 1882, Creek National Records, Foreign Relations, box 23, folder 8, doc. 30557, CRN 36, OHS; Snow Sells et al. to Samuel Checote, February 1, 1881, Creek National Records, Foreign Relations, box 23, folder 7, doc. 30457, CRN 36, OHS.

119. [Snow Sells] to Samuel Checote, April 9, 1882, Creek National Records, Foreign Relations, box 23, folder 8, doc. 30557, CRN 36, OHS.

120. C. H. Taylor to Samuel Checote, October 27, 1883, Creek National Records, Foreign Relations, box 23, folder 8, doc. 30596, CRN 36, OHS.

121. Debo, *Road to Disappearance*, 257.

Chapter 7

1. Alice Mary Robertson, "As the months passed . . . ," series I, box 2, folder 4, Alice Robertson Collection, McFarlin Library, University of Tulsa; William A. Phillips to Edward R. S. Canby, February 16, 1865, *WRB*, series 1, vol. 48, 1:870–872.

2. Report from the Committee on Indian Affairs, *USS*.H.exdoc. 1 (49-2) 2467:83.

3. Estate of Thompson Perryman, October 12, 1888, Proceedings of the Court of the District of Arkansas, Creek Nation, vol. 7, p. 4, CRN 18, OHS.

4. Report from the Committee on Indian Affairs, *USS*.H.exdoc. 1 (49-2) 2467: 83.

5. G. A. Alexander and E. B. Childers to the National Council, August 8, 1896, Creek National Records, Federal Relations, box 21, folder 7, doc. 30039, CRN 35, OHS.

6. List of property belonging to Sam and G. W. Grayson, December 23, 1891, doc. 39350, CRN 51, OHS.

7. Elsewhere, the commissioner claimed that one-quarter of the Muscogee population were day laborers, an assertion directly contradicted by the report of his own agent in the Creek Nation. Report from the Committee on Indian Affairs, *USS*.H.exdoc. 1 (49-2) 2467:83, 373.

8. R. C. McGee to John C. Lowrie, February 15, 1882, box F, vol. 1, no. 354, reel 23, PHS.

9. Samuel Checote to Ward Coachman et al., March 8, 1882, Creek National Records, Federal Relations, box 20, folder 4, doc. 29690, CRN 35, OHS.

10. Interview with Oliver Bagby, April 5, 1937, IPP, 4:21–26, OHS.

11. Robert Grayson et al. to the Supreme Court, October 10, 1882, Supreme Court Letters and Documents, Creek Nation, section X, doc. 28804, frame 395, CRN 16, OHS; H. F. O'Beirne and E. S. O'Beirne, *The Indian Territory: Its Chiefs, Legislators and Leading Men* (St. Louis: C. B. Woodward, 1892), 250–252; *Indian Journal* (Eufaula and Muskogee), January 9, 1878; Mary Jane Warde, *George Washington Grayson and the Creek Nation, 1843–1920* (Norman: University of Oklahoma Press, 1999), 92–93.

12. Annelle Sharp Lanford, "North Fork to Eufaula, 1836–1907" (M.A. thesis, University of Oklahoma, 1954), 87.

13. *Indian Journal* (Eufaula and Muskogee), April 26, 1877; *Indian Journal* (Eufaula and Muskogee), January 29, 1880.

14. Warde, *George Washington Grayson*, 99–100.

15. Ibid., 98–99, 167–171, 183–186.

16. Lanford, "North Fork to Eufaula," 78–79; Carolyn Thomas Foreman, "North Fork Town," *Chronicles of Oklahoma* 29, no. 1 (1951): 108–109.

17. R. C. McGee to John C. Lowrie, October 7, 1878, box E, vol. 1, no. 83, reel 22, PHS.

18. The definitive account of the Green Peach War is still Angie Debo, *The Road to Disappearance: A History of the Creek Indians* (Norman: University of Oklahoma Press, 1941), 268–284.

19. *Indian Journal* (Eufaula and Muskogee), August 16, 1883.

20. Ohland Morton, "The Government of the Creek Indians," *Chronicles of Oklahoma* 8, no. 2 (1930): 204–205.

21. G. W. Stidham to the National Council, October 12, 1883, Creek National Records, Elections, box 18, folder 1, doc. 29430, CRN 34, OHS; *Indian Journal* (Eufaula and Muskogee), September 20, 1883.

22. Carolyn Thomas Foreman, "Jeremiah Curtin," *Chronicles of Oklahoma* 26, no. 3 (1948), 348.

23. G. W. Stidham to the National Council, October 12, 1883, Creek National Records, Elections, box 18, folder 1, doc. 29430, CRN 34, OHS.

24. *Indian Journal* (Eufaula and Muskogee), January 3, 1884.

25. *AGWG*, 158.

26. Returns of General Election, September 3, 1883, Creek National Records, Elections, box 17, folder 8, CRN 33, OHS.

27. G. W. Stidham to the National Council, October 12, 1883, Creek National Records, Elections, box 18, folder 1, doc. 29430, CRN 34, OHS.

28. *Indian Journal* (Eufaula and Muskogee), July 26, 1883.

29. *AGWG*, 161.

30. Quoted in Foreman, "Jeremiah Curtin," 347.

31. Isparhecher to the National Council, October 8, 1884, Creek National Records, Federal Relations, box 21, folder 6, doc. 29934, CRN 35, OHS.

32. Tacky Grayson, card 452, Old Series Enrollment Cards, Freedmen, Records Relating to Creek Citizenship, box 15, entry 124, RG 75, NAFW.

33. Tacky Grayson case file, Western District Court of Arkansas, Fort Smith, jacket 72, series 3W51, RG 21, NAFW; J. G. Atkins et al. to Samuel Checote, no date, Creek National Records, Intruders, box 24, folder 8, doc. 31121, CRN 37, OHS.

34. *Indian Journal* (Eufaula and Muskogee), April 3, 1884; Criminal Docket, Creek Nation, vol. 14, p. 160, frame 262, CRN 18, OHS; Tackey Grayson case file, Western District Court of Arkansas, Fort Smith, jacket 72, series 3W51, RG 21, NAFW; Eli Grayson case file, Western District Court of Arkansas, Fort Smith, jacket 72, series 3W51, RG 21, NAFW; Seaborn Grayson case file, Western District Court of Arkansas, Fort Smith, jacket 72, series 3W51, RG 21, NAFW; Silla Grayson case file, Western District Court of Arkansas, Fort Smith, jacket 72, series 3W51, RG 21, NAFW; Cyrus Harrod case file, Western District Court of Arkansas, Fort Smith, jacket 84, series 3W51, RG 21, NAFW; *Indian Journal* (Eufaula and Muskogee), April 3, 1884; Samuel Checote to Eli Danly, January 9, 1881, Creek Courts, Deep Fork District, doc. 25935, frame 299, CRN 29, OHS.

35. James Grayson case file, Western District Court of Arkansas, Fort Smith, jacket 95, series 3W51, RG 21, NAFW.

36. *Indian Journal* (Eufaula and Muskogee), February 15, 1883; *Indian Journal* (Eufaula and Muskogee), December 11, 1884; Michael Bruner, jacket 7, Fort Smith Criminal Court, NAFW.

37. December 30, 1904, book 15, DGWG; March 24, 1905, book 15, DGWG; March 31, 1906, book 17, DGWG; September 4, 1906, book 18, DGWG.

38. Warde, *George Washington Grayson*, 166–175.

39. Robert Grayson et al. to the Supreme Court, October 10, 1882, Supreme Court Letters and Documents, Creek Nation, section X, doc. 28804, frame 395, CRN 16, OHS.

40. Quotations from Henry Thompson to N. B. Moore, April 17, 1890, series II, box 7, folder 1, doc. 843, Alice Robertson Collection, McFarlin Library, University of Tulsa. See also F. B. Severs to N. B. Moore, April 5, 1890, series II, box 6, folder 10, doc. 835, Alice Robertson Collection, McFarlin Library, University of Tulsa; L. C. Perryman to N. B. Moore and Kowe Harjo, April 11, 1890, series II, box 6, folder 8, doc. 838, Alice Robertson Collection, McFarlin Library, University of Tulsa; F. B. Severs to N. B. Moore, July 13, 1890, series II, box 6, folder 11, doc. 876, Alice Robertson Collection, McFarlin Library, University of Tulsa.

41. Addie Grayson to N. B. Moore, November 1, 1891, Creek Per Capita Payments, 1869–1904, doc. 35416, CRN 5, OHS.

42. Passage deleted from *AGWG*, courtesy of W. David Baird.

43. Jimmy M. Skaggs, *Prime Cut: Livestock Raising and Meatpacking in the United States, 1607–1983* (College Station: Texas A&M University Press, 1986), 58–60.

44. Ibid., 90–95.

45. Claim no. 1311, Thomas Adams, Records Relating to Loyal Creek Claims, 1869–1870, box 14, entry 687, RG 75, NA; *AGWG*, 130.

46. *AGWG*, 47–55.

47. Ibid., 141; *Indian Journal* (Eufaula and Muskogee), May 10, 1877.

48. Alice Robertson described the trading process at the general store of F. B. Severs. Alice Robertson manuscript, box 2, file 2, Alice Robertson Collection, OHS.

49. Sam Checote to W. Ingalls, February 1, 1875, LR, OIA, frames 431–434, reel 235, M-234, NA.

50. R. C. McGee to John C. Lowrie, February 15, 1882, box F, vol. 1, no. 354, reel 23, PHS; Creek National Records, Pensions, box 41, folder 5, doc. 35282, CRN 42, OHS.

51. Skaggs, *Prime Cut*, 65–66.

52. Michael Bruner, jacket 7, Fort Smith Criminal Court, NAFW; *Creasy and Emma Grayson v. Lige*, Creek Courts, Miscellaneous, doc. 29225, p. 215, frame 194, CRN 33, OHS; Estate of Jeanetta Grayson, Probate Case Files, case 3032, OKM 284, frame 1398, Muskogee Public Library, Oklahoma; Julia Casey to E. H. Leblance, March 4, 1890, Creek Courts, Muskogee District, doc. 26630, frame 226, CRN 30, OHS.

53. Warde, *George Washington Grayson*, 99.

54. List of property belonging to Sam and G. W. Grayson, December 23, 1891, doc. 39350, CRN 51, OHS.

55. The Creek Nation determined that a fence sufficient to pen livestock would need to be seven rails high. *Constitution and Laws of the Muskogee Nation, as Compiled by L. C. Perryman, March 1st, 1890* (1890; reprint, Wilmington, DE: Scholarly Resources, 1975), 100; Asa Wallace Dagley, "The Negro in Oklahoma" (M.A. thesis, University of Oklahoma, 1926), 10–11.

56. Interview with Mr. Van Crockran, May 4, 1937, IPP, 22:25–28, OHS.

57. *Clarence W. Turner v. the U.S. and the Creek Nation*, 30241, U.S. Court of Claims, General Jurisdiction Case Files, box 2087, entry 1, RG 123, NA.

58. Skaggs, *Prime Cut*, 58–60.

59. Mollie signed her letter as Mollie Haynes. Her maiden name was Grayson. Mollie Haynes to E. H. Leblance, February 22, 1890, Creek Courts, Muskogee District, doc. 26619, frame 210, CRN 30, OHS.

60. H. C. Reed et al. to E. H. Lerblance, July 21, 1890, Creek National Records, Pastures and Stock, box 40, folder 2, doc. 34834, CRN 42, OHS; S. B. Callahan to E. H. Lerblance, August 6, 1890, Creek National Records, Pastures and Stock, box 40, folder 2, doc. 34836, CRN 42, OHS.

61. Muskogee Nation v. H. B. Spaulding, August 19, 1892, Creek National Records, Pastures and Stock, box 40, folder 2, doc. 34882, CRN 42, OHS.

62. Vicy Whetherspoon to E. H. LaBlance, March 14, 1892, Creek Courts, Muskogee District, doc. 27016, frame 827, CRN 30, OHS.

63. Nany Grasom to E. blanc, March 27, 1892, Creek Courts, Muskogee District, doc. 27033, frame 849, CRN 30, OHS.

64. E. H. Lerblance to L. C. Perryman, May 6, 1892, Creek National Records, Pastures and Stock, box 40, folder 2, doc. 34854, CRN 42, OHS.

65. Ibid.

66. Creek National Records, Pastures and Stock, box 40, folder 3, doc. 34960, CRN 42, OHS.

67. Creek National Records, Pastures and Stock, box 40, folder 3, docs. 35002 and 35003, CRN 42, OHS.

68. Report of the Dawes Commission, *USS.S.doc.* 182 (54-1) 3353.

69. Mrs. G. W. Grayson, "Confederate Treaties," *Indian Journal* (Eufaula and Muskogee), May 9, 1914.

70. Two excellent studies of continuity in southeastern Indian communities are Theda Perdue, *Cherokee Women: Gender and Culture Change, 1700–1835* (Lincoln: University of Nebraska Press, 1998); and James Taylor Carson, *Searching for the Bright Path: The Mississippi Choctaws from Prehistory to Removal* (Lincoln: University of Nebraska Press, 1999).

71. The best-known example of a Creek taking the paternal surname while tracing decent through the maternal clan is Alexander McGillivray. Michael D. Green, "Alexander McGillivray," in *American Indian Leaders: Studies in Diversity*, ed. R. David Edmunds (Lincoln: University of Nebraska Press, 1980), 41–63.

72. Claimants' accounts, December 1825, LR, OIA, frames 761–762, reel 220, M-234, NA.

73. See Louisa Grayson's Dawes census card, by blood 1401.

74. See, for example, November 1, 1903, book 12, DGWG.

75. See, for example, Bond of Creasy Grayson, July 23, 1878, doc. 26254, CRN29, OHS; *Creasy and Emma Grayson v. Lige*, Creek Courts, Miscellaneous, doc. 29225, p. 215, frame 194, CRN 33, OHS; Summons of Julia Casey, August 1, 1892, Creek Courts, Muskogee District, doc. 27101, frame 942, CRN 30, OHS; *Alex Evans v. Julia Casey*, Criminal Docket, Creek Nation, vol. 1, p. 328, frame 307, CRN 18, OHS; Emma Grayson, no. 3649, by blood, Creek Allotment Records, entry 135, RG 75, NAFW; Vicey Weatherspoon, no. 2352, by blood, Creek Allotment Records, entry 135, RG 75, NAFW.

76. Tackey Grayson case file, Western District Court of Arkansas, Fort Smith, jacket 72, series 3W51, RG 21, NAFW.

77. Bond of Creasy Grayson, July 23, 1878, doc. 26254, CRN 29, OHS; *Creasy and Emma Grayson v. Lige*, Creek Courts, Miscellaneous, doc. 29225, p. 215, frame 194, CRN 33, OHS; *Creasy Grayson v. Elijah Johnson*, Proceedings of the Court of the District of Arkansas, May 5, 1879, pp. 94–95, Creek Nation, vol. 7, CRN 18, OHS.

78. Emma Grayson, no. 3649, by blood, Creek Allotment Records, entry 135, RG 75, NAFW.

79. Brenda E. Stevenson, *Life in Black and White: Family and Community in the Slave South* (New York: Oxford University Press, 1996), 222–223.

80. Mollie Haynes to E. H. Leblance, February 22, 1890, Creek Courts, Muskogee District, doc. 26619, frame 210, CRN 30, OHS.

81. Julia Casey to E. H. Leblance, March 4, 1890, Creek Courts, Muskogee District, doc. 26630, frame 226, CRN 30, OHS.

82. Nany Grasom to E. blanc, March 27, 1892, Creek Courts, Muskogee District, doc. 27033, frame 849, CRN 30, OHS.

83. On the "cult of domesticity," as historians call the nineteenth-century ideology that defined middle-class white womanhood, see Barbara Welter, "The Cult of True Womanhood: 1820–1860," *American Quarterly* 18 (1966): 151–174; Kathryn Kish Sklar, *Catharine Beecher: A Study in American Domesticity* (New Haven, CT: Yale University Press, 1973); and Nancy F. Cott, *The Bonds of Womanhood: Woman's Sphere in New England, 1780–1835* (New Haven, CT: Yale University Press, 1977).

84. Bettie Chambers to [?], Creek Courts, Miscellaneous, doc. 29225, p. 286, frame 263, CRN 33, OHS; [Bettie Chambers] to Mr. McGilbra, n.d., Creek National Records, Divorce, doc. 29262, frame 582, CRN 33, OHS.

85. William Chambers to Elick McIntosh, April 1894, Creek Documents, Divorce, doc. 29251, frame 566, CRN 33, OHS.

86. William Chambers to W. Ward, May 25, 1896, Creek Documents, Divorce, doc. 29253, frame 567, CRN 33, OHS.

87. Sharper Grayson case file, Western District Court of Arkansas, Fort Smith, jacket 72, series 3W51, RG 21, NAFW.

88. September 24, 1891, Sheri Siebold, *Genealogical Data extracted from Muskogee Weekly Phoenix, Indian Territory, 1888–1892* (Muskogee, OK: Muskogee County Genealogical Society, 1985).

89. Eva Island to Judge Mcine, Creek Documents, Divorce, doc. 29261, frame 581, CRN 33, OHS.

90. *Muskogee Nation v. Sunny Grayson*, September 16, 1892, Creek Courts, Muskogee District, doc. 27196, frame 1117, CRN 30, OHS; *Muskogee Nation v. R. S. Hawkins*, September 1892, Creek Courts, Muskogee District, doc. 27213, frame 1153, CRN 30, OHS.

91. For more on the relationship between economy and social organization among the Creeks in the eighteenth century, see Claudio Saunt, *A New Order of Things: Property, Power, and the Transformation of the Creek Indians, 1733–1816* (New York: Cambridge University Press, 1999).

92. September 4, 1906, book 18, DGWG.

93. December 22, 1915, book 42, DGWG.

Chapter 8

1. For an exploration of the changing meaning of freedom in American history, see Eric Foner, *The Story of American Freedom* (New York: Norton, 1998).

2. European countries first dressed colonialism in the clothes of philanthropy in the mid–nineteenth century. Howard Temperley, *White Dreams, Black Africa: The Antislavery Expedition to the River Niger 1841–1842* (New Yaven, CT: Yale University Press 1991); Suzanne Miers, *Britain and the Ending of the Slave Trade* (London: Longman, 1975); and Adam Hochschild, *King Leopold's Ghost: A Story of Greed, Terror, and Heroism in Colonial Africa* (Boston: Houghton Mifflin, 1998).

3. Quoted in Robert Winston Mardock, *The Reformers and the American Indian* (Columbia: University of Missouri Press, 1971), 17–18, 81. Mardock argues that many abolitionists later became Indian reformers, but see Francis Paul Prucha, *American Indian Policy in Crisis: Christian Reformers and the Indian, 1865–1900* (Norman: University of Oklahoma Press 1976), 26n52, who says that the relationship between abolitionists and Indian reformers was weaker than Mardock suggests.

4. The Fourteenth Amendment as adopted excluded from citizenship all Indians "not taxed." William E. Nelson, *The Fourteenth Amendment: From Political Principle to Judicial Doctrine* (Cambridge, MA: Harvard University Press, 1988), 102–103.

5. On reformers and Indians in the post–Civil War years, see Henry E. Fritz, *The Movement for Indian Assimilation, 1860–1890* (Philadelphia: University of Pennsylvania Press, 1963); Robert Winston Mardock, *The Reformers and the American Indian* (Columbia: University of Missouri Press, 1971); Francis Paul Prucha, *American Indian Policy in Crisis: Christian Reformers and the Indian, 1865–1900* (Norman: University of Oklahoma Press, 1976); Francis Paul Prucha, "The Board of Indian Commissioners and the Delegates of the Five Tribes," in *Indian Policy in the United States: Historical Essays* (Lincoln: University of Nebraska Press, 1981), 198–213; Robert H. Keller Jr., *American Protestantism and United States Indian Policy, 1869–82* (Lincoln: University of Nebraska, 1983); and Frederick E. Hoxie, *A Final Promise: The Campaign to Assimilate the Indians, 1880–1920* (1984; reprint, New York: Cambridge University Press, 1989).

6. Assimilation has long been a goal of liberal reformers in the United States. Even in 2003, David A. Hollinger's thoughtful essay on "ethnoracial mixture," invoking Wendell Phillips, among others, ends with the hopeful message that U.S. history is the "story of amalgamation." It is difficult to see how Indian nations fit into this narrative. Hollinger, "Amalgamation and Hypodescent: The Question of Ethnoracial Mixture in the History of the United States," *American Historical Review* 108 (2003): 1389.

7. Testimony of Siller Herrod, May 26, 1891, Creek Courts, Muskogee District, frame 790, CRN 31, OHS.

8. List of property belonging to Sam and G. W. Grayson, December 23, 1891, doc. 39350, CRN 51, OHS.

9. Angie Debo, *The Road to Disappearance: A History of the Creek Indians* (Norman: University of Oklahoma Press, 1941), 334.

10. Ibid., 326, 333–334; Danney Goble, *Progressive Oklahoma: The Making of a New Kind of State* (Norman: University of Oklahoma Press, 1980), 3–42.

11. Frederick Hoxie skillfully describes the promise and failure of allotment in *A Final Promise*.

12. *Twenty-ninth Annual Report of the Board of Indian Commissioners, 1897* (Washington, DC: Government Printing Office, 1898), 30.

13. Quoted in Mary Jane Warde, *George Washington Grayson and the Creek Nation, 1843–1920* (Norman: University of Oklahoma Press, 1999), 154. Warde includes an informative discussion of Wash's views on allotment. See pp. 153–158, 177–181.

14. Quoted in ibid., 181.

15. Sam Grayson's impeachment is described in Debo, *Road to Disappearance*, 348–360.

16. Journal of the House of Warriors, 1894–1895, section X, CRN 8, OHS. See also Creek National Records, Federal Relations, box 21, folder 8, doc. 30082, CRN 35, OHS.

17. Debo, *Road to Disappearance*, chaps. 10 and 11, is still the definitive account of the destruction of the Creek Nation.

18. Charles J. Kappler, *Indian Affairs: Laws and Treaties* (Washington, DC: Government Printing Office, 1904), vol. 1 (30 Stat., 495).

19. *Thirty-first Annual Report of the Board of Indian Commissioners, 1899* (Washington, DC: Government Printing Office, 1900), 78.

20. *AGWG*, 164.

21. May 12, 1900, book 5, DGWG.

22. Historians generally argue that race became an important element in determining tribal membership only after the Dawes Commission imposed racist guidelines on Indian nations at the turn of the nineteenth century. In fact, Indians were frequently as interested as the Dawes Commission in using race to define tribal membership. See Alexandra Harmon, "Tribal Enrollment Councils: Lessons on Law and Indian Identity," *Western Historical Quarterly* 32 (2001): 175–200.

23. The process of enrollment is described in detail in Kent Carter, "Snakes and Scribes: The Dawes Commission and the Enrollment of the Creeks," *Chronicles of Oklahoma* 75 (1997): 384–413.

24. W. A. Sapulpa et al. to the Dawes Commission, September 23, 1896, Creek National Records, Federal Relations, box 21, folder 7, doc. 30041, CRN 35, OHS. Ex-slaves were well aware of the possibility that they would be excluded from a final settlement between the Creek Nation and the United States. W. A. Rentie to the Dawes Commission, February 4, 1899, Dawes Commission, Creek Correspondence, 65-4, OHS; James L. Grayson to the Secretary of the Interior, February 25, 1899, Dawes Commission, Creek Correspondence, 65-4, OHS.

25. U.S. Census (11th) 1890, Extra Census Bulletin, *The Five Civilized Tribes in Indian Territory: The Cherokee, Chickasaw, Choctaw, Creek, and Seminole Nations* (Washington, DC: United States Census Printing Office, 1894), 3, 6.

26. Creek Field Jacket 3915, roll 355, M1301, NA.

27. Chaney Trent et al., jacket 78, roll 327, Applications for Enrollment of the Commission to the Five Civilized Tribes, 1898–1914, M1301, NA.

28. G. W. Grayson to Tams Bixby, June 17, 1899, Dawes Commission, Creek Correspondence, 65-8, OHS.

29. Lewis Hardridge, jacket 96, roll 328, Applications for Enrollment of the Commission to the Five Civilized Tribes, 1898–1914, M1301, NA. Leaders of the "colored" towns were frequently accused of enrolling noncitizens.

30. Quoted in Kent Carter, "Snakes and Scribes," 388.

31. [?] to Rolly McIntosh, August 29, 1896, doc. 36739, CRN 46, OHS; Lewis Hardridge, jacket 96, roll 328, Applications for Enrollment of the Commission to the Five Civilized Tribes, 1898–1914, M1301, NA.

32. Paro Bruner to the Dawes Commission, August 5, 1895, Dawes Commission, Creek Correspondence, 65-3, OHS.

33. John Q. Tufts to the Commissioner of Indian Affairs, June 10, 1885, box 48, Records of the Department of Interior, Indian Territory Division, Special Files, entry 713, RG 48, NA. Buck Colbert Franklin, the son of Choctaw slaves, observed a similar problem in the Choctaw Nation: "There was one outstanding fact that made it almost impossible for an allottee with any Negro blood to get on the Indian Roll, and that was prejudice." Buck Colbert Franklin, *My Life and an Era: The Autobiography of Buck Colbert Franklin*, ed. John Hope Franklin and John Whittington Franklin (Baton Rouge: Louisiana State University Press, 1997), 74.

34. Joe Grayson, jacket 92, roll 327, Applications for Enrollment of the Commission to the Five Civilized Tribes, 1898–1914, M1301, NA.

35. The Colbert Commission rejected 72 percent of ex-slave applications compared with 39 percent of by-blood applications. Carter, "Snakes and Scribes," 392.

36. Joe Grayson, jacket 92, roll 327, Applications for Enrollment of the Commission to the Five Civilized Tribes, 1898–1914, M1301, NA.

37. Testimony of Joe Grayson, Sr., Letters and Documents Relating to Citizenship in the Creek Nation, 1874–1895, Creek Citizenship, doc. 25415, frame 514, CRN 3, OHS.

38. J. R. Gregory to Isparhecher, September 28, 1899, Letters and Documents Relating to Citizenship in the Creek Nation, 1896–1910, Creek Citizenship, doc. 25330, CRN 4, OHS.

39. Maria Richardson to the Dawes Commission, December 5, 1899, Dawes Commission, Creek Correspondence, 66-4, OHS.

40. Letters and Documents Relating to Citizenship in the Creek Nation, 1874–1895, Creek Citizenship, doc. 25004, CRN 3, OHS. See also doc. 24950, CRN 3; docs. 25162, 25195, 25196, CRN 4; and J. E. Reed to Mr. Wright, February 13, 1909, frame 870, DC 71, Dawes Commission, Creek Correspondence, OHS.

41. Application of Thomas J. Grayson, July 12, 1895, Letters and Documents Relating to Citizenship in the Creek Nation, 1874–1895, Creek Citizenship, docs. 25045 and 25046, CRN 3, OHS; Dawes Commission, Citizenship Commission Record Book, vol. 82-8-12, A-6-86-5, RG 75, NAFW.

42. Thomas J. Grayson, case 61, 1896 Creek Applications, M1650, roll 23, NA.

43. John Grayson, no. 5714, by blood, Creek Allotment Records, entry 135, RG 75, NAFW.

44. Creek Field Jacket 3915, roll 355, M1301, NA.

45. Nelson McIntosh, jacket 1024, roll 335, Applications for Enrollment of the Commission to the Five Civilized Tribes, 1898–1914, M1301, NA.

46. Chaney Trent et al., jacket 78, roll 327, Applications for Enrollment of the Commission to the Five Civilized Tribes, 1898–1914, M1301, NA.

47. Martha Parker, jacket 209, roll 328, Applications for Enrollment of the Commission to the Five Civilized Tribes, 1898–1914, M1301, NA

48. The phrase comes from Merrill E. Gates, president of the Lake Mohonk Indian Conference in 1899. *Thirty-first Annual Report of the Board of Indian Commissioners, 1899*, 78.

49. *United States v. Kagama*, May 10, 1886, in Francis Paul Prucha, ed., *Documents of United States Indian Policy* (Lincoln: University of Nebraska Press, 195), 168–169. On plenary power, see Sidney L. Harring, *Crow Dog's Case: American Indian Sovereignty, Tribal Law, and United States Law in the Nineteenth Century* (New York: Cambridge University Press, 1994), 144–149.

50. Testimony regarding Rutherford B. Cravens and Alex H. Mike, July 2, 1902, Dawes Commission, Creek Correspondence, 67-6, OHS.

51. Visey Grayson, card 482, Old Series Enrollment Cards, Freedmen, Records Relating to Creek Citizenship, box 15, entry 124, RG 75, NAFW.

52. Eli Grayson, card 1517, Old Series Enrollment Cards, 1481–1720, Records Relating to Creek Citizenship, box 7, entry 124, RG 75, NAFW; Eli Grayson, card 495, Old Series Enrollment Cards, Freedmen, Records Relating to Creek Citizenship, box 15, entry 124, RG 75, NAFW.

53. G. W. Grayson to Tams Bixby, June 17, 1899, Dawes Commission, Creek Correspondence, 65-8, OHS.

54. Case 137, pp. 47–53, Dawes Commission, Citizenship Commission Record Book, vol. 82-8-12, A-6-86-5, RG 75, NAFW.

55. Creek by blood cards 1123, 654, 668, and 717, Enrollment Cards for the Five Civilized Tribes, 1898–1914, M1186, NA.

56. Mitchell Grayson, card 487, Old Series Enrollment Cards, Freedmen, Records Relating to Creek Citizenship, box 15, entry 124, RG 75, NAFW.

57. Pleasant Porter, the principal chief of the Creek Nation from 1899 until his death in 1907, explained that in all cases, if an applicant's mother was a Creek citizen, "all her children were Creek citizens, no matter where they came from." Lillian Lerblanche, jacket 2, roll 326, Applications for Enrollment of the Commission to the Five Civilized Tribes, 1898–1914, M1301, NA.

58. Creek by blood card, 669, Enrollment Cards for the Five Civilized Tribes, 1898–1914, M1186, NA.

59. Calculated from Leonard A. Carlson, *Indians, Bureaucrats, and Land: The Dawes Act and the Decline of Indian Farming* (Westport, CT: Greenwood Press, 1981), 204. Indian America is here defined as lands owned by Indian nations or held in trust by the federal government for individual Indians.

60. Figures calculated from Angie Debo, *And Still the Waters Run: The Betrayal of the Five Civilized Tribes* (Norman: University of Oklahoma Press, 1940), 6, 387–388; and Carlson, *Indians, Bureaucrats, and Land*, 184.

61. Debo, *And Still the Waters Run*, 92.

62. Emma Grayson, no. 3649, by blood, Creek Allotment Records, entry 135, RG 75, NAFW. The Timbered Ridge Cemetery is located in section 6, range 18 east, township 13 north. See James W. Tyner and Alice Tyner Timmons, *Our People and Where They Rest* (Norman: University of Oklahoma Press, American Indian Institute, 1972), 7:69.

63. Vicey Weatherspoon, no. 2352, by blood, Creek Allotment Records, entry 135, RG 75, NAFW; Eli Grayson et al., nos. 2202, 2203, 2204, 2205, by blood, Creek Allotment Records, entry 135, RG 75, NAFW; Mitchell Grayson et al., nos. 3530–3533, by blood, Creek Allotment Records, entry 135, RG 75, NAFW.

64. Julia and John were the children of Emma's sisters Katie and Judy. Julia Casey et al., nos. 2210–2212, by blood, Creek Allotment Records, entry 135, RG 75, NAFW; John Vann, nos. 957–958, by blood, Creek Allotment Records, entry 135, RG 75, NAFW; Onie Finniegan, no. 2206, by blood, Creek Allotment Records, entry 135, RG 75, NAFW.

65. Adeline was the daughter of Henderson Grayson. Adeline Grayson et al., nos. 9610–9613, by blood, Creek Allotment Records, entry 135, RG 75, NAFW.

66. Elizabeth was the daughter of William Grayson Jr. Elizabeth Williams, no. 3706, by blood, Creek Allotment Records, entry 135, RG 75, NAFW. Emma also had a daughter Mollie, who lived a few miles northwest of Muskogee, about ten miles away. Mollie Daniels et al., nos. 1973–1975, by blood, Creek Allotment Records, entry 135, RG 75, NAFW.

67. In 1891, Grayson Brothers owned four thousand head of cattle. List of property belonging to Sam and G. W. Grayson, December 23, 1891, doc. 39350, CRN 51, OHS.

68. J. D. C. Atkins to Sec. of Interior, September 28, 1886, enclosed in Report from the Committee on Indian Affairs, *USS*.H.exdoc. 1 (49-2) 2467, p. 83.

69. Mary Jane Warde notes that Grayson Brothers faced financial pressures other than the loss of pasture. Warde, *George Washington Grayson*, 185–186, 192. On the seizure of property, see chapter 22, sec. 300, of laws of the Muskogee Nation, in A. P. McKellop, *Constitution and Laws of the Muskogee Nation* (Muskogee, 1893; reprint, Wilmington, DE: Scholarly Resources, 1973), 106.

70. George W. Grayson et al., nos. 5189–5193, by blood, Creek Allotment Records, entry 135, RG 75, NAFW.

71. July 28, 1904, book 14, DGWG.

72. 32 Stat., 500.

73. In the first year of this program, 146 Creeks successfully petitioned to remove restrictions. Department of the Interior, *Annual Report of the Commissioner of Indian Affairs, 1905* (Washington, DC: Government Printing Office, 1906), 217.

74. 35 Stat., 312.

75. 33 Stat., 180; Debo, *And Still the Waters Run*, 114.

76. Alice Robertson to O. H. Platt, March 7, 1904, series II, box 9, folder 5, doc. 1168, Alice Robertson Collection, McFarlin Library, University of Tulsa.

77. 34 Stat., 137. Debo, *And Still the Waters Run*, 88–91, 115.

78. 35 Stat., 312.

79. Twenty-three percent of Creeks on the by-blood rolls were enrolled as less than half-blood. Ten percent were enrolled as at least half-blood but less than three-quarters. Statistics compiled by Jack D. Baker, Oklahoma City.

80. There were 2,926 people on the minor Creek, minor freedmen, newborn Creek, and newborn freedmen rolls.

81. Debo, *And Still the Waters Run*, 106.

82. Ibid., chap. 4.

83. The drilling of the first well in Red Fork is described in Kenny A. Franks, *The Rush Begins: A History of the Red Fork, Cleveland, and Glenn Pool Oil Fields* (Oklahoma City: Oklahoma Heritage Association, 1984), 10–16.

84. Quoted in ibid., 19.

85. Ibid.

86. Debo, *And Still the Waters Run*, 86–87; Franks, *The Rush Begins*, 132.

87. Debo, *And Still the Waters Run*, 200.

88. Donald L. Fixico, *The Invasion of Indian Country in the Twentieth Century: American Capitalism and Tribal Natural Resources* (Niwot: University Press of Colorado, 1998), chap. 2; Dennis McAuliffe, *The Deaths of Sybil Bolton: An American History* (New York: Times Books, 1994). For a fictionalized account of the Osage murders, see Linda Hogan, *Mean Spirit: A Novel* (New York: Atheneum, 1990).

89. Wiley Grayson, Creek 8808, Individual Indian Case Files, entry 552, RG 75, NAFW.

90. Ibid.

91. Sturgis Williams Darling, "Oktaha," 22, sec. X, towns—Oktaha, OHS; James M. Etter, *Oktaha: A Track in the Sand* (Oktaha, OK: Oktaha Historical Society, 1982), 61.

92. In 1904, between thirty thousand and fifty thousand bushels of corn shipped out of Oktaha. Application of Jeanetta Newberry, Dawes Commission Records, Creek Nation, Townsites, Oktaha, box 136, folder 3, OHS.

93. June 26, 1907, *Oktaha Democrat*.

94. "Oktaha: An Old Story in a New Country," September 15, 1905, *Oktaha American*.

95. June 26, 1907, *Oktaha Democrat*.

96. Eli Grayson et al., nos. 2202, 2203, 2204, 2205, by blood, Creek Allotment Records, entry 135, RG 75, NAFW; Mitchell Grayson et al., nos. 3530–3533, by blood, Creek Allotment Records, entry 135, RG 75, NAFW; Julia Casey et al., nos. 2210–2212, by blood, Creek Allotment Records, entry 135, RG 75, NAFW.

97. October 13, 1902, book 10, DGWG; November 15, 1902, book 10, DGWG; November 18, 1902, book 10, DGWG.

98. March 11, 1904, book 13, DGWG; Debo, *And Still the Waters Run*, 121–123.

99. May 5, 1903, book 11, DGWG.

100. March 12, 1904, book 13, DGWG; March 25, 1904, book 13, DGWG.

101. April 8, 1904, book 13, DGWG.

102. June 13, 1903, book 11, DGWG; July 3, 1903, book 11, DGWG.

103. November 1, 1903, book 12, DGWG.

104. December 30, 1904, book 15, DGWG.

105. December 31, 1904, book 15, DGWG.

106. June 26, 1905, book 15, DGWG.

107. August 14, 1905, book 16, DGWG.

108. January 25, 1906, book 17, DGWG.

109. May 2, 1907, book 20, DGWG; September 12, 1907, book 21, DGWG.

110. September 14 and September 18, 1908, book 23, DGWG; September 29, 1908, book 23, DGWG.

111. Angie Debo makes this observation about another Creek speculator, Pleasant Porter, Wash's old friend from Civil War days. Debo, *And Still the Waters Run*, 123.

112. Robert Grayson was the son of William and Judah's first son, William Jr.

113. Annie Grayson, jacket 982, roll 334, Applications for Enrollment of the Commission to the Five Civilized Tribes, 1898–1914, M1301, NA.

114. March 15, 1905, book 15, DGWG; G. W. Grayson to Tams Bixby, June 10, 1899, Dawes Commission, Creek Correspondence, 65-8, OHS.

115. August 13, 1900, book 5, DGWG.

116. Citizenship Commission Record Books, no. 82-8-12 (01890) and 100166, roll 7RA68-2, NAFW.

117. Ben T. DuVal to W. M. Springer, February 15, 1899, Dawes Commission, Creek Correspondence, 65-6, OHS.

118. August 13, 1900, book 5, DGWG.

119. On March 31, 1905, James Evans's sister Savannah married John Casey, the son of Julia, who was William and Judah's granddaughter. Creek by blood card 1119, Enrollment Cards for the Five Civilized Tribes, 1898–1914, M1186, NA.

120. Unpublished autobiography of George Washington Grayson, passage in possession of the author.

121. February 6, 1909, book 24, DGWG.

122. April 21, 1909, book 25, DGWG; April 24, 1909, book 25, DGWG; April 26, 1909, book 25, DGWG; April 27, 1909, book 25, DGWG.

123. May 17, 1909, book 25, DGWG; May 18, 1909, book 25, DGWG; May 21, 1909, book 25, DGWG; May 24, 1909, book 25, DGWG; May 26, 1909, book 25, DGWG; September 13, 1909, book 26, DGWG; November 13, 1909, book 27, DGWG.

124. September 13, 1909, book 26, DGWG.

125. December 20, 1909, book 27, DGWG.

126. July 13, 1910, book 29, DGWG.

Bob Littlejohn, July 1999 and June 2000

1. John S. Tomer and Michael J. Brodhead, *A Naturalist in Indian Territory: The Journals of S. W. Woodhouse, 1849–50* (Norman: University of Oklahoma Press, 1992), 137.

Chapter 9

1. Bryan F. Le Beau, *Currier and Ives: America Imagined* (Washington, DC: Smithsonian Institution Press, 2001), chap. 1.

2. John F. Kasson examines the relationship between technology and democracy in *Civilizing the Machine: Technology and Republican Values in America, 1776–1900* (New York: Penguin, 1976). For his comments on Palmer's lithograph, see pp. 178–179.

3. J. Valerie Fifer, *American Progress: The Growth of the Transport, Tourist, and In-formation Industries in the Nineteenth-Century West* (Chester, CT: Globe Pequot Press, 1988), 186, 200–204, 226, 403. For the Crofutt quotation, see Le Beau, *Currier and Ives*, 120–121.

4. The literature on the mythic West in American culture is vast. A brief introduc-tion can be found in Alan Trachtenberg, *The Incorporation of America: Culture and Society in the Gilded Age* (New York: Hill and Wang, 1982), chap. 1.

5. *Indian Journal* (Eufaula and Muskogee), August 28, 1876.

6. *Indian Journal* (Eufaula and Muskogee), March 27, 1879.

7. In the early 1900s, a number of Indian intellectuals rejected the idea of progress and affirmed the value of native cultures, as Frederick Hoxie notes in "Exploring a Cultural Borderland: Native American Journeys of Discovery in the Early Twentieth Century," *Journal of American History* 79 (1992): 969–995. In so doing, Philip Deloria points out, they reinforced stereotypes of the primitive Indian. Deloria, *Playing Indian* (New Haven, CT: Yale University Press, 1998), 121–127. The example of the Grayson family adds the element of race to this discussion of Indian responses to modernism. For a brief treatment of progressive Indians and racism, see Brian Dippie, *The Vanishing American: White Attitudes and U.S. Indian Policy* (Lawrence: University Press of Kansas, 1982), 263–269.

8. *AGWG*, 41; Annual Report of the Commissioner of Indian Affairs, *USS.S.exdoc.* 1 (33–1) 690:391–392.

9. Jedidiah Morse, *Geography Made Easy: Being an Abridgement of the American Universal Geography* (Troy, NY: Parker and Bliss, 1814).

10. *AGWG*, 31.

11. S. G. Goodrich, *Goodrich's Second Reader* (Boston: Otis, Broaders, and Com-pany, 1839), 130–132, 144.

12. In the early twentieth century, Charles Eastman, the Santee Sioux physician and writer, similarly struggled to come to terms with the tenets of progress, as is revealed in his autobiography, *Indian Boyhood*. See H. David Brumble III, *American Indian Au-tobiography* (Berkeley and Los Angeles: University of California Press, 1988), chap. 7.

13. G. W. Grayson to Col. Powell, May 11, 1885, Records of the Bureau of Amer-ican Ethnology, Correspondence, LR, 1879–1888, Smithsonian Institution, National Anthropological Archives.

14. G. W. Grayson to J. W. Powell, May 26, 1885, Records of the Bureau of Amer-ican Ethnology, Correspondence, LR, 1879–1888, Smithsonian Institution, National Anthropological Archives.

15. July 17, 1900, book 5, DGWG.

16. November 27, 1902, book 10, DGWG.

17. November 24, 1910, book 29, DGWG.

18. The best overview of the image of the vanishing American in popular culture is Dippie, *Vanishing American*.

19. February 10, 1899, book 2, DGWG.

20. John Beattie Crozier, *Civilization and Progress*, 4th ed. (London: Longmans, Green, 1898), 397–398.

21. May 29, 1900, book 5, DGWG.

22. Bernard Moses, *Democracy and Social Growth in America: Four Lectures* (New York: Putnam, 1898), 4–5.

23. Ibid., 6–7.

24. December 22, 1905, book 17, DGWG. Wash made a return visit a year later. February 18, 1907, book 19, DGWG.

25. Quoted in Curtis M. Hinsley Jr., *Savages and Scientists: The Smithsonian Institution and the Development of American Anthropology, 1846–1910* (Washington, DC: Smithsonian Institution Press, 1981), 113. Franz Boas, who proposed that all cultures were equal, never seriously influenced the National Museum. See Hinsley, *Savages and Scientists*, chap. 4.

26. September 25 to October 3, 1904, book 14, DGWG; December 22, 1905, book 17, DGWG; May 18, 1908, book 22, DGWG.

27. Paul Reddin, *Wild West Shows* (Urbana: University of Illinois Press, 1999), 53–157.

28. May 18, 1908, book 22, DGWG. Wash was not the only Indian to have attended a Wild West show. Joy S. Kasson, *Buffalo Bill's Wild West: Celebrity, Memory, and Popular History* (New York: Hill and Wang, 2000), 212.

29. December 22, 1905, book 17, DGWG.

30. May 18, 1908, book 22, DGWG. Historians did not speak about the invasion of America until 1975, when Francis Jennings published *The Invasion of America: Indians, Colonialism, and the Cant of Conquest* (Chapel Hill: University of North Carolina Press, 1975).

31. January 30, 1912, book 33, DGWG.

32. "Excerpts from a Typescript of a Script for the Musicale, 1911–1912," in Mick Gidley, *Edward S. Curtis and the North American Indian, Incorporated* (Cambridge: Cambridge University Press, 1998), 219.

33. On Curtis's musicale, see Gidley, *Edward S. Curtis*, chap. 7. For a highly critical examination of Curtis's photography, see Christopher M. Lyman, *The Vanishing Race and Other Illusions: Photographs of Indians by Edward S. Curtis* (Washington, DC: Smithsonian Institution Press, 1982).

34. April 25, 1914, book 39, DGWG.

35. Mary Holland Kinkaid, *The Man of Yesterday: A Romance of a Vanishing Race* (New York: Frederick A. Stokes, 1908), 66.

36. Ibid., 16.

37. Louis Owens, *Other Destinies: Understanding the American Indian Novel* (Norman: University of Oklahoma Press, 1992), chap. 3; Owens, *Mixedblood Messages: Literature, Film, Family, Place* (Norman: University of Oklahoma Press, 1998), chap. 3; Jace Weaver, *That the People Might Live: Native American Literatures and Native American Community* (New York: Oxford University Press, 1997), 104–110; Deloria, *Playing Indian*, 122–126. Arnold Krupat points out that much of the emphasis of current scholars on locating places of "hybridity" in early twentieth-century Indian literature is in fact ahistorical. Such places did not exist at the time. Krupat, *Red Matters: Native American Studies* (Philadelphia: University of Pennsylvania Press, 2002), 89–90. It is a striking fact that the literature on "mixed-bloods" never considers the position of Indians who are part African.

38. Kinkaid, *The Man of Yesterday*, 314.

39. Ibid.

40. Carl Snyder, *New Conceptions in Science, with a Foreword on the Relations of Science and Progress* (New York: Harper, 1903), 37.

41. Ibid., 35.

42. December 23, 1903, book 12, DGWG.

43. May 23, 1901, book 6, DGWG.

44. For a brilliant examination of the connection between the culture of imperialism and technology in the late nineteenth and early twentieth centuries, see Michael Adas, *Machines as the Measure of Men: Science, Technology, and Ideologies* (Ithaca, NY: Cornell University Press, 1989).

45. October 1, 1902, book 10, DGWG; March 7, 1908, book 22, DGWG.

46. July 10, 1909, book 26, DGWG.

47. December 26, 1909, book 27, DGWG.

48. May 4, 1911, book 31, DGWG.

49. October 16, 1911, book 32, DGWG.

50. January 25, 1913, book 36, DGWG.

51. February 3, 1913, book 36, DGWG.

52. Ibid.

53. June 18, 1908, book 22, DGWG.

54. R. Laurence Moore, *In Search of White Crows: Spiritualism, Parapsychology, and American Culture* (New York: Oxford University Press, 1977).

55. January 9, 1910, book 27, DGWG; January 16, 1910, book 27, DGWG; January 21, 1910, book 27, DGWG. Wash's first encounter with parapsychology was in 1908, when he asked a clairvoyant for information on his son Washie, who was then in the U.S. Army in the Philippines. April 17, 1908, book 22, DGWG.

56. January 9, 1910, book 27, DGWG; *Eternal Progress*, March 1909, xiii.

57. *Eternal Progress* (March 1909), 2, 4, 27.

58. *Eternal Progress* (May 1909), 4.

59. *Progress Magazine*, June 1909; *Progress Magazine*, August 1909; *Progress Magazine*, September 1909; *Progress Magazine*, October 1910.

60. *Progress Magazine* (October 1910). This special issue on American Indians reflected the low expectations that U.S. reformers had for native peoples. Frederick Hoxie describes their changing attitudes in Hoxie, *A Final Promise: The Campaign to Assimilate the Indians, 1880–1920* (Lincoln: University of Nebraska Press, 1984).

61. *Progress Magazine*, November 1910, 3.

62. January 22, 1911, book 30, DGWG.

63. November 2, 1904, book 15, DGWG.

64. Matthew Frye Jacobson, *Barbarian Virtues: The United States Encounters Foreign Peoples at Home and Abroad, 1876–1917* (New York: Hill and Wang, 2001), 105–178.

65. July 16, 1910, book 29, DGWG.

66. H. N. Hutchinson, J. W. Gregory, and R. Lydekker, *The Living Races of Mankind* (London: Hutchinson and Co., 1901), ii.

67. Ibid., 491.

68. Ibid., 290, 293.

69. Ibid., 529, 530, 532.

70. James Earl Fraser and other western artists are discussed in Dippie, *Vanishing American*.

71. November 2, 1904, book 15, DGWG.

72. Alexander Posey, *The Poems of Alexander Lawrence Posey* (Topeka, KS: Crane and Company, 1910), 104–105. Posey and Wash Grayson were both members of the Informal Club, a literary and political discussion group. Mary Jane Warde, *George Washington Grayson and the Creek Nation, 1843–1920* (Norman: University of Oklahoma Press, 1999), 236.

73. Daniel F. Littlefield Jr., *Alex Posey: Creek Poet, Journalist, and Humorist* (Lincoln: University of Nebraska Press, 1992), 147.

74. October 23, 1900, book 5, DGWG.

75. August 16, 1903, book 12, DGWG.

76. *AGWG*, 20.

77. Ibid., 71; December 11, 1905, book 17, DGWG.

78. May 21, 1903, book 11, DGWG.

79. "An Indian Army Officer," *St. Louis Globe*, n.d., Records of the Bureau of American Ethnology, Correspondence, LR, 1888–1906, Smithsonian Institution, National Anthropological Archives.

80. France and Britain had a long history of drawing troops from colonies to serve in other colonies. Julian Go, "Introduction: Global Perspectives on the U.S. Colonial State in the Philippines," in *The American Colonial State in the Philippines: Global Perspectives*, ed. Julian Go and Anne L. Foster (Durham, NC: Duke University Press, 2003), 20–21.

81. Peter G. Gowing, "Moros and Indians: Commonalities of Purpose, Policy and Practice in American Government of Two Hostile Subject Peoples," *Philippine Quarterly of Culture and Society* 8 (1980): 125–149.

82. Paul Barclay, " 'They Have for the Coast Dwellers a Traditional Hatred': Governing Igorots in Northern Luzon and Central Taiwan, 1895–1915," in *The American Colonial State in the Philippines: Global Perspectives*, ed. Julian Go and Anne L. Foster (Durham, NC: Duke University Press, 2003), 238–239.

83. Harold Hanne Elarth, *The Story of the Philippine Constabulary* (Los Angeles: Philippine Constabulary Officers Association, 1949), 48.

84. Edward Merrick to G. W. Grayson, August 6, 1904, Records of the Bureau of American Ethnology, Correspondence, LR, 1888–1906, Smithsonian Institution, National Anthropological Archives; G. W. Grayson to the Director of the American Bureau of Ethnology, August 9, 1904, Records of the Bureau of American Ethnology, Correspondence, LR, 1888–1906, Smithsonian Institution, National Anthropological Archives; the Director of the American Bureau of Ethnology to G. W. Grayson, August 30, 1904, Records of the Bureau of American Ethnology, Correspondence, LR, 1888–1906, Smithsonian Institution, National Anthropological Archives.

85. Robert W. Rydell, *All the World's a Fair: Visions of Empire at American International Expositions, 1876–1916* (Chicago: University of Chicago Press, 1984), chap. 6.

86. Timothy J. Fox and Duane R. Sneddeker, *From the Palaces to the Pike: Visions of the 1904 World's Fair* (St. Louis: Missouri Historical Society, 1997).

87. *The Greatest of Expositions Completely Illustrated: Official Views of the Louisiana Purchase Exposition* (St. Louis: Louisiana Purchase Exposition, 1904), 158.

88. Promotional brochure pictured in Eric Breitbart, *A World on Display: Photographs from the St. Louis World's Fair, 1904* (Albuquerque: University of New Mexico Press, 1997), 24; W. J. McGee, "Introduction," in *Louisiana and the Fair: An Exposition of the World, Its Peoples, and Their Achievements*, ed. J. W. Buel (St. Louis: World's Progress Publishing Company, 1904), xi–xii.

89. "Types and Development of Man," in *Louisiana and the Fair: An Exposition of the World, Its Peoples, and Their Achievements*, ed. J. W. Buel (St. Louis: World's Progress Publishing Company, 1904), frontispiece to volume 5.

90. Louisiana Purchase Exposition, *The Greatest of Expositions Completely Illustrated* (St. Louis: Official Photographic Company, 1904), 272.

91. Christopher A. Vaughan, "Ogling Igorots: The Politics and Commerce of Exhibiting Cultural Otherness, 1898–1913," in *Freakery: Cultural Spectacles of the Extraordinary Body*, ed. Rosemarie Garland Thomson (New York: New York University Press, 1996), 219–233; quotation on p. 225.

92. Ibid., 225–226.

93. Breitbart, *World on Display*, 43; Walter L. Williams, "United States Indian Policy and the Debate over Philippine Annexation: Implications for the Origins of American Imperialism," *Journal of American History* 66 (1980): 810–831.

94. Breitbart, *World on Display*, 33, 49.

95. September 25 to October 3, 1904, book 14, DGWG; G. W. Grayson to F. W. Hodge, October 7, 1904, Records of the Bureau of American Ethnology, Correspondence, LR, 1888–1906, Smithsonian Institution, National Anthropological Archives; March 23, 1905, book 15, DGWG.

96. July 5, 1903, book 11, DGWG; November 20, 1903, book 12, DGWG; May 25, 1905, book 15, DGWG.

97. June 12, 1906, book 18, DGWG.

98. January 17, 1907, book 19, DGWG.

99. Elarth, *Story of the Philippine Constabulary*, "Foreword."

100. October 11, 1909, book 26, DGWG; October 10, 1913, book 38, DGWG; January 15, 1914, book 38, DGWG.

101. January 15, 1914, book 38, DGWG.

102. Elarth, *Story of the Philippine Constabulary*, "Foreword."

103. On the relationship between domestic and foreign policy at the turn of the nineteenth century, see Jacobson, *Barbarian Virtues*; and Amy Kaplan, *The Anarchy of Empire in the Making of U.S. Culture* (New York: Cambridge University Press, 2002).

104. On the politics surrounding the creation of the state of Oklahoma, see Danney Goble, *Progressive Oklahoma: The Making of a New Kind of State* (Norman: University of Oklahoma Press, 1980); Philip Mellinger, "Discrimination and Statehood in Oklahoma," *Chronicles of Oklahoma* 49 (1971): 340–378; and Murray R. Wickett, *Contested Territory: Whites, Native Americans, and African Americans in Oklahoma, 1865–1907* (Baton Rouge: Louisiana State University Press, 2000).

105. Dippie, *Vanishing American*, 249–262.

106. Quoted in ibid., 250.

107. These events are chronicled in Arthur Tolson, "The Negro in Oklahoma Territory, 1889–1907: A Study in Racial Discrimination" (Ph.D. diss., University of Oklahoma, 1966), 34–41. See also Goble, *Progressive Oklahoma*, 135.

108. Quoted in Murray R. Wickett, "Contested Territory: Whites, Native Americans, and African Americans in Oklahoma, 1865–1907" (Ph.D. diss., University of Toronto, 1996), 376.

109. Interview with Anna McMahan and Sarah McConnell, August 11, 1937, IPP, 57:259–271, OHS.

110. Interview with Jenks Ross, September 5, 1969, T518-3, fiche 255, vol. 45, DU, WHC.

111. Interview with Nora DeBaun Eades, July 13, 1937, IPP, 27:3–16, OHS.

112. Interview with Adelia Thompson Greenley, April 22, 1938, IPP, 36:48–54, OHS.

113. Interview with Tom Hawkins, December 5, 1969, T545-2, fiche 82, vol. 15, DU, WHC.

114. Interview with James M. Etter, July 2, 1999; Application of Jeanetta Newberry, Dawes Commission Records, Creek Nation, Townsites, Oktaha, box 136, folder 3, OHS; Application of James McQueen, Dawes Commission Records, Creek Nation,

115. Philip Mellinger, "Discrimination and Statehood in Oklahoma," *Chronicles of Oklahoma* 49 (1971): 354.

116. Interview with John Dill, n.d., IPP, 24:357–365, OHS.

117. *Muskogee Cimeter*, June 2, 1904.

118. May 5, 1899, book 3, DGWG.

119. October 5, 1899, book 3, DGWG.

120. October 7, 1899, book 3, DGWG.

121. October 14, 1899, book 3, DGWG.

122. December 3, 1903, book 12, DGWG.

123. December 11, 1903, book 12, DGWG.

124. September 17, 1907, book 22, DGWG. Wash's comments about "real" Indians are ironic in light of a 1989 review of his autobiography that questioned his own Indian identity on the basis of his European ancestry. W. David Baird, "Are There 'Real' Indians in Oklahoma? Historical Perceptions of the Five Civilized Tribes," *Chronicles of Oklahoma* 68, no. 1 (1990): 4–23.

125. February 25, 1908, book 22, DGWG.

126. Alexia Kosmider writes that Alexander Posey displaced "Native people's phobias, fears, and desires onto blacks." Alexia Kosmider, *Tricky Tribal Discourse: The Poetry, Short Stories, and Fus Fixico Letters of Creek Writer Alex Posey* (Moscow: University of Idaho Press, 1998), 56. For an account of Posey's life, see Littlefield, *Alex Posey*. For an interpretation of Posey's writings, see Craig S. Womack, *Red on Red: Native American Literary Separatism* (Minneapolis: University of Minnesota Press, 1999).

127. Quoted in Littlefield, *Alex Posey*, 156.

128. Alexander Posey, *The Fus Fixico Letters*, ed. Daniel F. Littlefield Jr. and Carol A. Petty Hunter (Lincoln: University of Nebraska Press, 1993), 56, 62, 66.

129. June 17, 1903, book 11, DGWG.

130. November 3, 1905, book 16, DGWG.

131. Posey, *Fus Fixico Letters*, 109.

132. Ibid., 131.

133. Quoted in Warde, *George Washington Grayson*, 203.

134. February 3, 1904, book 13, DGWG.

135. Warde, *George Washington Grayson*, 203.

136. Posey, *Fus Fixico Letters*, 167.

137. Murray R. Wickett, *Contested Territory: Whites, Native Americans, and African Americans in Oklahoma, 1865–1907* (Baton Rouge: Louisiana State University Press, 2000), 175–180, 184–185; Mellinger, "Discrimination and Statehood in Oklahoma," 361; Franklin, *Journey toward Hope*, 13–17; Goble, *Progressive Oklahoma*, 92–93, 200; Alice Robertson to William E. Curtis, November 11, 1905, series II, box 2, folder 8, doc. LS-36, Alice Robertson Collection, McFarlin Library, University of Tulsa.

138. October 26, 1906, *Oktaha Democrat*; Wickett, *Contested Territory*, 180–185.

139. October 26, 1906, *Oktaha Democrat*.

140. September 1 and September 19, 1906, book 18, DGWG.

141. "White man's country" quoted in Franklin, *Journey toward Hope*, 39; William Murray quoted in Goble, *Progressive Oklahoma*, 144. See also Wickett, *Contested Territory*, 181–182.

142. July 12, 1910, book 29, DGWG.

143. *Checotah Times*, March 8, 1907.

144. Clarence B. Douglas, "The Dawn," *Muskogee Phoenix*, November 16, 1907, reprinted in Joseph B. Thoburn and Muriel H. Wright, *Oklahoma: A History of the State and Its People* (New York: Lewis Historical Publishing, 1929), 2:638–639.

Bob Littlejohn, June 2002

1. This information is gleaned from the following U.S. censuses: Pulaski County, Georgia, 1870; Dodge County, Georgia, e.d. 28, sheet 27, 1900; Dodge County, Georgia, e.d. 55, sheets 7 and 11, 1910; and Muskogee County, Oklahoma, Ogle Township, e.d. 74, sheet 4.

Chapter 10

1. The color line separated people who were often distantly and sometimes closely related. Several authors offer first-person testaments to this fact. In the process, they powerfully illustrate the arbitrariness of racial categories. See, for example, Gregory Howard Williams, *Life on the Color Line: The True Story of a White Boy Who Discovered He Was Black* (New York: Dutton, 1995); James McBride, *The Color of Water: A Black Man's Tribute to His White Mother* (New York: Riverhead Books, 1996); and Neil Henry, *Pearl's Secret: A Black Man's Search for His White Family* (Berkeley and Los Angeles: University of California Press, 2001).

2. The term "red nigger" was in use as early as the 1820s. The drafting of Jim Crow laws in the late nineteenth century separating public spaces into black and white must have given the phrase new significance. David R. Roediger, *The Wages of Whiteness: Race and the Making of the American Working Class*, rev. ed. (London: Verso, 1999), 22.

3. Philip Mellinger, "Discrimination and Statehood in Oklahoma," *Chronicles of Oklahoma* 49 (1971): 362–371; Arthur Tolson, "The Negro in Oklahoma Territory,

1889–1907: A Study in Racial Discrimination" (Ph.D. diss., University of Oklahoma, 1966), 125–130.

4. William H. Murray, "The Constitutional Convention," *Chronicles of Oklahoma* 9 (1931): 133; Blue Clark, "Delegates to the Constitutional Convention," *Chronicles of Oklahoma* 48 (1970–1971): 400–415D. Among those who claimed Indian ancestry was Robert Latham Owen Jr. Owen served as vice president of the campaign to elect Democratic delegates to the constitutional convention. He later became the state's first U.S. senator. Apart from William Murray, the most influential delegate to the constitutional convention was probably Charles N. Haskell, who later became the state's first governor. He was an outspoken opponent of black enfranchisement; at the same time, he maintained close ties to a number of Indian politicians. Kenny L. Born, "A Progressive from Oklahoma," *Chronicles of Oklahoma* 62 (1984): 234–237; Danney Goble, *Progressive Oklahoma: The Making of a New Kind of State* (Norman: University of Oklahoma Press, 1980), 140–141; Paul Nesbitt, "Haskell Tells of Two Conventions," *Chronicles of Oklahoma* 14 (1936): 189–217.

5. Francis W. Schruben, "The Return of 'Alfalfa Bill Murray,'" *Chronicles of Oklahoma* 41 (1963): 39.

6. Quoted in Richard B. Sherman, " 'The Last Stand': The Fight for Racial Integrity in Virginia in the 1920s," *Journal of Southern History* 54 (1988): 77.

7. Buck Colbert Franklin, *My Life and an Era: The Autobiography of Buck Colbert Franklin*, ed. John Hope Franklin and John Whittington Franklin (Baton Rouge: Louisiana State University Press, 1997), 121–122.

8. Quoted in Mellinger, "Discrimination and Statehood in Oklahoma," 351.

9. Jimmie Lewis Franklin, *Journey toward Hope: A History of Blacks in Oklahoma* (Norman: University of Oklahoma Press, 1982), 42–44.

10. Mellinger, "Discrimination and Statehood in Oklahoma," 373–374; Tolson, "The Negro in Oklahoma Territory, 1889–1907," 125–150.

11. David Grayson, Creek N.E., Individual Indian Case Files, entry 552, RG 75, NAFW.

12. November 8, 1910, book 29, DGWG.

13. In his memoirs, William Murray, president of the Oklahoma constitutional convention and former governor of the state, would list the Grayson family as among "prominent Indians and white men." He and Murray knew each other from the Sequoyah Convention of 1905, a movement to turn Indian Territory into a single state. William H. Murray, *Memoirs of Governor Murray and True History of Oklahoma* (Boston: Meador Publishing, 1945), 1:282–283.

14. July 1, 1908, book 22, DGWG; January 22, 1913, book 36, DGWG; June 18, 1915, book 41, DGWG; December 13, 1915, book 42, DGWG; December 22, 1915, book 42, DGWG.

15. October 14, 1908, book 23, DGWG.

16. December 3 and December 4, 1914, book 40, DGWG.

17. July 25, 1915, book 41, DGWG.

18. August 1, 1914, book 39, DGWG. Before 1907, there were at least seven lynchings in Indian Territory and Oklahoma Territory. After statehood, there were forty-one lynchings. Franklin, *Journey toward Hope*, 131–137. For an account of one 1898

lynching in Indian Territory, see Daniel F. Littlefield, *Seminole Burning: A Story of Racial Vengeance* (Oxford: University Presses of Mississippi, 1996).

19. April 28, 1900, book 4, DGWG.

20. June 5, 1902, book 9, DGWG; June 8, 1909, book 25, DGWG; May 15, 1911, book 31, DGWG.

21. May 29 and June 3, 1905, book 15, DGWG.

22. May 30, 1912, book 34, DGWG.

23. May 30, 1916, book 43, DGWG.

24. January 3, 1905, book 15, DGWG; May 26, 1905, book 15, DGWG; June 7, 1905, book 15, DGWG.

25. August 20, 1907, book 21, DGWG.

26. September 18, 1913, book 37, DGWG.

27. *AGWG*, 14–15.

28. Ibid., 20.

29. Ibid., 19, 20, 24, 25.

30. March 27, 1908, book 22, DGWG.

31. April 6, 1908, book 22, DGWG. The quotation is from the preface to *The Clansman: An Historical Romance of the Ku Klux Klan* (New York: Doubleday, 1905), Dixon's novel that was one of the sources of the play.

32. Quoted in Lawrence J. Oliver, "Writing from the Right during the 'Red Decade': Thomas Dixon's Attack on W. E. B. DuBois and James Weldon Johnson in *The Flaming Sword*," *American Literature* 70 (1998): 136.

33. Raymond Allen Cook, *Fire from the Flint: The Amazing Careers of Thomas Dixon* (Winston-Salem, NC: John F. Blair, 1968), chap. 6; John Hammond Moore, "South Carolina's Reaction to the Photoplay, *The Birth of a Nation*," in *The Proceedings of the South Carolina Historical Association, 1963* (Columbia: South Carolina Historical Association, 1964); John C. Inscoe, "*The Clansman* on Stage and Screen: North Carolina Reacts," *North Carolina Historical Review* 1987 (64): 139–161.

34. Mellinger, "Discrimination and Statehood in Oklahoma," 354.

35. May 12, 1909, book 25, DGWG.

36. May 28, 1909, book 25, DGWG; August 1, 1909, book 26, DGWG.

37. June 6, 1910, book 28, DGWG.

38. Margaret Gibbs, *The DAR* (New York: Holt, Rinehart and Winston, 1969), 22–31; Matthew Frye Jacobson, *Barbarian Virtues: The United States Encounters Foreign Peoples at Home and Abroad, 1876–1917* (New York: Hill and Wang, 2001), 152–163.

39. Daniel F. Littlefield Jr. and James W. Parins, eds., *Native American Writing in the Southeast: An Anthology, 1875–1935* (Jackson: University Press of Mississippi, 1995), 28.

40. January 17, 1907, book 19, DGWG.

41. December 4, 1915, book 42, DGWG.

42. A useful overview of Reconstruction historiography through the 1970s can be found in Eric Foner, "Reconstruction Revisited," *Reviews in American History* 10 (1982): 82–100. The best single work on Reconstruction is Eric Foner, *Reconstruction: America's Unfinished Revolution, 1863–1877* (New York: Harper and Row, 1988).

43. The view that Reconstruction was unjust is still not entirely extinct, in part because of the influence of *The Birth of a Nation*. John Hope Franklin, " 'Birth of a Nation': Propaganda as History," *Massachusetts Review* 20 (1979): 417–434; Mimi White, "*The Birth of a Nation*: History as Pretext," in *The Birth of a Nation: D. W. Griffith, Director*, ed. Robert Lang (New Brunswick, NJ: Rutgers University Press, 1994), 214–224. For an interesting examination of white supremacy and Griffith's early Biograph shorts on Native Americans, see Gregory S. Jay, " 'White Man's Book No Good': D. W. Griffith and the American Indian," *Cinema Journal* 39 (2000): 3–26.

44. December 4, 1915, book 42, DGWG.

45. Quoted in Michael Rogin, " 'The Sword Became a Flashing Vision': D. W. Griffith's *The Birth of a Nation*," *Representations* 9 (1985): 164.

46. For an exploration of *The Birth of a Nation's* sexual themes, see ibid.

47. E. G. Williams to Pleasant Porter, July 15, 1907, Records of the Chief of the Creek Nation, Correspondence, Records of Tribal Governments, entry 43, RG 75, NAFW.

48. September 17, 1907, book 21, DGWG. The copyedited and printed version of Wash's entry states that Porter had "a decided strain" rather than "streak" of "negro blood." Frederick Webb Hodge, ed., *Handbook of American Indians North of Mexico*, bulletin 30, Bureau of American Ethnology, 2nd ed. (Washington, DC: Smithsonian Institution Press, 1912), 2:287–288.

49. William Elsey Connelley, "Memoir of Alexander Lawrence Posey," in Alexander Lawrence Posey, *Alex Posey, the Creek Indian Poet* (Topeka, KS: Crane and Company, 1910), 6–7, 10.

50. October 25, 1910, book 29, DGWG.

51. Alice Robertson to Dr. Cain, June 17, 1909, series II, box 1, folder 11, doc. 1319, Alice Robertson Collection, McFarlin Library, University of Tulsa.

52. *Muskogee Times-Democrat*, December 8, 1909.

53. *Louis Hall v. Zur Eddleyman*, et al. District Court, Muskogee County, OK, case 819, April 15, 1909, OKN 100, LDS 1943668, Muskogee Public Library, Oklahoma.

54. "Jim Crow Case," *Oktaha Leader*, April 14, 1910.

55. *Lewis Pitman v. School District* no. 33, Civil Case Files, case 2313, reel 81, McIntosh County Courthouse, Eufaula, OK.

56. School Enumeration Reports, Muskogee County, dist. 54, 1913, OKN 5, Muskogee Public Library, Oklahoma.

57. School Enumeration Reports, Muskogee County, dist. 53, 1915, OKN 8, Muskogee Public Library, Oklahoma.

58. School Enumeration Reports, Muskogee County, dist. 63, 1912, OKN 2, Muskogee Public Library, Oklahoma.

59. School Enumeration Reports, Muskogee County, dist. 63, 1915, OKN 8, Muskogee Public Library, Oklahoma.

60. School Enumeration Reports, Muskogee County, dist. 63, 1917, OKN 11, Muskogee Public Library, Oklahoma; School Enumeration Reports, Muskogee County, dist. 63, 1918, OKN 13, Muskogee Public Library, Oklahoma.

61. School Enumeration Reports, Muskogee County, dist. 54, 1912, OKN 2, Muskogee Public Library, Oklahoma.

62. School Enumeration Reports, Muskogee County, dist. 54, 1913, OKN 5, Muskogee Public Library, Oklahoma.

63. School Enumeration Reports, Muskogee County, dist. 54, 1915, OKN 8, Muskogee Public Library, Oklahoma.

64. School Enumeration Reports, Muskogee County, dist. 54, 1917, OKN 11, Muskogee Public Library, Oklahoma.

65. School Enumeration Reports, Muskogee County, dist. 54, 1918, OKN 13, Muskogee Public Library, Oklahoma.

66. School Enumeration Reports, Muskogee County, dist. 54, 1920, OKN 18, Muskogee Public Library, Oklahoma.

67. School Enumeration Reports, Muskogee County, dist. 63, 1912, OKN 2, Muskogee Public Library, Oklahoma; School Enumeration Reports, Muskogee County, dist. 63, 1913, OKN 5, Muskogee Public Library, Oklahoma.

68. *Edmond Grayson v. Mariah Grayson*, Superior Court Cases, case 8664, OKN 89, LDS 1943657, Muskogee Public Library, Oklahoma.

69. School Enumeration Reports, Muskogee County, dist. 54, 1915, OKN 8, Muskogee Public Library, Oklahoma; School Enumeration Reports, Muskogee County, dist. 64, 1918, OKN 13, Muskogee Public Library, Oklahoma.

70. School Enumeration Reports, Muskogee County, dist. 64, 1920, OKN 18, Muskogee Public Library, Oklahoma.

71. School Enumeration Reports, Muskogee County, dist. 63, 1925, OKN 23, Muskogee Public Library, Oklahoma.

72. Scott Ellsworth, *Death in a Promised Land: The Tulsa Race Riot of 1921* (Baton Rouge: Louisiana State University Press, 1982), 66–69; Tim Madigan, *The Burning: Massacre, Destruction, and the Tulsa Race Riot of 1921* (New York: St. Martin's Press, 2001), 221–224.

73. Quoted in Ellsworth, *Death in a Promised Land*, 95. In addition to Ellsworth, see Alfred L. Brophy, *Reconstructing the Dreamland: The Tulsa Riot of 1921* (New York: Oxford University Press, 2002); and Madigan, *The Burning*. For a view of the riot written by a survivor, see Mary E. Jones Parrish, *Race Riot, 1921: Events of the Tulsa Disaster* (Tulsa, OK: Out on a Limb Publishing, 1998).

74. On Wash's uneventful term as principal chief, see Mary Jane Warde, *George Washington Grayson and the Creek Nation, 1843–1920* (Norman: University of Oklahoma Press, 1999), 242–247.

75. Frederick Hoxie, *A Final Promise: The Campaign to Assimilate the Indians, 1880–1920* (Lincoln: University of Nebraska Press, 1984), 178–187.

76. In an extensive genealogy compiled in the 1930s, James's great-grandmother is identified as an unknown woman from Ketchapataka, the tribal town of most of the Graysons after removal. Wash wrote in his unedited autobiography that Annie Grayson's descendants lived in the vicinity of Henryetta, Oklahoma, and were either Graysons or Barnetts. The descendants of the unknown woman from Ketchapataka also lived near Henryetta and used both the Grayson and Barnett surnames. See the Barnett genealogy compiled by Sim L. Liles of Sapulpa, Oklahoma, and now in archives of the OHS.

77. This account is based on *Blake et al. v. Sessions et al.*, 1924, Oklahoma Supreme Court, no. 11986, Archives and Records Division, Oklahoma Department of Libraries.

78. David Grayson, Creek 2099, Individual Indian Case Files, entry 552, RG 75, NAFW.

79. For an examination of twentieth-century court cases regarding the legality of interracial marriage, see Peggy Pascoe, "Miscegenation Law, Court Cases, and Ideologies of 'Race' in Twentieth-Century America," *Journal of American History* 83 (1996): 44–69.

80. *Blake et al. v. Sessions et al., 1924*, pp. 272, 280, and 296, Oklahoma Supreme Court, no. 11986, Archives and Records Division, Oklahoma Department of Libraries.

81. *Blake et al. v. Sessions et al., 1924*, p. 114, Oklahoma Supreme Court, no. 11986, Archives and Records Division, Oklahoma Department of Libraries.

82. Ibid., p. 125.

83. Ibid., p. 309.

84. Ibid., p. 299.

85. Ibid., p. 380.

86. *Brief and Argument of Plaintiffs in Error, Blake et al. v. Sessions et al., 1924*, pp. 6–7, Oklahoma Supreme Court, no. 11986, Archives and Records Division, Oklahoma Department of Libraries.

87. *Brief of Defendants in Error, Blake et al. v. Sessions et al., 1924*, p. 37, Oklahoma Supreme Court, no. 11986, Archives and Records Division, Oklahoma Department of Libraries.

88. *Blake et al. v. Sessions et al., 1924*, p. 121, Oklahoma Supreme Court, no. 11986, Archives and Records Division, Oklahoma Department of Libraries.

89. *Checotah Times*, March 8, 1907.

90. Estate of Jeanetta Grayson, Probate Case Files, case 3032, OKM 284, frame 1398, Muskogee Public Library, Oklahoma.

91. Estate of G. W. Grayson, Probate Case Files, case 2877, reel 48, McIntosh County Courthouse, Eufaula, OK.

92. December 16, 1916, book 44, DGWG.

93. Estate of Vicey Weatherspoon, Probate Case Files, case 5404, OKM 362, frame 1743, Muskogee Public Library, Oklahoma.

94. Estate of Eli Grayson, Probate Case Files, case 5601, Muskogee County Court House, Oklahoma.

95. Interview with Cooper Grayson, January 27, 1970, T553-1, fiche 165, vol. 29, DU, WHC.

96. Edmond Grayson, Probate Attorneys Case Files, entry 346, RG 75, NAFW.

97. Edmond Grayson to Harold Icks [sic], September 9, 1935, in Edmond Grayson, Probate Attorneys Case Files, entry 346, RG 75, NAFW.

98. Edmond Grayson to the Commissioner of Indian Affairs, July 13, 1935, in Edmond Grayson, Creek 2204, Individual Indian Case Files, entry 552, RG 75, NAFW.

99. J. M Stewart to Edmond Grayson, July 24, 1935, in Edmond Grayson, Creek 2204, Individual Indian Case Files, entry 552, RG 75, NAFW.

100. Edmond Grayson to Harold Icks [sic], September 9, 1935, and Harry Smith to Peter Deichman, August 1, 1933, in Edmond Grayson, Probate Attorneys Case Files, entry 346, RG 75, NAFW.

101. Edmond Grayson, Creek 2204, Individual Indian Case Files, entry 552, RG 75, NAFW.

102. It is a striking fact that the tremendous rise in the Native American population at the end of the twentieth century was largely due to Americans who for the first time identified themselves on the census as part Indian. There was no similar trend of white and Native Americans identifying themselves as part black. As David A. Hollinger points out, in the United States, the stigma of blackness is unique. David A. Hollinger, "Amalgamation and Hypodescent: The Question of Ethnoracial Mixture in the History of the United States," *American Historical Review* 108 (2003): 1368.

103. Warde, *George Washington Grayson*, 247–248.

104. Phone interview with John York, June 28, 1999.

105. Obituary of Edmond Grayson, October 22, 1963, *Muskogee Daily Phoenix*. Washie Grayson is buried in the Greenwood Cemetery in Eufaula, Oklahoma. Edmond Grayson is buried in the "Old Indian Cemetery near Oktaha," now called Grayson Cemetery.

Afterword

1. Posting by Willie, March 23, 2004, http://www.afrigeneas.com/forume/index.cgi?read=3012.

2. Posting by Eli Grayson, March 24, 2004, http://www.afrigeneas.com/forume/index.cgi?read=3013.

3. Posting by Willie, March 24, 2004, http://www.afrigeneas.com/forume/index.cgi?read=3015.

4. Posting by Willie, March 24, 2004, http://www.afrigeneas.com/forume/index.cgi?read=3019. "Willie" equated Indian identity with the possession of a tribal roll number, but the question of who is an Indian is far more complicated. Two books that address this question are Circe Sturm, *Blood Politics: Race, Culture, and Identity in the Cherokee Nation of Oklahoma* (Berkeley and Los Angeles: University of California Press, 2002); and Eva Marie Garroutte, *Real Indians: Identity and the Survival of Native America* (Berkeley and Los Angeles: University of California Press, 2003).

5. Posting by Eli Grayson, March 25, 2004, http://www.afrigeneas.com/forume/index.cgi?read=3020.

6. Constitution of the Muscogee (Creek) Nation, courtesy of the Muskogee (Creek) Nation, Okmulgee, Oklahoma.

7. Phone interview with Buddy Cox, July 31, 1999.

8. *Cherokee Nation Code, Annotated*, art. V, sec. 3; art. VI, sec. 2; art. IX, sec. 2; and *Cherokee Nation Code, Annotated, 1987 Supplement* (Orford, NH: Equity, 1987), 10-3-1; Constitution of the Choctaw Nation of Oklahoma, art. II, sec. 1, courtesy of the Choctaw Nation of Oklahoma, Talihina, Oklahoma.

9. *Riggs v. Ummerteskee* (2002).

10. "Cherokee Freedmen Caught in High-Level Dispute," August 20, 2003, Indianz.com, http://www.indianz.com/News/archives/000930.asp. This article included links to the following letters: Jeanette Hanna (director of the Eastern Oklahoma Regional Office of the BIA) to Chad Smith, July 11, 2003; Chad Smith to Jeanette Hanna, July 14, 2003 (source of quotation); and Chad Smith to Gale Norton, July 14, 2003.

11. "Senate Panel Approves Ross Swimmer Nomination," March 6, 2003, Indianz.com, http://www.indianz.com/News/show.asp?ID=2003/03/06/swimmer.

12. "Who Is a Seminole, and Who Gets to Decide?" *New York Times*, January 29, 2001; "The Seminole Tribe, Running from History," *New York Times*, April 21, 2002; *Davis v. United States*, No. 02-6198 (10th Cir. September 10, 2003).

13. Daniel F. Littlefield Jr., *The Chickasaw Freedmen: A People without a Country* (Westport, CT; Greenwood Press, 1980).

14. Federal Indian programs that determine eligibility using blood quantum include the Indian Hiring Preference, Employment Assistance for Adult Indians, Vocational Training for Adult Indians, Educational Loans and Grants, and Land Acquisition. Margo S. Brownell, "Who Is an Indian? Searching for an Answer to the Question at the Core of Federal Indian Law," *University of Michigan Journal of Law Reform* 34 (2000–2001): 280–282, 298–301.

15. 25 Code of Federal Regulations Part 83.7 (e).

16. The problem of identifying historical Indian tribes is explored in James Clifford, "Identity in Mashpee," in Clifford, *The Predicament of Culture* (Cambridge, MA: Harvard University Press, 1988), 277–346.

17. Brownell, "Who Is an Indian?" 307–308.

18. Any U.S. violation of Indian sovereignty on behalf of the civil rights of the descendants of slaves would have its own problems, for the United States would then be exploiting the very practices that it had forced onto Indian nations. For an analysis of similar colonial interventions in India, see Nicholas B. Dirks, "The Policing of Tradition: Colonialism and Anthropology in Southern India," *Comparative Studies in Society and History* 39 (1997): 182–212, especially 209–212. See also Dirks, "Castes of Mind," *Representations*, Special Issue: Imperial Fantasies and Postcolonial Histories, 37 (1992): 56–78.

19. Quoted in Brownell, "Who Is an Indian?" 307.

20. David A. Hollinger observes that the "differences in the historical experience of the several American minority descent groups sometimes have been hidden from view as we react in horror to the evils of white racism wholesale." He has in mind the stringent application of miscegenation laws to African Americans but not to Indians, Asian Americans, and Latinos. His observation might be extended by noting that the evils of white racism have also obscured the experiences of minorities within minority groups. Hollinger, "Amalgamation and Hypodescent: The Question of Ethnoracial Mixture in the History of the United States," *American Historical Review* 108 (2003): 1380.

A Note on Sources and Historiography

1. As far as I know, Wash Grayson's diary is the only one of its kind in existence. Don Talayesva, an educated Hopi, was reportedly paid by Yale sociologist Leo Simmons to begin keeping a diary in 1938. It eventually reached eight thousand pages, but unfortunately, it has been lost. H. David Brumble, *American Indian Autobiography* (Berkeley and Los Angeles: University of California Press, 1988), 105, 201n6.

2. Examples of oral histories include Two Leggings, *Two Leggings: The Making of a Crow Warrior* (Lincoln: University of Nebraska Press, 1967); Black Elk, *Black Elk Speaks: Being the Life Story of a Holy Man of the Oglala Sioux* (Lincoln: University of Nebraska Press, 2000); and Mary Crow Dog and Richard Erdoes, *Lakota Woman* (New York: Grove Press, 1990). For a comprehensive list of such accounts, see H. David Brumble

III, *An Annotated Bibliography of American Indian and Eskimo Autobiographies* (Lincoln: University of Nebraska Press, 1981).

3. Arnold Krupat, *For Those Who Come After: A Study of Native American Autobiography* (Berkeley and Los Angeles: University of California Press, 1985); Brumble, *American Indian Autobiography*.

Index

Adams, Chester, 108–110
Adams, Louis, 108
Adams, Mahala, 108
Adams, Thomas J., 108, 109
Adams, Washington, 108
Adkins, Richard, 157
Agassiz, Louis, 57
Alabama Emigration Company, 53
Alabama, role in removing Creeks, 37–38
allotment (1830s), 39–43
allotment (1890s), 152–168
Antony, Milton, 22
Arkansas College, 79, 91, 100
Arkansas Colored Town, 119, 125, 155, 156
Arnold, Edwin M., 163–164
Augusta, Georgia, 15
Autosee, 20

Ballentine, Mr., 69
Barnett, Ben, 126
Bartram, William, 13
Battle of Honey Springs, 101–103, 104, 106
Beggs, Oklahoma, 108, 109
Benson, Johnnie. See Tulwa Tustanagee
Benson, Mary, 49, 67
Benson family, 103
Big Warrior, 23, 26
Birth of a Nation, 200
Blake, W. R., 206, 208

Blunt, James G., 102, 107
Boggy Depot, 103
Brady, Adam, 138
Brady, Saucer, 80, 96, 101, 102, 105, 107
Broad, Philander, 50
Brown, John, 88
Bruner, Jacob, 103
Bruner, Lucy, 167
Bruner, Paro, 69, 155, 157–158
Bruner, Thomas, 94
Bush, George Herbert Walker, 86
Butler, Ed, 70

Caldwell, Charles, 56, 58
Canadian Colored Town, 119, 125, 135
Carolina, Tony, 70
Caruthers, Prissie, 120–121
Casey, John, 166, 203
Cass, Lewis, 50
Chambers, Bettie, 146
Chambers, William, 146
Checote, Sam, 117, 119, 122–125, 126, 134–136, 137
Cherokee Nation or Cherokees, 8, 64–65, 71, 74, 81
  and black Creeks, 126
  and the Civil War, 97, 98
  disenfranchises descendants of slaves, 214
  freed people in, 112
  joins the Confederacy, 92, 94

Chickasaw Nation or Chickasaws, 91–94,
      98, 215
   freed people in, 112, 114–115
Chimney Mountain, 44, 100, 101
Chinne Chotke. *See* Grayson, James
Choctaw Nation or Choctaws, 46, 61,
      70
   and the Civil War, 96, 104, 106
   freed people in, 112, 114–115
   joins the Confederacy, 92–94
   slave laws in, 62
   slavery in, 62, 70
Churchill, Ward, 8
Chustenahlah, 95
Cleveland, Grover, 132, 152
Clinton, William Jefferson, 86
Cody, Radmilla, 7
Colbert Commission, 155, 156
Columbus, Georgia, 30, 50, 51
Comanches, 71
Combe, George, 57
Cooney, Joseph, 96
Cooper, Douglas, 94, 95, 97
Cornsilk, David, 29
Cox, Buddy, 21, 128–131, 149–150
Cox, Claude, 47, 110, 128, 129, 149
Cox, Porter, 149
Cravens, M.A., 42
Crawford, T. Hartley, 58
Crawford, William 22
Creek Nation
   campaign against abolitionists in, 72–
      74, 76, 90
   in the Civil War, 95–96
   discovery of oil in, 163
   disenfranchises descendants of slaves,
      214
   emancipation in, 104, 113–116
   ex-slaves in (post-emancipation), 112–
      116, 119–121, 123–127, 134–136
   free blacks in (pre-emancipation), 35–
      36, 43, 75–79, 80, 89–91, 94, 96

   joins the Confederacy, 92–94
   land cessions by, 4, 18, 21, 30, 31, 34,
      37
   laws against free blacks in, 73, 75, 76
   matrilineality in, 143–147
   missionaries in, 35–36, 69, 71–74, 76,
      77–78, 90
   origins of racism in, 59–61
   population of slaves and Indians in, 66,
      68–69, 88
   ranching in, 139–143
   and the reconstruction treaties, 112–
      113, 115–116
   and removal treaty, 39–40
   schools in, 47, 72, 74, 78
   slave laws of, 23, 33, 74–75, 88–91
   slavery in, 10–11, 16–17, 25–26, 32,
      33, 38, 43–44, 46, 49, 67–79, 80–
      81, 94, 97–98
Creek War of 1836, 50–52
Crofutt, George, 173–174
Crowell, John, 38, 39
Currier and Ives, 173
Curtis Act, 153
Curtis, Edward S., 177
Curtis, Samuel, 106

Dale, E. E., viii, ix
Dannely, John, 38
Davenport, Don Little Cloud, 6, 7
Davis, Lucinda, 70, 101
Davis, Napoleon, 84–87
Dawes, Henry L., 152–152
Dawes Act. *See* General Allotment Act of
      1887
Dawes Commission, 153–154, 156–160,
      179
Debo, Angie, 152, 162
Descendants of the Freedmen of the Five
      Civilized Tribes, 65
Dick (Elizabeth Grayson's slave), 32, 33,
      43

Dixon, Thomas, 198–199, 200
Douglass, Frederick, 24, 35
Duncan, Turner, 125
Dunn, J. W., 119–120
Dunn Rolls, 120–121, 154, 156, 158
Durant, Monday, 112–113

Eades, Daniel, 14
Eades, John, 14
Early, Peter, 22
Ecunhutke, 20
Edwards, Elsie, 54
Elarth, Harold, 185
Emancipation Proclamation, 104, 113–114
environmentalism, 55–56, 58
Escoe, Lettie, 166
Eubanks, William, 199
Eufala (Creek town in Georgia), 51
Eufaula, Oklahoma, vii, viii, 135, 167, 179, 189
    becomes county seat, 167
    founding of, 133–134
    oil in, 165
    patriarchy in, 144
    racism in, 195, 198, 203
Evans, James, 166

Fanon, Frantz, 23
Fife, Joe, 94, 95
Fifteenth Amendment, 151
Finniegan, Onie, 160, 203
Finniegan, Phil, 160
First Indian Home Guards, 96–97, 100–101, 104, 107
First Kansas Colored Infantry Volunteers, 96, 100–102, 105
Fleetwood, Edmund, 137
Fleming, John, 72
Floyd, John, 20
Folsom, Jordan, 70
Foreman, Stephen, 98

Fort Gibson, 45, 53, 54, 61, 63, 72, 100–101, 102, 105, 115
Fort Mims, 19
Fort Scott, 97
Fort Smith, 61, 112, 113, 115, 137
Foster, Abraham, 93
Fourteenth Amendment, 104, 151

Gabler, Jack, 121
Garland, Samuel, 94
Garrison, Mrs., 90
General Allotment Act of 1887, 152–153
    and dispossession, 160, 161–163
Georgia, role in removing Creeks, 33–34, 37, 50
Glenn Pool, 163
Gomez, Jewelle, 7
Graham, William, 118
Grant, Ulysses S., 120
Grayson, Aaron, 84, 102
Grayson, Abby, 122
Grayson, Addie, 139
Grayson, Adeline (Emma's niece), 160
Grayson, Adeline (Katy's daughter), 81, 114
Grayson, Alfred, 124
Grayson, Annie (Katy's first daughter), 21, 22, 24, 49
    relatives and descendants of, 5, 205
Grayson, Annie (Wash's wife), vii, 67, 92, 166
    and patriarchy, 143, 145
    photographed, 122–123, 145
Grayson, Bailey, 41–42
Grayson, Ben (Jeanetta's son), 160
Grayson, Betsy, 108
Grayson, Burney, 135
Grayson, Caroline, 81, 114
Grayson, Charley (Jeanetta's son), 160
Grayson, Christie, 27
Grayson, Cilla, 124, 138, 152
Grayson, Clarissa, 103

Grayson, David, 19
  relatives and descendants of, 15
Grayson, Davy, 63
Grayson, Dick, 165
Grayson, Edmond (Eli's son)
  dispossession and death of, 209–211
  and Jim Crow, 204
  relatives and descendants of, 5
Grayson, Edmond (Watt's son), 133, 139
Grayson, Eli, 135
  and allotment, 152, 158–159, 160, 164
  death of, 209
  and Jim Crow, 201–202, 203, 204
  legal troubles of, 137, 138
  recalls Civil War, 102
  relatives and descendants of, 5
Grayson, Elizabeth (Emma's niece), 161
Grayson, Elizabeth (Katy's sister)
  marriage to William McIntosh, 27,
    233n6
  property stolen from, 32, 34
  relatives and descendants of, 15, 108
  and removal, 38–39, 40, 42–43, 49
  as slaveholder, 25–26, 31–32, 38, 43,
    44
Grayson, Emma
  and allotment, 152, 154, 156, 158–
    159, 160–161
  birth of, 33
  in the Civil War, 94, 96
  death of, 190, 208
  husband of, 80
  and Jim Crow, 186, 187
  legal troubles of, 136–138
  and matriarchy, 144, 146, 147
  and progress, 174
  as rancher, 140, 141, 142
  and the reconstruction of the Creek
    Nation, 112, 121, 122, 125
  relatives and descendants of, 5, 121,
    137, 138
  works as servant, 79, 91
Grayson, Franklin, 96, 105

Grayson, George, 110
Grayson, Hardy, 85
Grayson, Henderson, 35, 75, 94
  death of, 121
  in the First Indian Home Guards, 104,
    107
  possessions of, 80
  and the reconstruction of the Creek
    Nation, 121
  relatives and descendants of, 125
Grayson, Henry (Eli's son), 204
  relatives and descendants of, 5
Grayson, James (Katy's son), 78
  accompanies Wash to college, 79–80,
    82
  is given slave, 69
  marriage of, 67
  opposed to missionaries, 73
  relatives and descendants of, 4, 5
Grayson, James (Myrtle McNac's
    husband), 205–208
Grayson, James or Jim (Chinne Chotke),
    14, 25, 46, 97, 155, 193
Grayson, James (Wash's brother), 121
Grayson, Jeanetta, 121
  and allotment, 158, 159–160, 164
  death of, 209
  and Jim Crow, 201–202, 204
  legal troubles of, 137
  relatives and descendants of, 5
Grayson, Jennie. See Wynne, Jennie
Grayson, Jim (John Grayson's son), 124,
    138
Grayson, Joe, 155
Grayson, John (Katy's first son), 21, 22,
    24, 49
  in the Civil War, 102
  relatives and descendants of, 5, 124, 167
  and removal, 53
Grayson, Josh, 138
Grayson, Judah
  in the Civil War, 94, 95, 98
  emancipation of, 44

property stolen from, 32
relationship with William, 26, 31, 34,
    43–45
relatives and descendants of, 4, 5, 139,
    142, 144, 166, 167
subject to racist laws, 33, 73, 75, 78,
    89–91, 92–93
works as servant, 79
Grayson, Judy (Henderson Grayson's
    daughter), 121
Grayson, Judy (William and Judah's
    daughter), 75, 78, 94
    education of, 81
    possessions of, 80
    and the reconstruction of the Creek
        Nation, 112, 121
Grayson, Julia (descendant of Venus), 193
Grayson, Julia (William and Judah's
    granddaughter), 144, 160, 164
Grayson, Kate (William and Judah's great-
    granddaughter), 167
Grayson, Katie (Eli's granddaughter), 210
Grayson, Katie (William and Judah's
    daughter), 203
Grayson, Katy (William's sister), viii, ix,
    70
    in the Civil War, 94, 95, 98, 103
    and her black partner, 21, 24–25
    and her slaves, 25, 46, 67, 69, 78, 81,
        97, 155
    and John and Annie, 22, 24, 49, 55
    marries Johnnie Benson, 49
    and patriarchy, 143
    reasons for embracing slavery, 25, 49,
        68, 71
    relatives and descendants of, 4, 5, 15,
        108, 124, 167, 205
    and removal, 45, 53, 55
    rewarded by father, 25–26
    settles in Indian Territory, 61–62, 72
Grayson, Lucy, 85
Grayson, Maria (Eli's daughter-in-law),
    204

Grayson, Maria (William and Judah's
    daughter-in-law), 103
Grayson, Mary Ann, 103, 115, 121
Grayson, Mary (freedwoman), 67
Grayson, Mary (Matilda Grayson's
    daughter), 103
Grayson, Matilda, 102
Grayson, Mitchell, 103, 121, 138, 160
Grayson, Mitty, 121
Grayson, Mollie (rancher), 142, 144
Grayson, Molly (murder victim), 146
Grayson, Nannie, 142, 145
Grayson, Nelly, 164
Grayson, Peggie, 85
Grayson, Phil, 39
Grayson, Robert (Billy Grayson's son),
    103, 135, 137
    and allotment, 166–168
Grayson, Robert (d. 1823). See Grierson,
    Robert
Grayson, Robert (freeman), 97, 135
Grayson, Robert (Jeanetta's son), 160
Grayson, Sack, 96, 105
Grayson, Sam (Wash's brother)
    and allotment, 152
    business ventures of, 133–134, 140,
        141, 142
    and the Civil War, 103
    education of, 78
    legal troubles of, 138–139, 153
    and patriarchy, 143, 147
    and the reconstruction of the Creek
        Nation, 114, 121
Grayson, Samson, 42, 44, 73
Grayson, Sandy, Jr., 53
Grayson, Sandy, Sr., 19, 21, 25–26, 70,
    97
    relatives and descendants of, 15
    and removal, 39, 40, 42
Grayson, Sarah, 143
    relatives and descendants of, 15, 19,
        34, 69
Grayson, Seaborn, 137, 138, 142

Grayson, Sharper, 146

Grayson, Simpson, 80

Grayson, Sunny, 146

Grayson, Tacky, 137, 138, 142

Grayson, Thomas (imposter), 156

Grayson, Thomas (Katy's brother), 84
    relatives and descendants of, 15, 42
    and removal, 39, 44

Grayson, Vicey
    and allotment, 158–159, 160
    birth of, 78
    in the Civil War, 94
    death of, 209
    education of, 81
    and Jim Crow, 201–202
    legal troubles of, 136
    and matriarchy, 144, 146, 147
    possessions of, 80
    as rancher, 141, 142
    and the reconstruction of the Creek
        Nation, 112, 121, 122, 125
    relatives and descendants of, 5

Grayson, Wash (George Washington)
    and allotment, 152, 153–155, 161, 164–
        165, 166–168
    appointed principal chief, 205
    in Arkansas, 88, 91
    attitudes towards whites, 67
    autobiography of, vii-ix, 5, 25, 101,
        103–104, 166, 169, 171, 182, 198
    birth of, 67
    in the Civil War, 96, 99–104, 105–
        107
    death of, 209
    and dispute over election of 1883, 135–
        136
    education of, 78, 79, 81, 91, 174–175
    as election judge, 195
    on his black relatives, vii, ix, 44, 47–
        48, 103, 166–168, 198
    and Jim Crow, 186, 187–189, 195–
        201, 205
    legal troubles of, 136, 137, 138–139

as member of United Confederate
    Veterans, 197–198
as merchant, 133–134
and parapsychology, 180–181
and patriarchy, 143–144, 145, 147
and progress, 174–182
as rancher, 133, 140, 141, 142–143,
    161
and the reconstruction of the Creek
    Nation, 111–112, 114, 116–119,
    121–122, 124, 127
relatives and descendants of, 4–5
sees Birth of a Nation, 200
and technology, 178–180
traces Scottish ancestors, 198–199
visits John Ross, 81–83
visits the Louisiana Purchase
    Exposition, 183–185
visits William Grayson, 79–81
writes entries for Smithsonian
    Handbook, 200–201

Grayson, Washie (Washington)
    death of, 210–211
    in the Philippines, 183–185
    relatives and descendants of, 4, 5

Grayson, Watt
    in the Civil War, 96, 103
    property stolen from, 32
    provides capital to Wash Grayson, 139,
        140
    relatives and descendants of, 15, 108,
        133, 139
    and removal, 38, 40–42
    settles in Indian Territory, 62
    as slaveholder, 25, 46, 47, 69, 70, 92,
        160

Grayson, Wiley, 163–164

Grayson, William (Billy Grayson's son),
    103

Grayson, William, Jr. (Billy), 26, 75, 94,
    103, 121

Grayson, William (Katy's brother), ix, 55
    beaten by Creeks, 34–35

considers fate of his children, 68, 72, 78, 92
death of, 94
excluded from inheritance, 32
hosts Wash Grayson, 79–81
and matrilineal naming practices, 144
in the Redstick War, 20–21
relationship with Judah, 26, 31, 33, 43–45, 75
relatives and descendants of, 4, 5, 15, 108, 139, 142, 144, 166, 167
and removal, 38, 40, 42, 43, 44, 54
settles in Indian Territory, 44, 61, 62
Grayson Brothers Mercantile, 133–134, 139, 141, 147, 161
Grierson, Robert, viii, 3, 49
death of, 32
described by Wash, 182–183, 185, 198
in Hilabi, 11, 13–15
and his slaves, 16–17, 19, 21, 25–26, 31, 33, 46, 84, 97
in Jasper County, 21–22
and patriarchy, 17, 143
relatives and descendants of, 5, 15, 19, 27, 28, 34, 108, 233n6
and the Redstick War, 19–20
Griffith, D. W., 200

Hall, Louis, 202
Harrison, John, 70
Harrod, Mary, 80
Harrod, Steptney, 80
Hawkins, Benjamin, viii, 16–19, 25, 34
Hawkins, Daniel, 115
Hawkins, Pink, 69
Hawkins, Pinkey, 19, 34
Hawkins, Samuel, 32, 34, 69
Hawkins, Soda, 102
Hawkins, Stephen, 34
Hawkins, Sykie, 115
Hawkins, Tom, 187
Hay, Americus L., 78
Haynes, Alex, 70

Haynes, Delilah, 47
Henderson, James, 15
Henry, Hugh, 186
Herrod, Cyrus, 124, 126, 138
Hicks, Hannah, 98
Hilabi, 11–16, 32, 54, 119, 135
and the Creek War of 1836, 50, 52
and the Redstick War, 19–20, 49
and removal, 38, 42–43
Hillaby, Lotti, 102
Hitchcock, Ethan Allen, 68
Hogan, John, 50
Horseshoe Bend, 20
Howard, O. O., 119–120
Hutton, Everett, 47
Hutton, Jim (grandson of Venus), 46, 47
Hutton, Jim (slaveholder), 46
Hutton, Jim (son of Venus), 138
Hutton, Joe, 46, 47
Hutton, Nancy, 46
Hutton, Rudy, 46–48
Huttonville, 47

Indian Expedition, 96–98, 100
Intakhafpky, 49
Irving, Washington, 71
Island, Billy, 146
Island, Harry, 97
Isparhecher, 134–136

Jackson, Andrew, 19, 20, 21, 39, 50
Jasper County, Georgia, 20–22, 41
Jefferson, Thomas, 18, 56
Jeffersonian Indian policy, 18
Jesup, Thomas, 50, 51
Jim Crow, 48, 186–189, 195–205
Job, Leroy, 91

Katy Railroad. See Missouri, Kansas, and Texas Railroad
Kellam, Charles, 73–74
Kellam, E. L., 136–137
Kennard, Jim, 74

Kennard, Moty, 79, 92, 93, 95, 100
Kennard, Sophy, 74
Kernal, John, 125–126

Laflore, Michael, 115
Lake Mohonk Indian Conference, 153
Lawson, Curtis, 170
Lendly, Peter, 39
Lerblance, E. H., 142, 149–150
Lewis, Gilbert, 94, 95
Lewis (slave), 97
Lilley, John, 66
Lilley, Mrs., 69
Little Okfuskee, 20
Little Rock, Arkansas, 53
Littlejohn, Bob, 169–172, 192–193
Littlejohn, Cornelius, 170, 193
Logan, Mr., 39
Louisiana Purchase Exposition, 183–185
Lowery, George, 125
Lucky, Daniel, 126–127
Lumbees, 8

Macon County, AL, 55
Marshall, Benjamin, 97
Marshall, Lafayette, 102
Marshall, Mory, 102
Martin, L. M., 106
Mason, J. A., 74
May, John, 138
McAnally, Valentine N., 79, 81, 82
McBride, A. P., 165
McIntosh, Billy, 100
McIntosh, Chilly, 33, 34, 43
    in Civil War, 94, 99
    and land scams, 40
McIntosh, Daniel N., 94, 96, 97, 99, 116, 124
McIntosh, Ella, 120
McIntosh, Lewis, 115, 120
McIntosh, Roley, 72, 74, 139
McIntosh, Una, 117

McIntosh, William (Creek leader), 25, 27, 31, 33, 43
    death of, 34
    and land cessions, 32, 34, 37
    marriage to Elizabeth Grayson, 27, 233n6
McIntosh, William F. (judge), 142
McIntosh, William (leader of Arkansas Colored Town), 155, 157
McKellop, James, 111
McNac, Myrtle, 205–208
Memphis, Tennessee, 53
Menaway, 38
Miller, Edward, 158
miscegenation, origin of word, 90
Missouri, Kansas, and Texas Railroad (Katy Railroad), 134, 140, 141, 142, 164
Mitchell, David, 22, 23, 24
Mobile, Alabama, 50, 51
Montgomery, Alabama, 11, 31, 34, 43, 51
Mordecai, Abraham, 128, 149
Morrison, Vicey, 146
Morton, Samuel George, 57–58, 59, 68
Moss, Henry, 56
Murray, William, 189–190, 194–195
Murrell, George M., 81–82
Muskogee, Oklahoma, 37, 44, 47, 71, 84, 156, 204
    racism in, 125–126, 187–187, 189, 198, 199, 200, 201, 202
Myer, John, 96

Neamathla, 60, 61
Neha Micco, 39
New Yaucau, 19
North Fork Colored Town, 119, 125, 135
North Fork Town, 74, 79, 91, 92, 94, 125, 134
Northsun, Nila, 9

Oklahoma, discrimination in, 186–187,
    189–190, 194–195, 201–208
Oktaha, Oklahoma
    development of, 164
    Grayson homes near, 61, 121, 125,
        160
    racism in, 187, 202–204, 209–211
    ranching in, 141–142
    Wash Grayson visits, 166
    women in, 144, 146–147
Oktarsars Harjo (Sands), 113, 118, 119,
    120, 122–123, 134
Old Suttin (freedman), 114, 115
Opothleyahola, 34, 41, 43, 92, 104, 134
    leads exodus to Kansas, 95–96, 97

Park Hill, 81, 97, 98
Parker, Liza, 157
Patterson, Benjamin, 52
Perryman, Alex, 35
Perryman, Joseph M., 104–105, 135–136
Perryman, Legus C. (L. C.), 155, 171, 189
Perryman, Lewis, 170
Perryman, Mose, 70, 98, 117
Perryman, Sampson, 35
Perryman, Sanford, 117–118
Perryman, Thomas, 43
Phillips, Wendell, 151
Phillips, William, 107
phrenology, 57
Pike, Albert, 92, 97, 99
Pilot, Hutton, 47
Pittman, Lewis, 203
Porter, Pleasant, 70, 111, 163, 187–189,
    200
Posey, Alexander, 182, 188–189, 201
Powell, John Wesley, 175
Price, M. L., 78
Prince (freedman), 115

racism, scientific, 55–61, 63
Raines, A. J., 53–54

Randall, Sakay, 35
Red Fork, Oklahoma, 163
Redstick War, 18–21, 47
Reed, H. C., 142
Reeves, Ira, 201
removal, 38–45, 49, 51–55, 63
Rhoden, Mr., 39
Riggs, Bernice, 214
Roberts, Donna, 6–7
Robertson, Alice, 161
Robertson, William, 69, 99
Rollin, David, 72, 77
Roosevelt, Theodore, 174, 185, 200
Ross, John, 81–83, 92, 97
Rowland, 204
Rush, Benjamin, 56

Sands. See Oktarsars Harjo
Sanger, S. S., 91, 92
Sapulpa, William A., 93
Scales, Gray E., 122
Schley, William, 50
Schultz, Christie, 27
Scroggins, 51
Seminole Nation or Seminoles, 50, 60
    and the Civil War, 92, 95
    disenfranchises descendants of slaves,
        214, 215
    settles in Creek Nation, 77, 79, 99
Sequoyah, 56–57
Sessions, William, 206, 208
Shock, E. E., 167
Shorter, Eli, 22, 41–42
Shorter, Reuben, 22
Sinnugee, 3
    adopted into Creek clan, 11
    and patriarchy, 17
    relatives and descendants of, 5, 15, 19,
        28, 34
    and removal, 40, 54
    starts family, 14–15
Sitting Sun, Chief, 6

slavery
   Cherokee laws regarding, 74
   Choctaw laws regarding, 62, 72
   in the Choctaw Nation, 62, 70
   Creek laws regarding, 23, 33, 74–75,
     88–91
   in the Creek Nation, 10–11, 16–17, 25–
     26, 32, 33, 38, 43–44, 46, 49, 67–
     79, 80–81, 94, 97–98
   and kinship, 16–17
Smith, Chad, 214
Smith, E. Kirby, 106
Smith, James, 116
Smith, Samuel Stanhope, 55
Smock, Eloise, viii, ix
Smock, John, 165
Socapatoy, Alabama, 52
Sodom, Oklahoma, 47
Spaulding, H. B., 142
Standard Oil, 142
Steele, William
Steen, J. W., 163–164
Stephens, J. W., 93
Stidham, Annie. *See* Grayson, Annie
   (Wash's wife)
Stidham, G. W., 67, 93, 99, 117, 122,
   142
Stidham, Georgeanna. *See* Grayson, Annie
Stidham, Prince, 155, 158–159
Summit, Oklahoma, 144, 146, 160, 164
Swan, Caleb, 11
Swimmer, Ross, 214

Thirteenth Amendment, 104, 114
Thompson, Mrs., 69
Tiger, Stella, 166
Tobler, George, 114–115
Towns, Henry, 39
Troup, George M., 33–34, 35, 37, 49, 55
Tulsa Race Riot, 204–205.

Tulwa Tustanagee
   marries Katy Grayson, 49
   relatives and descendants of, 5, 67
Tustanarkchopko, 99
Tutu, Desmond, 86

United Confederate Veterans, 197–198,
   200
United States v. Kagama, 158

Vann, Cobb, 125
Vann, Ed, 125
Vann, James (of post-removal era), 126
Vann, James (of pre-removal era), 64
Vann, John, 126
Vann, Marilyn, 64–65
Venus (slave), 14, 25, 46, 97, 193

Wagoner, Oklahoma, 105
Walker, Henry, 21, 31
Walker, Tandy, 106
Wapanucka Academy, 103
Warrior, Robert, 9
Washington, George, 17
Watie, Saladen, 100
Watie, Stand, 97, 100
Weer, William, 97
Wewocau, 19
White, James, 20
Williams, Crocket, 197
Wilson, Sarah, 114
Wilson (slave), 69
Withington Station, 36
Wofford, Arceny, 120–121
Woodhouse, S. W., 169–170
Wright, J. Leitch, 7
Wynne, Jennie, 67, 78, 96, 103

Yuchi Town, 51